Origami to Astonish and Amuse

Jeremy Shafer

St. Martin's Griffin
New York

ORIGAMI TO ASTONISH
AND AMUSE

Library of Congress Cataloging-in-Publication Data

Shafer, Jeremy.
  Origami to astonish and amuse / Jeremy Shafer.ñ 1st ed.
    p. cm.
  ISBN 0-312-25404-0
  1. Origami. I. Title.

TT870 .S4443 2000
736'.982ñdc21

00-040266

10 9 8 7 6 5

To Margo, Rob, Mike,
and always, my bear,
Teddy!

FOREWORD

Jeremy Shafer burst on the origami scene like a tidal wave engulfing a crowd of happy surfers. Or perhaps he crept up silently, like a giant ant about to surprise a party of unsuspecting picnickers. However you choose to describe it, the origami world was simply not prepared for the brilliant and bizarre take on art and life that is uniquely Jeremy's. In case the reader of this book is similarly unprepared, a little warning is in order.

Jeremy was considerably less than twenty when we first met, at a gallery in San Francisco where about a dozen of us were exhibiting our work. The freshness of Jeremy's vision was instantly apparent. I remember even now his surfer conquering a huge wave, his working nail clippers, and several other creations with a distinctly Charles Addams-like feel. In the years since, Jeremy has continued to train one eye on the macabre and the other on the absurd in conjuring up hundreds of ingenious designs, many of which are in this, his first book. Little did I expect back then that the same febrile mind would one day produce the delightfully pointless Origami Square, Monolithic Rubblestone Boulder, and Carbon Atom!

How to explain Jeremy's wicked imagination and manic inventiveness? Perhaps the driving force behind Jeremy's work is his sheer pleasure in entertaining. In this, Jeremy shares a kinship with the other great paperfolder-magicians of the past, Robert Harbin, Adolfo Cerceda, and Harry Houdini. Many, if not most, of Jeremy's models have found a place in his performance repertoire, in between sessions of unicycling, juggling, sleight-of-hand, prestidigitation, fire-eating, and whatever else makes up his one-man-band street act. So there is almost always a storyline or drama to keep the viewers entertained—the evolving moods and escapades of Mr. Smiley, the darting eyes of the Glancer, the tragic heroes in the Man Swatter and Unfortunate Suitor, and the "in your face" action of the exploding Venus Flytrap, Heart Attack, and Flasher (co-designed with Chris Palmer). Jeremy's protean inventiveness is fueled by a restless desire to transform, and like the Cat in the Hat, who is not content just to stand on a ball and balance a goldfish on an umbrella and a cup on his hat, Jeremy is driven to top each of his creations with a newer one that jumps, changes color, folds in half to make a face, turns upside down, shrinks to become infinitesimally small or expands to be REALLY HUGE. Before he even puts the last fold into place on one model his mind is racing ahead to the next, and the next, and the next.

But there is much more than sheer entertainment value to Jeremy's work. Almost obscured by Jeremy's provocative choice of subject matter are his remarkable technical skill, mathematical ingenuity, and keen attention to craft. All of this is evidenced by the brilliance of his more "normal" models, such as the Waxing Waning Moon, the lyrical Double Yin Yang, the spirited Dancers, and the ingenious Swiss Army Knife, Star of David and Labyrinth Walker. As he mentions in the Introduction, it is this choice of new subjects, with their attendant design challenges, that propels him into the making of new forms. I am not surprised to read this, since without new challenges, any art form, origami included, cannot advance. In the case of origami, these challenges may come from a new choice of subject matter, a new aesthetic, a heightened attention to realism, or a new mathematical confrontation. Once the folder sets out on a new path, he or she cannot be faint of heart and turn back when obstacles arise, since it is the surmounting of those obstacles that defines the finished work of art, that gives it its particular form, proportions, and aesthetic. The artist is the one with the courage of his or her convictions, who perseveres to the bitter end. The work in this book is evidence that Jeremy is one such artist.

Where will origami go after Jeremy? Where will Jeremy go after origami? In this book, Jeremy has shown, like Marcel Duchamp, Jackson Pollock, or John Cage, not only how to produce extraordinary art, but also how to annihilate it in the process. Confronted with the work of these art-annihilators, audiences and critics have often wondered whether art would survive. It always does, and when it resurfaces, it takes off in new directions that could never have been imagined. So perhaps the warning at the beginning of this Foreword was not needed at all. Enjoy the work before you for its sheer entertainment and the pleasure of folding it, and be reassured that far from annihilating origami, Jeremy Shafer has given it a new burst of life.

—PETER ENGEL

ACKNOWLEDGMENTS

This book is the fruit of a passion, a labor of love, and a bridge from me to you. Since the age of ten, I've been happily obsessed with designing new origami models. Finally, the product of my seventeen years of folding, mostly by myself, can be shared with folders worldwide. So, first of all, I'd like to thank St. Martin's Press, and my editor Dorsey Mills, in particular, for helping make this book a reality.

Many people have influenced my work and are acknowledged throughout the book in the *Thoughts Behind the Folds* boxes. But I'm particularly indebted to the following people:

- John Montroll, my mentor, whose book *Origami for the Enthusiast* triggered my passion for origami;

- Peter Engel whose book *Folding the Universe: Origami from Angelfish to Zen* swept me out of my self-imposed folding isolation and into a book-buying frenzy from which I learned techniques used by the masters;

- Chris Palmer for our countless head-banging brainstorming sessions, especially around our quest for the Flasher pattern (see page 110);

- Mark Turner for his inspirational achievements and for founding the Bay Area Rapid Folders;

- The members of Bay Area Rapid Folders who regularly tried out my diagrams and gave me feedback;

- Sam Randlett, my copy editor, who tirelessly tested and proofed all the diagrams. He made many hundreds of corrections and insightful suggestions;

- Gay Merrill Gross, my proofreader, who further checked all of the diagrams multiple times;

- Camp Winnarainbow for nurturing my creativity and creating a safe space to try new things. In particular, my twelve summers at camp helped transform me into a fanatic juggler, unicyclist, origamist, vegan, and street performer;

- My folding friends in Colombia, Ecuador, Venezuela, Japan, England, France, Spain, and Italy for their hospitality, encouragement, and friendship;

- All my friends and family who over the years have thrown ideas at me and given enthusiastic feedback and inspired me to always try to take it one step further.

I must also mention that many of my models were designed at school, while sitting in the back of class secretly folding in my lap. So, in all fairness, I am indebted to the various teachers and professors of these classes for apparently not noticing my under-the-table operations.

On the other hand, I would like to thank two math professors at UC Santa Cruz, Dan Goldstein and Richard Montgomery, who not only noticed my work, but enthusiastically sponsored my origami independent studies. A special thanks goes to Chuck Atkinson, my writing professor at UC Santa Cruz, who assisted me in writing the introduction to this book, and encouraged me to be more personal in my writing style.

Most of all I am grateful to my parents and brother for supporting and even encouraging my eccentric passions. For their love and support this book is dedicated to them—Margo, Rob, and Mike.

Finally, I would like to thank all of you for taking an interest in origami so that St. Martin's Press would take the risk of accepting this zany book for publication. May the folds be with you!

CONTENTS

S = Simple
LI = Low Intermediate
I = Intermediate
HI = High Intermediate
C = Complex

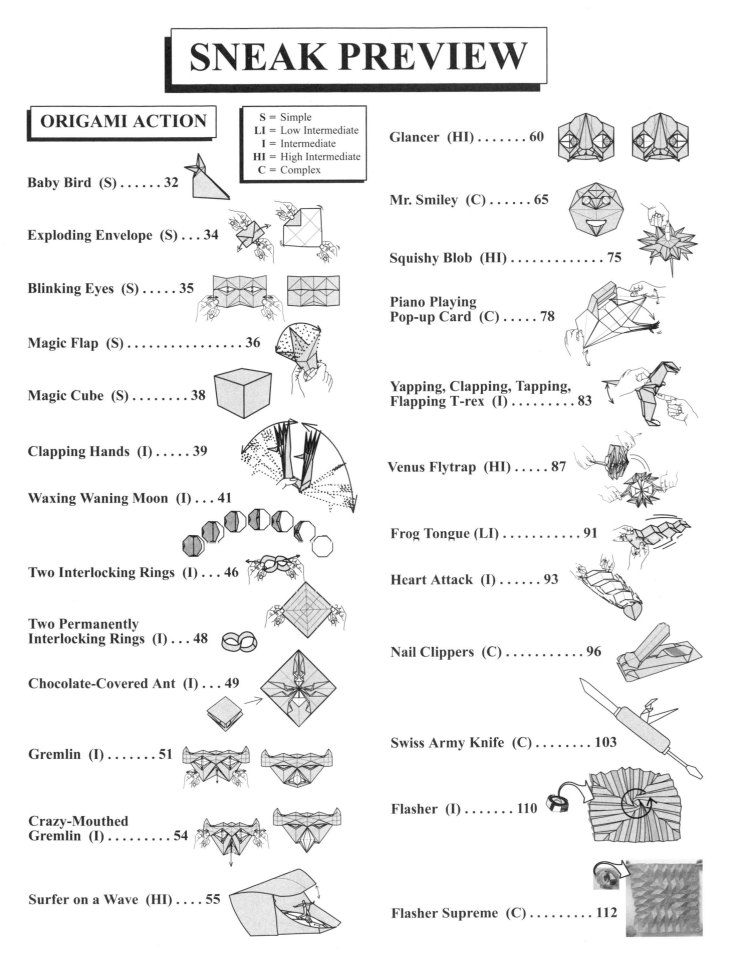

SNEAK PREVIEW

ORIGAMI ACTION

S = Simple
LI = Low Intermediate
I = Intermediate
HI = High Intermediate
C = Complex

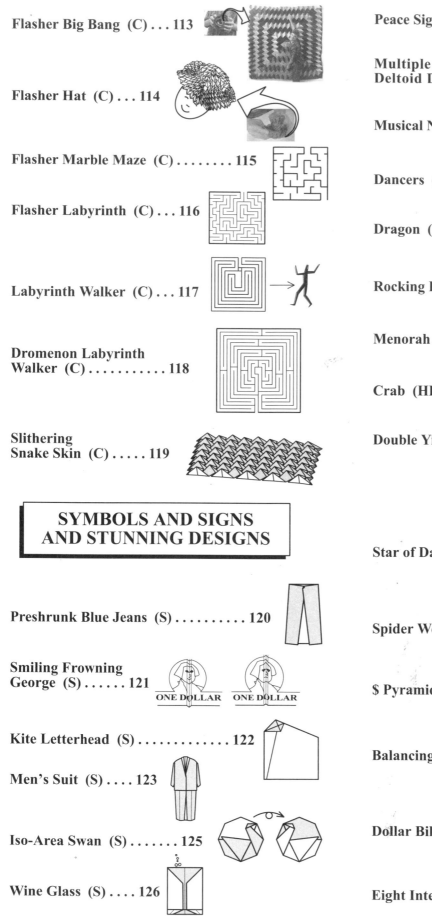

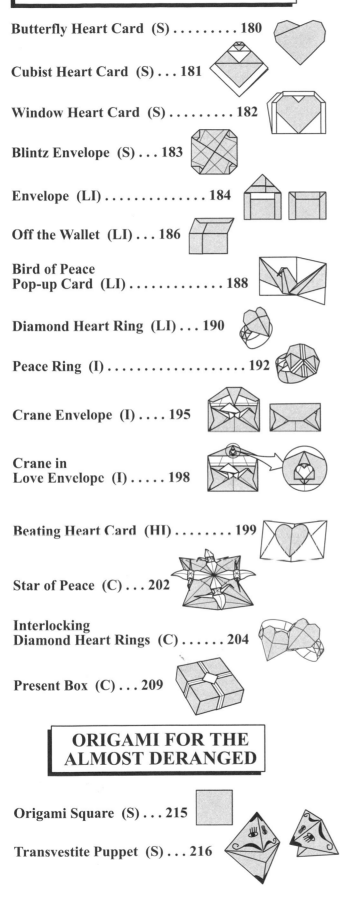

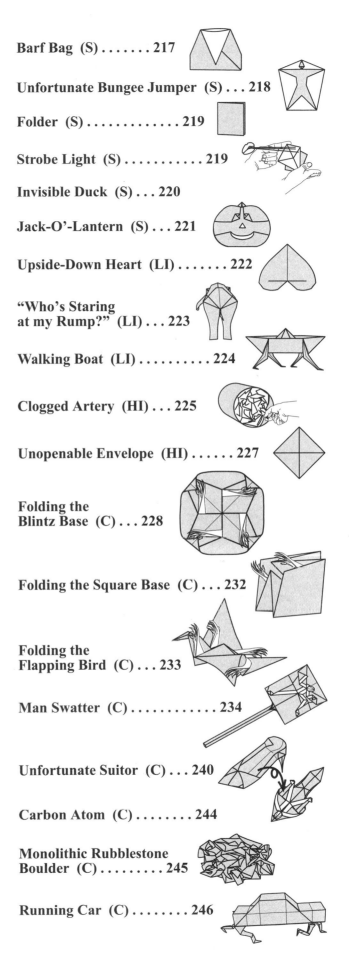

INTRODUCTION

Origami: A Personal Account

Like most folders throughout the world, origami found me on the playground. Paper airplanes, hats, cups, and "Cootie Catchers," are "playground folds" which we learned in elementary school and have been part of cultures throughout the world for centuries. For most adults, origami was simply a childhood pastime, one that they outgrew, but for me it grew to become a burning passion which is still flaming today. What I find so intriguing about origami is the infinite possibilities that can burst forth from folding a simple sheet of paper. Most of all, I love designing my own models and sharing them with other folders.

Imagine creating something that will live indefinitely and be appreciated and reproduced for generations to come. Origami is an endless forum for expressing creativity; there can never be enough new origami models. Through this book, I hope to inspire people of all ages to become passionate about origami and learn to design new models, so that we can share the fruits of discovery and further the world of folds.

Montroll's Grasshopper (fourth grade)

When I was ten, my parents gave me my first advanced origami book, *Origami for the Enthusiast*, by John Montroll, the only origami book that I would see for the next five years. The first model that I tried out of this book was the grasshopper; it was the last and most difficult model in the book. Although my finished model did not look nearly as good as the one pictured in the book, it was my first exposure to advanced folding techniques and allowed me to take off into a new world of designing origami. It was from the first folds of the grasshopper that I designed my first origami model, a "five-headed bird." I figured it out by looking at the grasshopper base and noticing that it looked just like a Bird Base but with four extra points; I thought, why not turn these extra points into heads? The result was a five-headed bird.

After folding only a few models from the Enthusiast book, I stopped using the book and instead focused on designing my own models. I simply liked folding by instinct rather than by following directions. I clung to the ideal of exploring my own personal unknown.

Part of what allowed me to stay away from diagrams was that my expectations of quality weren't very high. The fact that my designs were unrefined didn't bother me; it was not the final outcome of the models that was important to me, but rather the process of designing them. I loved the idea of folding something that probably no one had ever folded before. Most of my finished models were imaginary creatures and didn't look like anything recognizable. My folding premise was that anything could be made into a creature, and my designing method was to keep folding a piece of paper any which way until there were enough appendages sticking out to make a creature. No matter where the appendages ended up, I would turn them into arms, legs, wings, heads, and tails, and then presto, I would have a creature. Sometimes it would even turn out to be almost recognizable: "Look mom, it's a kangaroo pegasus!"

During eighth and ninth grades, I went through a phase where I would go through the dictionary and try to design origami models of whatever words had pictures by them. This is when I first started having specific forms in mind before sitting down to fold. In general, I would tend to fold animals, but I also branched out into other themes such as houses, boats, and furniture. I used to declare that nothing is impossible to represent by folding one uncut square piece of paper. Of course, I was aware that some subjects are more difficult and less worthwhile to try to represent than others. So rather than trying to fold amoebas, barbed-wire fences, restaurants, or shopping malls, I tended to stick to the familiar, straightforward theme of animals.

I was aware that many of the animal subjects I had been folding could already be found in other advanced origami books, but because I enjoyed designing my own models, I tried to keep away from these books. I was worried that if I were to be exposed to all of the amazing models out there, I would be less inspired to design my own models, for I would see how mediocre my own models were. My whole self-protective philosophy changed in the tenth grade when I discovered *Folding the Universe: Origami from Angelfish to Zen,* by Peter Engel. What made this origami book different from others I had glanced at was that it had an extensive section relating origami to such unlikely topics as music, Buddhist philosophy, and psychology of creativity. It looked so fascinating I could not resist buying it.

Lanky Pegasus (seventh grade)

Creature (seventh grade)

Flying Walking Whale (eighth grade)

Kangaroo Pegasus (eighth grade)

Wild Boar (ninth grade)

I learned so much from reading Peter Engel's book that I soon realized how silly and unproductive my boycott of origami books actually was. I decided to go on a quest for origami knowledge. I decided that I could better forge my own path if I let myself be given the tools used by the origami experts. I went on an origami book shopping spree; I bought all of the advanced books I could find and studied the different authors' methods of folding. After coming in contact with this garden of origami knowledge, I stopped designing animal models, as I felt overwhelmed by all of the exquisite, extremely polished animal designs in the books. I felt that whatever animal subjects I could design had already been designed perfectly by the experts. Despite causing me to bid animal folding goodbye, on the whole these books actually expanded my repertoire of folding. It was no longer enough to just design a new way to fold a certain subject; the new challenge was to come up with new subjects that had never been folded. I forced myself to branch out as far as I could beyond animal themes and instead try to fold scenes, ideas, and symbols. One of my main strategies was to try to fold already commonly folded subjects such as cranes, hearts, and people, using only part of the paper, so that I could then use the rest of the paper to fold some sort of surrounding scene. For instance, after discovering how to fold a person using only two corners of the square, I was able to apply this method to make a whole variety of models of people doing things (e.g., *Surfer on a Wave, Person on a Balance Beam*). This general method of creating new models I called "isolating squares," or "isolating points."

Person Stranded on a Desert Island
1990 (undiagrammed)

The isolation method enabled me to reach outside the existing bounds of origami and define my own style. It also enabled me to manifest my personality in my origami models. Some common themes I liked to inject into my models were the 'ridiculously extreme' (e.g., *25-headed crane*), the 'ridiculously oxymoronic' (e.g., *Surfer on a Still Lake*), and the 'outrageously ridiculous' (e.g., *Baby Contemplates Suicide after Running over Mother with Baby Carriage)*. These *ridiculous* themes tended to reflect my other interests: caricature acting, juggling, unicycling, and clowning.

Soon after delving into the world of origami books, I came out of the origami closet even further by putting on a display for the public at Kasuri Dyeworks, a decorative paper and fabric store in Berkeley, California (my home town). This was the first time my origami was viewed by a wide audience. Eunice Lew, a member of the San Francisco Origami Group (SFOG), saw my display, phoned me, and told me about the group. I started attending the monthly meetings where for the first time I folded with an actual group of origamists.

At first, I was surprised to find that I was one of the few who actually designed origami models. Most members of the club just folded from diagrams and were amazed to see all the models I had created myself. Before going there, I hadn't realized that designing origami models was uncommon. Since it was my primary experience, I was under the impression that it was what everybody did.

At the meetings I got to teach many of my original models, which gave me new insights into origami designing. From trying unsuccessfully to teach some of my earlier, less-guidelined models, I learned how important it was when designing to guideline each fold. For instance, I found that instructions like, "Fold this flap to right about here," were far less effective than instructions like, "Valley-fold the tip of the wave down to meet the right edge of the base of the wave." I found that the more each design had clear landmarks at each step (i.e., "fully guidelined"), the easier it would be to teach.

Goofing around at an OrigamiUSA Convention

At the San Francisco Origami Group, I was told about The Friends of The Origami Center of America (now Origami USA), and in 1990 I attended my first origami convention in New York City. It was a dream-come-true to meet and fold with so many people who were all there for a common purpose: to be "wrapped up" in origami. Imagine a huge gym filled with hundreds of folders exchanging ideas and teaching each other their favorite models. It was especially satisfying for me to meet so many origami designers.

The biggest highlight for me was meeting my mentor, John Montroll. I took his *Origami Chessboard* class. At first I was nervous, being aware of how famous he was in the origami world, but my nervousness disappeared when class started and I saw how friendly he was. He constantly made puns and light-heartedly teased everybody, including himself. Rather than interacting on a master-student level, we quickly became pals. After I completed the chessboard, we sat down for a game of chess (he beat me with ease). In addition to origami and chess, we both had common interests in math, whistling, and Gilbert and Sullivan.

Attending the New York origami convention made me aware of how popular origami was on the east coast, as well as how relatively sparse it was on the west coast, at least in Berkeley, my home town, and in Santa Cruz, where I went to college. The San Francisco Origami Group was great while it lasted, but alas, it *folded* (I couldn't resist).

Luckily, soon after, a new origami group, Bay Area Rapid Folders (BARF—a revolting play on "BART": Bay Area Rapid Transit) was formed by Mark Turner, an extremely outgoing and inspiring folder who, tragically, had been diagnosed with AIDS. Over his brief origami career, Mark's accomplishments were awesome. Throughout the three years from the time he was diagnosed with AIDS to the time he passed away, he organized the monthly BARF meetings, wrote and published the monthly newsletter, organized numerous origami exhibits, and most amazing of all, learned how to design his own models and wrote his own origami book, *Garden Folds*.

The area of origami in which Mark and I related most was designing models. At the 1993 origami convention in New York, Mark and I dormed together and over the course of the weekend spent a lot of time discussing origami design. Before the convention, Mark had folded an amazing number of highly complex models from diagrams (probably more than I had in my ten years of folding), but he had folded practically no models of his own.

The second night of the convention, we stayed up late into the night designing an *"Old Man with a Cane"* to be displayed in the origami exhibit the next day. From deciding what base to use, to figuring out how to form the different appendages and perfect the final model, I guided him through each stage of the design. When we finished, we had a model we were both quite pleased with, and he exclaimed, "That wasn't so hard!" It seemed as if origami designing, to him, had suddenly become demystified.

I don't think that during our designing session I taught Mark anything that he didn't already understand; I think his revelation was more just a matter of finally sitting down and "going for it." While I'm sure that his previous folding

Mark Turner

experience provided him with helpful design techniques, I can honestly say that in a single weekend Mark became a prolific designer; six months later he was at the BARF meeting selling his own origami book (it's taken me six years to complete this book). My experience helping Mark take the final step into the realm of origami design has led me to believe that there are many folders out there who are ready to take this same step and just need to "go for it." It has also shown me that designing origami is not as difficult as people make it out to be and is far from an innate ability that only some folders happen to have. If more folders would just "go for it," we would have a lot more origami creators as well as more origami creations in the world today.

After Mark passed away in April, 1994, I assumed the position of editor of the *BARF Newsletter*. This has been a wonderful experience, for it has helped keep the club together and has kept me busy diagramming my models. Mark would be happy to know that Bay Area Rapid Folders is still going strong, carrying on his legacy into which he so devotedly and generously put his heart. I am especially grateful to Mark for forming the group; it has kept me in touch with the local origami community, and let me know that while not as widespread as on the east coast, origami is certainly alive and well in the San Francisco Bay Area.

Designing origami for me has always been a form of self-expression. The process of teaching and diagramming my own models, and following other people's diagrams has been a way for me to connect with other folders. Even more satisfying than designing origami models has been sharing them with others. That is why I feel extremely fortunate that my folding path eventually led me into a far greater, much brighter world of worldly origami.

Designing Origami

There are enough fabulous origami models out in the world, already exquisitely designed and diagrammed to keep a fanatic folder occupied for years. Many folders would rather spend their time folding these ready-to-fold, guaranteed-to-delight models than labor for hours trying to design something that might not turn out at all. Yes, it's a hard job, but somebody's got to do it. No, really, it's not as hard as you may think, and it's so rewarding. A folded origami frog may last a bit longer than a balloon animal, but an origami design, diagrammed and published, could last an eternity. Designing origami grants you posterity, expresses your creativity, and furthers origami as an art.

Following are some tips and techniques that I use which might help make the path of designing a little more clear. However, keep in mind that no matter how much you read about origami designing techniques, learning to use them can only begin once you sit down with a piece of paper.

One method of going for it is "freefolding." Start folding a paper without any goal in mind and let your imagination fly. With enough imagination anything can be made, and everything you make can be anything. Get zany: "Look, it's Calvin Klein underwear before he became famous!"

Another wonderful opportunity to use your imagination is when you get stuck following diagrams. Rather than gnash your teeth, curse the author, smash the model and throw it away, you could stop right where you are and exclaim, "Look, it's a pogosticking one-legged giraffe!" Imagination is not only useful in moments of exasperation. It can also be exercised whenever you fold; you never know what new models you may spontaneously see in the folds.

If you would rather not design all your models by accident, there are more deliberate methods. The approach that I most often use involves three major stages: Deciding what to design, actually designing it, and finally, refining and perfecting the design until I'm satisfied with the final outcome.

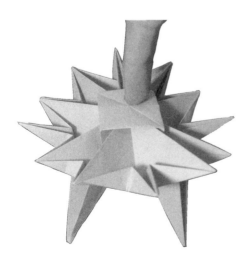

Squishy Blob (page 75)
Designed via free-folding

For the first stage, deciding what to fold, one must come up with an idea and assess whether it's practical. An important factor governing my decision to attempt to fold a given idea is whether I feel the idea is original enough. Since most animal forms have already been designed over and over by numerous experts, I shy away from them; why put so much effort into designing a model that someone else has already managed to successfully achieve through painful labor?

Venus Flytrap (page 87)
Designed via free-folding

Some origami designers will say that just because there are so many origami animal designs already out there is no reason for someone not to design animal models; each person's folding style has its own special qualities and is valuable to origami as a whole. While I agree that designing animal models makes for good tangible practice, I encourage designers to branch out into the endless other themes waiting to be folded. I feel that it is of more value to the world of origami to expand the pool of new origami ideas than it is to expand the pool of, say, new origami fish.

It is not difficult to come up with new folding themes. Even just looking around my room, I see ideas I have never folded or heard of anyone else folding: computer, video camera, TV, ruler, globe, toothbrush, somebody drinking, window with curtains. Going outside, the foldable world opens up. Throughout this book are boxes called *Thoughts Behind the Folds* which include ideas for new designs. I have found that there are endless ideas out there that haven't been folded yet, and I think that by trying to cultivate some of these ideas rather than struggling with old ones, the process of designing is more satisfying, and also furthers the art.

More difficult than coming up with new ideas is actually folding them. Although this requires spatial awareness, a lot of designing ability comes naturally through experimentation and experience following diagrams. The more folding experience you have, the easier it should be to make your models look like what you are trying to represent; the less folding experience, the more you might have to use your imagination. When I first started designing (in the fourth grade), I had little spatial awareness, and my models didn't look like much, but it was still fun to explore the infinite folding possibilities.

Once an idea has been chosen, there are many possible techniques to design the model. One technique is to blindly start folding and pray. A slightly more practical method is to start with the standard bases and see if any of them can be transformed into your target model. If this doesn't work, you can try starting with bases from other models you've folded, or try to make up your own base.

If the model has a clear form, a useful technique before making any folds is to try to map out on the square roughly where each appendage will come from when the model is folded. The goal is to plot the points of the appendages on the paper in such a manner that when folded, the model will waste the least paper and come out as large as possible. For instance if you were to try to design a table it would make sense to plot the four legs at the four corners. For most animals, it is easiest to plot the head and tail at two opposite corners since most animals have their head farthest from their tail.

Once you have a general idea where on the square each appendage of your model will come from, the next important technique is to isolate those points. This involves attaching the points with creases and then using those creases to fold up the model in such a way that the points stick out.

After you have achieved the general form of a model, the final step is to refine it so that it can be diagrammed and taught to other people. This entails giving all folds clear landmarks, and reducing them to simple folding operations such as "rabbit ear," "reverse fold," and so on. Sometimes altering a model to make it more foldable will involve compromising your own artistic tastes. But keep in mind that a major part of what makes a model aesthetically pleasing is its foldability, and in this sense, simplifying a model is a major plus. For instance, you could design a three-dimensional book without actually having to give it separate pages.

Man Swatter (page 234)
Evolved from a rockclimber, which wasn't worth diagramming or photographing

One general technique I almost always use in some way is the process of evolution. I use it in refining designs, but more importantly, I use it in branching out to make entirely new models. For instance, the Unfortunate Suitor evolved out of the Man Swatter which was an offshoot of a Rock Climber (undiagrammed). In the *Thoughts Behind the Folds* boxes are many ideas for how to branch out into new directions.

One difficulty that a lot of people seem to have when starting to design their own models is achieving satisfaction with their final product. I've found it easier to achieve satisfaction by folding original ideas (like a flying tomato or a hitchhiking hand)—there's nobody else's model for comparison.

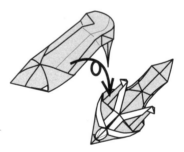

Unfortunate Suitor (page 240)
Evolved from the Man Swatter

More generally, to avoid frustration, I suggest focusing not so much on the final product as on the fun of the designing process itself. Origami is like playing competitive sports in that the main fun should not lie in winning but rather in playing the game. If you can enjoy origami designing simply for the process itself, then pleasing results will come naturally.

Mastering the techniques of origami design is a gradual process which cannot be done overnight. No matter how good someone is at designing, there will still be times of head-banging and frustration. But overall, the rewards of coming up with an original origami model far outweigh the tribulations.

Origami Purism

For centuries, origami has involved cutting, gluing, and using more than one sheet, and in many folding circles, it still does. But, over the last fifty years, origami has been taken up by scientists and mathematicians, who have found it more satisfying to restrict themselves to one square, no cuts. In "A Brief History of Origami," Robert Lang recounts,

> As origami designers' abilities improved, there arose an unofficial set of rules governing what was allowed and what wasn't, particularly in the West. In general, an origami figure from an uncut sheet was better than one from a cut sheet; a single sheet was more desirable than two; and a fold from a square was preferred over any other starting shape. (*Origami Sculptures,* by John Montroll, page 9)

As an origami designer, I am what people call an origami purist, for I strictly adhere to the above rules and regard them as a code of ethics. I subscribe to origami purism because I find this type of origami to be more aesthetically pleasing than non-pure forms, and the methods of designing more cohesive, structured and tangible. In fact, with certain models, such as the Eight Interlocking Rings, it is the fact that the model has been folded from just one square piece of paper that so astonishes people. When people discover that my models are from just one uncut square they are often very surprised. "How can you do that?" they ask me, and then the more bold ask, "Why?" These are the same questions I get asked when I tell people that I'm vegan, i.e., I eat no animal products.

I equate origami purism and veganism, two seemingly unrelated concepts because they have actually both affected me in similar ways. Although for many, veganism and origami purism might seem restricting and difficult to adhere to, they have both given me a foundation from which I can eat and fold to my full potential. By including an explanation of my vegan philosophy, I feel I can better explain origami purism.

I used to be a hamburger and hot dog junkie. I hated mixing foods, would steer clear of most vegetables and often would fill my plate with nothing but hamburger and catsup. It was clear to me that my diet was less than varied, not healthy and needed to change. When I decided to become vegetarian and again when I became vegan, I began eating new and healthier foods. I discovered delicious plant-based foods that I'd never even heard of. Although on one level, I was placing restrictions on my diet, in reality, my diet became more varied, balanced, and wholesome. Almost all animal-based foods have plant-based substitutes that are healthier, and, in my opinion, taste better as well. Veganism set down a foundation for my diet for it made me avoid unhealthy foods and gave me simple guidelines for what foods were good for me and for the environment as well.

Although origami purism is less political and certainly less environmental-minded than veganism, many of the ideas governing each are parallel. Both doctrines set guidelines which narrow sets of possibilities by ruling out certain elements and in doing so make more tangible those that remain. There are already so many possible ways to fold most models using only one square and no cuts, that when you lose these restrictions you lose a sense of direction. When setting out to design a model from one square no cuts, the designer has a set of guidelines in which to work; he is aware of exactly how much paper he has to work with and has a set goal in mind—to fold the most well-proportioned, realistic-looking, efficient model using the most aesthetically pleasing, easily foldable method. If cutting or using more than one piece of paper is permitted, then the effort the designer puts into so carefully rationing out the paper to fit the different appendages becomes meaningless. For the paper cutter, it matters not how many appendages a given model requires, because with only a few cuts, the right number can easily be achieved.

What did the out-of-line folder say to the purist?
"Can I please have cuts?"

Just as I feel that when animal products are used, the wholesomeness of the food is lost, as an origami purist I believe that when scissors are employed, the integrity of the paper is lost. There are few if any folding subjects that could benefit from the use of scissors (origami "confetti" comes to mind). When non-purists cut paper, they are actually cutting up the art, destroying the wholeness of the art. The origami purist, on the other hand, sees the beauty and wonder of an endless array of representations of life springing out of the simple square. Why use scissors, or more than one sheet, when one uncut square suffices? A similar question is asked by vegans, "Why eat animal products when plant-based foods suffice?"

Another reason that I object to the use of cutting in origami is that it falsely represents origami. Just as one cannot see directly the suffering and environmental harm that went into a plate of meat, most origami viewers cannot see when a model has been cut. I remember once, a long time ago, I attempted to fold the traditional crab from a beginning origami book because I thought the crab shown in the picture looked really neat. It was a huge let down when I came to the step where you need to make four cuts in order to turn the four legs into eight. I was so disappointed that I didn't even finish the model, for inside of me there had already sprouted an origami code of ethics. Besides treating the paper disrespectfully, the widespread use of cutting in traditional origami has made the public view origami as a craft where cutting is okay. As a result, when people see the modern purist origami, they can't appreciate it as much for what it is, for they just assume that it too involves cutting.

Why did the almost deranged folder fold razor sharp paper?

Because he wanted a paper cut.

But then why would he use scissors?

Because he wanted a paper cut.

But then why did he take it all to a professional?

Because he wanted to pay per cut.

Many of my arguments against cutting also apply to using more than one sheet of paper. Using two sheets is most commonly found in animal designs where the head and front legs are folded from one sheet and the body and hind legs are folded from the other. Even the world-renowned Japanese folder, Akira Yoshizawa, requires two sheets to fold many of his animals, possibly because it makes the models easier for others to fold.

But being easier to fold should not justify using more than one sheet. There are many alternative approaches to designing simple origami that can be done with one sheet. One approach is to use fewer appendages. For example, there is a wonderful traditional three-legged giraffe model which is also very realistic-looking. Simplifying a design can also be achieved by shortening the appendages. Although this will usually make the model look more abstract, it can also give the model a more artistic look. In general, designing a model that is easier to fold, entails making it less realistic-looking. However, abstract models are valuable to both designers and folders and are a much better solution to simplifying a model than using scissors or more than one piece of paper.

How many modular origami folders does it take to make a 20 ft. high sculpture?

"I don't know... I can't manage to get their arms and legs to stay interlocked, and using superglue would be inhumane and impure."

It all comes down to a simple question: Why fold a model out of two sheets when you can fold it out of one? American folders John Montroll and Robert Lang have demonstrated that folding practically any species of animal out of just one square is not only possible, but also well worth the effort. Many people will argue that for many species of animals, it is easier to fold a realistic-looking final product out of two sheets of paper than out of one. But for me, the challenge of designing purist origami is part of what makes it fun. Meeting that challenge is extremely satisfying because not only am I unlocking new doors inside myself, but I'm opening them up to the world of folders as well. Relating this to veganism, meeting the challenge of eating vegan in a meat-based society, is enjoyable and satisfying to me.

Once diagrammed, an origami model will potentially outlive its designer. In designing models that require cutting, one is sending out a message to future generations, "I didn't have the ability or the ambition to fold this without cutting, but I hope you'll still fold it." But if a designer is not willing to meet the challenge and put in the time it takes to make an aesthetically pleasing model, then why should folders take the time to fold it? There are plenty of designers out there who have the ability and the ambition to make pure, wholesome, **UNCUT** origami and it is these folders—not the cutters—who further origami as an art.

The origami purist doctrines adhere to the idea that origami is not just an art where what you see is what you get: there are many folds hidden behind the visible folds, which although unseen by the viewer, contribute to the overall integrity of the design. Since origami is more about folding than viewing, it is of utmost importance that the folding procedure be as aesthetically pleasing as possible. Cutting is the least aesthetic folding operation of all because it destroys the wholeness of the paper. Although origami with cutting is traditional and has been viewed for centuries as a sacred craft, I see the cutting part of it as a primitive attribute, ready to be outgrown. I like to think of the origami paper as sacred and from this point of view I see cutting the paper as sacrilege.

• Since writing the above, I've modified my folding morals and my diet to occasionally include rectangles and honey respectively.

Ethics and Politics in Origami

One of the greatest rewards of creating models is that it furthers the world of origami. This should be the ultimate goal of designing models, for the more selfless we can be, the easier it is to work together, exchange ideas and grow from each other. I am greatly fulfilled when I see what could be my influence in other people's work, whether or not I'm credited for it. When the origami world becomes an open forum for exchanging ideas and knowledge, each of us can achieve the most and contribute the most to the art.

The most fruitful collaboration I have ever experienced was with my very good friend Chris Palmer. During the three years that we both lived in Santa Cruz, we had countless sessions folding together and bouncing ideas back and forth. Our biggest joint discoveries were in the realms of flashers and tessellations. By working together, we were able to use each other's insights to open doors that we might never have discovered by ourselves.

Unfortunately, not all origami relationships between people are as fruitful. In many cases the politics of origami achievements gets in the way of working together and sometimes causes bitterness and distrust. In general, the more people are concerned with who gets credit for what, the more people will be protective of their models and less willing to share their ideas. In *Folding the Universe: Origami from Angelfish to Zen,* Peter Engel, in his section called, "The Case of the Purloined Pig," discusses the dispute between Akira Yoshizawa and Alfredo Cerceda where each claimed to be the creator of the same origami pig. Besides general bitterness, one of the outcomes was that they both became more protective of their models and less willing to share their new designs with the origami community. This kind of dispute can alienate folders and hinder the progress of the art.

The conflict between Yoshizawa and Cerceda is an extremely rare case in that the two pigs were identical. However, when designers' models are similar, disputes of origami ownership are all too common. Oftentimes, folders get caught up in the personal gratification of origami: "Hey look, I am the first one who ever did this; I hope everyone sees, but nobody copies me." Many people feel that it is not safe to show a model before it is published. They are worried that people will see it, and just by looking at it, be able to figure out how to fold it and then claim they designed it. One might think that this never happens, for origami is a peaceful art and most folders are kind and sensitive, but the problem is that possible scenarios for infringement are not black and white; there is a lot of gray in-between. What might be a completely original model to one folder might be considered a mere variation by another.

Iso-Area Twist Octagons
(identical on both sides)
This tessellation, which Chris Palmer folded from one square, was one of our a collaborative efforts.

I advocate being overly sensitive about this issue. I feel it is of extreme importance for us to go out of our way to give credit where it is due. Throughout the model diagrams in this book I've included special boxes discussing my influences. Citing our influences in depth is beneficial to us, to those we cite, and to those who fold our models. It also promotes mutual cooperation and appreciation among designers. People enjoy getting history about what inspired us to try to create a given model and what method we used.

It is a fact of human interaction that when we come in contact with each other's work, we are bound to be influenced by it. That is a good thing. Origami is an art where we can all learn and grow from each other. When we cooperate and share our ideas and breakthroughs, the most progress can be made.

Now, with no further ado, on with the folds!

NOTATION

Line Styles

Valley Fold	------------
Mountain Fold	-·-·-·-·-·-
Crease	————
Covered up edges or folds or where the paper ends up	···················

Arrows and Symbols

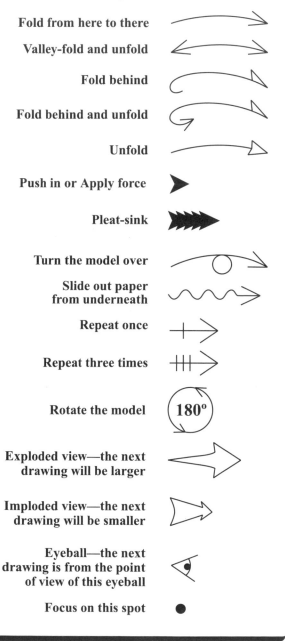

Fold from here to there

Valley-fold and unfold

Fold behind

Fold behind and unfold

Unfold

Push in or Apply force

Pleat-sink

Turn the model over

Slide out paper from underneath

Repeat once

Repeat three times

Rotate the model 180°

Exploded view—the next drawing will be larger

Imploded view—the next drawing will be smaller

Eyeball—the next drawing is from the point of view of this eyeball

Focus on this spot

Basic Folds Index

In addition to the Basics section on the following pages, basic folds instructions are also integrated into the model diagrams in the form of cartoon clouds. This is so that you can get straight to folding models. Below is a list showing where each fold is explained.

Anatomy of the Origami Diagram

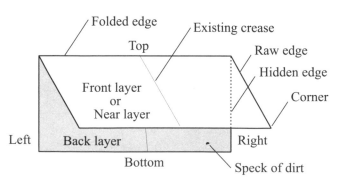

Folded edge · Existing crease · Top · Raw edge · Hidden edge · Corner · Front layer or Near layer · Left · Back layer · Right · Bottom · Speck of dirt

Basics

This is a pictorial glossary showing how to do the basic folds which appear throughout origami diagrams. All origami maneuvers can be broken down into mountain folds and valley folds. Mountain folds, indicated by dot-dot-dash lines, are convex like a mountain ridge. Valley folds, indicated by dash-dash lines, are concave, like a valley.

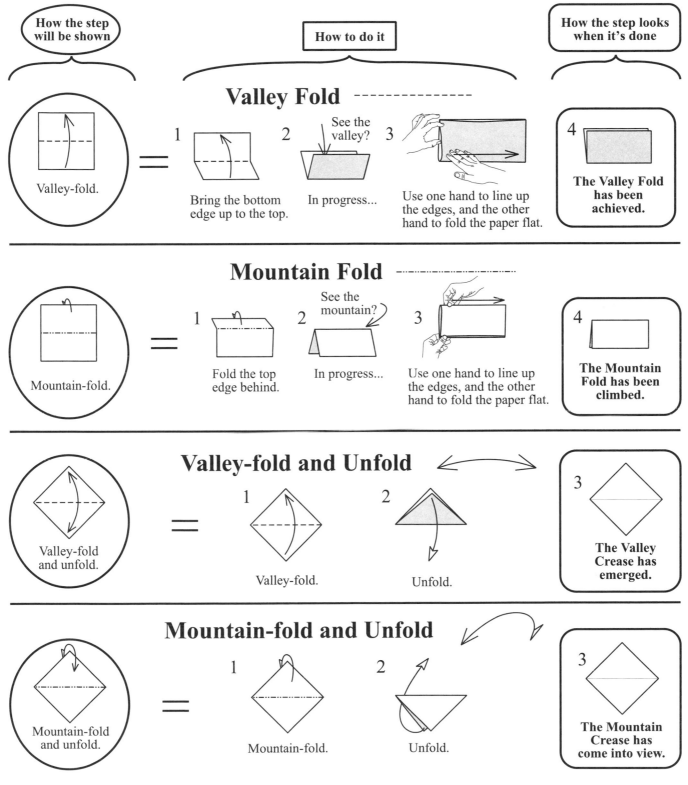

How the step will be shown

How to do it

How the step looks when it's done

Valley Fold

Valley-fold.

= 1 Bring the bottom edge up to the top.

2 See the valley? In progress...

3 Use one hand to line up the edges, and the other hand to fold the paper flat.

4 The Valley Fold has been achieved.

Mountain Fold

Mountain-fold.

= 1 Fold the top edge behind.

2 See the mountain? In progress...

3 Use one hand to line up the edges, and the other hand to fold the paper flat.

4 The Mountain Fold has been climbed.

Valley-fold and Unfold

Valley-fold and unfold.

= 1 Valley-fold.

2 Unfold.

3 The Valley Crease has emerged.

Mountain-fold and Unfold

Mountain-fold and unfold.

= 1 Mountain-fold.

2 Unfold.

3 The Mountain Crease has come into view.

Blintz Base

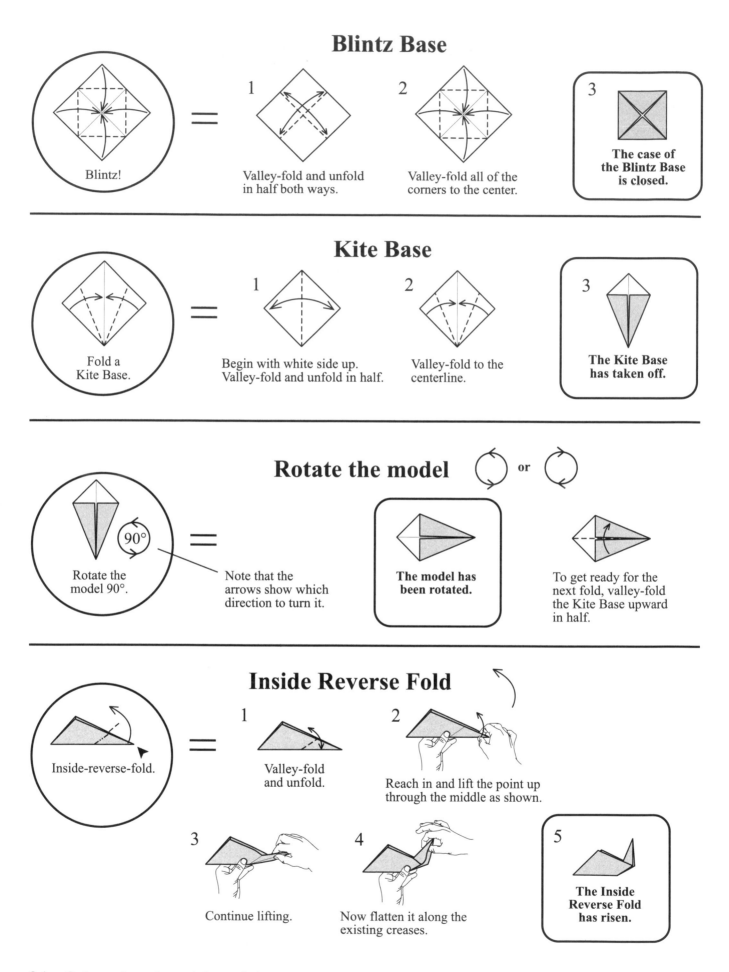

Blintz! =

1 Valley-fold and unfold in half both ways.

2 Valley-fold all of the corners to the center.

3 The case of the Blintz Base is closed.

Kite Base

Fold a Kite Base. =

1 Begin with white side up. Valley-fold and unfold in half.

2 Valley-fold to the centerline.

3 The Kite Base has taken off.

Rotate the model or

Rotate the model 90°. =

Note that the arrows show which direction to turn it.

The model has been rotated.

To get ready for the next fold, valley-fold the Kite Base upward in half.

Inside Reverse Fold

Inside-reverse-fold. =

1 Valley-fold and unfold.

2 Reach in and lift the point up through the middle as shown.

3 Continue lifting.

4 Now flatten it along the existing creases.

5 The Inside Reverse Fold has risen.

Outside Reverse Fold

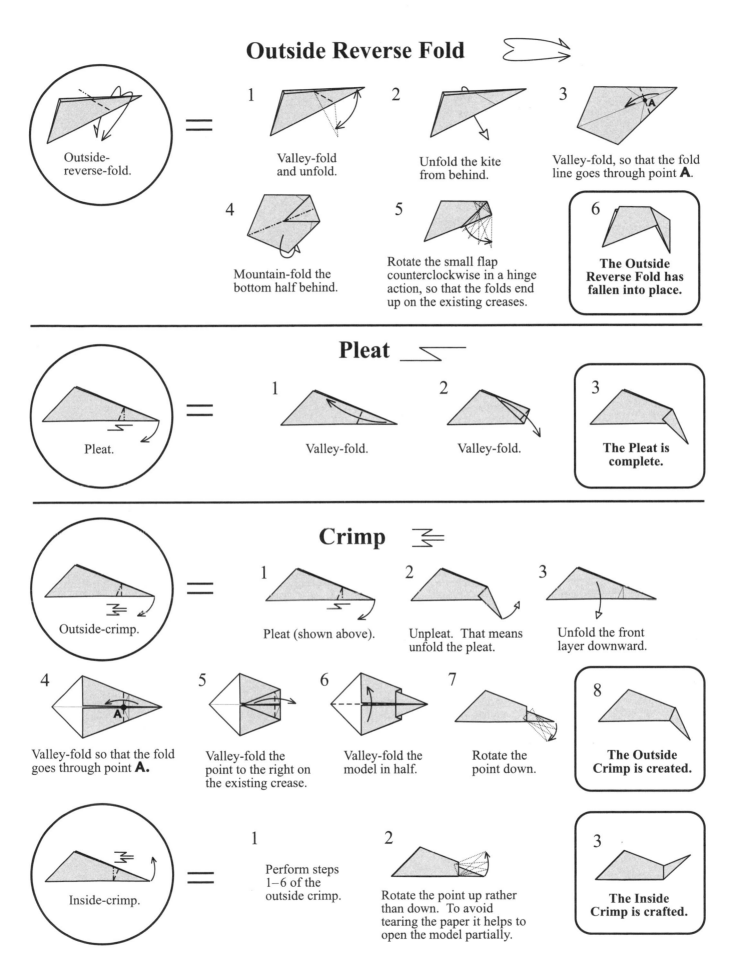

Outside-reverse-fold.

=

1 Valley-fold and unfold.

2 Unfold the kite from behind.

3 Valley-fold, so that the fold line goes through point **A**.

4 Mountain-fold the bottom half behind.

5 Rotate the small flap counterclockwise in a hinge action, so that the folds end up on the existing creases.

6 **The Outside Reverse Fold has fallen into place.**

Pleat

Pleat.

=

1 Valley-fold.

2 Valley-fold.

3 **The Pleat is complete.**

Crimp

Outside-crimp.

=

1 Pleat (shown above).

2 Unpleat. That means unfold the pleat.

3 Unfold the front layer downward.

4 Valley-fold so that the fold goes through point **A.**

5 Valley-fold the point to the right on the existing crease.

6 Valley-fold the model in half.

7 Rotate the point down.

8 **The Outside Crimp is created.**

Inside-crimp.

=

1 Perform steps 1–6 of the outside crimp.

2 Rotate the point up rather than down. To avoid tearing the paper it helps to open the model partially.

3 **The Inside Crimp is crafted.**

Squash Fold

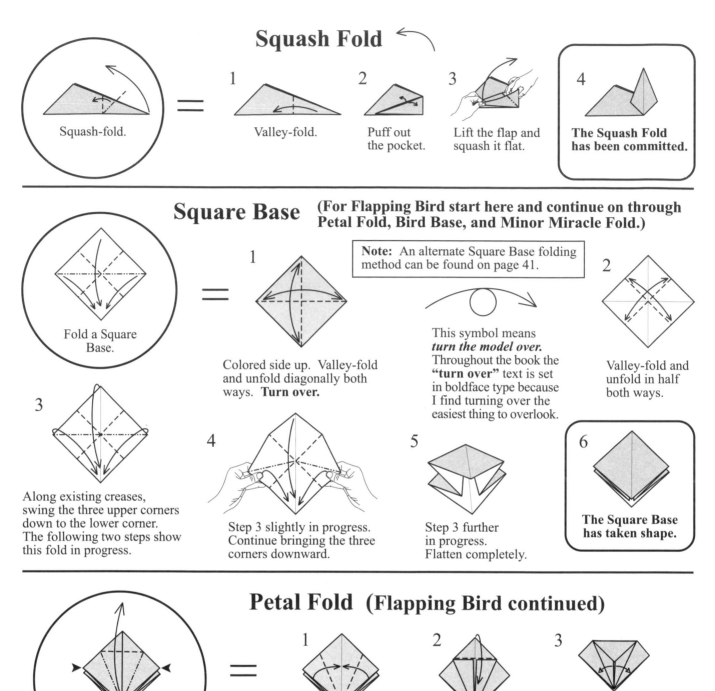

Squash-fold.

=

1 Valley-fold.

2 Puff out the pocket.

3 Lift the flap and squash it flat.

4 The Squash Fold has been committed.

Square Base

(For Flapping Bird start here and continue on through Petal Fold, Bird Base, and Minor Miracle Fold.)

Fold a Square Base.

=

1 Colored side up. Valley-fold and unfold diagonally both ways. **Turn over.**

Note: An alternate Square Base folding method can be found on page 41.

This symbol means *turn the model over.* Throughout the book the **"turn over"** text is set in boldface type because I find turning over the easiest thing to overlook.

2 Valley-fold and unfold in half both ways.

3 Along existing creases, swing the three upper corners down to the lower corner. The following two steps show this fold in progress.

4 Step 3 slightly in progress. Continue bringing the three corners downward.

5 Step 3 further in progress. Flatten completely.

6 The Square Base has taken shape.

Petal Fold (Flapping Bird continued)

Petal-fold.

=

1 Begin with a Square Base. Valley-fold the left and right front flaps to middle crease.

2 Valley-fold the top down.

3 Unfold the two flaps but leave the top folded down.

4 Lift the front flap slightly.

5 Keep lifting.

6 Here we have a boat. Collapse the sides of the boat to the middle line.

7 The Petal Fold has blossomed. For Flapping Bird, now skip to Bird Base step 2.

Bird Base (Flapping Bird continued)

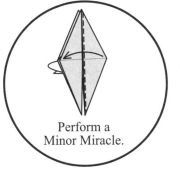

Fold a Bird Base.

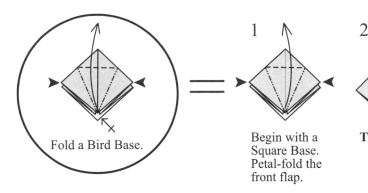

1 Begin with a Square Base. Petal-fold the front flap.

2 **Turn over.**

3 Petal-fold as before. If you forgot how to do a petal fold, go back a page to Petal Fold step 1.

4 **The Bird Base has landed.**

Minor Miracle Fold (Flapping Bird cont.)

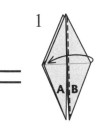

Perform a Minor Miracle.

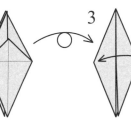

1 Begin with a Bird Base. Notice there are two legs at the bottom, **A** and **B**. Valley-fold one side flap from right to the left.

2 **Turn over.**

3 Valley-fold one flap from right to the left.

4 **A Minor Miracle has been worked:** The legs are now shorter and on top. WOW!

Flapping Bird

(Begin with Square Base on page 26 and continue on through Petal Fold, Bird Base, and Minor Miracle Fold.)

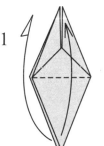

1 Fold up the front flap in front and the back flap to the back.

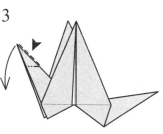

2 Rotate the two inner flaps down to the positions shown by the dotted lines. Then flatten the model.

3 Inside-reverse-fold to form the head. See page 24 for how to do an inside reverse fold.

4 Valley-fold and unfold the front wing. Repeat behind.

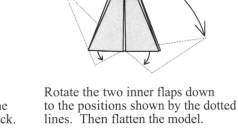

5 Holding exactly as shown, put your finger in the pocket and then take it out. Repeat behind.

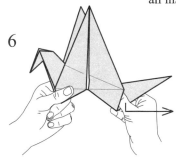

6 Hold firmly as shown. To make the wings flap, pull your right hand straight down and then to the right.

7 **The Bird has been flapped.** Pull the tail out and push it in, flapping to your heart's content.

Fish Base or Rabbit Ear

Note: A rabbit ear is just one side of a Fish Base.

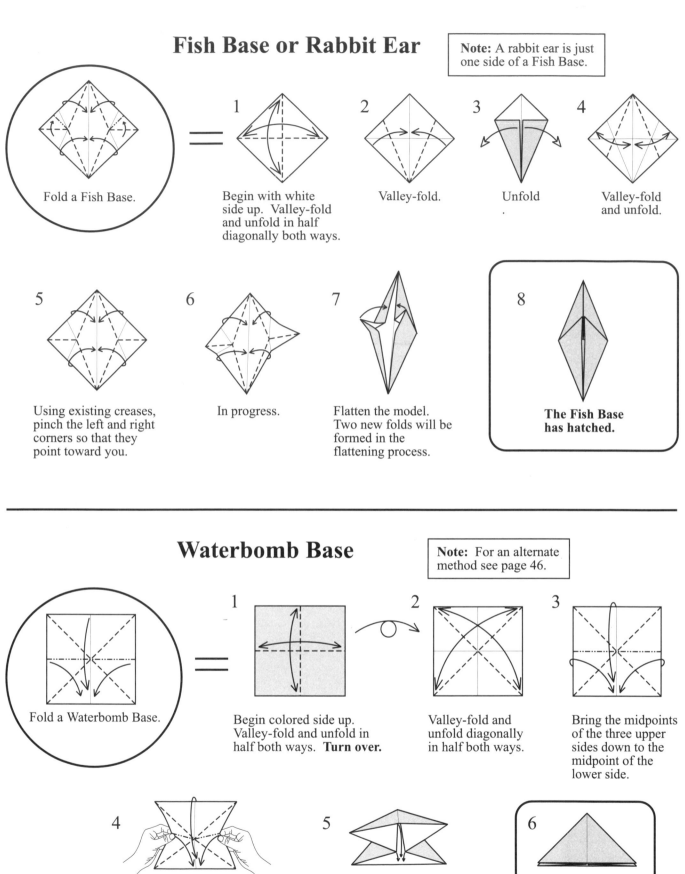

Fold a Fish Base.

1 Begin with white side up. Valley-fold and unfold in half diagonally both ways.

2 Valley-fold.

3 Unfold.

4 Valley-fold and unfold.

5 Using existing creases, pinch the left and right corners so that they point toward you.

6 In progress.

7 Flatten the model. Two new folds will be formed in the flattening process.

8 **The Fish Base has hatched.**

Waterbomb Base

Note: For an alternate method see page 46.

Fold a Waterbomb Base.

1 Begin colored side up. Valley-fold and unfold in half both ways. **Turn over.**

2 Valley-fold and unfold diagonally in half both ways.

3 Bring the midpoints of the three upper sides down to the midpoint of the lower side.

4 In progress.

5 Even more progressive!

6 **The Waterbomb Base has exploded into existence.**

Sink

Note: The sink arrowhead is also used when a point gets reverse-folded into the model.

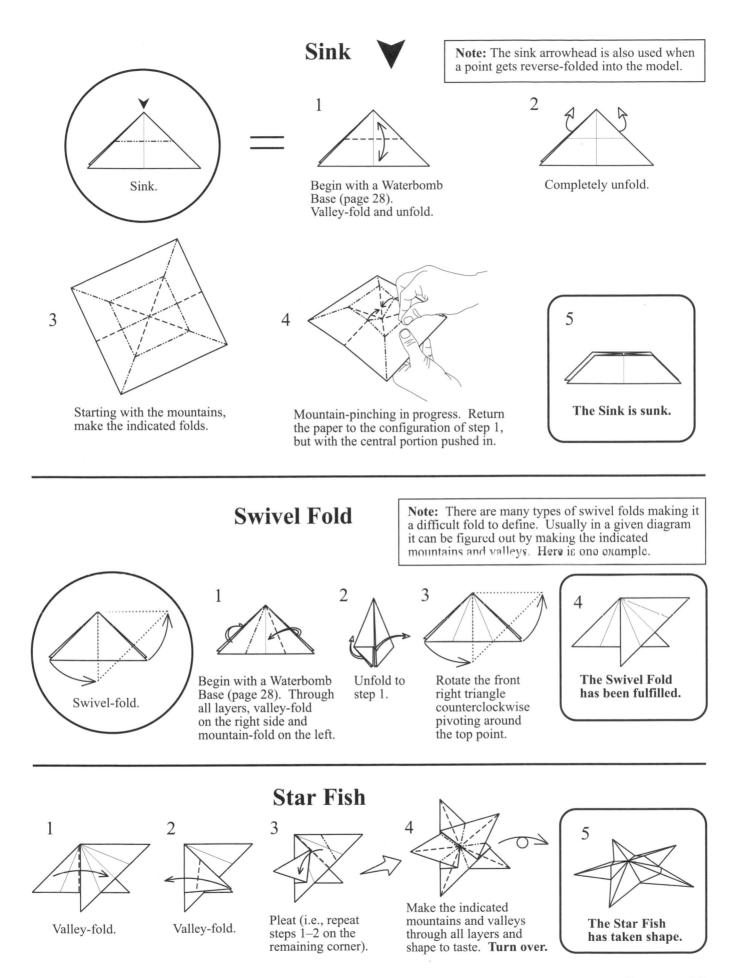

Sink.

1
Begin with a Waterbomb Base (page 28). Valley-fold and unfold.

2
Completely unfold.

3
Starting with the mountains, make the indicated folds.

4
Mountain-pinching in progress. Return the paper to the configuration of step 1, but with the central portion pushed in.

5
The Sink is sunk.

Swivel Fold

Note: There are many types of swivel folds making it a difficult fold to define. Usually in a given diagram it can be figured out by making the indicated mountains and valleys. Here is one example.

Swivel-fold.

1
Begin with a Waterbomb Base (page 28). Through all layers, valley-fold on the right side and mountain-fold on the left.

2
Unfold to step 1.

3
Rotate the front right triangle counterclockwise pivoting around the top point.

4
The Swivel Fold has been fulfilled.

Star Fish

1
Valley-fold.

2
Valley-fold.

3
Pleat (i.e., repeat steps 1–2 on the remaining corner).

4
Make the indicated mountains and valleys through all layers and shape to taste. **Turn over.**

5
The Star Fish has taken shape.

Choosing Paper

The following is a run-down on papers most commonly used for origami. Throughout many of the model diagrams, suggestions are given for what type of paper to use.

Origami paper (a.k.a. Kami): Paper squares colored on one side only, usually imported from Japan. Origami paper can be found at art stores and toy stores. The sizes available range from 1.5" to 14" squares.

Japanese foil: Foil origami paper from Japan. It's white paper on one side and foil on the other. If you don't like the shininess of foil, you can color/paint the white side and use that side instead. With acrylic paint, both sides of the foil can be colored. Japanese foil can be found at most art stores in packages of 3", 5", 6", and 10" squares. In addition, large sheets of silver and gold can often be found in the bulk paper section of the art store.

American foil: Foil produced in the United States. It's heavier than Japanese foil and tends to flake off. The only place I've ever seen this paper sold is at Origami USA conventions. But, then again, I haven't really looked for it since I prefer Japanese foil.

Tissue foil: Aluminum foil laminated on both sides with tissue paper. This foil is not sold in stores, but is not hard to make. Using the adhesive of your choice (spray glue works well), simply paste tissue paper onto both sides of a sheet of aluminum foil. If you overlap the aluminum foil, you can make huge sheets.

Florists' foil: The foil used to wrap flowers. It's strong, comes in large sizes, comes in many pretty colors and is foil on both sides. It's good for complex models. It's available at florist shops—imagine that!

Wyndstone Marble Light paper: A heavy, durable, smooth paper that is the same color on both sides. It's a high quality paper ideal for all Flasher designs and just about any model that does not require two colors. It's available at many major art stores.

Typing paper: You all know what that is (even though no one ever types onto it anymore).

Card Stock: Thick paper used for cards and covers. It's not commonly used for folding but works beautifully for the Frog's Tongue, Heart Attack, and giant Magic Flap (11" x 11").

Wallpaper: A heavy, durable paper available in huge sizes. Also, wallpaper scraps (or samples) are often given out freely at wallpaper stores. Ask to see their dumpster.

Sheet metal: Copper or brass sheet metal and metal mesh sold for industry by special sheet metal retailers, but also sold at many hobby shops. Metal is a great origami medium for the serious sculptor, but many varieties are available—some not so good, so make sure to get a sample before buying.

Magazine and junkmail paper: Cheap, colorful, abundant paper that we ought to be putting to good use.

Dollar bills: High quality paper that some people even still use to buy things with. One drawback is that it's quite expensive. However, each rectangle can be cut into two or more squares to economize!

Tips for Following Diagrams

Make folds as precise as possible. Carefully line up each fold making sure it's exactly where it's supposed to be. Never approximate unless the diagram calls for it. Most of the models in this book are fully guidelined (i.e., there are landmarks for every fold). Any error made will get magnified; if the beginning folds of a model are off, the end folds will be REALLY off!

Look ahead to the next step. If, for instance, you're on step 4 of the Exploding Envelope, your goal is to make the model look like the diagram in step 5. So before doing step 4, you should look at the diagram in step 5 to see what you're aiming for.

Orient the paper. Make sure the paper is oriented exactly as it is shown in the diagram.

Fold on a flat surface. Most folders, including myself, fold on a flat surface simply because it's easier. However, grand master Akira Yoshizawa encourages origamists to fold in the air so that they can surround the paper and breathe life into it on all sides. So the choice is yours.

Make Sharp Folds (unless otherwise stated). Fingernails are a good tool.

Don't get in over your head. All the models in the Table of Contents and Sneak Preview are labeled Simple (S), Low Intermediate (LI), Intermediate (I), High Intermediate (HI), and Complex (C).

If you are a beginning folder, it's a good idea to start with the simple models. You're welcome to start out with the complex diagrams, but if you get stuck, before you start cursing, please come back and attempt something easier.

Tips for Tackling Tough Steps

Fold the mountains and valleys piecewise. Since all diagrams are made up of mountains and valleys, if you get stuck on a step, break it down. In other words, pinch all mountains and valleys as they are shown in the diagram. Then, like pieces of a puzzle, try to make them fit together.

Read the text. Ideally, origami is an illustrated language, but sometimes reading the text can clear up confusion.

Take a break and come back to it. Sometimes it is frustration that impedes one's effort. After a snack break, a stretch break or a visit to an origami therapist, you might feel as good as new and ready once more to try to conquer the fold.

Consult other folders. See if there is an origami club in your area. Sometimes commiserating with other folders is beneficial. For regional group information visit Joseph Wu's webpage: **www.origami.vancouver.bc.ca** or contact:

OrigamiUSA
15 West 77 Street New York, NY 10024-5192
Telephone: (212) 769-5635

Try something easier. How about brain surgery?

Origami Action

If you were an origami model which would you rather be,
a sad stationary model that has to sit idle on a display shelf
getting dusty and neglected, or a happy action model
that frequently gets to frolic in the hands of a folder
and give moving performances that astonish and amuse?

Of course you would opt for being the action model.
Whether it be in the folding of origami,
the mailing of envelopes,
or the turning of pages in a book,
the message is the same:

Paper was meant to move,
and this movement we
as folders must embrace.

In the words of Moses, "Let my Paper go!"
Stationery should not have to stay stationary!

As origami moves forward in time, we folders must do our part
to help as many pieces of paper as possible
fulfill their dream of becoming action models.
So don't hesitate—join the paper movement today
and do unto paper as you would it do unto you!
The following diagrams will serve as your guide
to becoming a paper activist.
May you be moved!

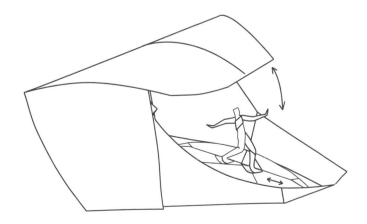

Baby Bird

We burst forth into action with this Baby Bird which opens and closes its beak and, with the help of a ventriloquist, cries out, "Feed me!"

1

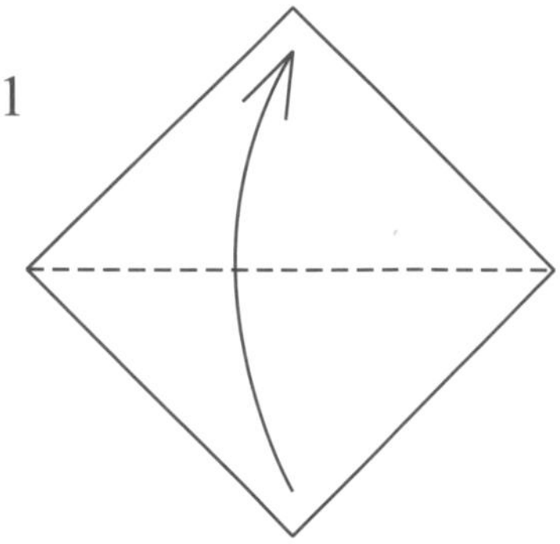

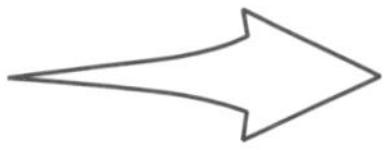

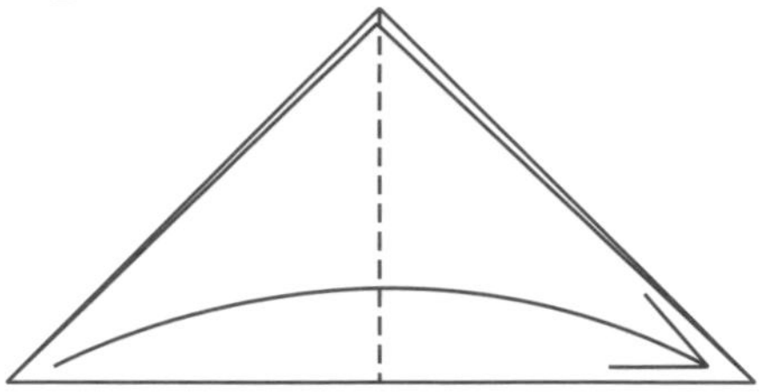

Begin white side up. Valley-fold the paper diagonally in half.

This symbol is telling you the next drawing will be larger.

2

Halve it again. Go to step 3 at the bottom of the page.

Pinch and Unpinch

3a₁
This cloud shows how to do step **3a**. Bring the front flap to the left edge, but do not crease! Instead...

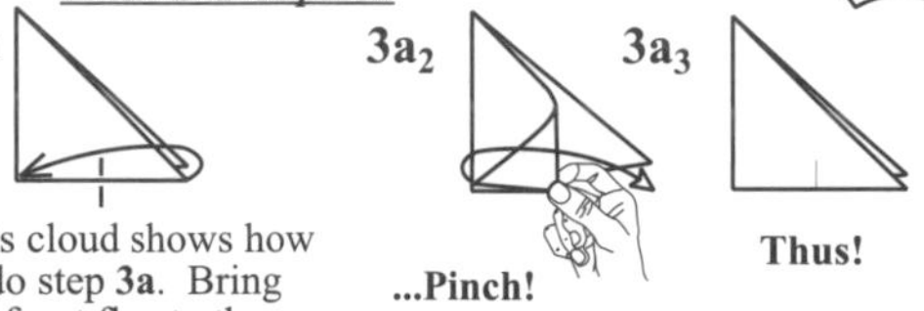

3a₂
...Pinch! Now, unfold the flap.

3a₃
Thus!

3a
This cloud shows how to do step 3. First pinch and unpinch to achieve the half mark. For help doing this, consult the next cloud up.

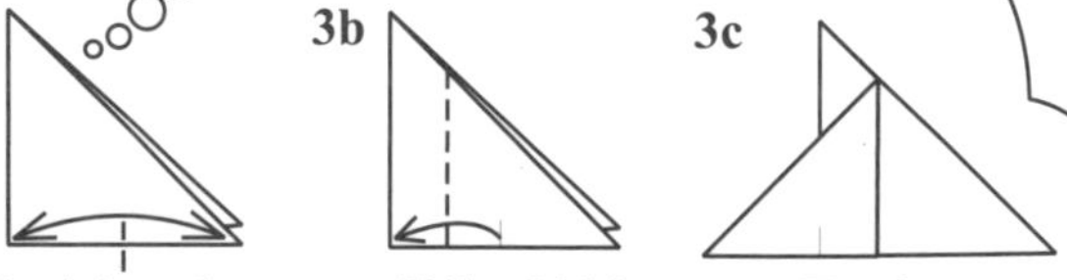

3b
Valley-fold the front flap to the left, lining up the half mark with the left edge.

3c
Thus! Go on to step 4.

Repeat Step 3 Behind

4a
Whenever a diagram says, *repeat behind*, the first thing to do is get behind the model. The easiest way to do this is by **turning it over!**

4b
Now you need to make this side look like the front side. You can do this with a simple valley fold. **Note:** When repeating steps behind, you must do each step in mirror image of the way it's shown in the diagram: whatever went to the left, now must go to the right and vice versa.

4c
Now that both sides are matched, it's time to walk back around to the front of the model. In other words, **turn it over!**

4d
The repeat is complete! Go on to step 5.

3

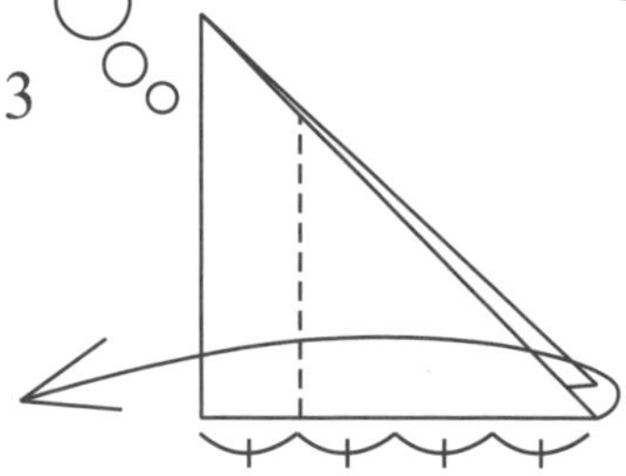

Valley-fold the front flap to the left. Supposing the base is four units in length, make the fold one unit from the left edge. If you haven't the foggiest idea how to do this, venture into the cloud to clear things up.

4

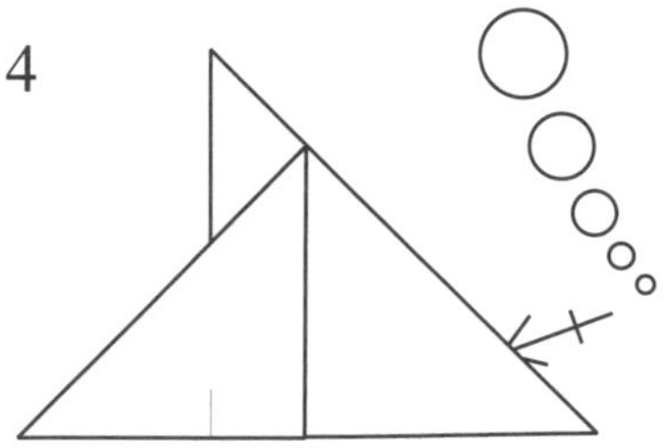

Repeat step 3 behind. If you've never repeated behind, look up at the cloud.

5

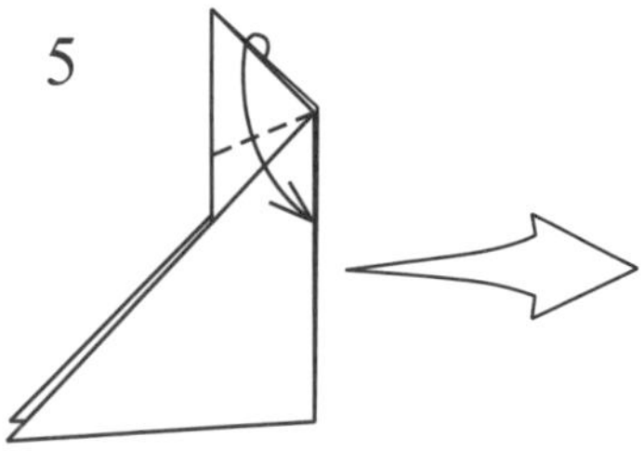

Valley-fold, lining up edge-to-edge. Crease sharply! Take a closer look at the model.

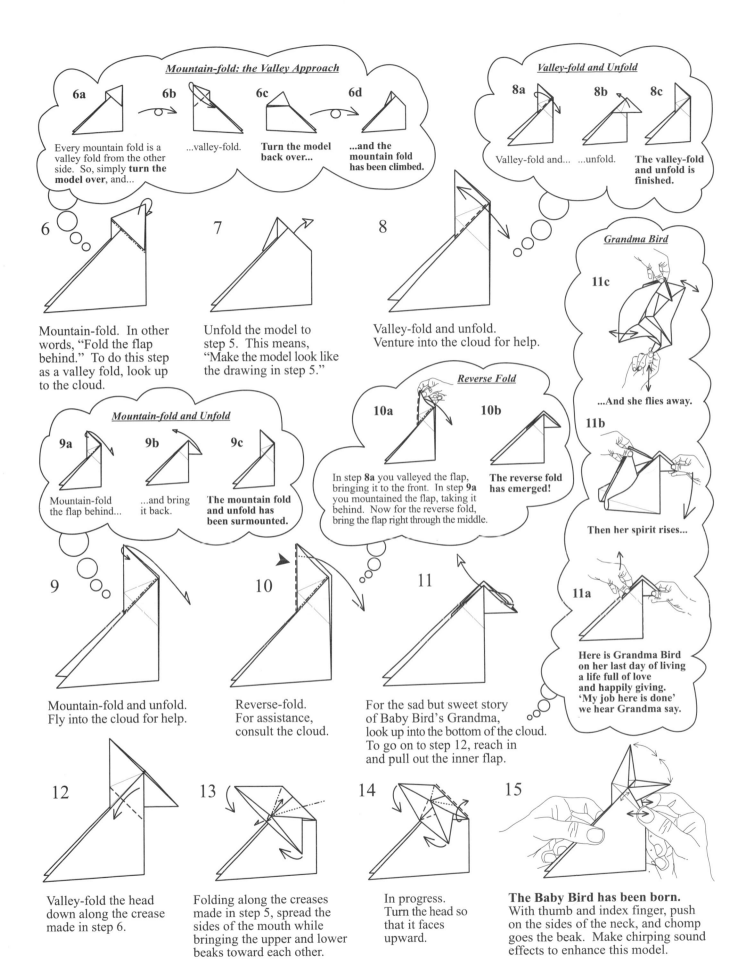

Mountain-fold: the Valley Approach

6a 6b 6c 6d

Every mountain fold is a valley fold from the other side. So, simply **turn the model over**, and...

...valley-fold.

Turn the model back over...

...and the mountain fold has been climbed.

Valley-fold and Unfold

8a 8b 8c

Valley-fold and... ...unfold. **The valley-fold and unfold is finished.**

6

Mountain-fold. In other words, "Fold the flap behind." To do this step as a valley fold, look up to the cloud.

7

Unfold the model to step 5. This means, "Make the model look like the drawing in step 5."

8

Valley-fold and unfold. Venture into the cloud for help.

Grandma Bird

11c

...And she flies away.

11b

Then her spirit rises...

11a

Here is Grandma Bird on her last day of living a life full of love and happily giving. 'My job here is done' we hear Grandma say.

Mountain-fold and Unfold

9a 9b 9c

Mountain-fold the flap behind...

...and bring it back.

The mountain fold and unfold has been surmounted.

Reverse Fold

10a 10b

In step **8a** you valleyed the flap, bringing it to the front. In step **9a** you mountained the flap, taking it behind. Now for the reverse fold, bring the flap right through the middle.

The reverse fold has emerged!

9

Mountain-fold and unfold. Fly into the cloud for help.

10

Reverse-fold. For assistance, consult the cloud.

11

For the sad but sweet story of Baby Bird's Grandma, look up into the bottom of the cloud. To go on to step 12, reach in and pull out the inner flap.

12

Valley-fold the head down along the crease made in step 6.

13

Folding along the creases made in step 5, spread the sides of the mouth while bringing the upper and lower beaks toward each other.

14

In progress. Turn the head so that it faces upward.

15

The Baby Bird has been born. With thumb and index finger, push on the sides of the neck, and chomp goes the beak. Make chirping sound effects to enhance this model.

Baby Bird **33**

Exploding Envelope

No longer is it necessary to use combustible material to make an envelope explode.... This model explodes with the simple pull of a tab!

1

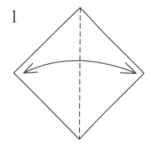

Works well out of Kami, Wyndstone or typing paper. Consider first writing a letter on the paper before you begin folding it. White side up, lightly valley-fold and unfold diagonally in half.

2

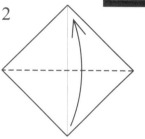

Valley-fold diagonally in half.

Thoughts Behind the Folds

Discovery of the Exploding Envelope was a result of experimenting. I was just trying to make a quick, simple envelope and this one appeared. Then, when I tried to open it, it exploded— a new model!
Exercise: See what other models you can "explode" by pulling at two opposite ends.

3

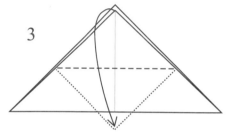

Valley-fold one flap down to just beyond the bottom.

4

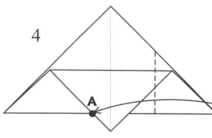

Valley-fold the right corner to point **A**.

5

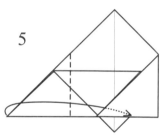

Valley-fold the left flap similarly, slipping it inside the right flap.

6

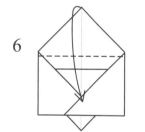

Now is a good time to fill the envelope with goodies— origami models, class notes, baseball cards, gum wrappers, birdseed, thumbtacks, etc. Also remember, a well packed envelope makes a more dramatic explosion. When the envelope is sufficiently filled, valley-fold the top flap down, so that it covers up the white and a little bit more.

7

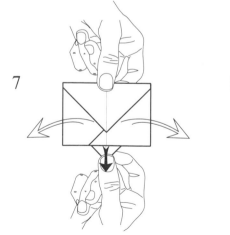

The Exploding Envelope has been built.
To explode it, pull on the white tab. To avoid tearing, explode the envelope slowly at first and help the paper to open out. Once the envelope has been trained, it can be exploded quickly and safely.

8

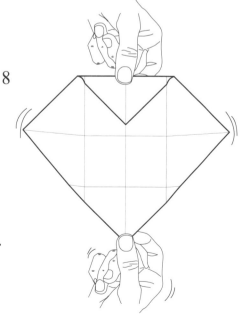

The Exploded Envelope has BURST forth!

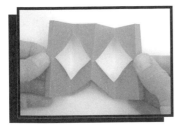

Blinking Eyes

This is a good model to teach on a first date. Upon completing the models you can hold a friendly staring contest and then compliment each other on what beautiful eyes you both have.

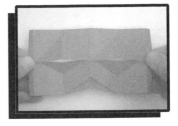

1

Begin white side up. Valley-fold and unfold in half both ways.

2

Valley-fold the top edge of the paper to the center crease.

3

Valley-fold the bottom edge slightly past the center crease, slipping it behind the upper flap.

4

Roll the sides behind with mountain folds. Crease sharply.

5

Valley-fold and unfold the corners, bisecting the indicated angles. Mountain-fold the left side of the model behind.

6

Valley-fold and unfold the left corner through all layers. Unfold to step 5.

7

Valley-fold the sides to the center and partially unfold. Take a slightly closer look at the model.

8

Valley-fold and unfold again, but this time lift the upper eyelids upward along existing creases to reveal the white surface behind. It's really easier to do this when the paper is partially closed.

9

Pull the lower eyelids frontward to reveal even more white. They don't need to be pulled as far forward as the upper eyelids. By making reverse folds you can form a mouth, but this is optional since it's not in the title and it might even detract from the eyes.

10

The Blinking Eyes have seen the light! Pull the sides out and in and the eyes will blink. Can you make the blinker wink?

11

"Hey, who turned out the lights?"

Thoughts Behind the Folds

The Blinking Eyes came out of an attempt to fold a mouth. I looked at the opening and closing mouth and asked myself what else it could be. I answered, "An eye!" Then the obvious question arose: "Could I make two eyes?" And so, in the blink of an eye, a new model was born. **Exercise:** Incorporate the Blinking Eyes into your own designing of faces or, better yet, of famous personalities. **Challenge:** Can you design a Barber Shop Quartet?

Magic Flap

Astonishing, simple-to-make, and perfect for parties, this model creates the illusion of one flap swinging back and forth through another flap.

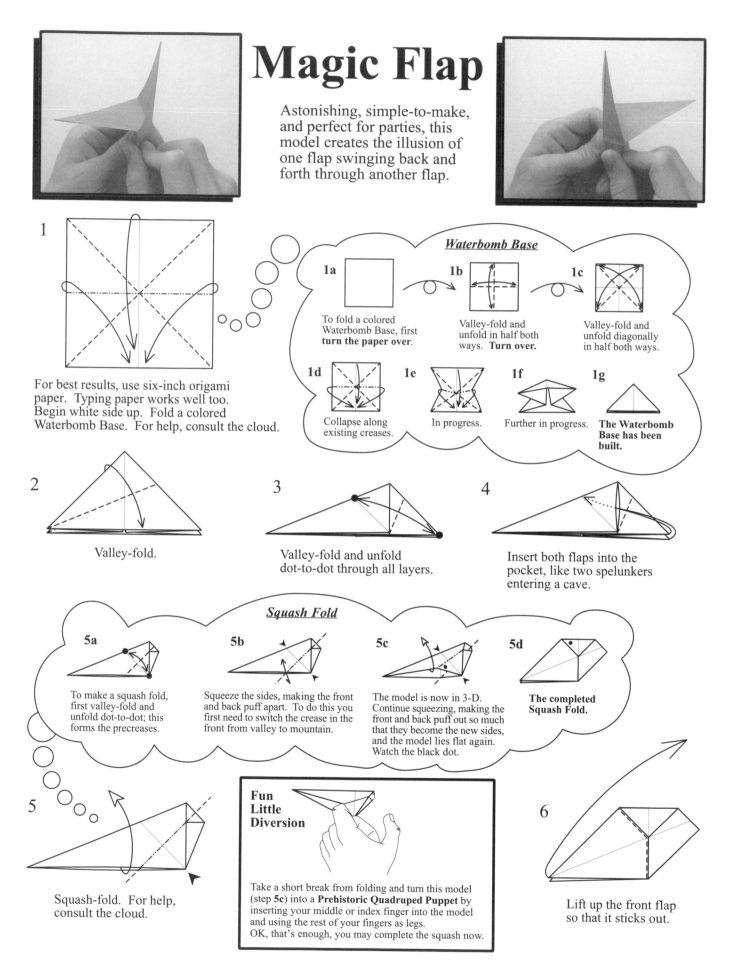

1

For best results, use six-inch origami paper. Typing paper works well too. Begin white side up. Fold a colored Waterbomb Base. For help, consult the cloud.

Waterbomb Base

1a To fold a colored Waterbomb Base, first **turn the paper over**.

1b Valley-fold and unfold in half both ways. **Turn over.**

1c Valley-fold and unfold diagonally in half both ways.

1d Collapse along existing creases.

1e In progress.

1f Further in progress.

1g The Waterbomb Base has been built.

2 Valley-fold.

3 Valley-fold and unfold dot-to-dot through all layers.

4 Insert both flaps into the pocket, like two spelunkers entering a cave.

Squash Fold

5a To make a squash fold, first valley-fold and unfold dot-to-dot; this forms the precreases.

5b Squeeze the sides, making the front and back puff apart. To do this you first need to switch the crease in the front from valley to mountain.

5c The model is now in 3-D. Continue squeezing, making the front and back puff out so much that they become the new sides, and the model lies flat again. Watch the black dot.

5d The completed Squash Fold.

5 Squash-fold. For help, consult the cloud.

Fun Little Diversion

Take a short break from folding and turn this model (step **5c**) into a **Prehistoric Quadruped Puppet** by inserting your middle or index finger into the model and using the rest of your fingers as legs.
OK, that's enough, you may complete the squash now.

6 Lift up the front flap so that it sticks out.

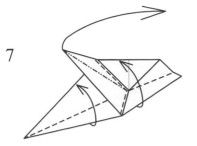 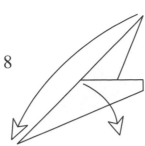 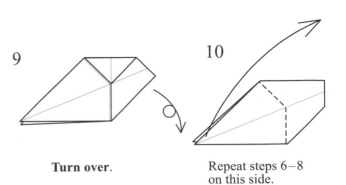

7

3-D view. On the protruding flap, pinch a mountain fold along the existing crease. Continue to swing this flap to the right, while folding the rest of the model in half. Then flatten the model.

8

Unfold the model to step 6.

9

Turn over.

10

Repeat steps 6–8 on this side.

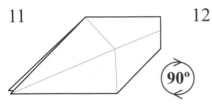 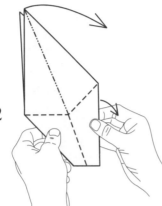

11

Repeat steps 6–10 many times, continually creasing sharply. Then press the model flat as can be. Rotate 90° clockwise.

12

Hold the left side still with the left hand. With the right hand, bend the right side toward yourself, making the front flap pop out while the back flap stands still. If the front flap doesn't pop out as it's supposed to, simply repeat step 11 once and try again.

Thoughts Behind the Folds

The Magic Flap came about from experimenting with action. I first discovered the effect using a much simpler base: Fold a square diagonally in half and then in half again. See how that looks like step 6? After I discovered the basic effect, finding which base to use and the best folding method took a lot of further experimentation.

Cute Little Mean Trick: Ask a friend to "Grab this flap." When s/he reaches for the flap, flip the flap to the other side and say, "No, not that flap... (turn the model)... THIS ONE!" Repeat the trick over and over until your friend gets annoyed or you get bored.

Fun Little Diversion:
Try inside-reverse-folding the ends of the two flaps—"Two Battling Birds!" Or, try outside-reverse-folding the ends of the two flaps and turning the model upside down to create the lower torso of a walking Charlie Chaplin.

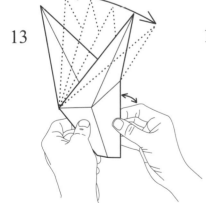 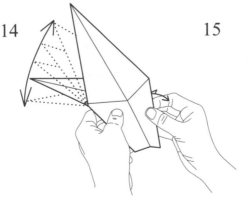

13

Holding the left hand still, swing the front flap by slightly wiggling the right hand. See how far you can swing the front flap without making the back flap move.

14

Now see how far you can swing the back flap without making the front flap move.

15

The Magic Flap has materialized.
Holding the left side still, wiggle the right side rapidly, making the flaps take turns. This creates the stunning illusion of a Magic Flap swinging back and forth through a stationary flap. The illusion is most effective with the stationary hand facing toward you and the moving hand toward your viewer.

Magic Cube

Here's an optical illusion, a magical model that senses your every movement, and, without your even touching it, moves whenever you move! Add a personalized greeting to make it a perfect gift.

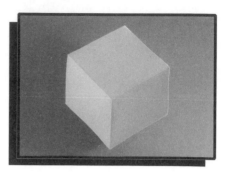

1

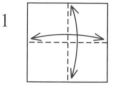

Works best out of five-inch foil or smaller. Colored side up, valley-fold and unfold in half both ways.

2

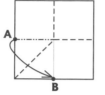

Valley-fold point **A** to point **B**. The model will not lie flat.

3

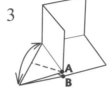

We are now in 3-D. Valley-fold and unfold the left flap.

4

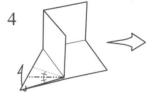

Mountain-fold.

5

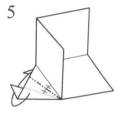

Mountain-fold.

6

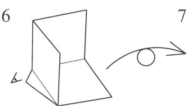

The next view is from behind, so **turn the model over.**

7

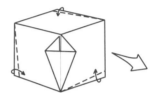

It's time to put this model in perspective. Valley-fold three edges in, creasing sharply. Guidelines for these folds are to taste.

Thoughts Behind the Folds

The idea to design the Magic Cube came from seeing an exhibit at the Exploratorium, an ongoing science fair in San Francisco.
Challenge: See what other shapes or designs you can fold inverted to give them this effect. **Ideas:** cone, polyhedrons, book, mask, nose, eye, heart, soul.

8

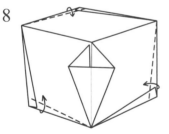

Now for more perspective... Valley-fold the other three edges in. Make sure these folds get the royal fingernail treatment.

9

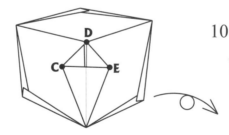

The Magic Cube is finished, but facing the wrong way. So, **turn it over** and stand it up on triangle **CDE**.

10

The Magic Cube has appeared. To see the magic, first, **close your eyes** and start rocking side to side. Then, still rocking, open one eye and look at the cube. Be astonished as the cube comes to life, and starts rotating whichever way you move!

If that didn't work, keep staring at the model with one eye open until it looks like a real cube, with Point **G** popping out at you, as in the diagram. Once you see it as a cube, move your head and say, "Wow! Magical!" Now try to touch it. To make the illusion more effective, write a personal greeting on it in perspective by following the golden rule: *'The closer to G, the bigger they be.'*

Note: This optical illusion also works with the back side of almost any mask. Using one eye, visually invert the mask, just as you did with the cube. Then, move your head around and the mask will come alive!

How to make this into a magic trick...

To set up for the trick, station the model in the corner of the room so that everyone will be able to see point **G** at all times. Make sure there are no shadows on the cube. Cover the model with a box. To perform the trick, say to your audience, "Inside here is a magical cube that will rotate whichever way you move. I'll let you see it, but first you must cover up one eye and start rocking back and forth. Now let's all say the magic words, TAHINI CUBINI, BAFFLE HOUDINI!" Uncover the model and watch as everyone gasps in amazement!

Clapping Hands

Here's a model that's very handy. Whether you're too lazy to lift your hands, or you just need a self-esteem boost, this model can fulfill all of your clapping needs. In addition, this is one of the few models that can actually show its appreciation for having been folded.

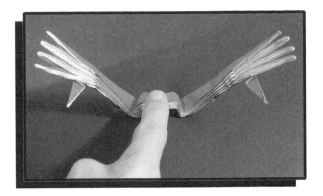

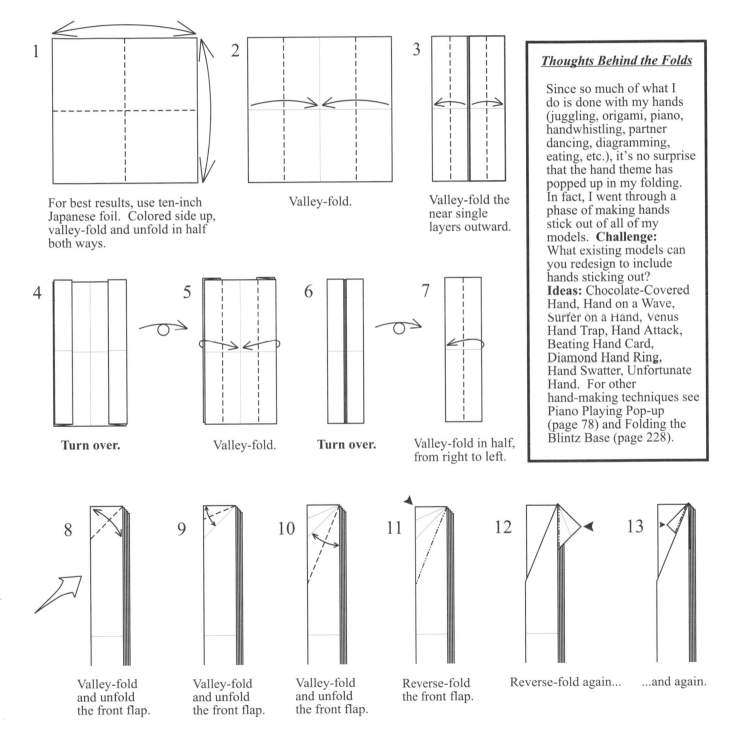

1

For best results, use ten-inch Japanese foil. Colored side up, valley-fold and unfold in half both ways.

2

Valley-fold.

3

Valley-fold the near single layers outward.

4

Turn over.

5

Valley-fold.

6

Turn over.

7

Valley-fold in half, from right to left.

8

Valley-fold and unfold the front flap.

9

Valley-fold and unfold the front flap.

10

Valley-fold and unfold the front flap.

11

Reverse-fold the front flap.

12

Reverse-fold again...

13

...and again.

Thoughts Behind the Folds

Since so much of what I do is done with my hands (juggling, origami, piano, handwhistling, partner dancing, diagramming, eating, etc.), it's no surprise that the hand theme has popped up in my folding. In fact, I went through a phase of making hands stick out of all of my models. **Challenge:** What existing models can you redesign to include hands sticking out? **Ideas:** Chocolate-Covered Hand, Hand on a Wave, Surfer on a Hand, Venus Hand Trap, Hand Attack, Beating Hand Card, Diamond Hand Ring, Hand Swatter, Unfortunate Hand. For other hand-making techniques see Piano Playing Pop-up (page 78) and Folding the Blintz Base (page 228).

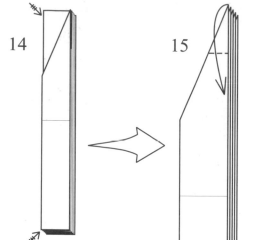

14 Repeat steps 8–13 on the seven remaining corners.

15 Valley-fold the front flap. Repeat below.

16 Valley-fold. Repeat below.

This symbol is telling you that the next drawing will be smaller.

17

Valley-fold sharply through all layers.

18 Valley-fold all layers, Repeat below.

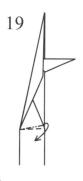

19 Pull the central right (multiple-layer) corner downward and flatten to form a pleat. Repeat below.

20 Spread out the fingers. Repeat below. Say out loud, "What is the sound of one hand clapping?"

Ah, good question. You shouldn't need to worry about it if you've been repeating below.

21 **Turn the hand over.** Repeat below! Flatten it however you see fit. Ironing it, hammering it, or driving over it with a pickup truck are just a few ideas. Repeat below.

22 Make two pleats near the center of the model. Make sure these pleats are extra sharp.

23 Squeeze the center of the model, making two sharp, curved mountain folds. Swing the hands together. Rounding out the hands and arms will enhance the shapeliness, sturdiness and effectiveness of the model.

24

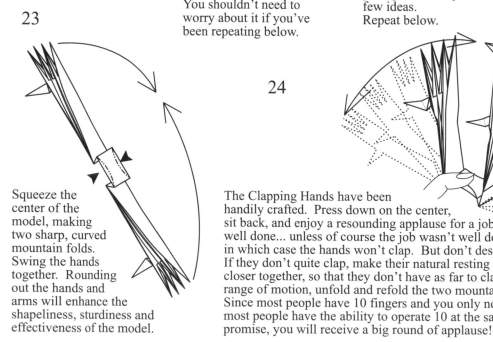

The Clapping Hands have been handily crafted. Press down on the center, sit back, and enjoy a resounding applause for a job well done... unless of course the job wasn't well done, in which case the hands won't clap. But don't despair! If they don't quite clap, make their natural resting position closer together, so that they don't have as far to clap. To give the hands a greater range of motion, unfold and refold the two mountains in step 22 a bunch of times. Since most people have 10 fingers and you only need one to operate this model, most people have the ability to operate 10 at the same time... AND, if you do so, I promise, you will receive a big round of applause!

Waxing Waning Moon

Witness the stages of the moon captured in this single transforming model.

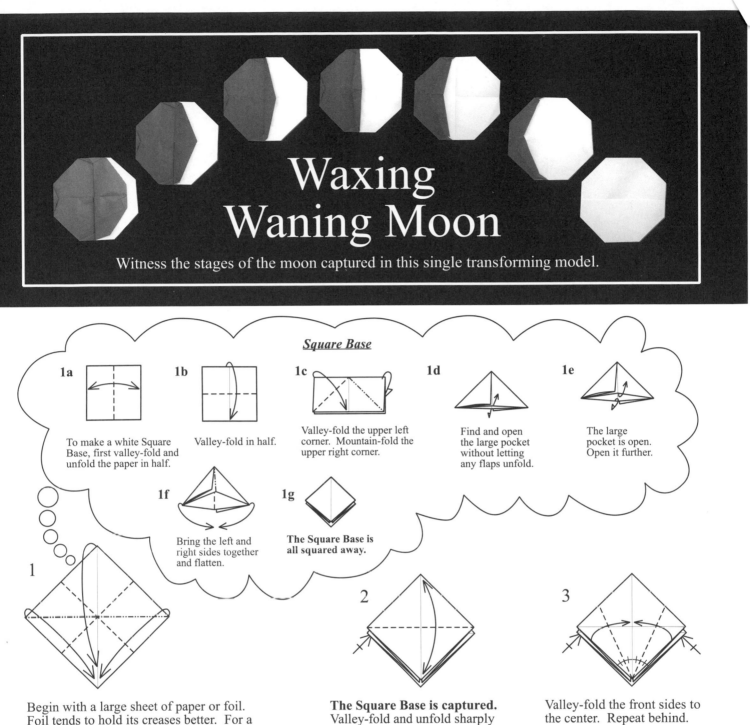

Square Base

1a
To make a white Square Base, first valley-fold and unfold the paper in half.

1b
Valley-fold in half.

1c
Valley-fold the upper left corner. Mountain-fold the upper right corner.

1d
Find and open the large pocket without letting any flaps unfold.

1e
The large pocket is open. Open it further.

1f
Bring the left and right sides together and flatten.

1g
The Square Base is all squared away.

1
Begin with a large sheet of paper or foil. Foil tends to hold its creases better. For a really neat effect, use glow-in-the-dark paper painted black on the back. Fold a white Square Base. For help, look up to the cloud.

2
The Square Base is captured. Valley-fold and unfold sharply through all layers. Repeat behind (i.e., mountain-fold through all layers).

3
Valley-fold the front sides to the center. Repeat behind.

4
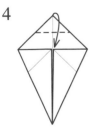
Valley-fold the top downward as shown.

5
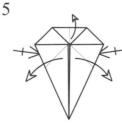
Unfold the model to step 3.

6
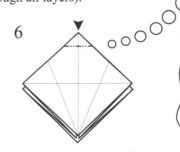
Sink the top corner. The following cloud shows how to do this.

Sink

6a
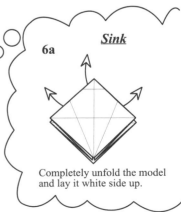
Completely unfold the model and lay it white side up.

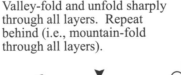
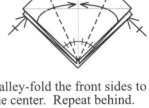

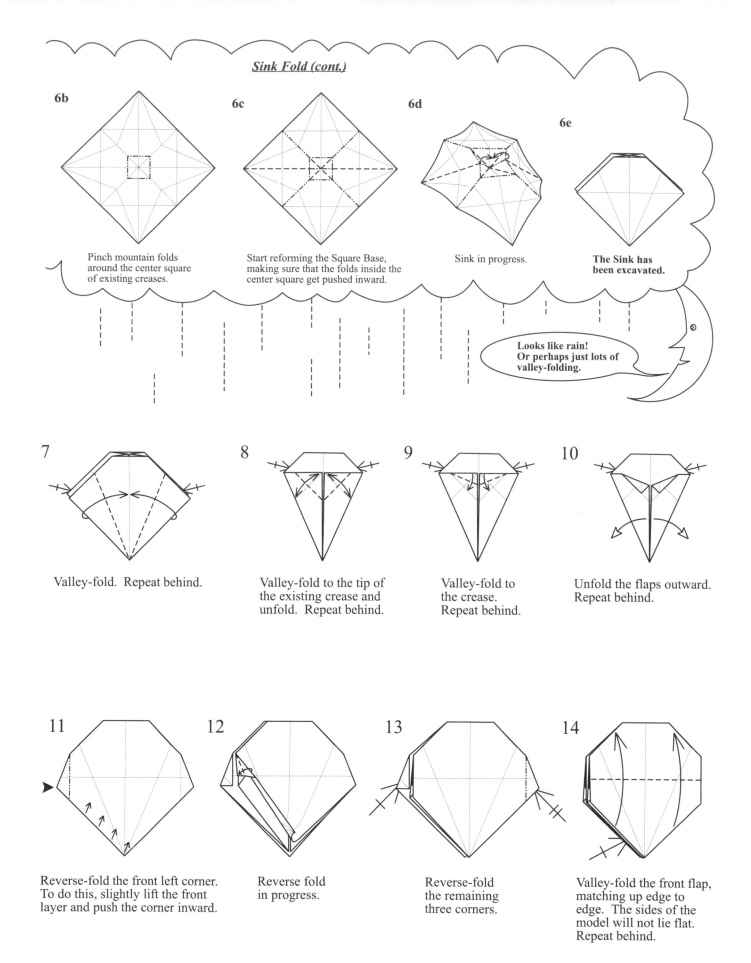

Sink Fold (cont.)

6b

Pinch mountain folds around the center square of existing creases.

6c

Start reforming the Square Base, making sure that the folds inside the center square get pushed inward.

6d

Sink in progress.

6e

The Sink has been excavated.

Looks like rain! Or perhaps just lots of valley-folding.

7

Valley-fold. Repeat behind.

8

Valley-fold to the tip of the existing crease and unfold. Repeat behind.

9

Valley-fold to the crease. Repeat behind.

10

Unfold the flaps outward. Repeat behind.

11

Reverse-fold the front left corner. To do this, slightly lift the front layer and push the corner inward.

12

Reverse fold in progress.

13

Reverse-fold the remaining three corners.

14

Valley-fold the front flap, matching up edge to edge. The sides of the model will not lie flat. Repeat behind.

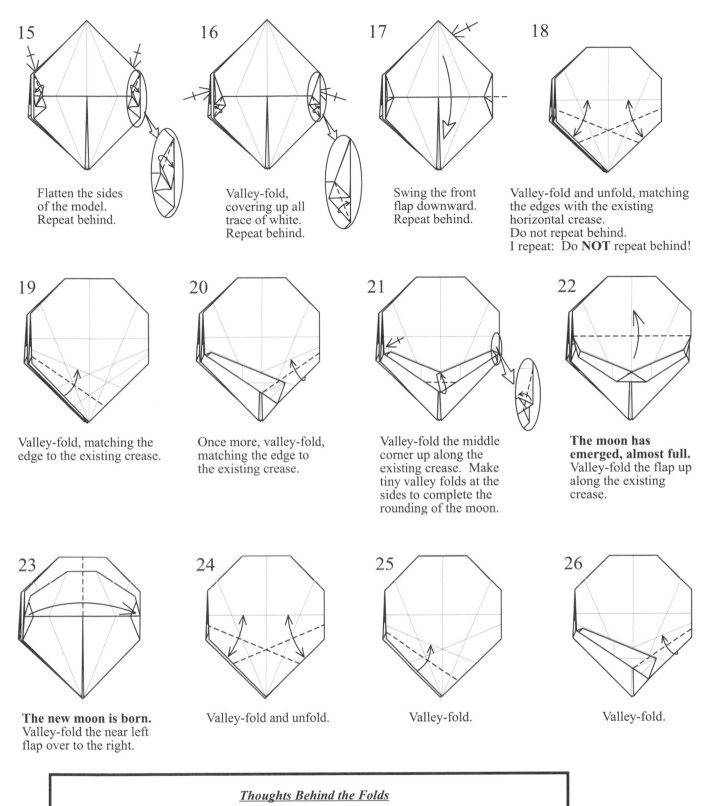

15 Flatten the sides of the model. Repeat behind.

16 Valley-fold, covering up all trace of white. Repeat behind.

17 Swing the front flap downward. Repeat behind.

18 Valley-fold and unfold, matching the edges with the existing horizontal crease. Do not repeat behind. I repeat: Do **NOT** repeat behind!

19 Valley-fold, matching the edge to the existing crease.

20 Once more, valley-fold, matching the edge to the existing crease.

21 Valley-fold the middle corner up along the existing crease. Make tiny valley folds at the sides to complete the rounding of the moon.

22 **The moon has emerged, almost full.** Valley-fold the flap up along the existing crease.

23 **The new moon is born.** Valley-fold the near left flap over to the right.

24 Valley-fold and unfold.

25 Valley-fold.

26 Valley-fold.

Thoughts Behind the Folds

The Waxing Waning Moon started out as an attempt to fold a moon. Working from a Square Base (a good launching pad for thoughtless experimenting), it was very easy to make the basic arc of the moon. A few valley folds on one of the corners did the trick, and I still had three other corners to work with! When a solution is too easy, chances are the problem was also too easy. So to make the moon problem harder I set off to see how many stages of the moon I could fold, hence this model. **Challenge:** What other transforming subjects could be folded in origami? **Ideas:** Butterfly emerging from a cocoon, egg hatching, person aging, flower blossoming.

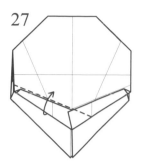

27

Valley-fold.

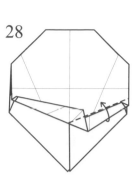

28

Valley-fold.

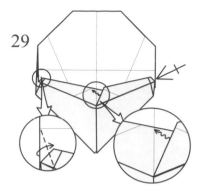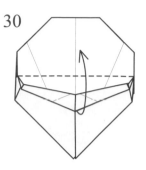

29

Make tiny valley folds at the sides. Then "wrinkle-fold" the indicated edge to make it vertical. In other words, roll the edge leftward, pulling paper out from underneath.

30

Another stage of the moon has been reached. Valley-fold the flap up along the existing crease.

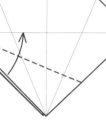

31

We set foot on yet another stage of the moon. Turn the model over.

32

Valley-fold.

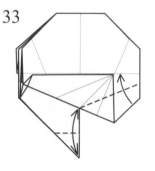

33

Valley-fold on the right. Valley-fold and unfold the bottom corner.

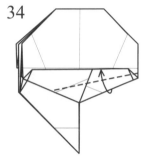

34

Valley-fold.

Solar Variation

Didier Piguel of France brought to my attention that the Waxing and Waning Moon can also be presented as a solar eclipse simply by performing steps 45–53 in reverse. To complete the solar eclipse he turns out the light!

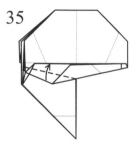

35

Valley-fold.

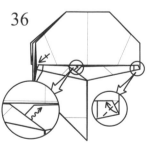

36

Make tiny valley folds on the sides. Then do another wrinkle fold as in step 29.

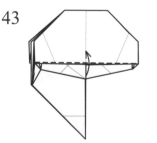

43

The half moon is established. Valley-fold the flap up.

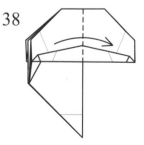

38

Behold another lunar stage. Valley-fold the near left flap to the right.

---

44 *Origami to Astonish and Amuse*

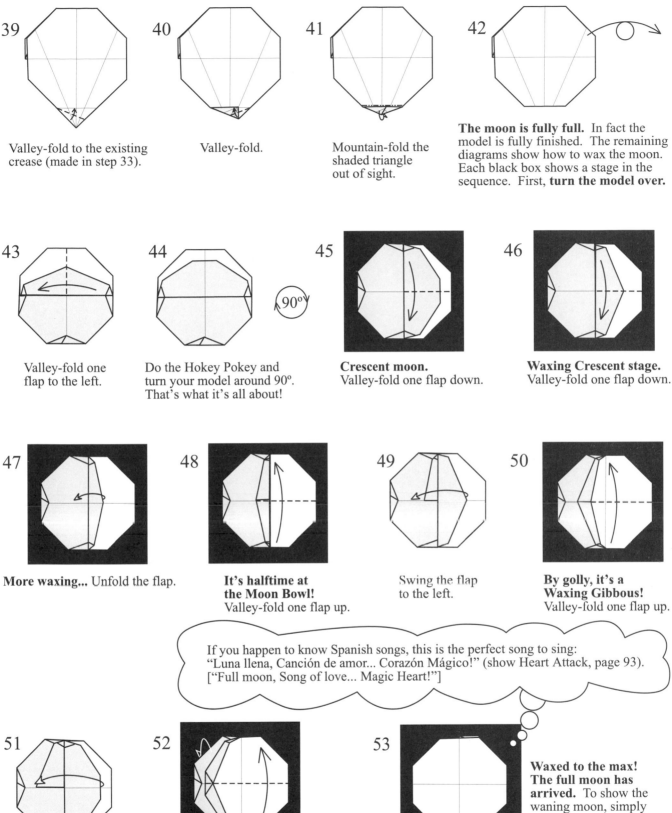

39 Valley-fold to the existing crease (made in step 33).

40 Valley-fold.

41 Mountain-fold the shaded triangle out of sight.

42 **The moon is fully full.** In fact the model is fully finished. The remaining diagrams show how to wax the moon. Each black box shows a stage in the sequence. First, **turn the model over.**

43 Valley-fold one flap to the left.

44 Do the Hokey Pokey and turn your model around 90º. That's what it's all about!

90º

45 **Crescent moon.** Valley-fold one flap down.

46 **Waxing Crescent stage.** Valley-fold one flap down.

47 **More waxing...** Unfold the flap.

48 **It's halftime at the Moon Bowl!** Valley-fold one flap up.

49 Swing the flap to the left.

50 **By golly, it's a Waxing Gibbous!** Valley-fold one flap up.

If you happen to know Spanish songs, this is the perfect song to sing: "Luna llena, Canción de amor... Corazón Mágico!" (show Heart Attack, page 93). ["Full moon, Song of love... Magic Heart!"]

51 Swing the flap to the left.

52 **Well-waxed moon.** To turn this into the full moon you could just turn the model over, but it looks better to your audience if you valley-fold the lower half of the model up while letting only the back flap swing down.

53 **Waxed to the max! The full moon has arrived.** To show the waning moon, simply rotate the model 180º and perform the whole sequence backwards so that the crescent ends up on the left. If you wax and wane the moon again, so that the crescent ends up back on the right, you will have completed a full lunar cycle!

Two Interlocking Rings

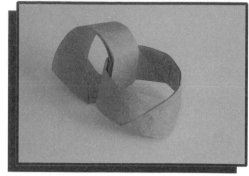

Here's an entertaining model for parties (or weddings), because everyone thinks it's two separate loops. But then miraculously the loops are pulled apart and shown to be just one square sheet!

1

Tyvek® (express envelope paper) is ideal for this model. Begin by folding a Waterbomb Base. For a neat way to do this, hike up into the clouds.

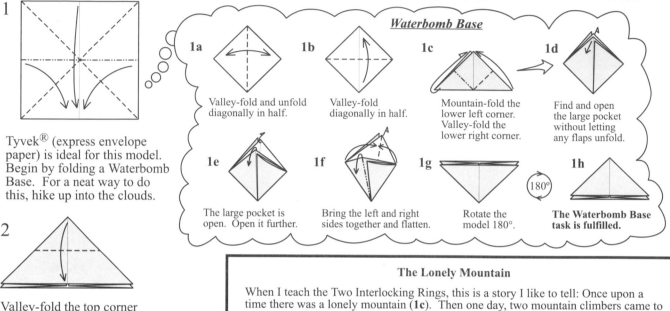

Waterbomb Base

1a Valley-fold and unfold diagonally in half.

1b Valley-fold diagonally in half.

1c Mountain-fold the lower left corner. Valley-fold the lower right corner.

1d Find and open the large pocket without letting any flaps unfold.

1e The large pocket is open. Open it further.

1f Bring the left and right sides together and flatten.

1g Rotate the model 180°.

1h **The Waterbomb Base task is fulfilled.**

2

Valley-fold the top corner down to the bottom.

3

Valley-fold same corner up to the top.

4

Like this. **Turn the model over.**

5

Valley-fold the entire top half down to the bottom.

6

The Waterbomb Base has been pleated. (For skinnier rings you can make more pleats.) Now, without hesitation, unfold the model completely.

The Lonely Mountain

When I teach the Two Interlocking Rings, this is a story I like to tell: Once upon a time there was a lonely mountain (**1c**). Then one day, two mountain climbers came to visit the mountain. One climbed up in front, and the other in back (**1c**). Unfortunately they weren't very careful and caused an avalanche that made the mountain no longer look very much like a mountain (**1d**). So, the mountain got angry, opened its mouth (**1e**), and shouted, "GET OFF THIS MOUNTAIN!" (**1f**). And the mountain blew the climbers into outer space and recovered its shape as a mountain (**1h**). But as time passed, the mountain grew lonely again and began looking all over for some friends. It looked down to the ground (2). It looked on top (3). It turned around to look behind (4). It looked on the ground again, but still no sign of any friends (5). The mountain was very sad and no longer felt tall like a mountain. It cried out, "I look like a plateau!" (6). So one day it decided to pack its bags and head to town to find some friends and start a new life. Luckily the mountain remembered to bring a street map of town so it wouldn't get lost (7). Disguised as a large table, the mountain started walking to the middle of town. It decided to walk on every street so as to try to meet everyone (8). The table walked passed many people, but couldn't find any friends, and soon got tired from all the walking (9). It decided it needed to grow longer legs (10). But still, the table couldn't find anyone to be its friend, and was even more tired from all the walking (11). So it decided to grow even longer legs (12). But still, nobody would be its friend. Perhaps it was just that nobody wanted to sit at a walking table. Finally, the table collapsed right in the center of town (13), and decided to become a walking stick (14). But just as the stick started walking, it realized it was walking side-by-side with another walking stick (15). They fell in love, and vowed to **stick** together forevermore (16). "Not even death do us part!" (17).

7

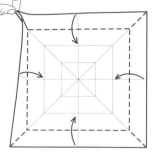

Valley-fold the four sides in along existing creases while pinching the corners so that they stick out. The model will look like an upside-down table with very short legs.

8

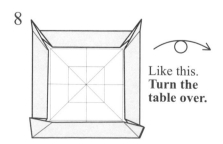

Like this. **Turn the table over.**

9

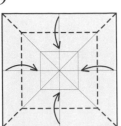

Valley-fold the four sides in along existing creases while pinching the corners, as was done in step 7.

10

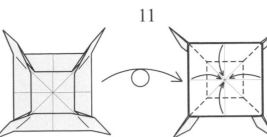

We now have a smaller upside-down table with longer legs. **Turn the table over.**

11

Valley-fold the four sides in along existing creases while pinching the corners, as was done in step 7.

12

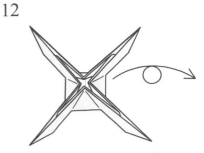

We now have a very small table with extremely long legs—excellent for racing! **Turn the table over.**

13

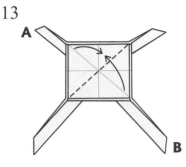

Valley-fold the top square diagonally in half so that the two opposite table legs **A** and **B** stick up.

14

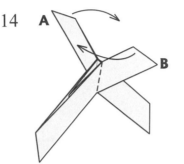

Swing legs **A** and **B** horizontally clockwise like screwing in a wing nut. This creates two overlapping strips that lie flat.

15

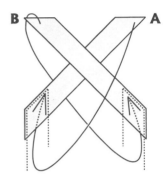

Siamese Worms! Turn the worms into interlocking rings by **inserting the shorter ends into the longer ends** at an angle.

16

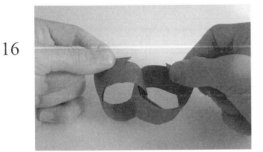

Two Interlocking Rings have emerged. And now for the dramatic action. In one quick motion, completely unfold the model! This might seem like a waste of time, but since the audience believes that there are two distinct loops, for them it is a stunning effect. Here's how to unfold the model: Holding at the ends of the loops, start pulling outwards, first letting the two shorter ends slip out (thus undoing step 15). Then continue pulling the longer ends apart until...

17

WHOOSH!... The model suddenly unfolds, revealing to the startled audience that the two loops are really just one square of paper! Later, at your convenience, refold the model for your next audience. This time it should be much easier, since all the creases are already in place.

Thoughts Behind the Folds

The Two Interlocking Rings is a variation of the Four-Link Chain by Iris Walker (*British Origami Society Spring 1981 Convention Book*). No doubt she has also done a two-link chain. However my rings are different in the locking device, the pulling apart action and the name. **Border Variation:** Start by folding a border around the paper (see Peace Sign, page 127). Then fold as shown in this model. **Zig-zag Border Variation:** Start with a Blintz Base. Follow steps 1–17, but before doing step 7, pleat the blintzed corners along existing creases. The pleats go behind.

Two Permanently Interlocking Rings

For those of you who like to keep your models folded, here's a nice way to lock the ends together.

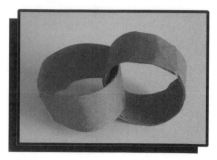

15

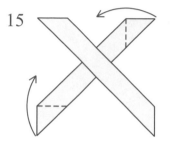

Begin with step 15 of Two Interlocking Rings. Valley-fold both ends of the back strip toward the shorter end of the front strip.

16

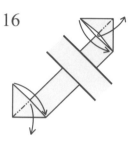

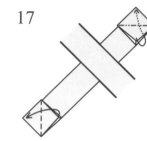

In progress.

Open and squash-fold both ends of the back strip. It's like squashing the fruit on a cactus!

17

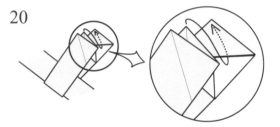

Valley-fold the single layer of the *small flap* on the longer end and mountain-fold the *small flap* on the shorter end, tucking it away safely in its pocket.

18

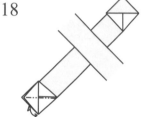

Mountain-fold and unfold the white square diagonally in half, making a **sharp** crease.

19

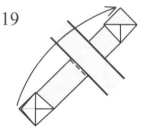

Valley-fold the bottom strip in half, bringing both ends together.

20

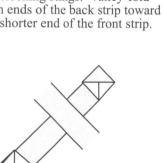

Insert only the *small flap* into the other *small flap's* pocket so that both *small flaps* can finally be united, happily bonded forever.

21

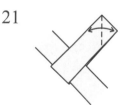

Valley-fold and unfold, with all your might, along the **sharp** crease made in step 18.

22

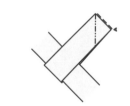

Reverse-fold into any one of the three most convenient slots. Basically, just push the thing in and it's bound to work.

23

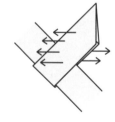

By golly, they're locked! It must be magic! Open up and round out the ring.

24

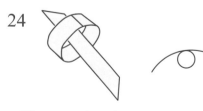

It's a worm jumping through a hoop! **Turn the model over.**

25

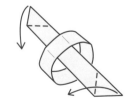

It's a worm hoolahooping! Enthusiastically repeat steps 15–23 on the other strip.

26

Behold, Two Interlocking Ring Worms bonded forever in holy happiness. Sorry folks, no action here!

Chocolate-Covered Ant

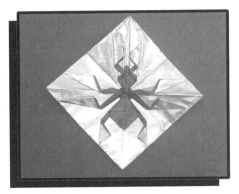

Author's disclaimer: No ants were injured in the designing, folding or diagramming of this model. Furthermore, the chocolate is fully organic—free of pesticides and genetic engineering. Yum!

1

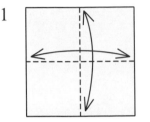

A ten-inch paper makes a jumbo morsel. Begin with a sheet of brown paper or foil brown side up (see note in square). If you would rather not have an albino ant, paint the white side black. Valley-fold and unfold in half both ways.

2

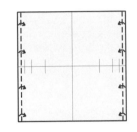

Create an equal border around the square with valley folds, starting at the left and right. These folds are to taste, but an ideal thickness for the border is 1/32 of the side of the square.

3

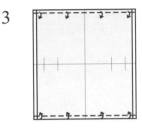

Valley-fold at the top and bottom to complete the border.

4

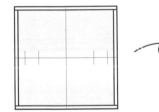

The Border Base has come about. **Turn the model over.**

5

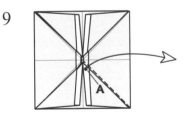

Valley-fold the sides together.

6

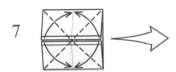

Valley-fold the top and bottom together.

Note: If you are upset by the fact that foil doesn't come in black or brown, either write your congressman or consider painting both sides of the foil the appropriate colors. Acrylic paint works well.

7

Valley-fold the four near corners as shown.

8

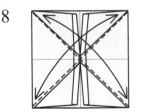

Valley-fold and unfold in half both ways, through all layers.

9

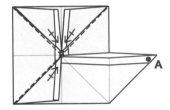

Slide out point **A**.

10

Repeat step 9 on the other three corners.

11

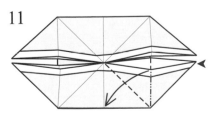

This is the Pinwheel Base. Lift, open out, and squash.

12

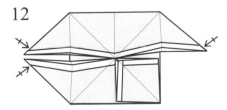

Like this. Now, squash the other three corners.

13

Rotate the model 45°.

14

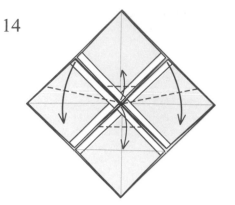

And just like that, we have eight long narrow appendages to do with as we'd like. The varieties of bug splats possible from this base are endless. To make the ant, valley-fold four flaps to taste.

15

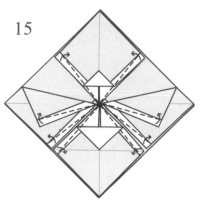

Narrow the appendages even more by valley-folding along the diagonal of each leg.

16

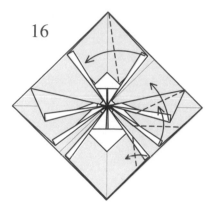

Focusing on the right side, make more valley folds, succulently to taste.

17

18

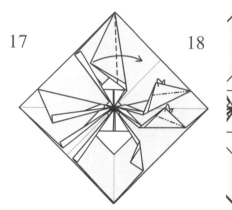

Valley-fold at the top to make an ant antenna. Shorten the legs on the right side with mountain folds.

Valley-fold the antenna gently.

19

Fine tune the antenna with a mountain fold to taste.

20

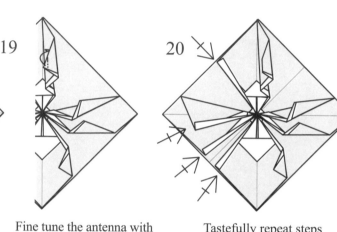

Tastefully repeat steps 16–19 on the left side.

Thoughts Behind the Folds

The Chocolate-Covered Ant emerged from playing around with the Border Base (step 4), a base I discovered when designing the Peace Sign, page 127. In my play, I folded a squashed Pinwheel Base (step 13), and suddenly saw eight narrow appendages—an insect designer's dream-come-true! **Exercise:** Try folding the Border Base into other bases and see what models you can come up with. **Ideas:** hieroglyphics, alphabet letters, highway, tic tac toe board, company logos.

21

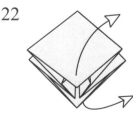

The fat and juicy Chocolate-Covered Ant is captured! Now for the icing on the cake... I mean, the chocolate on the ant. Blintzing would work, but, generally, ants prefer to be wrapped in a chocolate Square Base. Gourmet!

22

And so the model is complete...ly tasteless, but only slightly less appealing than a real chocolate-covered ant. Reopen to reveal to your audience the juicy nugget of insect flesh preserved within this luscious base of chocolate-colored paper. A delicious delicacy!

23

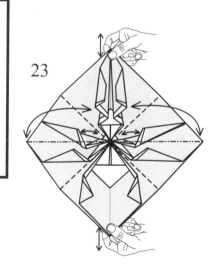

To make the Chocolate-Covered Ant clap, hold at the top and bottom and push inward.

If bug splats are more your thing, you can transform this model into a tremendous bug splat explosion by simply grasping any two opposite ant appendages and pulling outward at great velocity. See what other models you can "explode" in this manner.

Gremlin

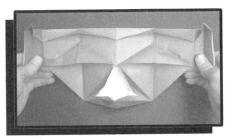

Perfect for Halloween, this eye-opening, jaw-dropping creature is sure to scare the living daylights out of any unsuspecting viewer. **WARNING:** This model is not intended for children under 18. It's too scary! Parental discretion is advised.

1
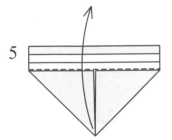
Works well out of paper or foil. White side up, valley-fold and unfold in half both ways.

2
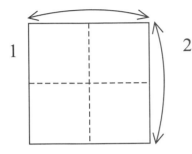
Valley-fold.

3
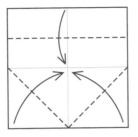
Valley-fold the top edge downward and unfold.

4
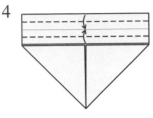
Valley-fold the top edge down to the crease. Valley-fold the raw edge up to the crease.

5
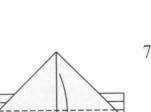
Valley-fold.

6
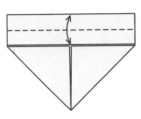
Valley-fold, matching the existing horizontal folded edge.

7
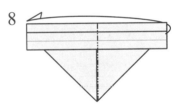
Unfold the white strip downward.

8
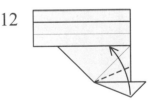
Mountain-fold the right half behind.

9
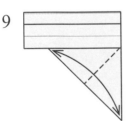
Valley-fold and unfold.

10
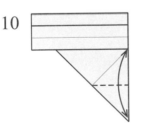
Valley-fold and unfold.

11
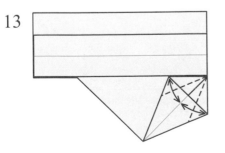
Valley-fold.
Stop slouching.

12
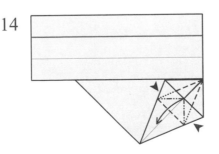
Valley-fold.

13
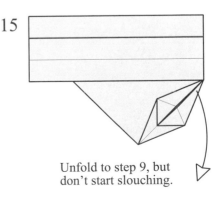
Valley-fold and unfold.

14
Petal-fold (page 26).

15
Unfold to step 9, but don't start slouching.

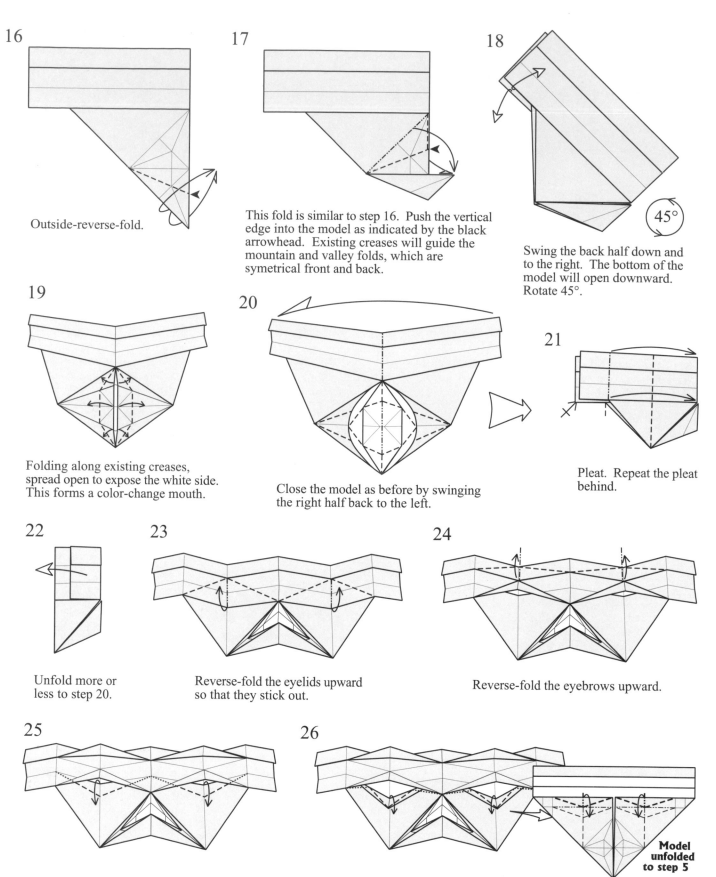

16

Outside-reverse-fold.

17

This fold is similar to step 16. Push the vertical edge into the model as indicated by the black arrowhead. Existing creases will guide the mountain and valley folds, which are symetrical front and back.

18

45°

Swing the back half down and to the right. The bottom of the model will open downward. Rotate 45°.

19

Folding along existing creases, spread open to expose the white side. This forms a color-change mouth.

20

Close the model as before by swinging the right half back to the left.

21

Pleat. Repeat the pleat behind.

22

Unfold more or less to step 20.

23

Reverse-fold the eyelids upward so that they stick out.

24

Reverse-fold the eyebrows upward.

25

Reverse-fold the lower eyelids downward. This is just like step 24, but more difficult as you have to reach underneath the upper eyelid. You may need to unfold a little to complete this step cleanly.

26

Model unfolded to step 5

This step, which color changes the lower eyelid, is rather difficult, and can be skipped if it can't be tackled. Pull out the inside of the lower eyelid (the raw edge of the paper), and reverse-fold it down. To do this cleanly, it's necessary to unfold to step 5. After making the new reverse folds (in bold), fold the model back up along existing creases.

27

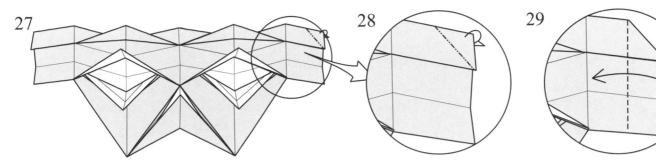

The eyes are fully visible.
Now for the ears...

28

Mountain-fold.

29

Valley-fold.

30

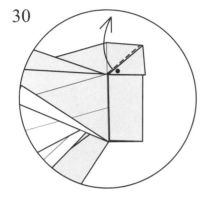

Free the trapped corner and bring it up.
Watch the black dot.

31

Open out the ear.

32

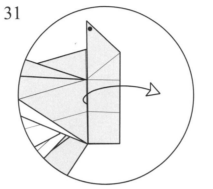

Reverse-fold to make the ear appear
larger. This fold does not lie flat.

33

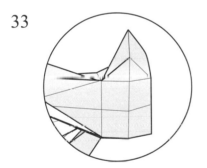

Like this. Repeat steps 28–32 on the
left side to form the other ear.

34

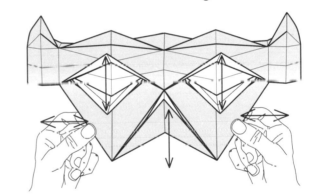

A Gremlin has been fashioned, open-eyed, ready for action.
When the sides are brought out and in, the Gremlin blinks its
eyes and opens and closes its mouth.

35

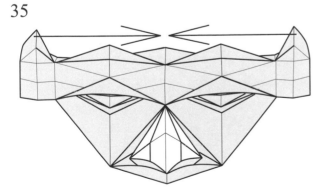

The well-worked Gremlin, yawning, ready for sleep.
To close the Gremlin so that it lies flat, push the sides
all the way together as in step 22.

36

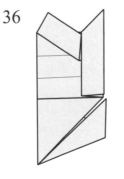

**The retired Gremlin,
ready for hibernation
in a pocket.**

___

Thoughts Behind the Folds

The Gremlin was the
Blinking Eyes taken one
step further. The goal was
to make a color-changed,
moving mouth.
Challenge: Can you make
a full Gremlin (face and
body) from one square?

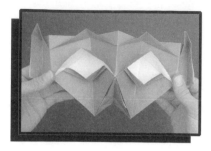

Crazy-Mouthed
Gremlin

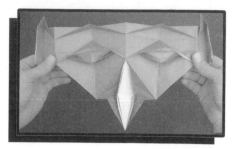

In the ordinary Gremlin, the blinking eyes are what grab people's attention. Here is a variation that will instead make the mouth the real jaw dropper.

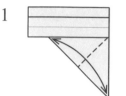

1

Begin by folding steps 1–9 of the Gremlin.

2

Valley-fold and unfold.

3

Valley-fold and unfold. Repeat behind.

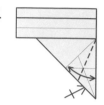

4

Valley-fold and unfold. Repeat behind.

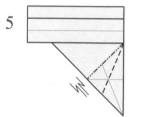

5

Inside-crimp (page 25).

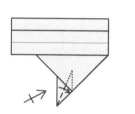

6

Reverse-fold internally on existing creases. Repeat behind.

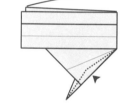

7

Push in on the middle layer (white). These folds are new. Swing out the back flap. The model will not lie flat.

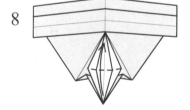

8

We are in 3-D. Close the mouth.

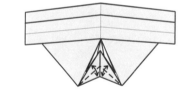

9

Valley-fold and unfold through all layers. These creases are crucial to the action mechanism and should be reinforced whenever the mouth refuses to close.

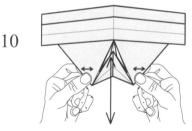

10

Get a feel for the mouth by pulling gently on the sides. With the slightest hand action the mouth should open and close like crazy! Open and close it 666 times or until craziness is achieved.

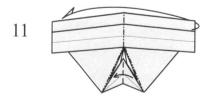

11

Swing the right side to the back while valley-folding the mouth in half. Since the rest of the model is no different, continue with steps 21–33 of the normal Gremlin.

12

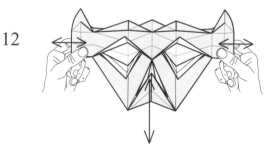

The Crazy Mouthed Gremlin has hatched. Since the mouth is hypersensitive, it's best to hold the Gremlin by the ears. With this variation, you might find it difficult to coordinate the mouth and eyes, but BOY, is that mouth crazy!

Surfer on a Wave

"Hey dude, check this out! It's an origami surfer riding a knarly wave. Like totally tubular, dude!!" But do I surf? So many people have asked me that when they see this model that finally I decided to take a surfing class, so now I say, "Yes, I do surf!... Like gag me with a wave, dude!"

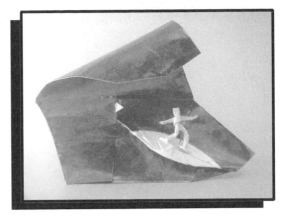

1

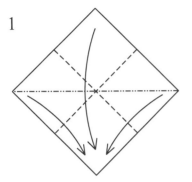

For best results, use six-inch Japanese foil or ten-inch American foil. Begin by folding a Square Base (page 26).

2

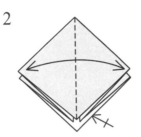

Valley-fold and unfold the near layer. Repeat behind.

3

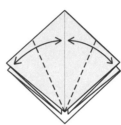

Valley-fold and unfold.

4

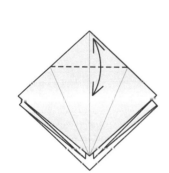

Valley-fold down and unfold.

5

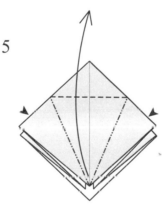

Petal-fold.

6

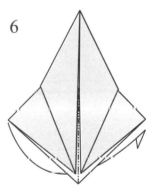

Swing the left flap behind to the right.

7

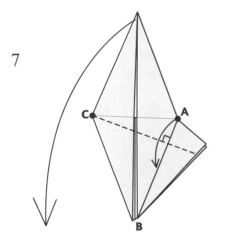

Valley-fold the top down through all layers so that the fold line goes through point **C** and is perpendicular to the line segment **AB.**

8

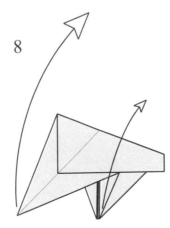

Unfold, letting one additional flap swing up.

9

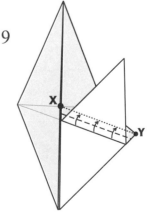

Valley-fold up to the imaginary line, **XY**.

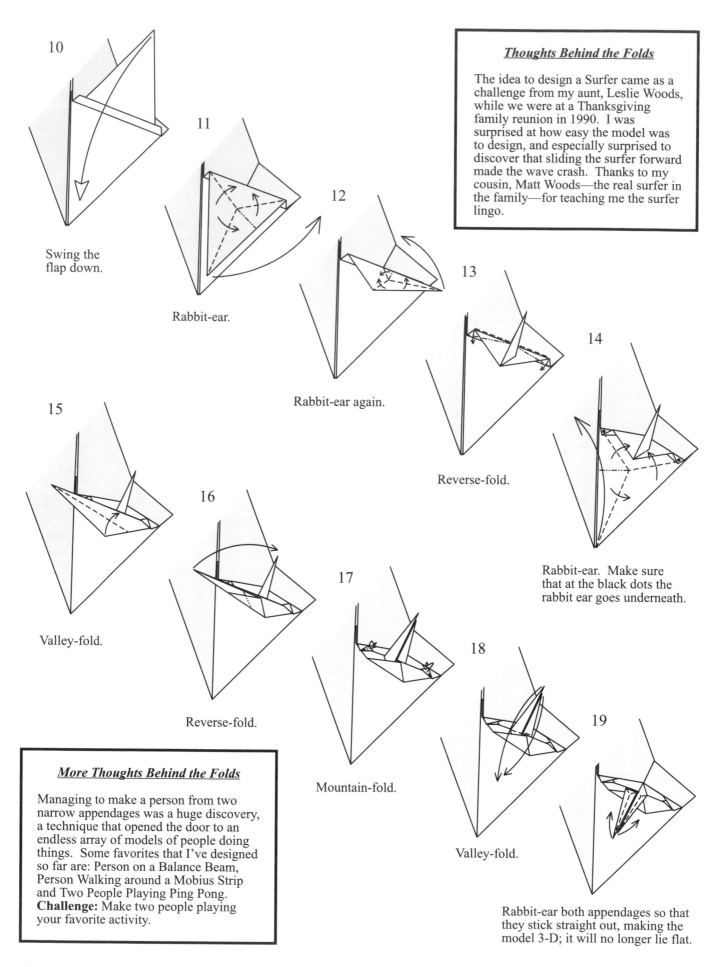

10

Swing the
flap down.

11

Rabbit-ear.

12

Rabbit-ear again.

13

Reverse-fold.

14

Rabbit-ear. Make sure
that at the black dots the
rabbit ear goes underneath.

15

Valley-fold.

16

Reverse-fold.

17

Mountain-fold.

18

Valley-fold.

19

Rabbit-ear both appendages so that
they stick straight out, making the
model 3-D; it will no longer lie flat.

Thoughts Behind the Folds

The idea to design a Surfer came as a
challenge from my aunt, Leslie Woods,
while we were at a Thanksgiving
family reunion in 1990. I was
surprised at how easy the model was
to design, and especially surprised to
discover that sliding the surfer forward
made the wave crash. Thanks to my
cousin, Matt Woods—the real surfer in
the family—for teaching me the surfer
lingo.

More Thoughts Behind the Folds

Managing to make a person from two
narrow appendages was a huge discovery,
a technique that opened the door to an
endless array of models of people doing
things. Some favorites that I've designed
so far are: Person on a Balance Beam,
Person Walking around a Mobius Strip
and Two People Playing Ping Pong.
Challenge: Make two people playing
your favorite activity.

20

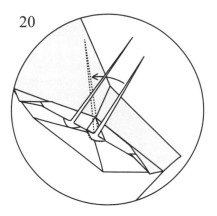

Those are some pretty skinny ears, eh? Begin to form the body of the surfer by bending the right ear behind the left ear.

21

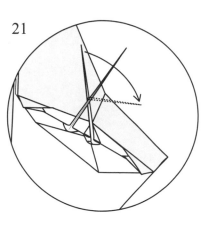

Wrap it around...

22

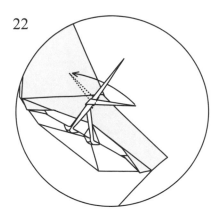

...and around.

23

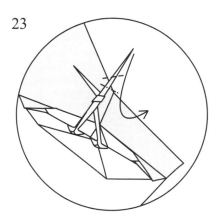

Fold the longer flap behind and then to the right, forming the surfer's head and other arm.

24

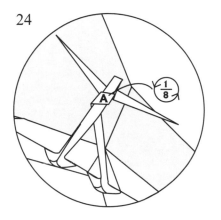

By bending, twisting and pinching, mold the surfer to taste. A good way to shape the legs is to pinch hard at point **A** and rotate counter-clockwise while holding the surfboard still with the other hand.

25

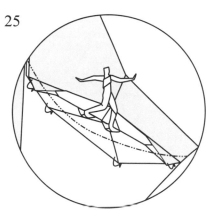

Make the board round with mountain folds. The center of the board is awfully thick, so needle-nose pliers might come in handy.

26

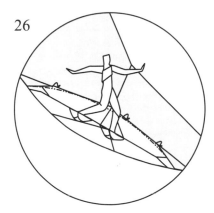

Round out the other side of the board.

27

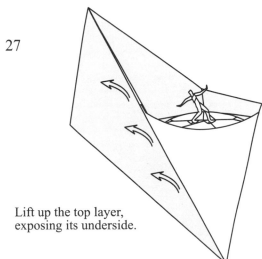

Lift up the top layer, exposing its underside.

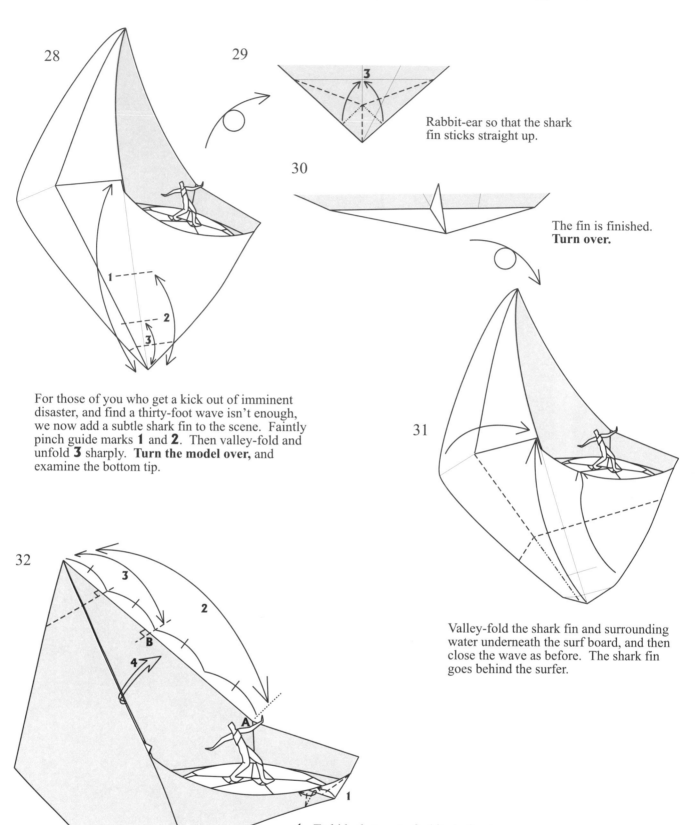

28

29

Rabbit-ear so that the shark fin sticks straight up.

30

The fin is finished. **Turn over.**

For those of you who get a kick out of imminent disaster, and find a thirty-foot wave isn't enough, we now add a subtle shark fin to the scene. Faintly pinch guide marks **1** and **2**. Then valley-fold and unfold **3** sharply. **Turn the model over,** and examine the bottom tip.

31

Valley-fold the shark fin and surrounding water underneath the surf board, and then close the wave as before. The shark fin goes behind the surfer.

32

1. To hide that spot of white in front of the surfer, pull on the near colored edge and swivel it counterclockwise as shown.
2. Make guide mark, **B**, by bringing the tip of the wave down to point **A**.
3. Valley-fold and unfold the tip of the wave down to **B**.
4. Lift up the right layer of the wave.

33

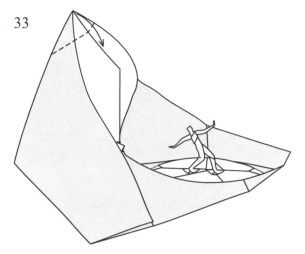

Valley-fold along the crease made in step 32.

34

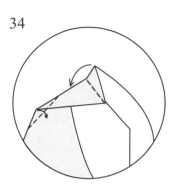

Magnified view. Close the wave and round the top to taste with at least one more valley fold.

35

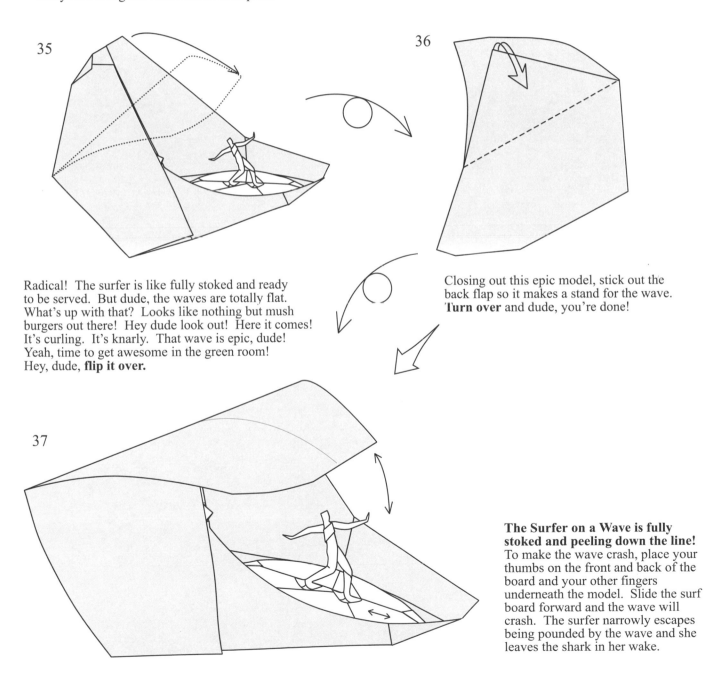

Radical! The surfer is like fully stoked and ready to be served. But dude, the waves are totally flat. What's up with that? Looks like nothing but mush burgers out there! Hey dude look out! Here it comes! It's curling. It's knarly. That wave is epic, dude! Yeah, time to get awesome in the green room! Hey, dude, **flip it over.**

36

Closing out this epic model, stick out the back flap so it makes a stand for the wave. **Turn over** and dude, you're done!

37

The Surfer on a Wave is fully stoked and peeling down the line! To make the wave crash, place your thumbs on the front and back of the board and your other fingers underneath the model. Slide the surf board forward and the wave will crash. The surfer narrowly escapes being pounded by the wave and she leaves the shark in her wake.

Glancer

Perfect for a haunted house, this creature looks as if it moves its eyes all by itself. Whether it's haunting a house, acting paranoid, watching ping pong, or flirting with passersby, this glancer will seize on any chance to glance.

1

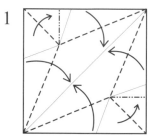

Begin with ten-inch paper or foil, white side up. Fold a Fish Base (page 28).

2

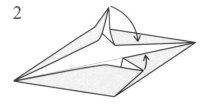

Fish Base in progress.

3

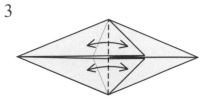

Valley-fold the middle flaps to the left side and then swing them back to the right side.

4

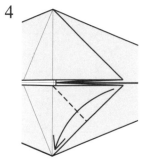

Valley-fold.

5

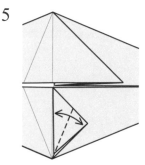

Valley-fold and unfold.

6

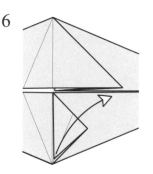

Unfold.

7

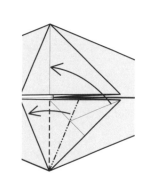

Lift, open slightly, and squash.

8

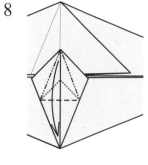

Petal-fold.

9

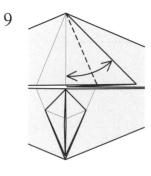

Valley-fold and unfold.

10

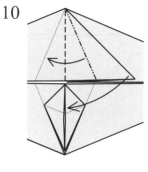

Lift and squash the nose-to-be.

11

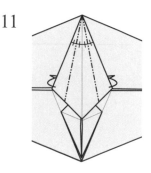

Mountain-fold the nose-to-be.

12

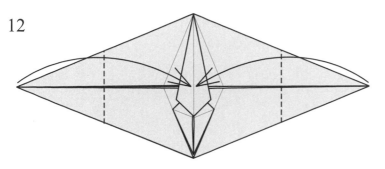

The nose is mostly done.
Valley-fold the ends to the center.

13

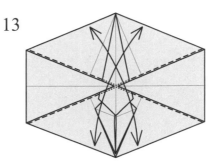

Valley-fold and unfold, but try
to avoid creasing on the nose.

14

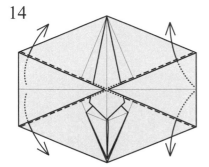

Pull out paper from inside the
two near flaps, valley-folding a
single layer as indicated.

15

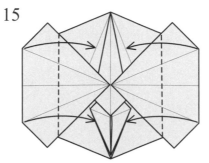

Valley-fold.

16

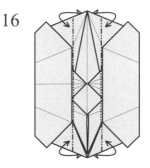

Mountain-fold and unfold
through the back layers.

17

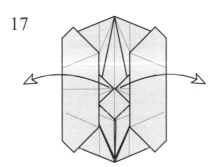

Unfold, letting the single-layer
corners swing out as well.

18

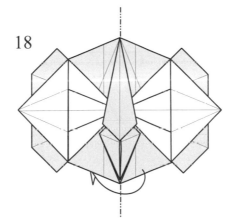

My, what big eyes you have!
Mountain-fold the right half behind.

19

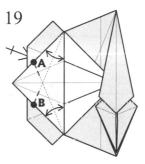

Bringing edge to edge,
valley-pinch at points **A**
and **B** only. Repeat behind.

20

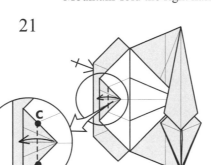

Valley-fold through points
A and **B**. Repeat behind.

21

Magnified view. Valley-fold
through points **C** and **D**.
Repeat behind.

22

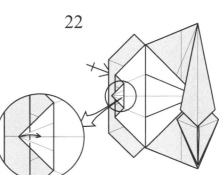

Magnified view. Valley-fold the tip,
matching up with the folded edge.
Repeat behind.

Glancer **61**

23

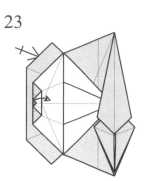

Swing the small flap rightward. The very tip stays fold. Repeat behind.

24

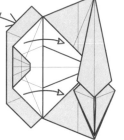

Swing the left flap to the right. Repeat behind.

25

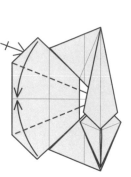

Valley-fold. Repeat behind.

26

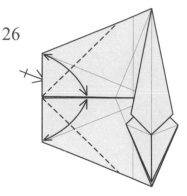

Valley-fold and unfold, bisecting the right angles. Repeat behind.

27

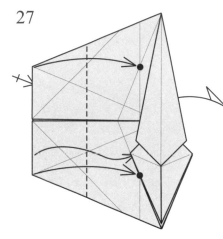

Valley-fold the corners to meet the existing crease. Repeat behind. OK, enough repeating behind! Swing the back flap to the right.

28

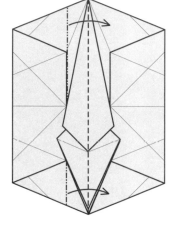

Pleat.

29

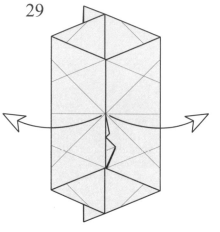

Swing the near flaps back outward from the middle.

Design note: The valley folds in step 32 are an example of what I call Bar Technique: When designing action models, the use of long slender folds helps build good bone structure and tends to enhance action mechanisms.

30

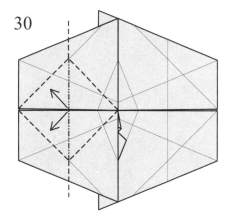

Valley-fold the left flap back to the center, incorporating two reverse folds on the near layer. The eyelids will not lie flat.

31

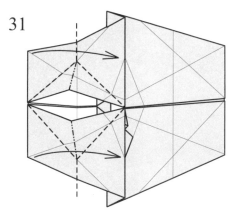

In progress.

32

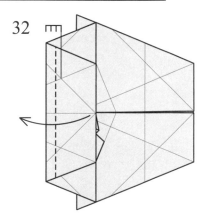

Valley-fold the front flap to the left, being careful to NOT crease the back layer of the model! The distance of this fold line from the left edge should be two thirds of the way to the intersection of creases. The model will not lie flat.

33

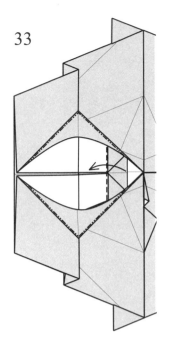

Valley-fold the small central flap to the left, to begin formation of the iris; allow the flap behind the iris to swing to the right. Define the outer edges of the eyelids with mountain folds.

34

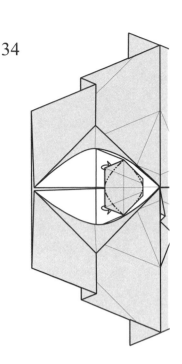

Optional: Round out the iris to taste using mountain folds. Avoid putting creases at the base of the iris flap.

35

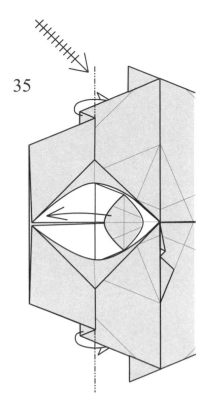

Swing the iris to the left, **while at the same time** swinging the back flap to the right. At all costs, avoid putting creases on the iris flap! When it looks like the next diagram, come back and repeat this step at least ten times, making the iris go back and forth in conjunction with the back flap. Make the creases super sharp.

36

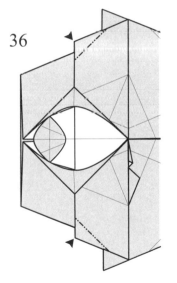

Reverse-fold, incorporating the existing crease. If the iris is hitting the eyelids, mountain-fold the inner edges of the eyelids just enough to get them out of the way.

37

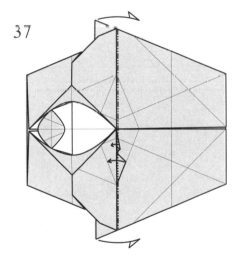

Swing the rear flap to the right, allowing the tiniest flaps to swing leftward.

38

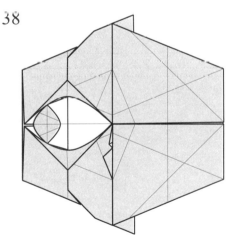

Repeat steps 30–36 on the right side.

Thoughts Behind the Folds

The Glancer evolved out of an attempt to design an eyeball. But an eyeball by itself is static and boring (unless it's being juggled) so I dropped the ball part and focused instead on making the iris move. Once I got one moving iris from a Kite Base, I doubled it using a Fish Base, and then made a nose and mouth from the two extra flaps in front. **Challenge:** How about designing a four-eyed glancer from a Bird Base?

39

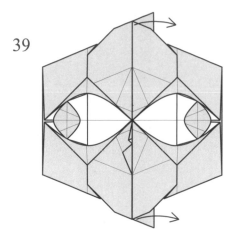

Swing open the middle of the model, moving the right half toward the right to expose the nose.

40

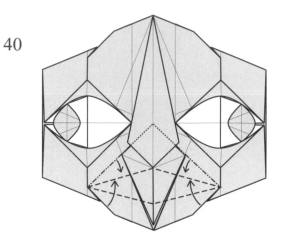

Make the indicated creases to form a mouth that will open when you pull at its sides. The mouth will not lie flat.

41

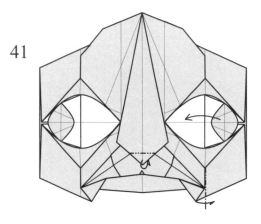

Mountain-fold the tip of the nose inside. Operating the back flap (see step 35), make the Glancer glance to the right (from its point of view).

42

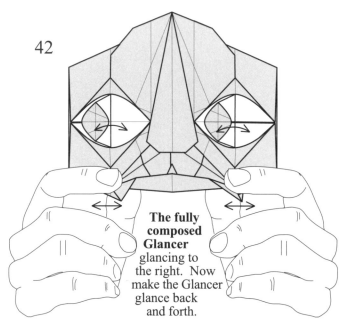

The fully composed Glancer glancing to the right. Now make the Glancer glance back and forth.

43

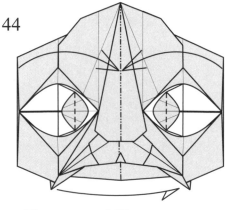

The fully composed Glancer glancing to the left.

44

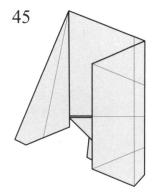

The cross-eyed Glancer. To store the Glancer, push the sides together, making the model lie flat.

45

The hibernating Glancer, waiting for another chance to glance.

Mr. Smiley

More than just a smiley face, this model contains a crazy cast of characters, including multiple personalities, weird animal forms, amusing action models and an environmental fable to tie them together. When I perform the Story of Mr. Smiley, I use a sixteen-inch model made from a twenty-seven-inch sheet of Wyndstone.

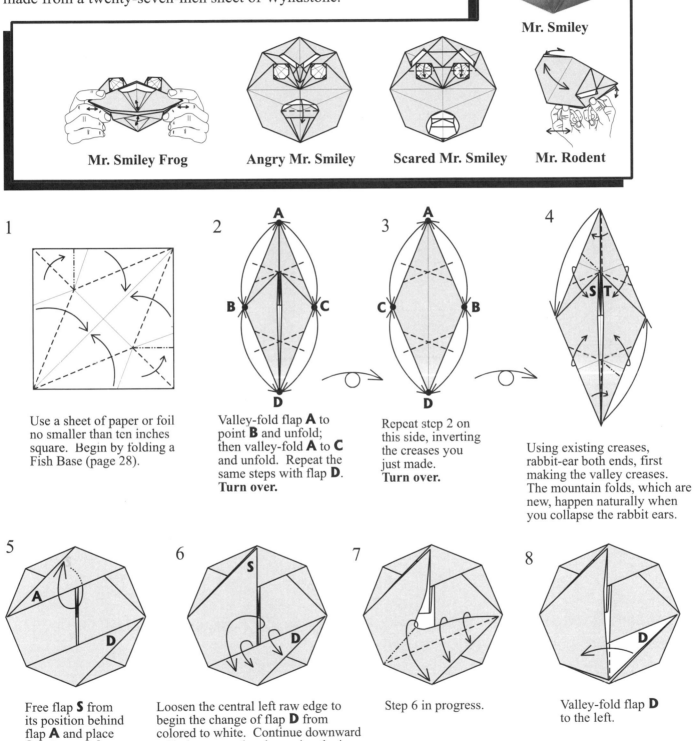

Mr. Smiley

Mr. Smiley Frog

Angry Mr. Smiley

Scared Mr. Smiley

Mr. Rodent

1

Use a sheet of paper or foil no smaller than ten inches square. Begin by folding a Fish Base (page 28).

2

Valley-fold flap **A** to point **B** and unfold; then valley-fold **A** to **C** and unfold. Repeat the same steps with flap **D**. **Turn over.**

3

Repeat step 2 on this side, inverting the creases you just made. **Turn over.**

4

Using existing creases, rabbit-ear both ends, first making the valley creases. The mountain folds, which are new, happen naturally when you collapse the rabbit ears.

5

Free flap **S** from its position behind flap **A** and place **S** in front of **A**.

6

Loosen the central left raw edge to begin the change of flap **D** from colored to white. Continue downward with the same edge, loosening the inner layer of **D**. Wrap this inner layer down around the near side of **D**.

7

Step 6 in progress.

8

Valley-fold flap **D** to the left.

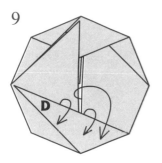

9

Repeat the actions of steps 6 and 7 to whiten the remaining side of flap **D**.

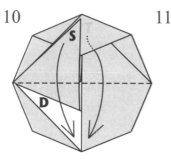

10

Free flap **T** from its position behind flap **A** and then fold **S** and **T** downward all the way.

11

Repeat steps 6–10 to whiten both sides of flap **A**. When you fold flap **T** back upward, tuck it under flap **A**.

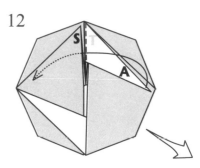

12

Swing the upper white flap to the left and place it behind the left flap.

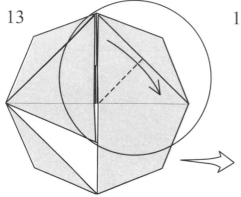

13

Valley-fold the right flap in half.

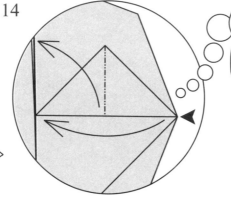

14

Lift, open slightly and squash-fold.

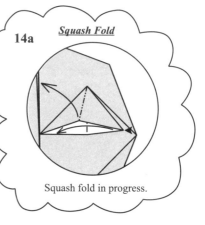

14a

Squash Fold

Squash fold in progress.

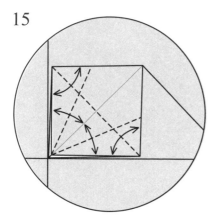

15

Valley-fold and unfold on the front two layers.

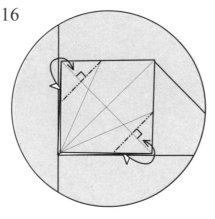

16

Mountain-fold and unfold, making the creases start at the ends of the kite-shaped creases.

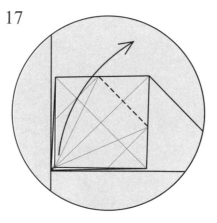

17

Open up the flap as if making a petal fold, but don't collapse it.

Thoughts Behind the Folds

The idea to fold a smiley face came from my high school friend, Sally Picciotto, who used to walk around giving smiley face stickers to everyone she passed. Over the next eight years, I kept on giving Mr. Smiley more transforming facial features, and made up a story to link them all together. I have performed it at birthday parties, street performances, and origami conventions.

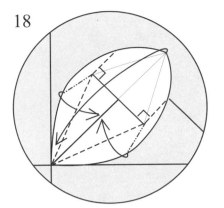

18

Collapse the flap back down along existing valley folds. The two mountains will get formed in the collapse.

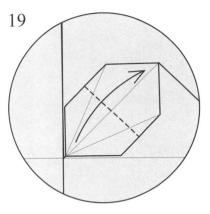

19

Valley-fold.

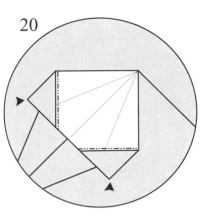

20

Reverse-fold.

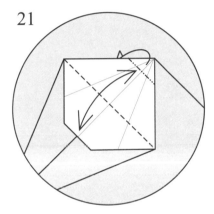

21

Mountain-fold the very tip behind by matching it with the opposite white folded edge.

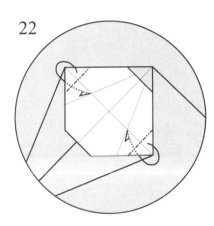

22

Mountain-fold the remaining tips behind to round out the eye. The guide mark is the intersection of existing creases.

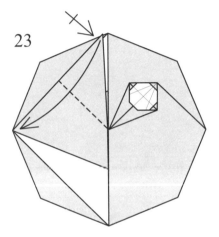

23

One eye is done. Fold the other eye by repeating steps 13–22 on the left side.

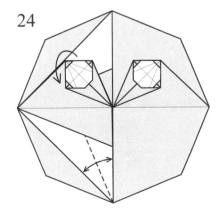

24

Bring the upper white flap in front of the eye. Valley-fold and unfold the lower white flap.

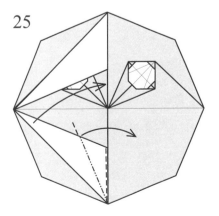

25

Lift, open, and squash.

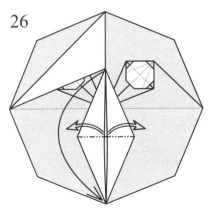

26

Fold downward in half while pulling the central edges outward.

Mr. Smiley **67**

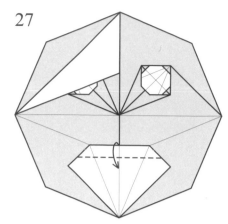

27

Valley-fold the flap as far down as possible.

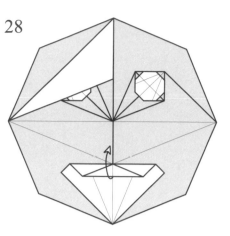

28

Swing the flap back up.

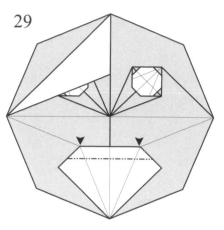

29

Closed-sink, i.e., shove in the upper lip.

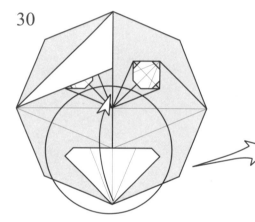

30

Petal-fold the mouth up, but do not flatten.

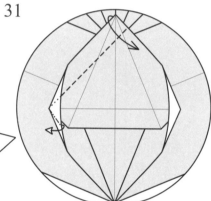

31

Starting from the top, fold the left edge downward toward the right; flatten the left corner outward.

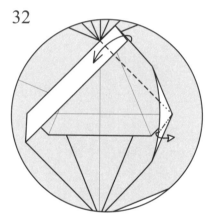

32

Repeat with the right edge.

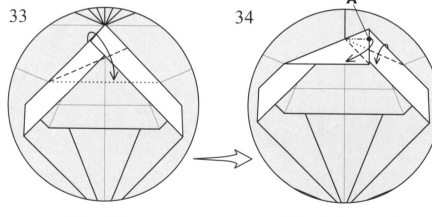

33

Valley-fold to the dotted line.

34

Pull point **A** toward the center as shown; flatten as shown in step 35.

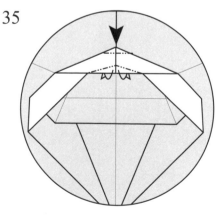

35

Round out the frown by closed-sinking the tip of the top of the lip, and mountain-folding the bottom edges behind.

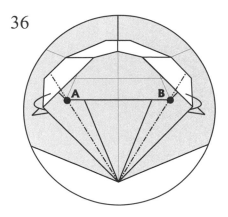

36

Mountain-fold through
points **A** and **B**.

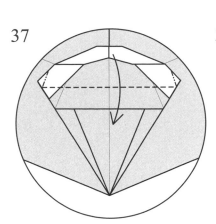

37

Valley-fold the frown down
on the existing crease,
petal-folding at the sides.

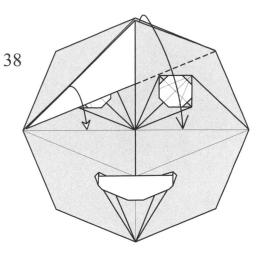

38

Say "Cheese!" The smile is captured.
Now for the eyebrows. Swing down
the white flap, opening it as shown.

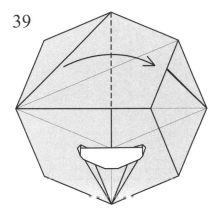

39

Swing the flap from left to right.

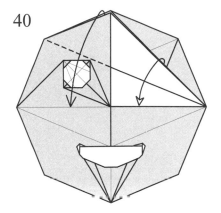

40

Swing down the white flap.

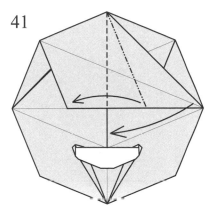

41

Lift, open, and squash.

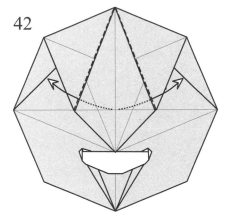

42

Pull out the inner layers.

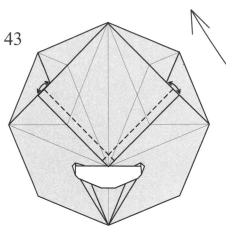

43

Valley-fold and unfold.

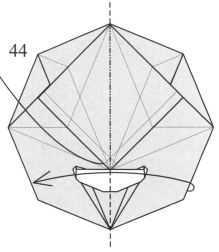

44

Valley-fold the model in half, while
opening the near central flap and
pulling it clockwise up to the left.

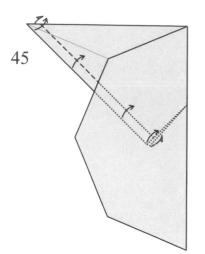

45

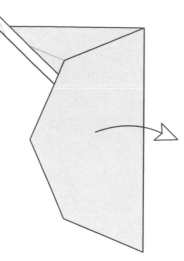

46

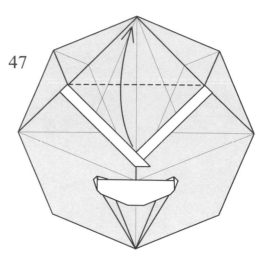

47

Keeping the model as closed as possible, plain-old-valley-fold along existing creases. Repeat behind, outside-reverse-folding at the tip.

Open the model back up, bringing the flap back down.

Valley-fold up the front flap, including the two flaps beneath it.

48

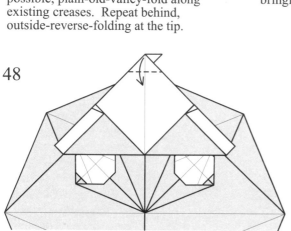

49

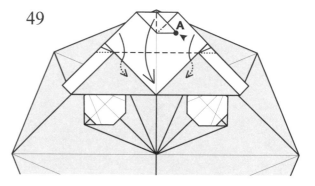

Valley-fold so that the top of Mr. Smiley's head appears.

Do away with point **A** with a tiny squash fold. Then, valley-fold the top flap underneath the white eyebrows.

50

51

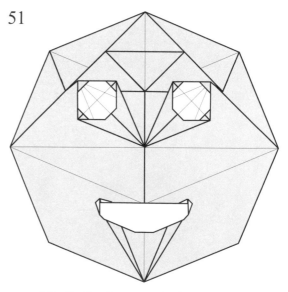

Mountain-fold the eyebrows behind, tucking them into the pockets. Bring the eyes in front.

**Mr. Smiley is very well done,
But we've only just begun.
Here comes the story in all of its glory,
A cornucopia of fun!**

Transforming Mr. Smiley...

The following diagrams show how to turn Mr. Smiley into a wild assortment of crazy characters that can be used for storytelling. Along the right side of the diagrams is a story I use when performing with Mr. Smiley.

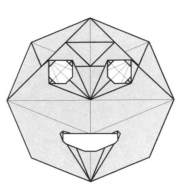

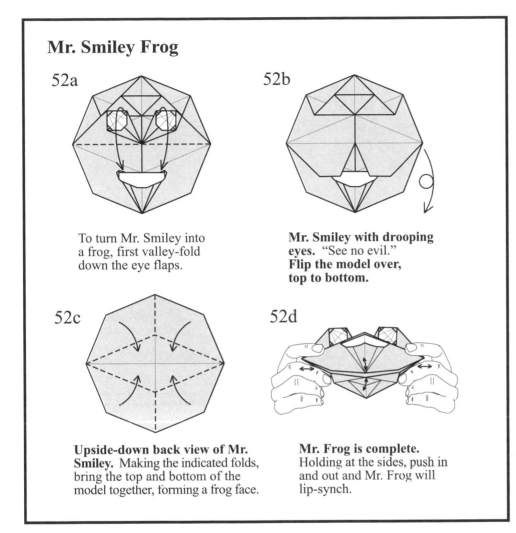

Mr. Smiley Frog

52a

To turn Mr. Smiley into a frog, first valley-fold down the eye flaps.

52b

Mr. Smiley with drooping eyes. "See no evil." **Flip the model over, top to bottom.**

52c

Upside-down back view of Mr. Smiley. Making the indicated folds, bring the top and bottom of the model together, forming a frog face.

52d

Mr. Frog is complete. Holding at the sides, push in and out and Mr. Frog will lip-synch.

The Story of
Mr. Smiley

Once upon a time...

In the Brazilian rainforest, there lived a lumberjack named Mr. Smiley {52a}. Mr. Smiley was known for being the quickest strongest happiest lumberjack in all the land. So thorough was Mr. Smiley in his work that he not only clear-cut all the trees in his path, but he also clear cut all the shrubs and shaved the ground bare with a razor.

One day Mr. Smiley was walking along when all of a sudden a huge frog {52d} jumped out in front of him.

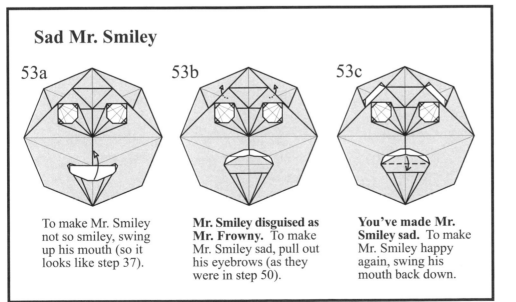

Sad Mr. Smiley

53a

To make Mr. Smiley not so smiley, swing up his mouth (so it looks like step 37).

53b

Mr. Smiley disguised as Mr. Frowny. To make Mr. Smiley sad, pull out his eyebrows (as they were in step 50).

53c

You've made Mr. Smiley sad. To make Mr. Smiley happy again, swing his mouth back down.

"Help! Help!" cried the frog, "I beg you! You've chopped down all the trees around the lake, and left no shade for us poor frogs to protect ourselves from the sun. We're all gonna die of sunstroke! Please help!"

Mr. Smiley, who was no longer so smiley {53b}— in fact he was a little sad {53c}—said...

Talking Mr. Smiley

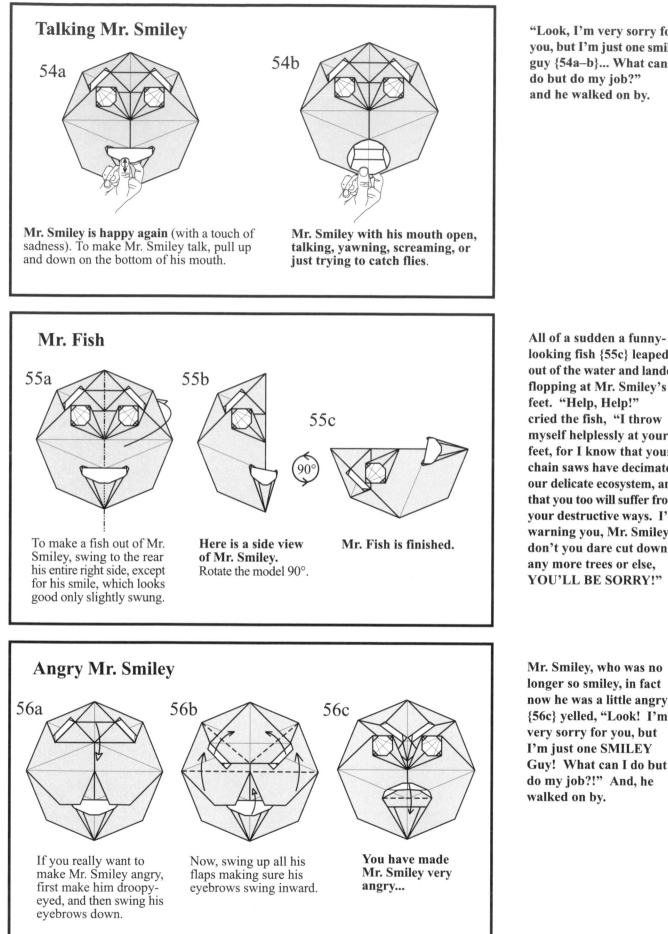

54a

54b

Mr. Smiley is happy again (with a touch of sadness). To make Mr. Smiley talk, pull up and down on the bottom of his mouth.

Mr. Smiley with his mouth open, talking, yawning, screaming, or just trying to catch flies.

"Look, I'm very sorry for you, but I'm just one smiley guy {54a–b}... What can I do but do my job?" and he walked on by.

Mr. Fish

55a

55b

55c

90°

To make a fish out of Mr. Smiley, swing to the rear his entire right side, except for his smile, which looks good only slightly swung.

Here is a side view of Mr. Smiley. Rotate the model 90°.

Mr. Fish is finished.

All of a sudden a funny-looking fish {55c} leaped out of the water and landed flopping at Mr. Smiley's feet. "Help, Help!" cried the fish, "I throw myself helplessly at your feet, for I know that your chain saws have decimated our delicate ecosystem, and that you too will suffer from your destructive ways. I'm warning you, Mr. Smiley, don't you dare cut down any more trees or else, YOU'LL BE SORRY!"

Angry Mr. Smiley

56a

56b

56c

If you really want to make Mr. Smiley angry, first make him droopy-eyed, and then swing his eyebrows down.

Now, swing up all his flaps making sure his eyebrows swing inward.

You have made Mr. Smiley very angry...

Mr. Smiley, who was no longer so smiley, in fact now he was a little angry {56c} yelled, "Look! I'm very sorry for you, but I'm just one SMILEY Guy! What can I do but do my job?!" And, he walked on by.

Mr. Killer Bee

57a

... or, perhaps, **schemishly evil.** To make Mr. Smiley transform into a killer bee, first shave off his eyebrows as well as the top of his head with a sharp mountain fold.

57b

Mr. Smiley with an amputated brain. Mountain-fold the model in half. Folding and unfolding this mountain becomes the wing action for the killer bee.

57c   ### 57d
90°

Mr. Smiley further amputated. Rotate what's left 90°.

Mr. Killer Bee has come to be. Flapping his "wings" (alternate between 57b and 57d) and adding sound effects will help make this model more convincing.

Scared Mr. Smiley

58

Mr. Smiley is scared (54b). Valley-fold to make him close his eyes in fear.

Mr. Rodent

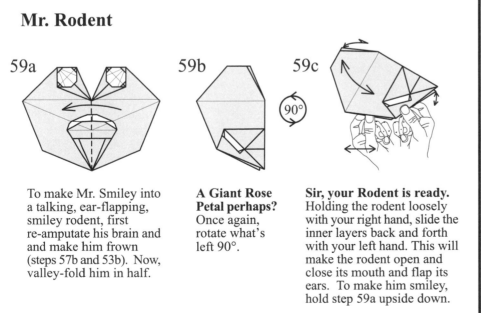

59a

59b
90°

59c

To make Mr. Smiley into a talking, ear-flapping, smiley rodent, first re-amputate his brain and and make him frown (steps 57b and 53b). Now, valley-fold him in half.

A Giant Rose Petal perhaps? Once again, rotate what's left 90°.

Sir, your Rodent is ready. Holding the rodent loosely with your right hand, slide the inner layers back and forth with your left hand. This will make the rodent open and close its mouth and flap its ears. To make him smiley, hold step 59a upside down.

The very next tree that Mr. Smiley cut down happened to be infested by a huge swarm of killer bees {57d}, and the killer bees chased Mr. Smiley deep into the rainforest where he got lost.

He cried out, "Help! Help!" {58} but there was no one there to help him.

Finally, a passing Amazon rodent {59c} heard him and said as he wiggled his ears, "I'm very sorry for you, but I'm just one smiley rodent {briefly show 59a upside down}. What can I do but do my job?" and he went off to eat more food.

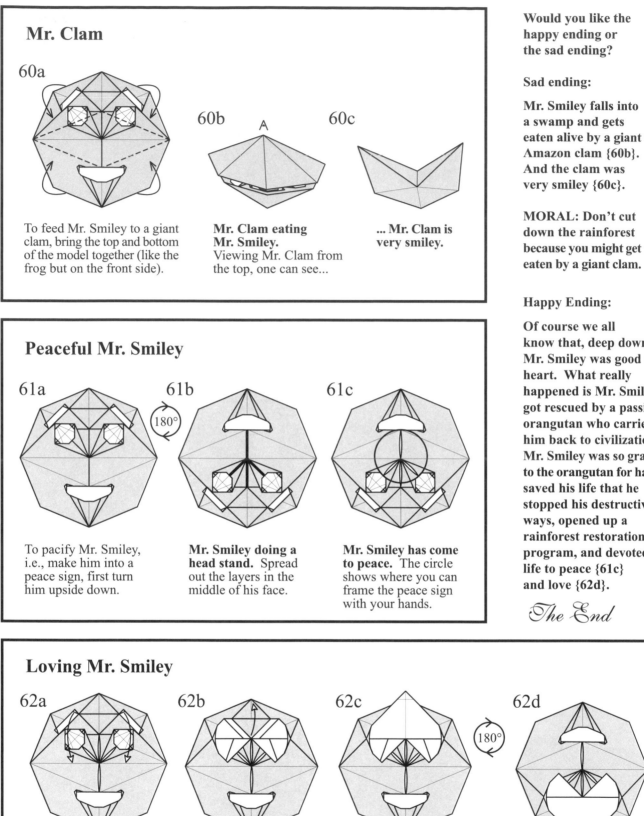

Mr. Clam

60a

To feed Mr. Smiley to a giant clam, bring the top and bottom of the model together (like the frog but on the front side).

60b

Mr. Clam eating Mr. Smiley. Viewing Mr. Clam from the top, one can see...

60c

... Mr. Clam is very smiley.

Peaceful Mr. Smiley

61a

To pacify Mr. Smiley, i.e., make him into a peace sign, first turn him upside down.

61b

Mr. Smiley doing a head stand. Spread out the layers in the middle of his face.

61c

Mr. Smiley has come to peace. The circle shows where you can frame the peace sign with your hands.

Loving Mr. Smiley

62a

To give Mr. Smiley a heart, first give him a pair of sunglasses by bringing down the front layers of his eyebrows over his eyes.

62b

Mr. Styley, ready to sunbathe. Completely unfold that middle flap.

62c

Mr. Smiley with an upside-down heart on his head. Turn Mr. Smiley upside down.

62d

Mr. Smiley upside down in love.

Would you like the happy ending or the sad ending?

Sad ending:

Mr. Smiley falls into a swamp and gets eaten alive by a giant Amazon clam {60b}. And the clam was very smiley {60c}.

MORAL: Don't cut down the rainforest because you might get eaten by a giant clam.

Happy Ending:

Of course we all know that, deep down, Mr. Smiley was good at heart. What really happened is Mr. Smiley got rescued by a passing orangutan who carried him back to civilization. Mr. Smiley was so grateful to the orangutan for having saved his life that he stopped his destructive ways, opened up a rainforest restoration program, and devoted his life to peace {61c} and love {62d}.

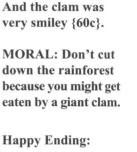

The End

Squishy Blob

What's that? It's a pointy thingamajig that bounces up and down like a trampoline. Its primary use is as a finger exercising device. However, it can also be used as a trampoline for your Mexican jumping bean.

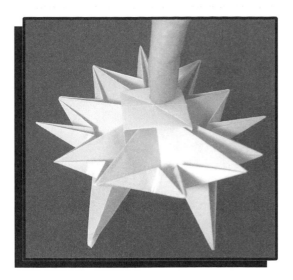

1

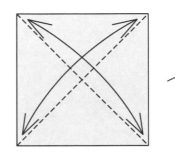

Works best folded from six-inch paper. Colored side up, valley-fold and unfold diagonally in half both ways. **Turn over.**

2

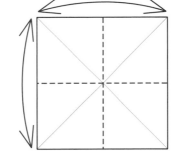

Valley-fold and unfold in half both ways.

3

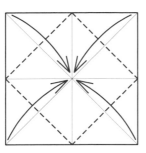

Blintz!

4

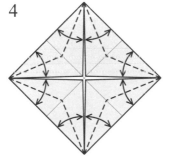

Valley-fold and unfold on the front layer only.

5

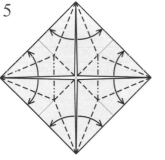

Along existing creases, make rabbit ears out of the corners.

6

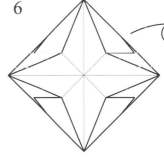

Like this. **Turn over.**

7

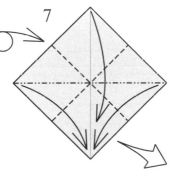

Form a Square Base.

8

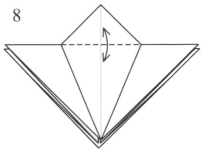

Valley-fold and unfold.

9

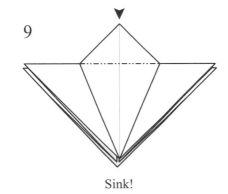

Sink!

10

Valley-fold. Repeat behind.

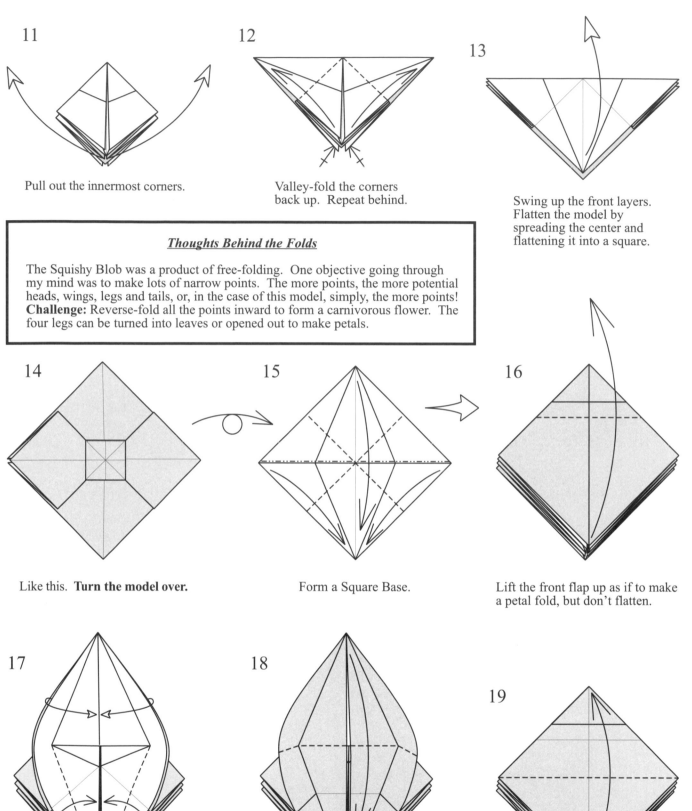

11

Pull out the innermost corners.

12

Valley-fold the corners back up. Repeat behind.

13

Swing up the front layers. Flatten the model by spreading the center and flattening it into a square.

Thoughts Behind the Folds

The Squishy Blob was a product of free-folding. One objective going through my mind was to make lots of narrow points. The more points, the more potential heads, wings, legs and tails, or, in the case of this model, simply, the more points! **Challenge:** Reverse-fold all the points inward to form a carnivorous flower. The four legs can be turned into leaves or opened out to make petals.

14

Like this. **Turn the model over.**

15

Form a Square Base.

16

Lift the front flap up as if to make a petal fold, but don't flatten.

17

Erase all the white by bringing the raw edges together.

18

Fold the flap back down. Repeat steps 16–18 on the other three such flaps.

19

Valley-fold the front flap. Repeat on the other three such flaps.

20

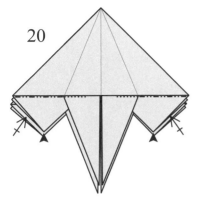

Reverse-fold.

21

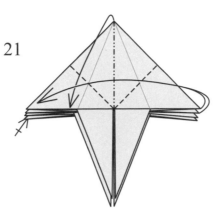

Swing the two front right corners to the left incorporating a reverse fold. Balance the model by repeating behind.

22

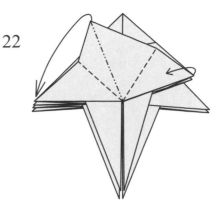

Step 21 in progress.

23

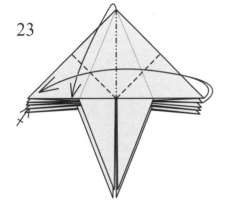

Repeat step 21 with the next set of flaps. The first set of step 21 reverse folds will come undone. Repeat behind.

24

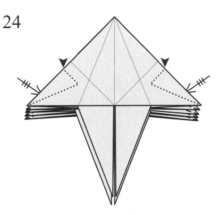

Make eight lovely little reverse folds. See the circled area in step 26 for an example in perspective.

25

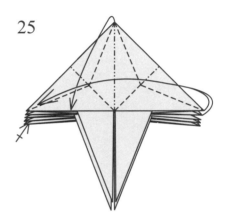

Repeat step 21 again, this time incorporating in addition the four remaining lovely little reverse folds. The model will now take shape.

26

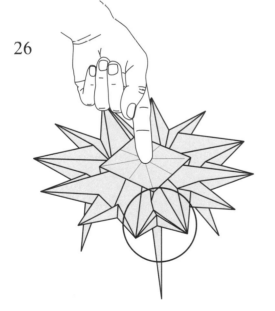

The Squishy Blob Trampoline has been constructed. Shrink yourself to the weight of a pencil and bounce bounce bounce, or more simply, bounce on it with your finger as shown.

27

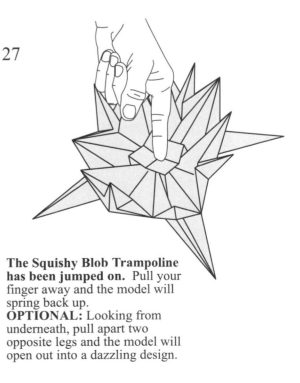

The Squishy Blob Trampoline has been jumped on. Pull your finger away and the model will spring back up.
OPTIONAL: Looking from underneath, pull apart two opposite legs and the model will open out into a dazzling design.

Piano Playing Pop-up Card

Not only is this model cheaper than a Steinway, it's also easier to make, easier to play and takes less space to store! Why would anyone buy a real piano when they can make this one?!

1

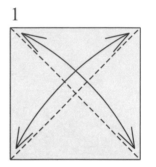

Use paper or foil no smaller than ten inches square. Colored side up, valley-fold and unfold diagonally in half both ways.

2

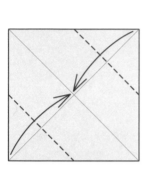

Valley-fold opposite corners to the center.

3

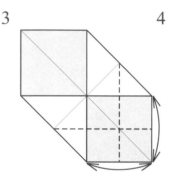

Valley-fold and unfold.

4

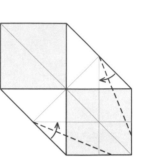

Valley-fold the edge to the crease line.

5

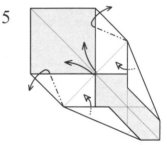

Slide out the paper from behind the near flaps.

6

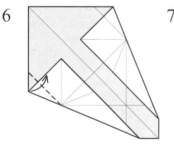

Valley-fold the left point on the existing crease.

7

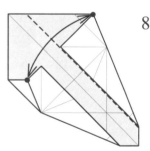

Valley-fold and unfold dot-to-dot.

8

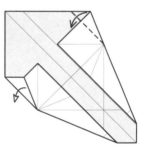

Unfold the left point. Valley-fold the right point on the existing crease.

9

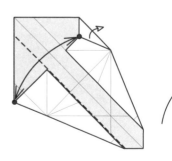

Valley-fold and unfold dot-to-dot. Unfold the little flap. **Turn over.**

10

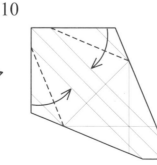

Valley-fold edge-to-crease.

11

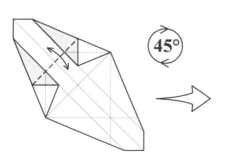

Valley-fold and unfold. Rotate the model 45°.

12

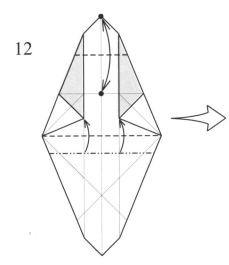

Valley-fold and unfold on top. Pleat in the middle, making the valley and then the mountain.

13

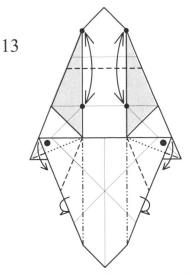

Valley-fold and unfold, dot-to-dot. Then mountain-fold the left edge to the back as shown; the upper left corner of the flap will be pulled counterclockwise. Watch the black dot and flatten. Repeat on the right.

14

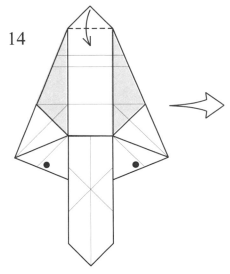

Valley-fold.

15

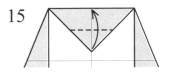

Valley-fold.

16

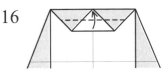

Valley-fold.

17

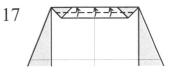

Valley-fold.

18

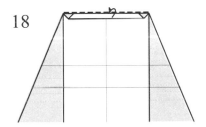

Swing the flap behind.

19

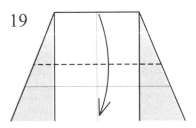

Valley-fold on the existing crease made in step 12.

20

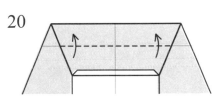

Valley-fold, lining up with the crease underneath (made in step 13).

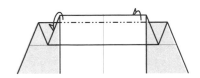

Mountain-fold the top edge inside.

22

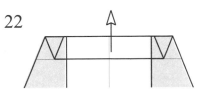

Unfold the pleat, but don't unfold the mountain you just made. The next diagram is looking at the model from an angle.

23

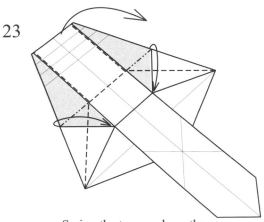

Swing the top up along the indicated existing folds.

24

Swing the top down along the indicated existing folds.

25

Fold the keys inside the piano. For a way to do this that will best avoid accidentally tearing the paper, go to the cloud, **turn the model over**, and look at the underneath side of just the piano.

25a

We're now looking underneath the piano. Swivel-fold on both sides. See page 229 to get the hang of swivel-folding.

25b

Pleat on the existing creases to fold the keys inside.

25c

The keys are all tucked away. **Turn the piano back over.**

26

Turn the model over.

27

Color-change the indicated flaps, and that does not mean use a pen! Free the single layer from behind the flaps and bring it around to the front. To do this cleanly it's necessary to unfold the model partially.

28

Bring the color-changed flaps to the front if they are not already there.

29

Pull the edges out, releasing paper from behind each flap. Watch the black dots.

30

Rotate the model 180° and look at it from an angle.

31

180°

Close the card by making the indicated folds.

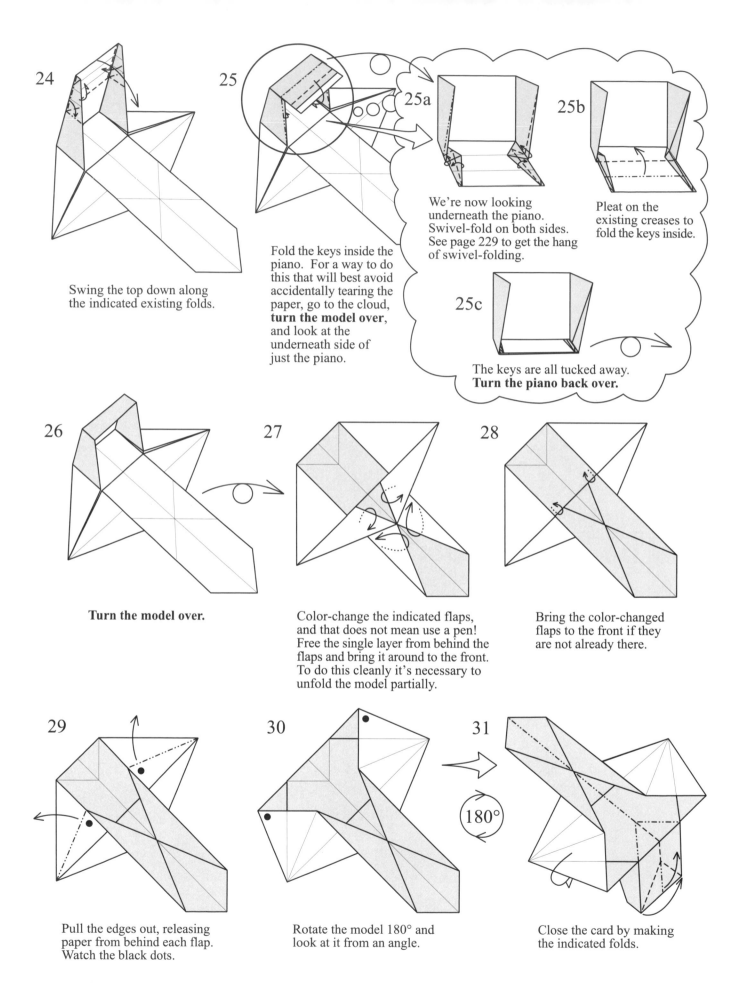

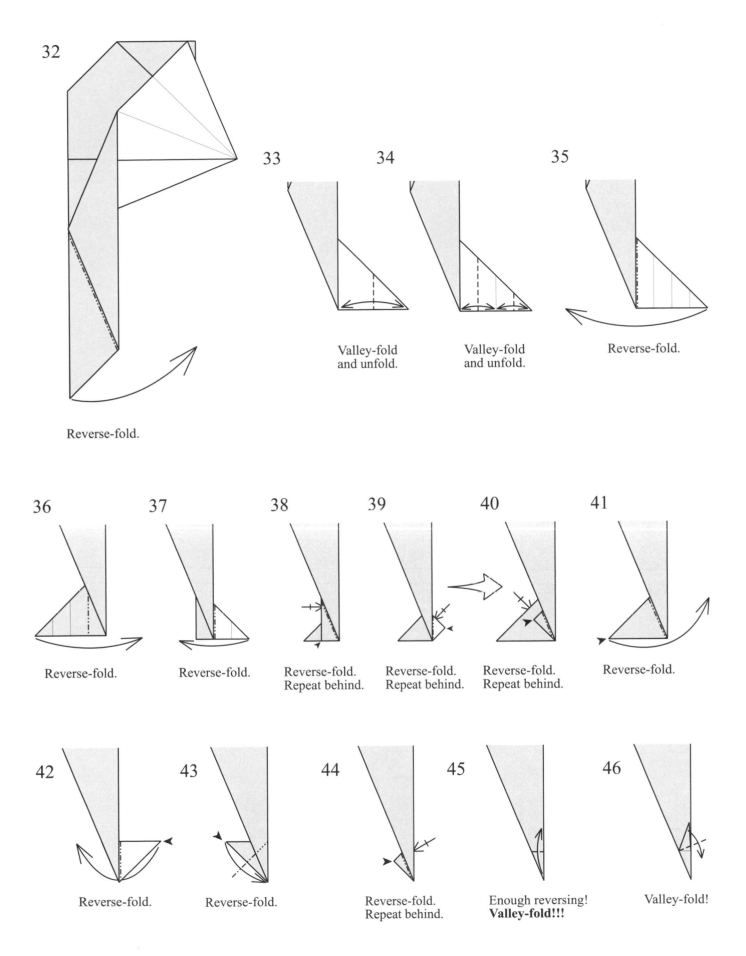

32

Reverse-fold.

33

34

Valley-fold
and unfold.

Valley-fold
and unfold.

35

Reverse-fold.

36

Reverse-fold.

37

Reverse-fold.

38

Reverse-fold.
Repeat behind.

39

Reverse-fold.
Repeat behind.

40

Reverse-fold.
Repeat behind.

41

Reverse-fold.

42

Reverse-fold.

43

Reverse-fold.

44

Reverse-fold.
Repeat behind.

45

Enough reversing!
Valley-fold!!!

46

Valley-fold!

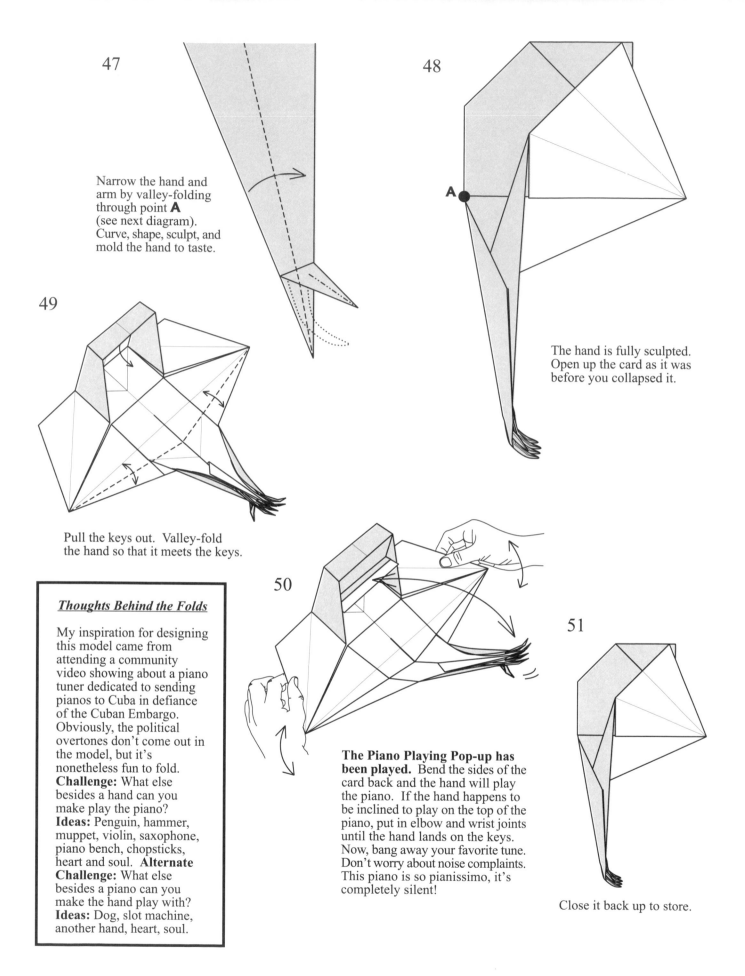

47

Narrow the hand and arm by valley-folding through point **A** (see next diagram). Curve, shape, sculpt, and mold the hand to taste.

48

A

The hand is fully sculpted. Open up the card as it was before you collapsed it.

49

Pull the keys out. Valley-fold the hand so that it meets the keys.

50

The Piano Playing Pop-up has been played. Bend the sides of the card back and the hand will play the piano. If the hand happens to be inclined to play on the top of the piano, put in elbow and wrist joints until the hand lands on the keys. Now, bang away your favorite tune. Don't worry about noise complaints. This piano is so pianissimo, it's completely silent!

51

Close it back up to store.

Thoughts Behind the Folds

My inspiration for designing this model came from attending a community video showing about a piano tuner dedicated to sending pianos to Cuba in defiance of the Cuban Embargo. Obviously, the political overtones don't come out in the model, but it's nonetheless fun to fold. **Challenge:** What else besides a hand can you make play the piano? **Ideas:** Penguin, hammer, muppet, violin, saxophone, piano bench, chopsticks, heart and soul. **Alternate Challenge:** What else besides a piano can you make the hand play with? **Ideas:** Dog, slot machine, another hand, heart, soul.

Yapping, Clapping, Tapping, Flapping T-rex—All when you Punch him in his Stomach

In terms of action, this model is full of it.
If all T-rexes had been this active,
they would have never become extinct.

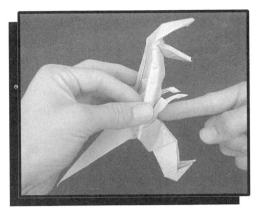

1

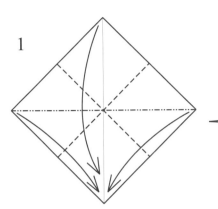

White side up. Fold a Square Base.

2

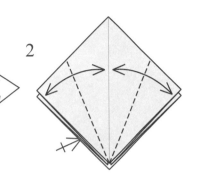

Valley-fold and unfold. Repeat behind.

3

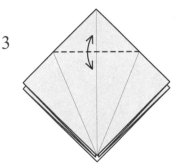

Valley-fold and unfold.

4

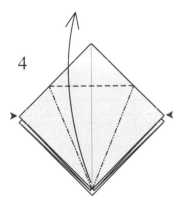

Petal-fold.

5

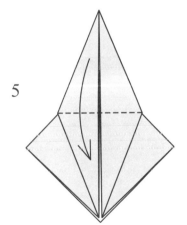

Valley-fold the flap down.

6

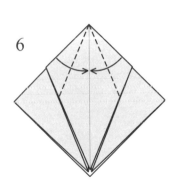

Valley-fold.

7

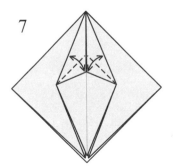

Valley-fold and unfold.

8

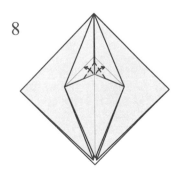

Valley-fold the tips to the creases
so that the two shaded triangles are isosceles
(i.e., two of the three sides have equal lengths).

9

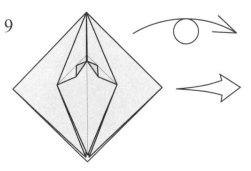

Like this. **Turn over.**

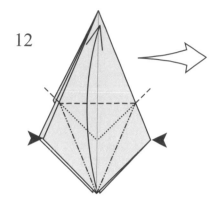

10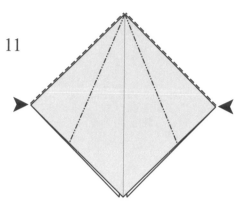

Valley-fold and unfold.

11

Reverse-fold.

12

Petal-fold the front flap.

13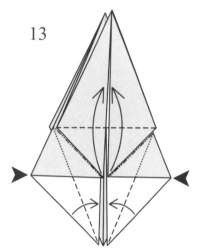

Petal-fold the middle flaps.

14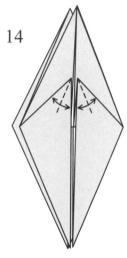

Valley-fold and unfold.

15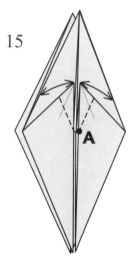

A

Anchoring at point **A**, valley-fold and unfold each flap to the side of the model.

16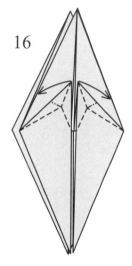

Using the creases made in steps 14 and 15, rabbit-ear the flaps to the sides of the model.

17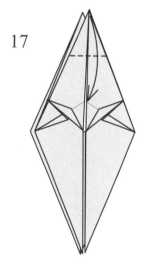

Valley-fold to the crease marks.

18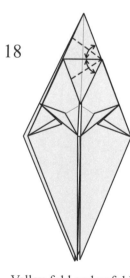

Valley-fold and unfold.

Thoughts Behind the Folds

This T-rex is a remnant of my prehistoric days of folding. I went through a phase of folding creatures. I believed that any folded form could be called a creature, especially if there were lots of wings, legs, heads, and tails. None of the moving features of the T-rex were intentional, which just goes to show that by playing around with the way the paper moves, sooner or later an action model is bound to jump out.

Exercise: Practice free-folding (folding with no intent), but continually move the paper in different ways, and let your imagination fly. With enough imagination, anything can be folded, and every fold can be anything!

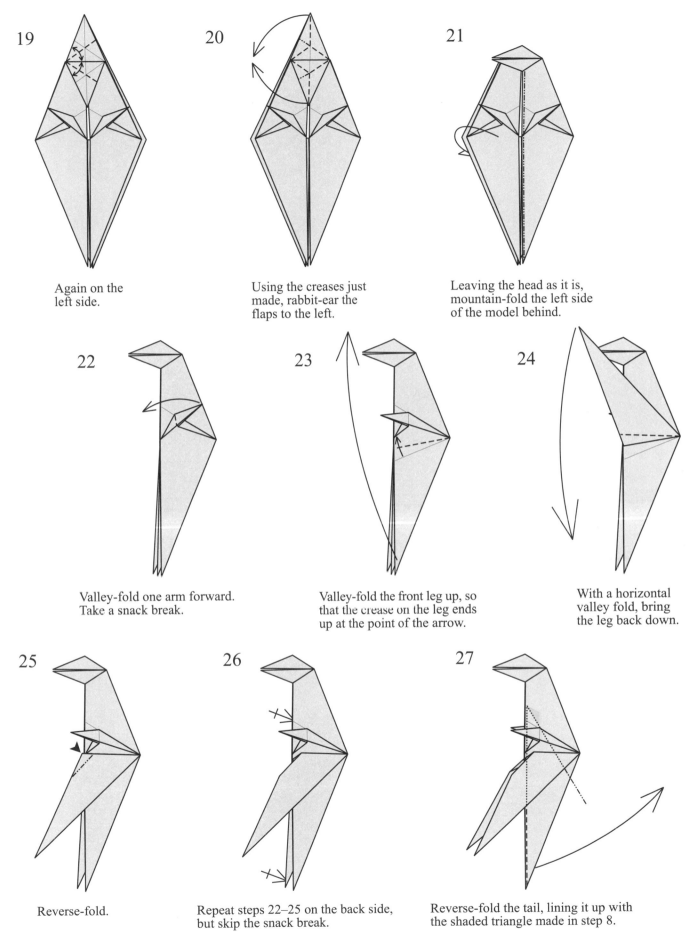

19

Again on the
left side.

20

Using the creases just
made, rabbit-ear the
flaps to the left.

21

Leaving the head as it is,
mountain-fold the left side
of the model behind.

22

Valley-fold one arm forward.
Take a snack break.

23

Valley-fold the front leg up, so
that the crease on the leg ends
up at the point of the arrow.

24

With a horizontal
valley fold, bring
the leg back down.

25

Reverse-fold.

26

Repeat steps 22–25 on the back side,
but skip the snack break.

27

Reverse-fold the tail, lining it up with
the shaded triangle made in step 8.

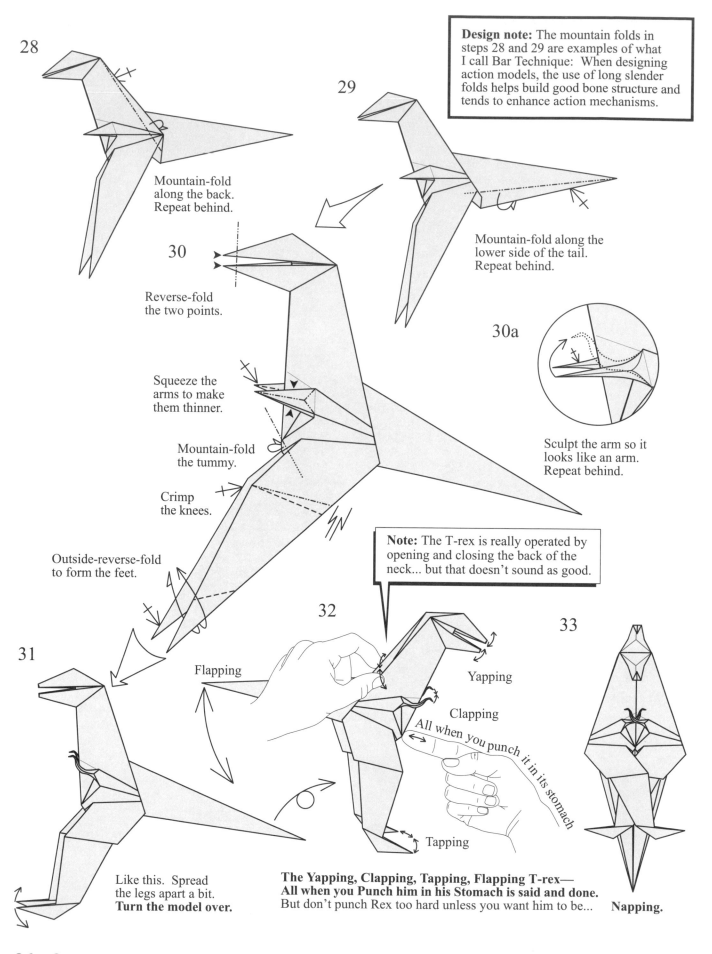

28

Mountain-fold
along the back.
Repeat behind.

29

Design note: The mountain folds in steps 28 and 29 are examples of what I call Bar Technique: When designing action models, the use of long slender folds helps build good bone structure and tends to enhance action mechanisms.

Mountain-fold along the
lower side of the tail.
Repeat behind.

30

Reverse-fold
the two points.

Squeeze the
arms to make
them thinner.

Mountain-fold
the tummy.

Crimp
the knees.

Outside-reverse-fold
to form the feet.

30a

Sculpt the arm so it
looks like an arm.
Repeat behind.

Note: The T-rex is really operated by opening and closing the back of the neck... but that doesn't sound as good.

31

Flapping

32

Yapping

Clapping

All when you punch it in its stomach

Tapping

Like this. Spread
the legs apart a bit.
Turn the model over.

**The Yapping, Clapping, Tapping, Flapping T-rex—
All when you Punch him in his Stomach is said and done.**
But don't punch Rex too hard unless you want him to be...

Napping.

33

Venus Flytrap

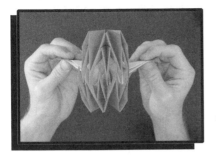

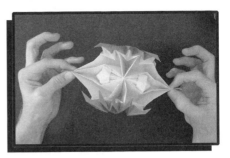

This creature doesn't really fly, but it might catch a fly if you try folding it out of sticky, smelly paper. Then again, I'm vegetarian, so I haven't tried.

1

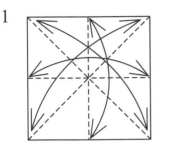

White side up, valley-fold and unfold in half every which way.

2

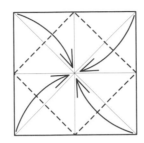

Blintz the four corners.

3

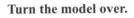

Turn the model over.

4

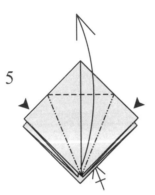

Fold a Square Base.

5

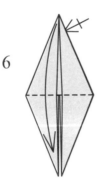

Petal-fold the front and back flaps to form a Bird Base.

6

Fold the flaps down.

7

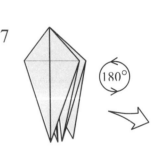

Rotate the model 180°.

8

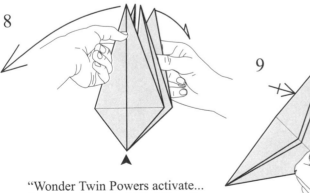

"Wonder Twin Powers activate... form of a Stretched Bird Base." To do this, hold on to the front and back flaps, and pull them as far apart as possible without ripping the paper. The model will not lie flat.

9

Now collapse the central region in rabbit ear fashion, and lay the flaps down toward the right.

10

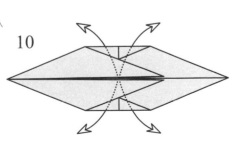

The Stretched Bird Base has been activated. Liberate the blintzed corners which are trapped behind the model. Partially unfolding the model makes this liberation easier.

11

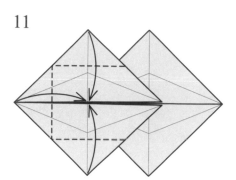

Blintz the three left corners.

12

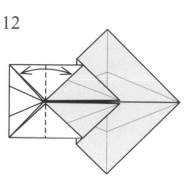

Valley-fold and unfold.

13

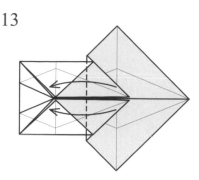

Swing the center flaps to the left.

14

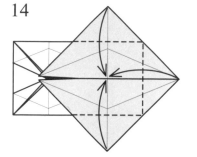

Blintz the three right corners.

15

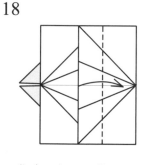

Valley-fold and unfold.
Turn over from top to bottom.

16

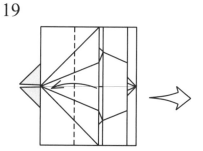

Valley-fold and unfold
through all layers, bisecting
each of the four corners.

17

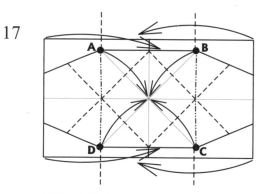

Valley-fold the left and right sides inward
(they will overlap), while at the same time
lifting and folding points **A**, **B**, **C**, and **D**
to the center along existing creases.

18

Swing the top flap over
as far as it will go, but
you needn't crease it—
just get it out of the way
so we can see underneath.

19

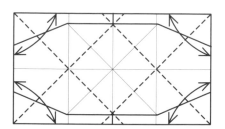

Do the same with this flap.

Thoughts Behind the Folds

The Venus Flytrap started out as a free-folding exercise—folding without a set goal in mind.
When I happened to fold a stretched blintzed Bird Base (step 11), I noticed what looked like
two squares of origami paper. I set out to try to fold each one of those into a blintzed Bird
Base which resulted in the Venus Flytrap. The action was pure chance, but no miracle, as
I'm always moving the paper in different ways looking for an action model to pop out.
Exercise: What else can you design from the stretched blintzed Bird Base?
Ideas: Siamese twins, Siamese cranes, Siamese anything-of-your-choice.

20

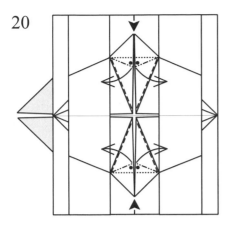

We will now perform oral surgery on the Venus Flytrap. Squash-fold the tonsils. Watch the black dots.

21

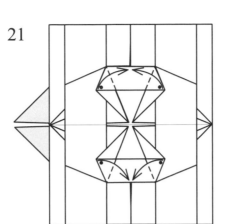

Valley-fold the surrounding glandular tissue.

22

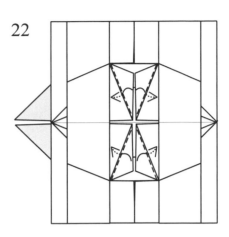

Valley-fold the four glandular flaps, inserting them into the **REAR** pockets.

23

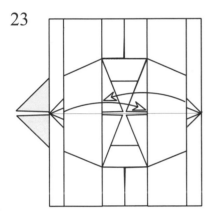

Return the two edges to their original positions, thus completing the throat surgery.

24

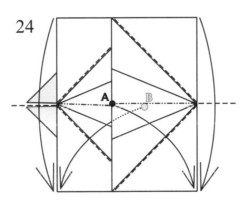

Now for the gums. Valley-fold the top down to the bottom, while at the same time lifting and pulling forward points **A** and **B**. This action is like that of step 17.

25

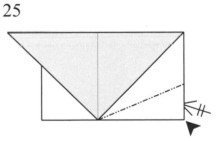

Reverse-fold the three corners.

26

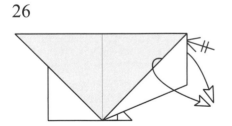

Release the three trapped corners. Partially unfolding the model makes this easier.

27

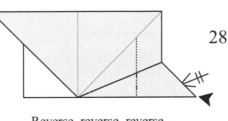

Reverse, reverse, reverse.

28

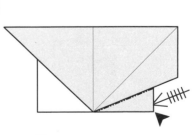

Reverse, reverse, reverse, reverse, reverse, reverse.

Venus Flytrap **89**

29

Valley-fold. Repeat behind.

30

Swing the flap to the right.
Repeat behind.

31

Repeat steps 25–29 on the left side.

32

Rotate the model 90°.

90°

OPTIONAL

Very Scary Variation

32a

32b

For a less cute, much scarier, more
realistic-looking Venus Fly Trap,
outside-reverse-fold the teeth.
You can also outside-reverse-fold
the arms to form leaves.

Thus!

33

Ready...

Set...

Feed me Seymour!

Note: This model can
double as a hat if
folded from large
enough paper.
Of course, any model
can be a hat—just
stick it on your head
—but this model
works especially well.

The Venus Flytrap, more
affectionately known as Space
Monster, has come into being.
Pull out on the arms and the monster
dramatically opens its mouth.

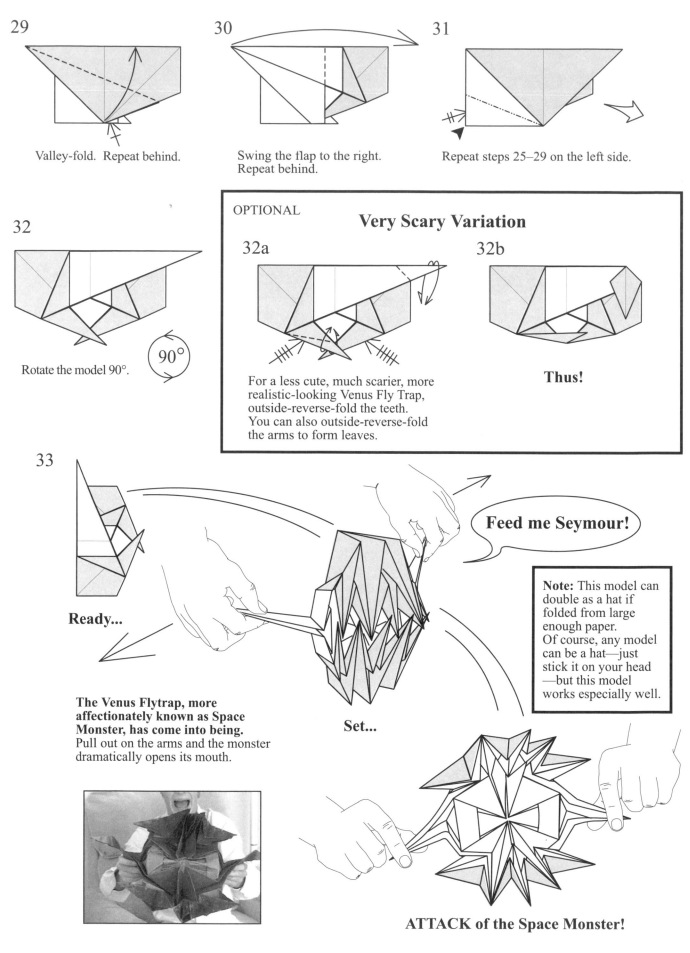

ATTACK of the Space Monster!

Frog Tongue

This hyper-action model won't actually catch insects, but it can give your friend (enemy-to-be) a nice knock on the nose. The model requires starting out with a 2½-inch by 8½-inch rectangle of **cardstock** or **contruction paper.** Normal paper just won't work. Cardstock, which is available at any office supply or copy store, comes in letter size paper (8½-inch by 11-inch). So just use the extra strip you get when you cut the paper square, or you can cut off a 3-inch by 11-inch rectangle to create a longer more impressive tongue. But remember, the longer the tongue, the more likely it will collapse, have a break down, and never serve you again.

1
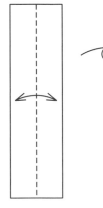
Valley-fold and unfold in half the long way. **Turn over.**

2
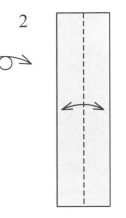
Valley-fold and unfold, inverting the existing crease from mountain fold to valley fold. Repeat steps 1 and 2 ten times, so that the crease is completely androgynous (neither mountain or valley). **Turn over.**

3

Valley-fold in half and **don't** unfold.

4
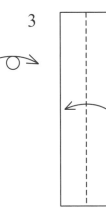
Valley-fold the lower right corner to the upper left.

5
Valley-fold bottom to top. Try to be as centered as possible.

6
Valley-fold the front flap to the bottom.

7
Mountain-fold, lining up with the previous fold. (step 6).

8
Unfold to step 4, and orient the paper horizontally.

9
Pleat the model along existing creases (as shown to the right). Unfold it again to step 4.

10
Pleat it again, this time inverting all the creases. Repeat steps 9–10 till all the creases are as soft as oatmeal.

11
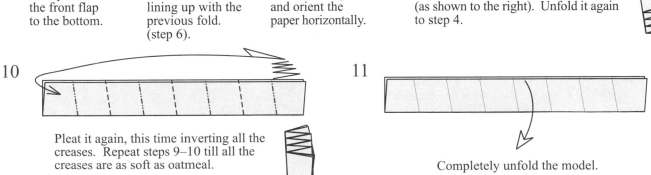
Completely unfold the model.

12

Flip the model over, left to right.

13

Make the indicated folds along the existing creases.
IMPORTANT: Do not alter the angle of these creases. They need to be slightly slanted, **NOT** vertical.

14

The model should look like this. You could stop here, and the model would work (skip to step 19), but the tongue isn't very shapely, so we continue... Flatten the model.

15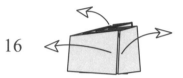

Valley-fold, edge-to-edge and repeat behind. This sequence of folds (15–17) will improve the shape of the tongue, make it sturdier, and make the starting length shorter so that it shoots out even further.

16

Completely unfold (for the last time).

17

Mountain-fold along existing creases.

18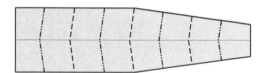

Remake the indicated folds. Give the rightmost mountain fold the royal loose-as-soggy-couscous treatment.* The last segment of the tongue has no weight to support, so the more flimsy it can be made, the more the tongue will shoot out.

19

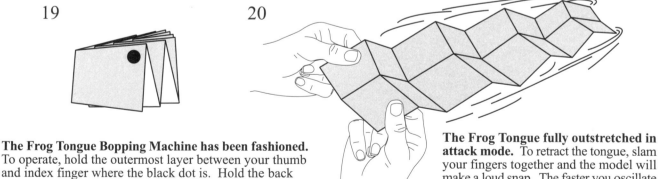

20

The Frog Tongue Bopping Machine has been fashioned. To operate, hold the outermost layer between your thumb and index finger where the black dot is. Hold the back similarly with the other hand. Say to your victim, "I would like you to examine this model very closely..." When your victim comes within range, abruptly pull your hands apart, and be prepared to apologize profusely for any noses you bonk.

The Frog Tongue fully outstretched in attack mode. To retract the tongue, slam your fingers together and the model will make a loud snap. The faster you oscillate the tongue, the louder the noise, and the further the extension. The extension also improves the more the tongue is exercised.

*__Loose-as-soggy-couscous treatment:__ The reversing back and forth of a crease until it is thoroughly loose.

Heart ATTACK!

Lonely? Heartbroken? Well, don't just sit there feeling sorry for yourself. It's time to reach out your heart and grab some love!

Important: Fold a Frog's Tongue before trying to make yourself have a Heart Attack.

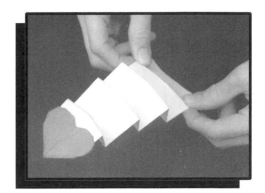

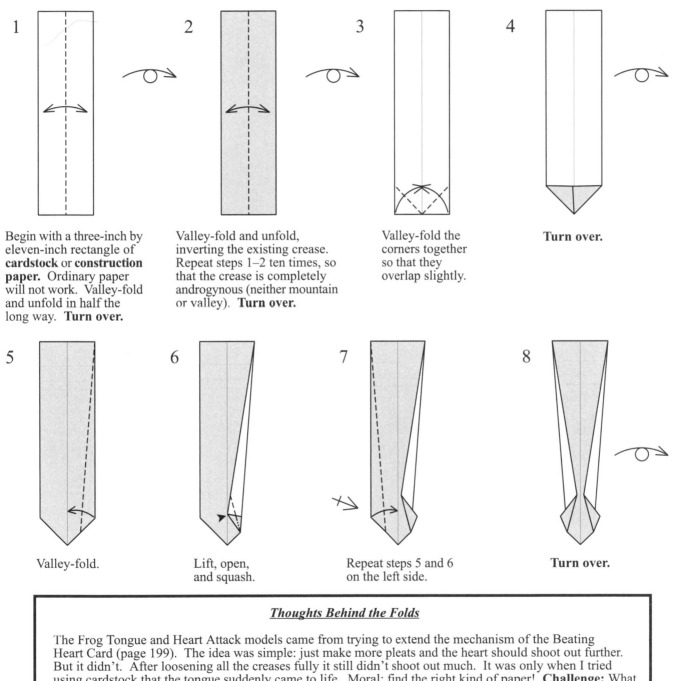

1

Begin with a three-inch by eleven-inch rectangle of **cardstock** or **construction paper.** Ordinary paper will not work. Valley-fold and unfold in half the long way. **Turn over.**

2

Valley-fold and unfold, inverting the existing crease. Repeat steps 1–2 ten times, so that the crease is completely androgynous (neither mountain or valley). **Turn over.**

3

Valley-fold the corners together so that they overlap slightly.

4

Turn over.

5

Valley-fold.

6

Lift, open, and squash.

7

Repeat steps 5 and 6 on the left side.

8

Turn over.

Thoughts Behind the Folds

The Frog Tongue and Heart Attack models came from trying to extend the mechanism of the Beating Heart Card (page 199). The idea was simple: just make more pleats and the heart should shoot out further. But it didn't. After loosening all the creases fully it still didn't shoot out much. It was only when I tried using cardstock that the tongue suddenly came to life. Moral: find the right kind of paper! **Challenge:** What else can you fold out of the front of the tongue? **Ideas:** Fly, hand, monster, lips, eyes, bull, Cupid's arrow, vampire teeth, boxing glove, boxing giraffe.

9

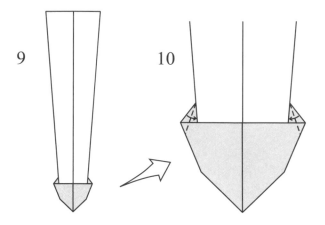

Like this. View
explosion imminent...

10

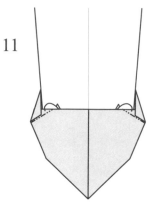

Exploded view.
Valley-fold.

11

Mountain-fold. To do
this you have to release
paper from behind the
valley fold made in the
last step and tuck it
behind the heart.

12

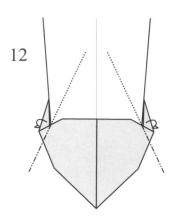

Mountain-fold,
folding behind as
much flap as you can.

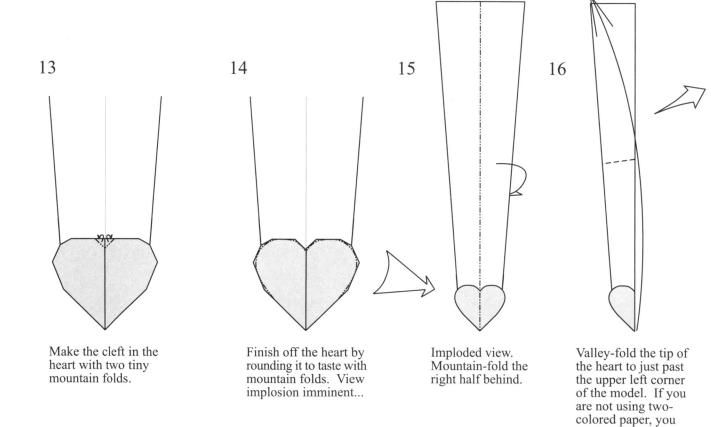

13

Make the cleft in the
heart with two tiny
mountain folds.

14

Finish off the heart by
rounding it to taste with
mountain folds. View
implosion imminent...

15

Imploded view.
Mountain-fold the
right half behind.

16

Valley-fold the tip of
the heart to just past
the upper left corner
of the model. If you
are not using two-
colored paper, you
can fold it exactly to
the corner.

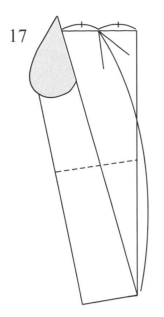

17

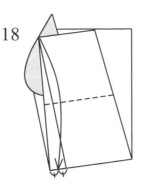

18

Valley-fold the near flap down so that the left corner lands on the midpoint of the indicated segment.

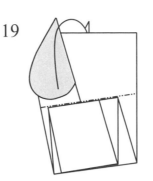

19

Mountain-fold the upper half behind, lining it up with the fold made in the last step.

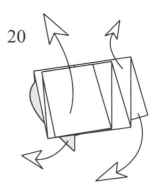

20

Unfold the model to step 15.

Valley-fold the lower right corner to the midpoint of the top edge.

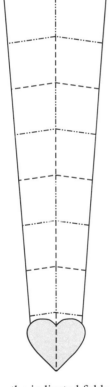

21

Make the indicated folds along the existing creases. **IMPORTANT:** Do not alter the angle of these creases. They need to be slightly slanted, **NOT** horizontal. To make the finished model extend further, reverse each fold back and forth several times, thereby loosening the hinges.

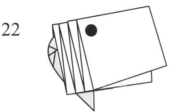

22

The Heart Attack is prepared and ready to execute. Hold the outermost layer between your thumb and index finger where the black dot is. Hold the back in the same way with the other hand. Say to your dearest love, "I have something very special to show you." When your dearest comes within range, abruptly pull your hands apart and say, "I'm so sorry! But, in your presence, I simply can't control my heart!"

23

Front view of the Heart Attack recoiled, ready for some attackin'.

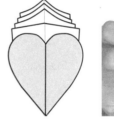

24

The Heart Attack fully extended in attack mode.

Nail Clippers

These clippers really will cut soggy noodles, but if you need them to cut nails, use a sheet of stainless steel and keep it soft with a blow torch. But if your sole purpose is to cut nails, 79¢ at your local drug store should suffice, or else you could just bite them off. To make Nail Clippers three inches long, use a piece of Japanese foil ten inches square. American foil just won't cut it.

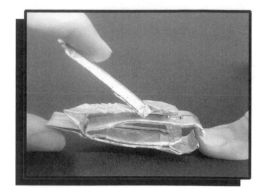

1

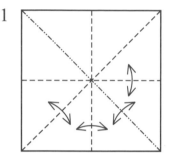

White side up. Fold the model in half in all directions: three valley folds and one diagonal mountain fold.

2

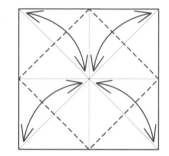

Blintz and unblintz.

3

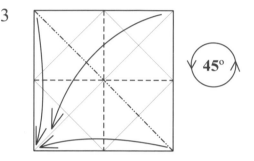

Fold a Square Base. Rotate the base **45°** counterclockwise.

4

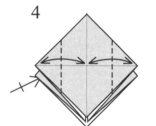

Valley-fold and unfold. Repeat behind.

5

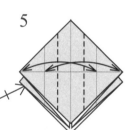

Valley-fold and unfold. Repeat behind.

6

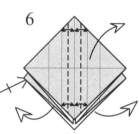

Once more, valley-fold and unfold. Repeat behind. Unfold the model completely.

7

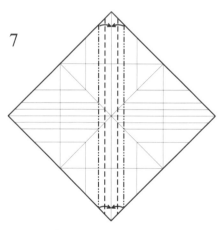

Pleat on existing creases.

8

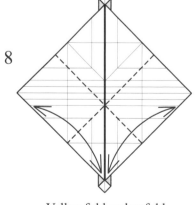

Valley-fold and unfold using existing creases.

9

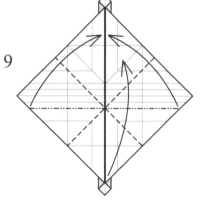

Fold a Square Base along existing creases.

10

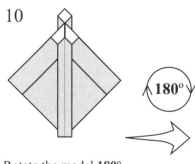

Rotate the model **180°**.

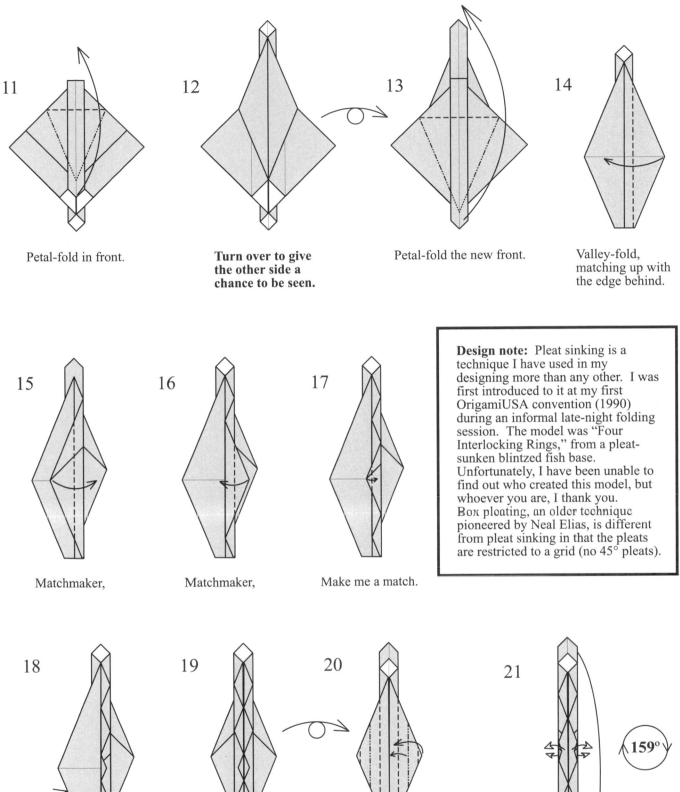

11 Petal-fold in front.

12 **Turn over to give the other side a chance to be seen.**

13 Petal-fold the new front.

14 Valley-fold, matching up with the edge behind.

15 Matchmaker,

16 Matchmaker,

17 Make me a match.

Design note: Pleat sinking is a technique I have used in my designing more than any other. I was first introduced to it at my first OrigamiUSA convention (1990) during an informal late-night folding session. The model was "Four Interlocking Rings," from a pleat-sunken blintzed fish base. Unfortunately, I have been unable to find out who created this model, but whoever you are, I thank you. Box pleating, an older technique pioneered by Neal Elias, is different from pleat sinking in that the pleats are restricted to a grid (no 45° pleats).

18 Play matchmaker on the left side (repeat steps 14–17).

19 **Turn over.**

20 Play matchmaker again (Repeat steps 14–18). Note: there are fewer matches to be made on this side.

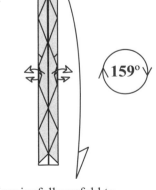

21 Now joyfully unfold to step 9, and rotate the model about 159° clockwise.

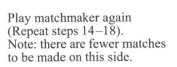

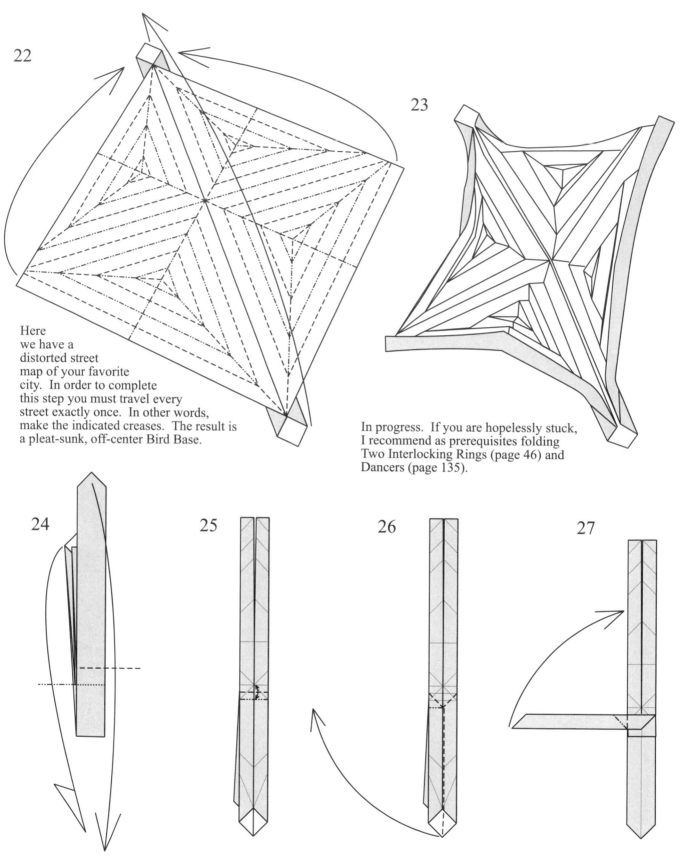

22

Here we have a distorted street map of your favorite city. In order to complete this step you must travel every street exactly once. In other words, make the indicated creases. The result is a pleat-sunk, off-center Bird Base.

23

In progress. If you are hopelessly stuck, I recommend as prerequisites folding Two Interlocking Rings (page 46) and Dancers (page 135).

24

The pleat-sunk off-center Bird Base is com**pleat**. Valley-fold the front flap as far down as it will go. Do the same with the back flap.

25

Make and unmake the indicated pleat.

26

Rabbit-ear, lining up with the valley crease made in the last step. That's one long rabbit ear, eh?

27

Lift and squash, lining up the center crease of the flap with the left edge of the model.

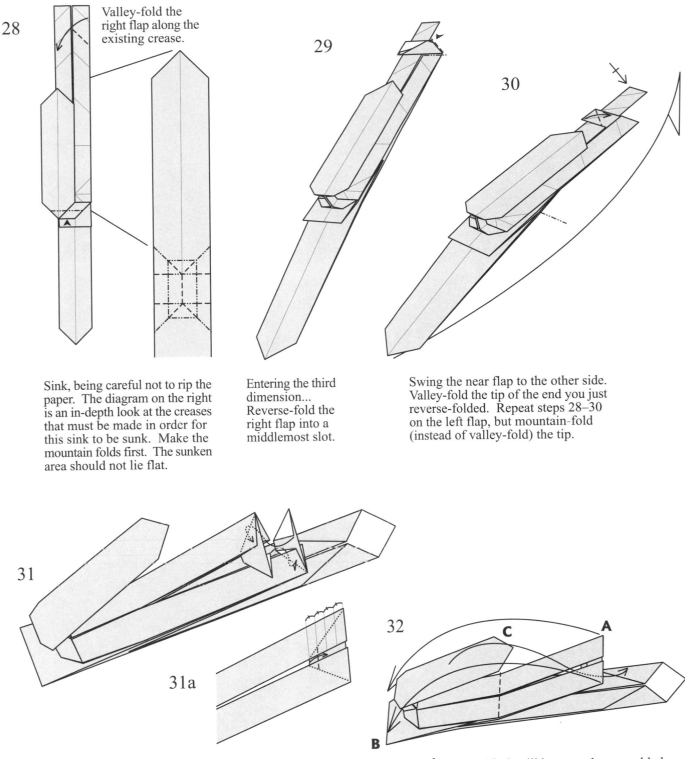

28 Valley-fold the right flap along the existing crease.

29 Entering the third dimension... Reverse-fold the right flap into a middlemost slot.

30 Swing the near flap to the other side. Valley-fold the tip of the end you just reverse-folded. Repeat steps 28–30 on the left flap, but mountain-fold (instead of valley-fold) the tip.

Sink, being careful not to rip the paper. The diagram on the right is an in-depth look at the creases that must be made in order for this sink to be sunk. Make the mountain folds first. The sunken area should not lie flat.

31

31a

Lock together the upper and lower right flaps by inserting each of their end points (the original corners of the square) into the slots provided by their opposite flap. Once they are inside the slots, wrap the corners behind the interior edge. This step is difficult to execute, and tweezers might be helpful. It also helps to open the slots as much as possible. To further enhance this lock, make a tiny valley fold as shown in 31a. If you can't figure out this lock, try to make up your own; there are lots of possibilities, and the flaps don't really need to lock well.

32 **C** **A** **B**

Flap **A**, now unified, will become the upper blade of the Nail Clipper. So take this upper-blade-to-be and swing it leftward across the model so that it is adjacent to the lower-blade-to-be, flap **B**. To do this you must pull flap **C** (lever-to-be) through the slit in the middle of flap **A**.

33

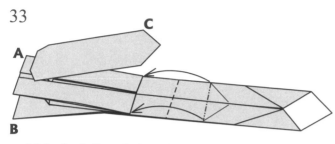

Make the indicated pleat, first making the mountain fold, and then folding it over to the hinge between the upper and lower blades.

34

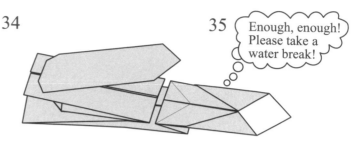

Like this.

35

36

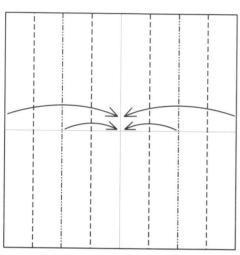

Solemnly unfold the model completely and make the indicated creases. **Just kidding!** Rather, take a scrap square of paper and make the indicated folds. The purpose of steps 36–41 is to illustrate a technique for locking together two ends, a technique which will then be applied six times in step 42.

37

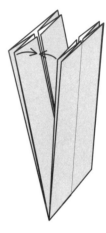

Valley-fold, but do not flatten.

38

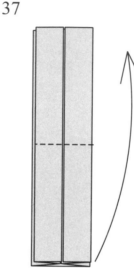

Bring together the two innermost layers.

39

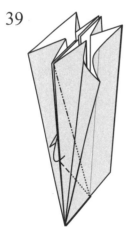

Treating the two innermost layers as one, make a pleat as shown. Needle-nose pliers make this fold a cinch.

40

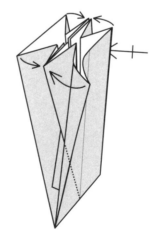

The two front flaps are locked. Now close the model. Repeat steps 39–40 on the two back flaps.

41

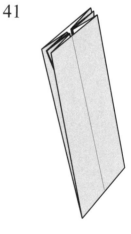

The two ends are safely locked.

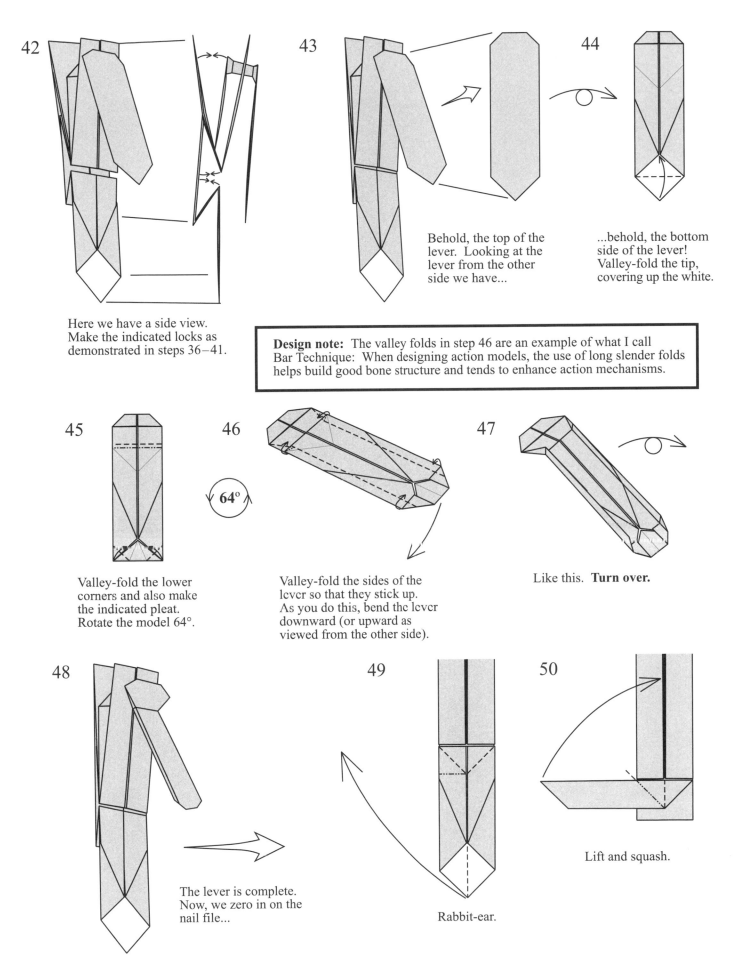

42

Here we have a side view.
Make the indicated locks as
demonstrated in steps 36–41.

43

Behold, the top of the
lever. Looking at the
lever from the other
side we have...

44

...behold, the bottom
side of the lever!
Valley-fold the tip,
covering up the white.

Design note: The valley folds in step 46 are an example of what I call
Bar Technique: When designing action models, the use of long slender folds
helps build good bone structure and tends to enhance action mechanisms.

45

Valley-fold the lower
corners and also make
the indicated pleat.
Rotate the model 64°.

46

64°

Valley-fold the sides of the
lever so that they stick up.
As you do this, bend the lever
downward (or upward as
viewed from the other side).

47

Like this. **Turn over.**

48

The lever is complete.
Now, we zero in on the
nail file...

49

Rabbit-ear.

50

Lift and squash.

51

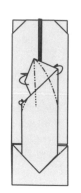

Mountain-fold.

52

Make a
neat pleat.

53

Round off the end of
the file with lots of
mountain folds.

54

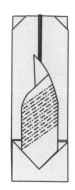

Pleat to your
heart's content.

55

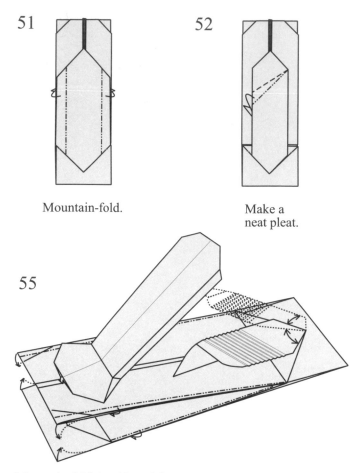

Mountain-fold the sides of the upper blade to cover up all those ugly
pleats. Cover up any ugly pleats on the lower blade by mountain-
folding them to the underside of the model. Bend together the ends
of the upper and lower blades. It should be possible to slide the nail
file out. The more you slide it in and out the easier it gets.

Thoughts Behind the Folds

The idea of folding nail clippers came to me
from looking around my dorm room for
something to fold. Paper of course!... but what
subject? My eyes hit the nail clippers on my
desk and the rest is history. In designing the
model, I started out with a pleat-sunken Bird
Base, which happened to give me all the
needed appendages, but at the wrong lengths.
So I then tried using an off-center Bird Base
which ended up making all the lengths perfect.
Challenge: What other household items can
you make? **Ideas:** Stapler, tweezers, toaster,
scissors, mechanical pencil, razor, garlic press,
unicycle.

56

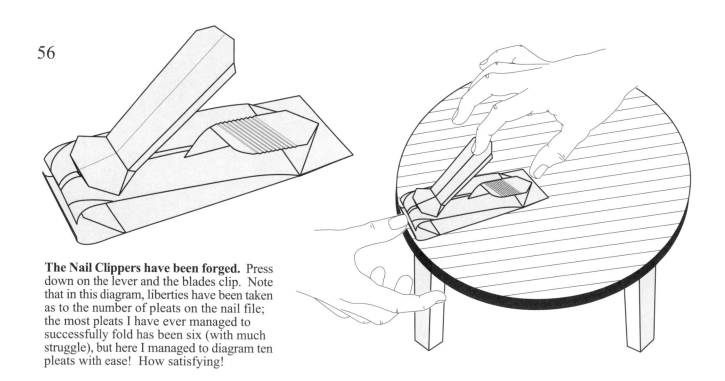

The Nail Clippers have been forged. Press
down on the lever and the blades clip. Note
that in this diagram, liberties have been taken
as to the number of pleats on the nail file;
the most pleats I have ever managed to
successfully fold has been six (with much
struggle), but here I managed to diagram ten
pleats with ease! How satisfying!

Swiss Army Knife

It not only looks realistic... it even opens and closes! But still you may ask, what good is an origami Swiss Army Knife? Believe it or not, the tools on this knife actually work! The knife can slice through even the thickest strands of spider web, the screwdriver can drive screws deeply into sand, the can opener **can open** just about any greeting card, and best of all, the awl can pop soap bubbles.

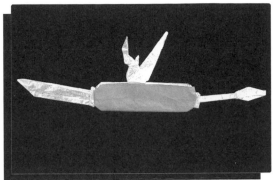

1

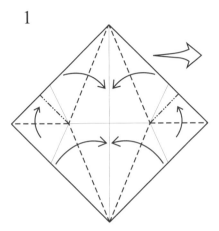

For best results, use ten-inch silver Japanese foil and paint the white side red. Starting silver side up, fold a red Fish Base.

2

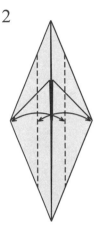

Valley-fold and unfold in thirds.

3

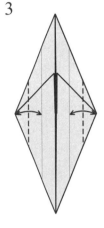

Valley-fold and unfold, and then completely unfold the model.

4

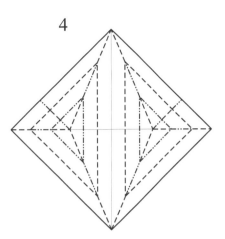

Fold a pleat-sunk Fish Base by folding the indicated mountains and valleys. If you've never pleat-sunk before, I advise first folding the Two Interlocking Rings (page 46), and Dancers (page 135).

5

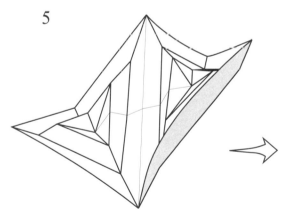

Pleat-sinking in progress.

6

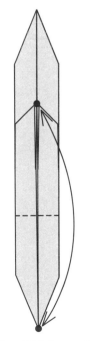

Valley-fold dot-to-dot and unfold.

7

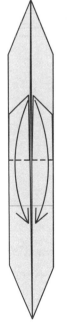

Bring both flaps down as far as possible.

8

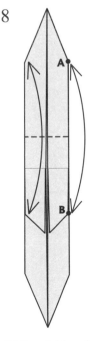

Valley-fold and unfold, bringing point **A** to point **B**.

9

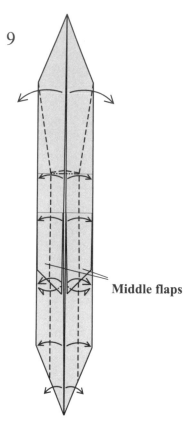

Middle flaps

Valley-fold the front layer. Outside-reverse-fold the **middle flaps**, turning them inside out. Be careful not to tear the foil. The top and bottom of the model will not lie flat.

10

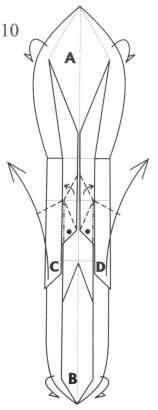

A

C D

B

Turn **A** and **B** inside out by wrapping the raw edges behind, but don't flatten yet. Valley-fold the middle flaps, **C** and **D**, outward at the indicated place and angle, first pinching the mountain folds, and then helping the valley folds to form as you flatten the central area. Watch the black dots.

11

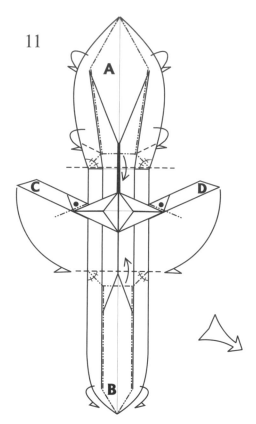

A

C D

B

Collapse **A** and **B** by mountain-folding the raw edges behind and flattening them. Then, noting carefully their positions, form the remaining mountains and valleys, thereby allowing the model to fully lie flat. Mountain-fold **C** and **D** so that they lie along the sides of the model.

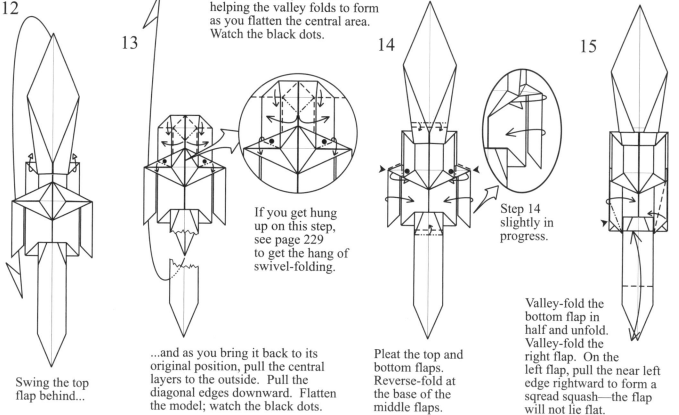

12

13

If you get hung up on this step, see page 229 to get the hang of swivel-folding.

Swing the top flap behind...

...and as you bring it back to its original position, pull the central layers to the outside. Pull the diagonal edges downward. Flatten the model; watch the black dots.

14

Step 14 slightly in progress.

Pleat the top and bottom flaps. Reverse-fold at the base of the middle flaps.

15

Valley-fold the bottom flap in half and unfold. Valley-fold the right flap. On the left flap, pull the near left edge rightward to form a sqread squash—the flap will not lie flat.

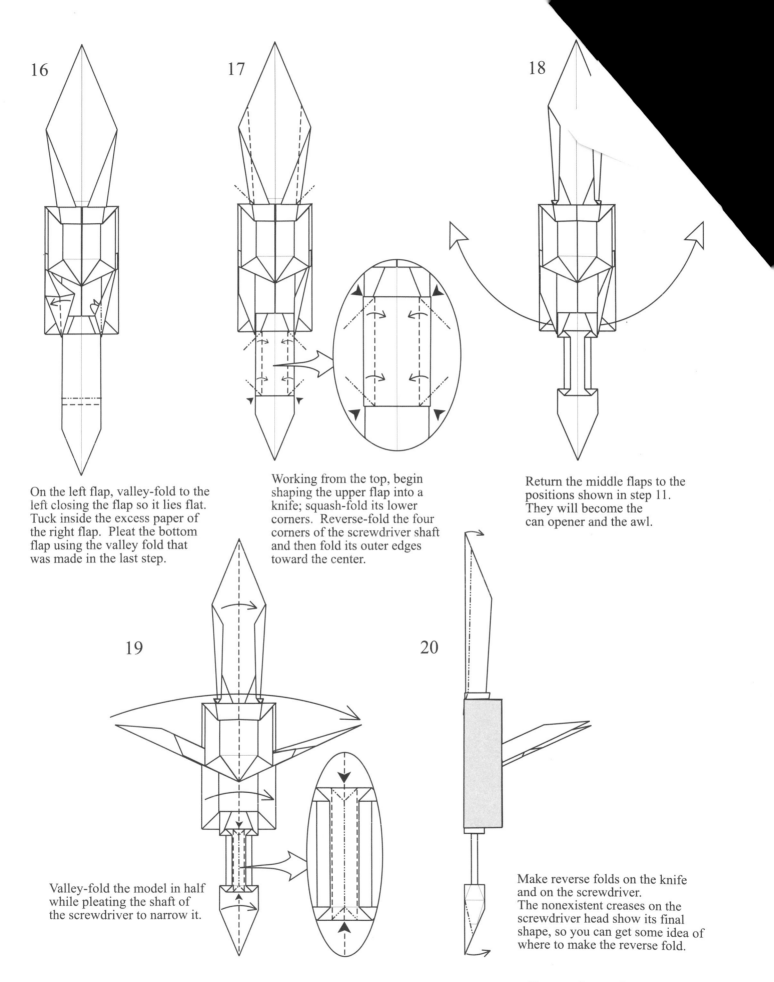

16

On the left flap, valley-fold to the left closing the flap so it lies flat. Tuck inside the excess paper of the right flap. Pleat the bottom flap using the valley fold that was made in the last step.

17

Working from the top, begin shaping the upper flap into a knife; squash-fold its lower corners. Reverse-fold the four corners of the screwdriver shaft and then fold its outer edges toward the center.

18

Return the middle flaps to the positions shown in step 11. They will become the can opener and the awl.

19

Valley-fold the model in half while pleating the shaft of the screwdriver to narrow it.

20

Make reverse folds on the knife and on the screwdriver. The nonexistent creases on the screwdriver head show its final shape, so you can get some idea of where to make the reverse fold.

Thoughts Behind the Folds

Like the Nail Clippers, the idea of folding a Swiss Army Knife came from looking around the room for subjects to fold. The Swiss Army Knife on my desk jumped out and attacked me figuratively. The design process was quite involved and it evolved over the course of five years. One of the big changes was to make it a bicolor model. Once I was satisfied with the design, I then had to figure out the most diagrammable procedure, which turned out to be a major part of the design process. **Question:** What's sitting around your room waiting to be folded?

21

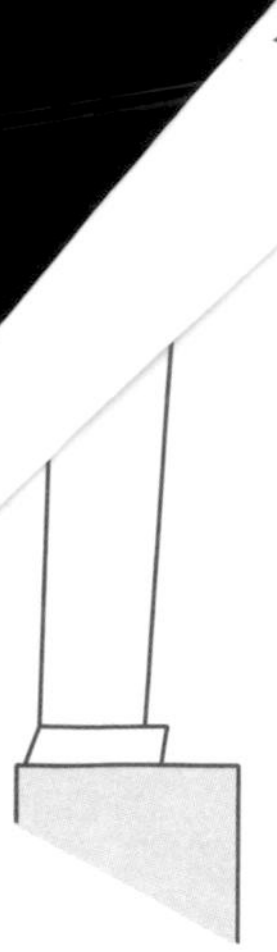

Reverse-fold intuitively.

22

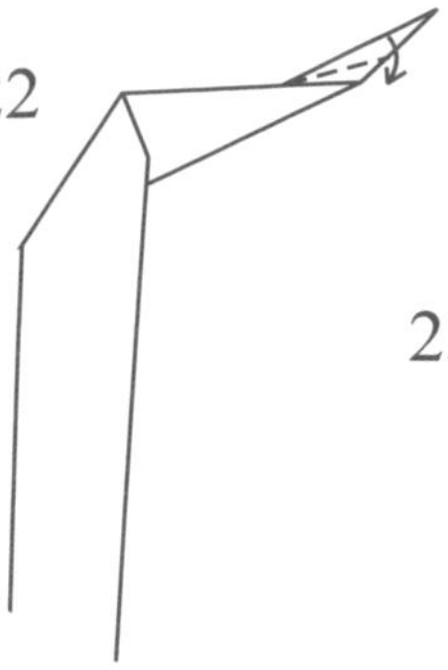

Valley-fold.

23

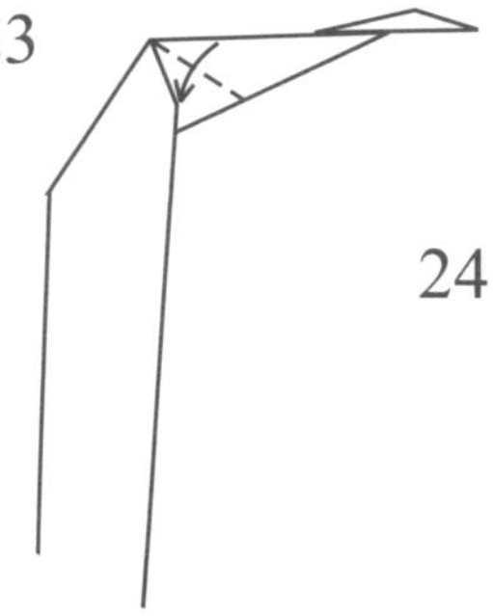

Valley-fold.

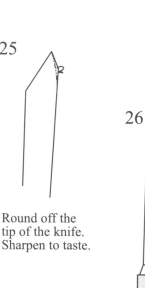

24

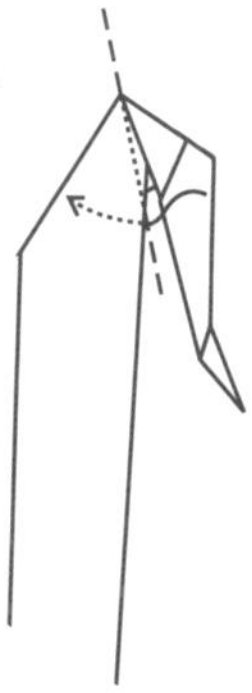

Valley-fold, tucking the twisted appendage inside the knife.

25

Round off the tip of the knife. Sharpen to taste.

26

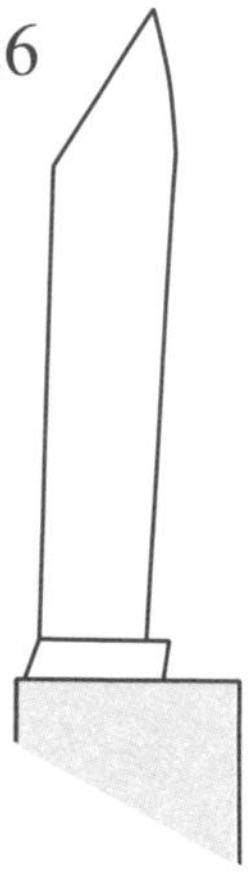

The knife is fully forged.

27

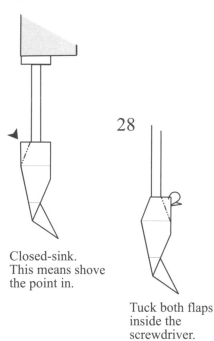

Closed-sink. This means shove the point in.

28

Tuck both flaps inside the screwdriver.

29

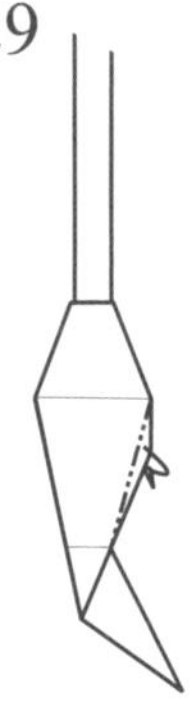

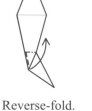

And again here.

30

Reverse-fold.

31

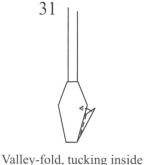

Valley-fold, tucking inside whatever sticks out.

32

The screwdriver is well-built.

Further Thoughts Behind the Folds

I designed the first version of the Swiss Army Knife in 1992 and the same year displayed it at the OrigamiUSA Convention. Two years later, in the Japanese origami magazine, *ORU*, there was a two-page spread of Swiss Army Knives designed by various Japanese folders. If they by chance got the idea from me, I would be greatly honored. I encourage people to use my ideas to further their own.

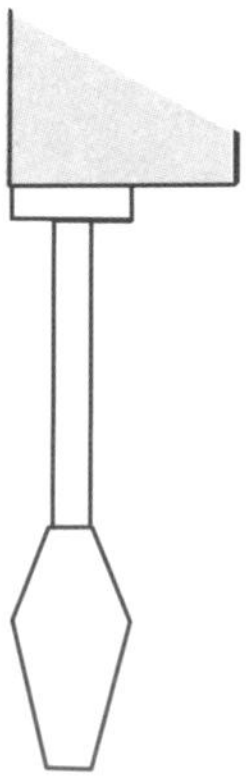

33

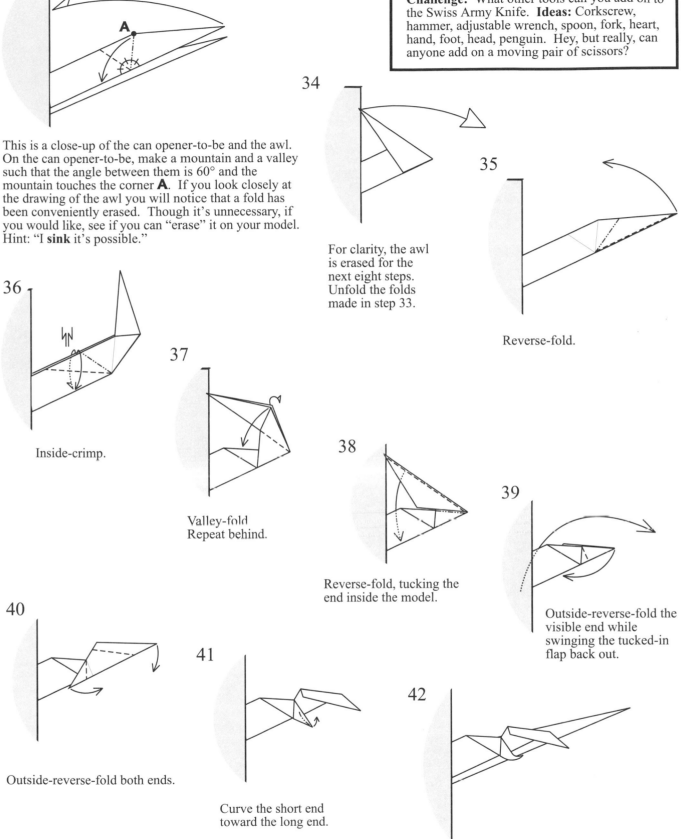

Even More Thoughts Behind the Folds

Challenge: What other tools can you add on to the Swiss Army Knife. **Ideas:** Corkscrew, hammer, adjustable wrench, spoon, fork, heart, hand, foot, head, penguin. Hey, but really, can anyone add on a moving pair of scissors?

This is a close-up of the can opener-to-be and the awl. On the can opener-to-be, make a mountain and a valley such that the angle between them is 60° and the mountain touches the corner **A**. If you look closely at the drawing of the awl you will notice that a fold has been conveniently erased. Though it's unnecessary, if you would like, see if you can "erase" it on your model. Hint: "I **sink** it's possible."

34

For clarity, the awl is erased for the next eight steps. Unfold the folds made in step 33.

35

Reverse-fold.

36

Inside-crimp.

37

Valley-fold
Repeat behind.

38

Reverse-fold, tucking the end inside the model.

39

Outside-reverse-fold the visible end while swinging the tucked-in flap back out.

40

Outside-reverse-fold both ends.

41

Curve the short end toward the long end.

42

The can opener is complete.

Swiss Army Knife **107**

43

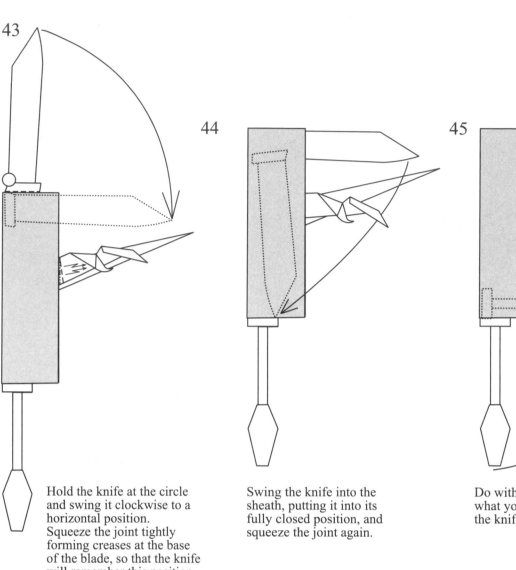

Hold the knife at the circle and swing it clockwise to a horizontal position. Squeeze the joint tightly forming creases at the base of the blade, so that the knife will remember this position. Crimp the can opener.

44

Swing the knife into the sheath, putting it into its fully closed position, and squeeze the joint again.

45

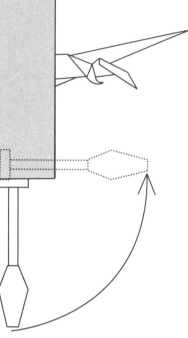

Do with the screwdriver what you just did with the knife, like this...

46

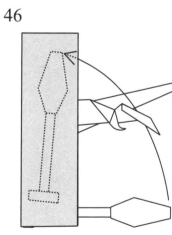

...and this.

47

Give the sheath thickness by slightly flattening the left edge. This will let the tools slide in and out more easily.

48

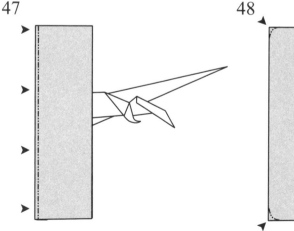

Round the corners of the sheath with tiny reverse folds, and shape them to taste. On the right, there are three possible slots to contain the reverse-folded corners. I recommend choosing the middle slot.

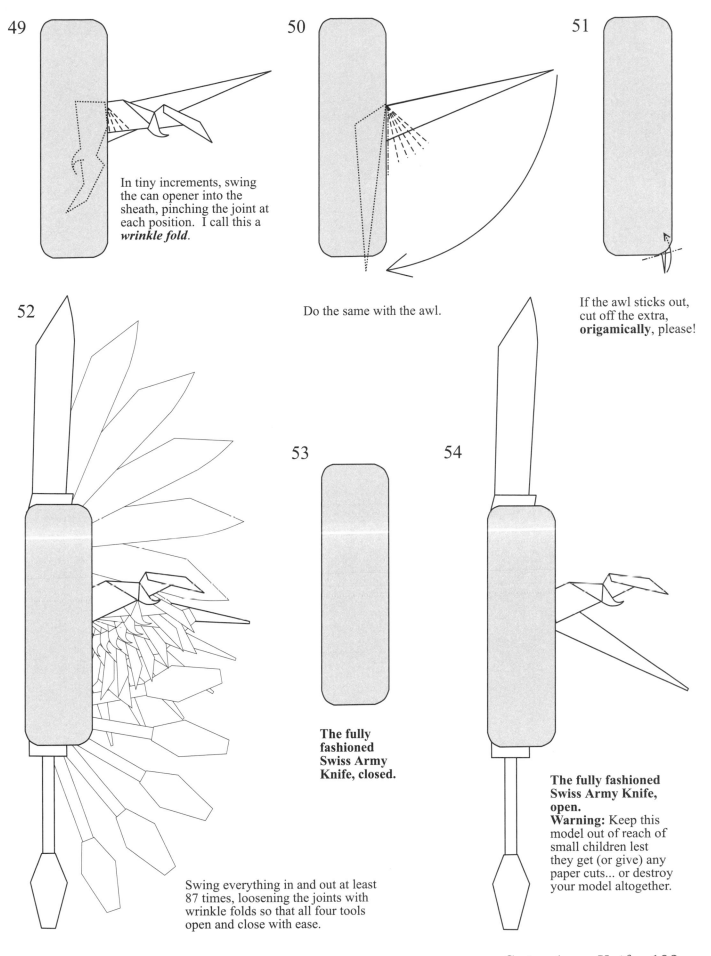

49

In tiny increments, swing the can opener into the sheath, pinching the joint at each position. I call this a *wrinkle fold*.

50

Do the same with the awl.

51

If the awl sticks out, cut off the extra, **origamically**, please!

52

Swing everything in and out at least 87 times, loosening the joints with wrinkle folds so that all four tools open and close with ease.

53

The fully fashioned Swiss Army Knife, closed.

54

The fully fashioned Swiss Army Knife, open.
Warning: Keep this model out of reach of small children lest they get (or give) any paper cuts... or destroy your model altogether.

Flasher

Don't worry, there's nothing unseemly about this Flasher. It's merely an entertaining 'hyper-action' geometric model that expands and contracts. Chris Palmer and I designed it together, using as a base Kawasaki's iso-area twist folding (*Origami for the Connoisseur*).

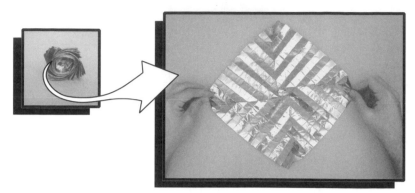

1

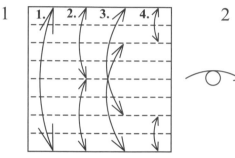

A sheet of Wyndstone paper works best, the larger the more impressive. With the white side up, divide the paper into eighths by folding it in half, then in quarters and then in eighths. **Turn over.**

2

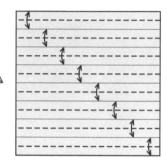

With colored side up, divide the paper into sixteenths by putting a valley fold in between each pair of mountain creases, making a paper fan.

3

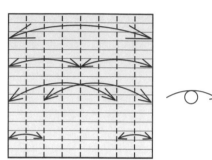

Repeat step 1 with the colored side up, making the valley folds perpendicular to the existing creases. **Turn over.**

4

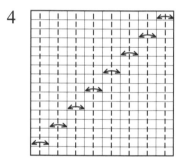

With the white side up, put a valley fold in between each pair of mountain creases from step 3, making a paper fan in the other direction.

5

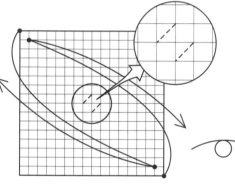

Following the fold-and-unfold arrows, pinch two tiny valley creases in the center. **Turn over.**

6

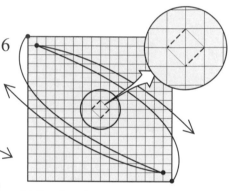

Following the arrows, pinch two tiny valley creases in the center.

7

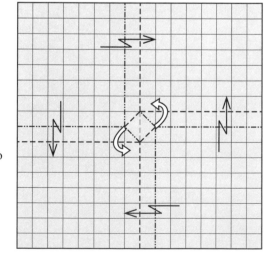

Using existing creases, make the indicated mountain and valley folds. This will cause the little square in the center to make a quarter turn. Toshikazu Kawasaki calls this fold an 'iso-area square twist.' 'Iso-area' means, 'both sides look the same but are opposite in color and orientation.'

8

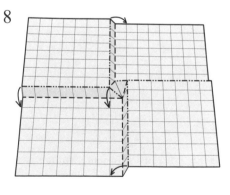

Iso-area square twist in progress.

9

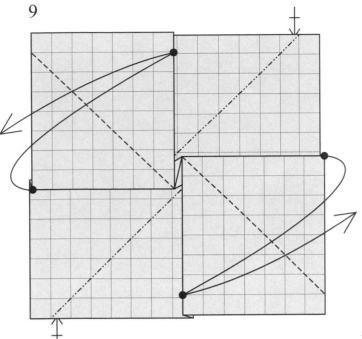

Following the arrows, make the diagonal valley creases. Repeat behind for the mountain folds. Note that these creases do not touch the corners of the model.

10

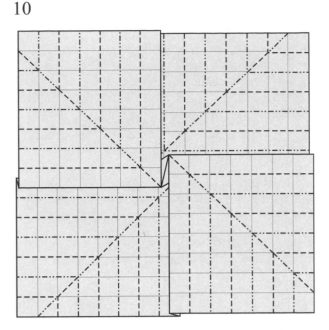

Make the indicated folds, starting from the center and moving out. The diagonal folds will form themselves naturally as you squeeze together the existing horizontal and vertical folds. It's easiest to pleat each of the four quadrants separately before collapsing the model. After all of the folds are in place, twist the center to make the sides come together as if they are being sucked into a spiraling black hole.

11

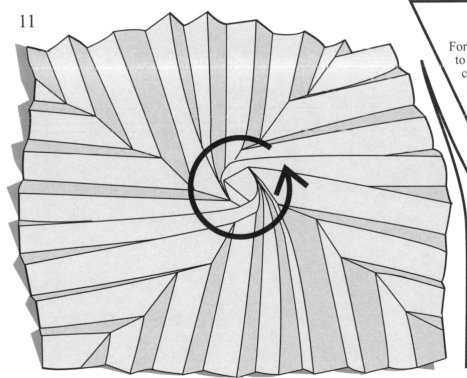

Thoughts Behind the Folds

For a long time, I had a passionate desire to fold a model that would expand and contract. I shared my obsession with my very good friend and folder, Chris Palmer. Together, we had many unfruitful, head-banging sessions. Then Chris came back from the OrigamiUSA Convention ('94), with Kawasaki's new rose base, which he sensed held the solution to our problem. In one collaborative evening the Flasher was born.

12

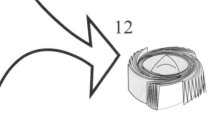

Finished Flasher open. Mathematically speaking this model has a very interesting property. Imagine the fold pattern extended infinitely in all four directions on an infinitely large piece of paper that had zero thickness. When all the folds are made, the infinite paper would have shrunk down to a finite area. **Wetfolding approach:** Once together, tie rubber bands around the model, dunk it in water, and set it out to dry in the sun. This process will make the model spring closed by itself.

Finished Flasher closed.
Open and close rapidly to flash-dazzle the audience. This model can also be used in storytelling as an explosion, a whirlpool, or a time machine.

Flasher Supreme

This is a Flasher variation that is composed of only two spiral arms (one mountain spiral and one valley spiral). It's also especially special in that it's purely iso-area (i.e., same on both sides). The basic Flasher is not iso-area in the very center. I diagrammed only the crease pattern, because the easiest way to go about folding it is crease by crease. One way to fold this model is to copy this page, cut out the square and pinch along the mountains and valleys. But, for the more standard approach...

Wyndstone paper is ideal for all Flashers. Begin by folding a 16-by-16 grid of genderless creases (i.e., every crease should be both mountained and valleyed). Starting at the sides and moving inward, pinch the boldly diagrammed spiral creases (you might want to pencil them in). Then, working on one section at a time (moving inward again), make all the indicated folds, gradually pushing the model together as you go. **Wetfolding approach:** See bottom of page 111.

Flasher
Big Bang

This model is really just the Flasher Supreme, but with twice as many iterations; it is consequently double the trouble, but also twice as nice, and much more almost deranged. I folded the huge seven-foot Big Bang pictured at the right at the last minute (or rather, the last 72 hours) to present on *The Carol Duvall Show*. As usual, I used the wetfolding approach, but the night before the shooting, it still hadn't dried. So, I resorted to using the hotel hair dryer and sunlamp, and almost burned it up. A year later, the bag it was in was stolen in the Singapore Airport.

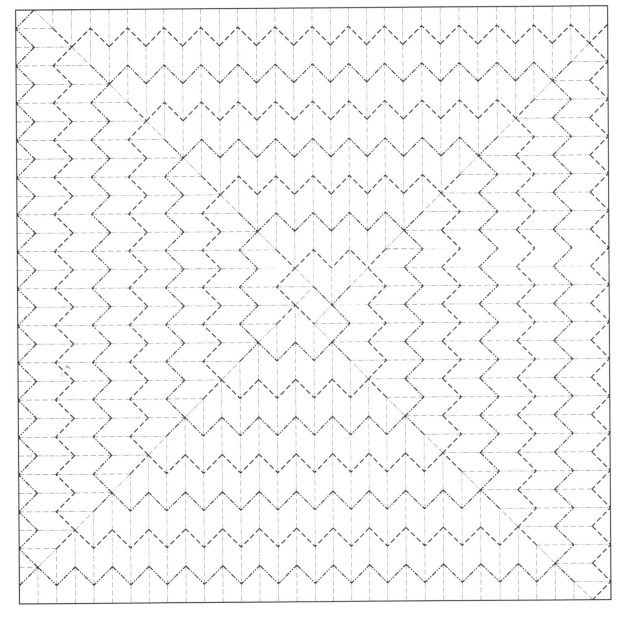

Begin by folding a 32-by-32 grid: every crease should be both mountained and valleyed. Starting at the sides and moving inward, pinch the boldly diagrammed spiral creases (you might want to pencil them in). Then, working on one section at a time (moving inward again), make all the indicated folds, gradually pushing the model together as you go. **Wetfolding approach:** See page 111.

Flasher Hat

Here's a collapsible sun hat that fits in your pocket. A seemingly sensible idea but almost derangedly difficult to fold. Make sure that you have completed all the other Flashers before attempting this one. A 28-inch square makes a nice hat size. The side shown in the diagram below will become the top of the hat.

Begin by creasing a 32-by-32 grid with every crease being both mountained and valleyed. Next, valley-fold the square diagonally in half both ways. Then pleat a diagonal grid that divides each diagonal of the square by 64. Make the indicated folds starting with the boldly diagrammed creases, which already exist in the diagonal grid (nothing needs to be reversed!). Push the model together and the hairline creases should form (with a little coaxing). **Wetfolding approach:** See page 111.

Flasher Marble Maze

A collapsible maze! Use Wyndstone paper (ideal) or any paper.
Begin by folding the basic Flasher. Open it out but don't flatten.
Make the indicated folds, starting with the bold mountains.
Many of the folds form naturally as you push the model together.
Notice that the center of the Flasher gets folded in half, making
the closed state more compact than that of the basic Flasher.
When open, it is a good marble maze, especially when held by
four hands (one hand per corner). When the model is closed, a
marble will fit nicely in its center to be used later.

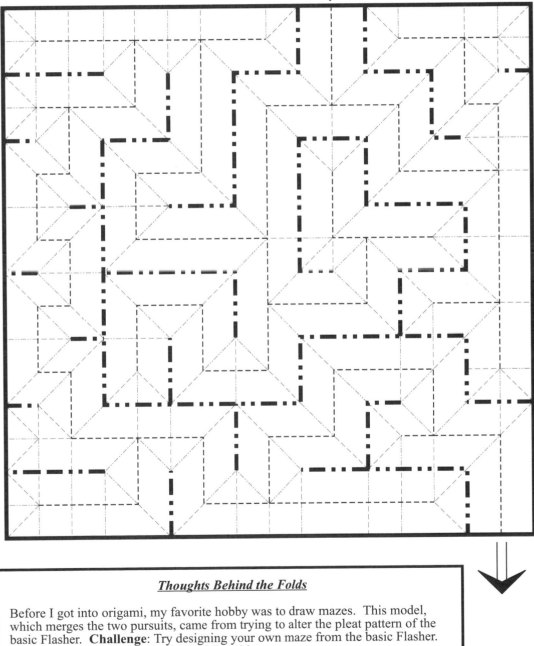

Thoughts Behind the Folds

Before I got into origami, my favorite hobby was to draw mazes. This model,
which merges the two pursuits, came from trying to alter the pleat pattern of the
basic Flasher. **Challenge**: Try designing your own maze from the basic Flasher.
You might find it even easier than folding this maze.

Flasher Labyrinth

A collapsible labyrinth! Begin by folding a 32-by-32 grid: every crease should be both valleyed and mountained. Then fold the Flasher Marble Maze. Open the model (but don't press flat) and open-sink along the entire path of the maze, creating two separate paths. Join the two paths at the end of the maze to form the labyrinth.

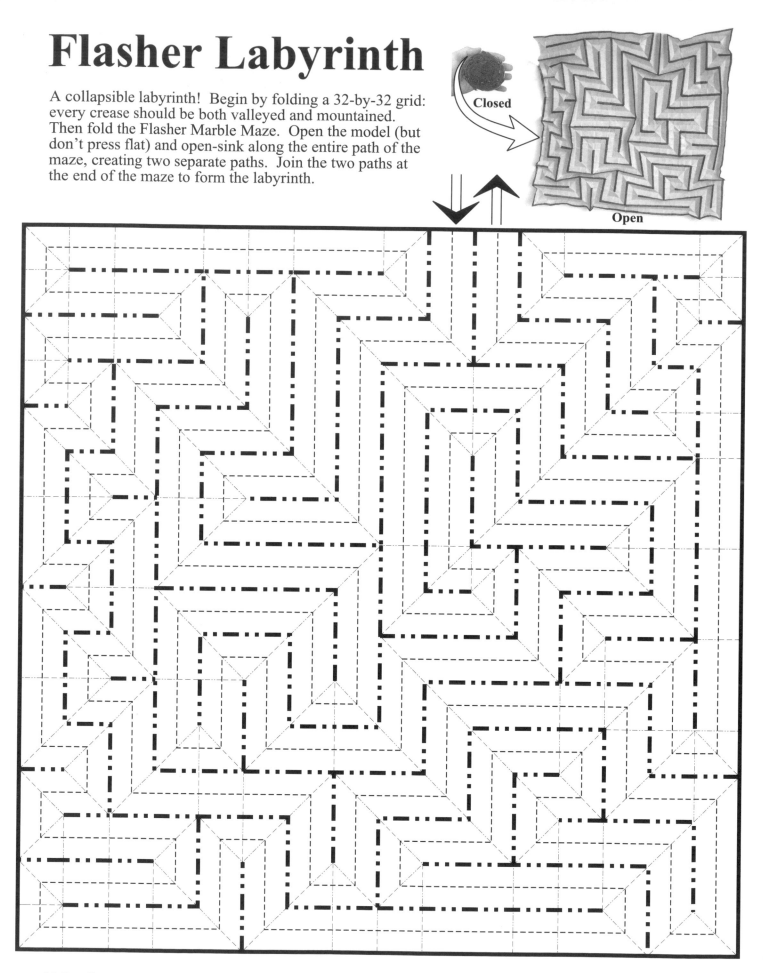

Closed

Open

Labyrinth Walker

On the outside, this model looks like any old box-pleated stick figure, but inside it reveals itself as the classical 5000-year-old Cretan Labyrinth; we can walk deep within it and feel it deep within us.

1

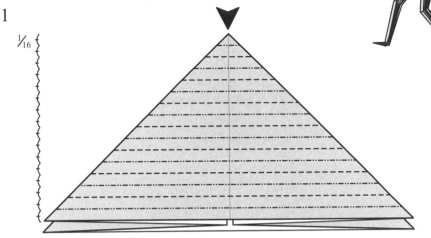

Begin by folding a Waterbomb Base, colored side out. Divide its height into sixteenths with pleats as shown above. Then unfold the pleats and pleat-sink along the existing creases (see pages 46–47, 103, and 135). Then completely unfold the pleat-sunk Waterbomb Base and make the folds indicated below. Really only the folds in the top middle need to be changed.

2

Using the existing creases as a framework, make the indicated folds.

Thoughts Behind the Folds

The idea of folding a labyrinth came from Camp Winnarainbow, a circus camp where I work at every summer teaching kids to juggle, unicycle, and fold. The Cretan Labyrinth is the spiritual center of the camp, making it a prime subject for me to try to fold. Amazingly the labyrinth practically folded itself. All I did was translate the ancient pattern into creases, made it square (instead of round), and then tried to fold it. Not only did it fold but by chance it turned into a person! I had a similar experience trying to make the Dromenon Labyrinth Walker (next page). Some folds are just meant to be!

3

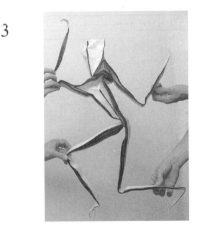

The Labyrinth Walker is discovered. Make bends in the arms and legs as you see fit. Now that all the folds have been made you can pull the model apart to reveal the labyrinth. Rest assured, putting it back together will be easier than before, for as a Zen master would say, "Once a labyrinth walker, always a labyrinth walker."

Dromenon
Labyrinth Walker

Here's an origami version of the classical Dromenon Labyrinth, found in many churches around the world. Begin by doing step 1 of the Labyrinth Walker (previous page), but divide the height into twenty-fourths instead of sixteenths. Pleat-sink, completely unfold, and then 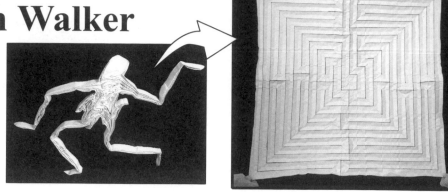 make the indicated folds. If you don't mind drawing on origami, draw in the labyrinth as it is pictured to the right. These lines are the mountains. As for the valleys, there's really just one long valley that goes through the whole labyrinth, like the dividing line of a highway. There are lots of other little folds that need to be made, but those will become apparent when you start pushing the model together.

Slithering Snake Skin

At first glance, this model might seem abhorrently laborious, but its startling undulating action makes every crease worthwhile!

1

First fold this model from a very large three-by-seven rectangle. (Make the paper four by eight and cut one strip off both width and length.) Then fold it from a dollar bill shortened slightly to the same proportion, as indicated above. **Turn over.**

2

Divide the width into thirds, then into fourths, and finally into twelfths— making in all a total of eleven evenly-spaced vertical valley folds. **Turn over.**

3

Make thirty-eight diagonal valley creases.

4

Make nine horizontal mountain creases.

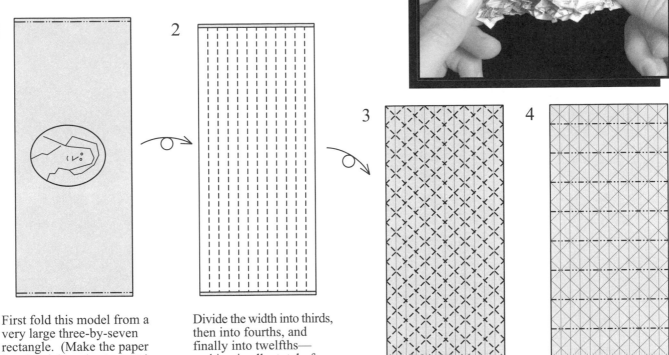

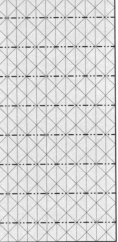

5

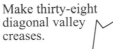

Make the indicated folds along existing creases. This is easier than it looks, as only a few creases are inverted and no new folds need be made.

Thoughts Behind the Folds

The Slithering Snake Skin came out of a search for new Flasher pleat patterns. Unfortunately it would make for an awkward Flasher because when the pleats are stretched the plane of folds is distorted. But, to tell you the truth, I don't recall ever actually trying it (I got so sidetracked playing with the toy). So... **Challenge:** Try to incorporate this pleat pattern into a Flasher.

6

The Slithering Snake Skin has been shed into existence. When the skin is convex, it spreads out. When it's concave, it contracts. When moved in a wavy manner, it resembles a snake swallowing its prey!

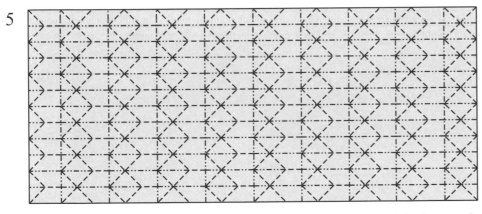

Symbols and Signs and Stunning Designs

As the years go by, we hope to see thousands of
stunning new designs emerge—
a fiesta of fabulous fun-filled folds. This section serves
to signal symbolically our forward motion in time.

Preshrunk Blue Jeans*

Machine washing these jeans is not recommended.
If soiled or stained, dry clean only, or better yet, refold the model!

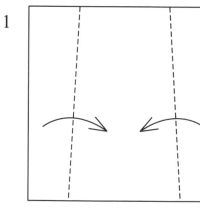

1

Begin with blue paper white side up.
Valley-fold the sides inward, slightly
overlapping at the top.

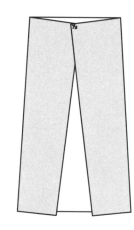

2

Valley-fold the button.

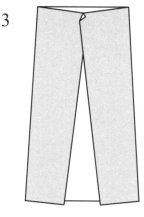

3

**The Preshrunk Blue Jeans have
been well tailored.** Fold simply that
others may simply fold.

*License to manufacture this garment design will not be sold to any multinational corporation known to use sweatshop or child labor.

Smiling Frowning George

Traditional North American model.
(Must be!....No one else plays so much with money!)

This model is a big hit at parties. With just three folds you can make George Washington smile and frown and your friends die of laughter. Any piece of paper with a face on it works. British currency is especially funny— the smiling/sneering queen.

1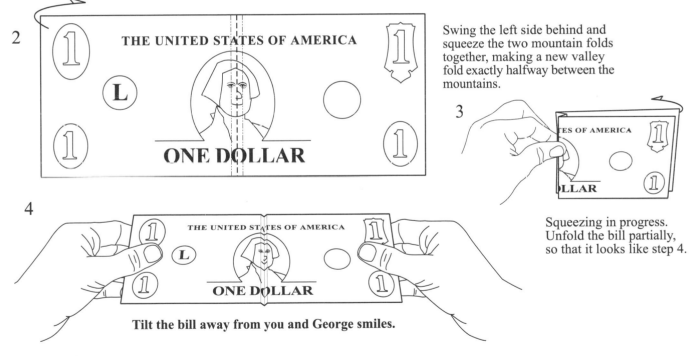

Begin with one dollar. Coins won't work! Make two sharp vertical mountain creases that intersect the pupils of the eyes.

2

Swing the left side behind and squeeze the two mountain folds together, making a new valley fold exactly halfway between the mountains.

3

Squeezing in progress. Unfold the bill partially, so that it looks like step 4.

4

Tilt the bill away from you and George smiles.

5

Tilt the bill toward you and George frowns. For extra laughs, try it with a five-dollar bill—Abe is hysterical!

Kite Letterhead

This model is great to fold on a windy day, for if you let it go in the right wind, the kite will really fly.....away.

1

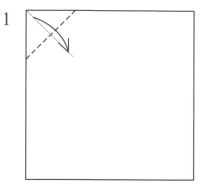

White side up. Valley-fold the corner to taste... a bigger flap will result in a bigger kite.

2

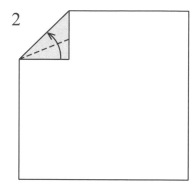

Valley-fold edge-to-edge.

3

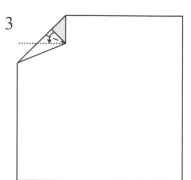

Valley-fold so that the edge becomes horizontal.

4

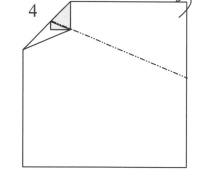

Mountain-fold the top behind.

5

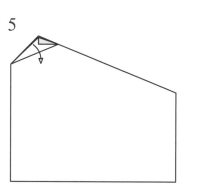

Unfold the top flap.

Thoughts Behind the Folds

The Kite Letterhead came from an exercise to see what I could make out of a corner. In college, one of my pranks was to sneak up in the middle of the night to the provost's office and do intricate corner folds on announcements posted on the door. **Exercise:** See what you can make out of a corner. **Ideas:** flying heart, smoking pipe, clenched fist, monster face, self-portrait, lightning bolt, eagle feather, fish lips, goose bump, rabbit ear.

6

Make sharp mountain creases that stick up so as to define the kite structure and the string. For a narrower letterhead, mountain-fold the right side behind.

7

Dear Mabel,

How beautifully blue the sky,
The kite is rising very high.
Continue fine I hope it may,
Although it went up yesterday.
Tomorrow it may fly again
(I hear that kites are very in)
Yet people say I know not why
That we shall have no wind to fly.

Love,
Frederic

The Kite Letterhead is fabricated, ready to be lettered with writing.

Men's Suit

Just what dad needs... a new suit! Even better than buying one, now you can give him a suit that you made yourself—the perfect gift! I designed this model to squeeze my way on to the Father's Day episode of the Carol Duvall Craft Show on Home & Garden TV. As a guest on the show, I taught several models, and showed many more.

Looks great both day and night!

1

White side up.
Valley-fold and unfold both ways in half.

2

Valley-fold the sides to the center so that they overlap by about a millimeter.

3

Valley-fold and unfold.
Turn over!

4

Valley-fold to the creases made in the last step.

5

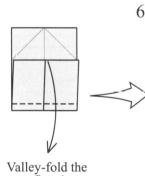

Valley-fold the near flap down.
The fold line is just above the bottom edge.

6

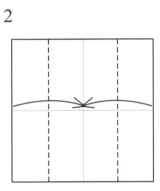

Valley-fold the sides exactly to the center.

7

Valley-fold and unfold through all layers. The folds do not go above the black dots. **Turn over.**

8

Valley-fold the corners to the sides to form the collar. These folds extend just down to the existing crease.

Thoughts Behind the Folds

The Carol Duvall Show had already invited me to be the guest artist on one episode. It just happened that they were to shoot the Father's Day episode on the same day as mine, and they asked me if I had anything father-related I could show on it. I told them "Perhaps the Preshrunk Blue Jeans, but that's too simple. Let me think about it and get back to you." I needed something more advanced than the Jeans, but still simple enough to teach on the show. "Oh," I thought, "extend the top edge of the jeans and perhaps I can design a suit!" which is exactly what I did. I called them right back... "Yes I do have something for Father's Day!"

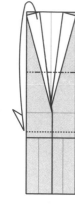 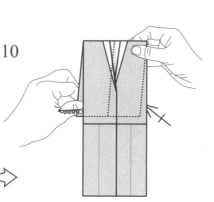 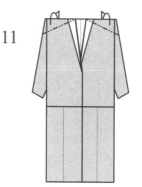 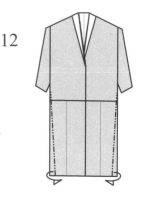

9

10

11

12

Mountain-fold the top behind to the dotted line. It should go to just above the bottom of the jacket.

Holding the model as shown, use your thumb to roll out paper so as to form an arm. Then form the other arm.

Mountain-fold the shoulders behind.

Narrow the sides of the pants with mountain folds.

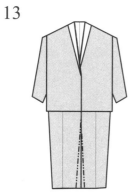  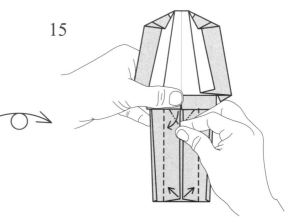

13

14

15

Mountain-fold the inseam of the pants. The easiest way to do this is to pinch the folds through all layers and then fold behind just the near layer.

The suit is sewn. To make it stand up, **turn the model over.**

Holding down the back of the jacket with one hand, slide out paper from underneath and make the flap stick straight out.

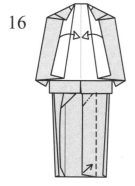 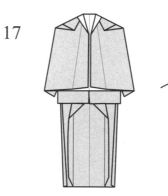 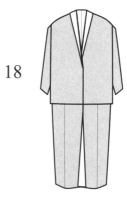

16

17

18

Repeat step 15 on the other side. For the sake of aesthetics, close the flaps on the jacket.

The top looks like a blouse! **Turn the model over** and shape it to taste.

The Men's Suit is in good standing. Bring him outside and he'll *really* **stand out**. **Outstanding!** I just can't **stand** it! Talk about **stand** up comedy! How about a **standing** ovation?!

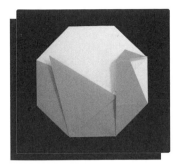

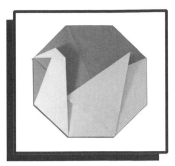

Iso-Area Swan

Iso-area means that the front and back are identical in shape but opposite in color and orientation. If you consider each side as a separate model, then iso-area folding in effect achieves two models from one sheet—in this case, a swan and its mate.

1

Valley-fold
and unfold.

2

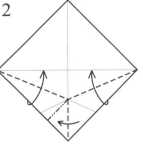

Rabbit-ear.

3

Turn over.

4

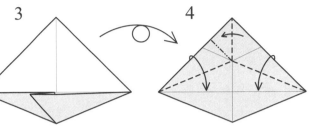

Rabbit-ear.

5

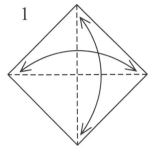

The Iso-Area Fish Base
has spawned. **Turn over
left to right.**

6

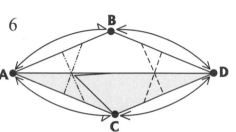

Looks similar, eh?
Mountain-fold point **A** to point **B** and unfold.
Mountain-fold point **A** to point **C** and unfold.
Valley-fold point **D** to point **B** and unfold.
Valley-fold point **D** to point **C** and unfold.

7

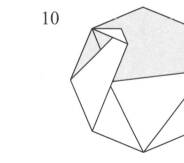

Using existing creases,
make the indicated
rabbit cars.

8

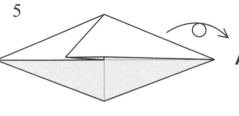

Outside-reverse-fold the head.
Adjust the angle of the wing.
Repeat behind.

9

**The Iso-Area Swan has swum
into existence. Turn over top to
bottom** to reveal her soul mate.

10

The soul mate unveiled.
Gay Merrill Gross, my proofreader,
suggests the following for presenting
the Iso-Area Swan: Fold from blue
paper, white on the reverse side.
Hold up finished model and say,
"This is a swan gliding across the
crystal blue water of the lake. When
the sun goes down {Show step 9},
we see the silhouette of the swan by
the light of the moon."

Thoughts Behind the Folds

The Iso-Area Swan came from experimenting with the
Iso-Area Fish Base (step 5). I was trying to make a model
simpler than the Yin Yang (page 155). **Challenge:** Can
you design an iso-area model even simpler than this?
Ideas: Iso-area penguin, fish, wave, heart, log, square.

Wine Glass

This is a pureland model: the term was borrowed from Buddhism by John S. Smith of England to describe models folded with valleys and mountains only. It's a perfect model for any special or not-so-special occasion. So toast to simplicity, fold, drink, and be merry. But don't really try to fill this wine glass or you'll end up with soggy paper and spilled wine.

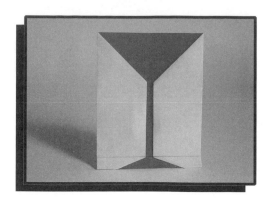

1

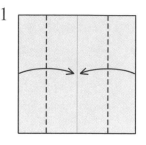

Begin with colored side up. Valley-fold the sides inward almost, but not quite, to the center line. The width between the two folded edges is the width of the wine glass stem.

2

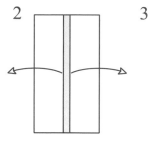

Unfold the model to step 1.

3

Valley-fold the top corners. Valley-fold and unfold the bottom corners.

Thoughts Behind the Folds

The Wine Glass came out of a search for simple Pureland folds. I was experimenting with shapes I could make by folding in the edges of the paper to form an outline. In a sense the technique was to try to fold what isn't the wine glass to form what is. See the Chocolate-Covered Ant (page 49) for a related idea. **Challenge:** What other shapes can be outlined in this manner? **Ideas:** Bull's head, guard dog, vegan butterfly, vehicular intersection, Florida, Cuba, golf green, alphabet, volcano, colliding rockets.

4

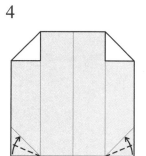

Valley-fold.

5

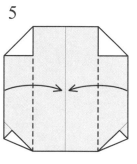

Valley-fold.

6

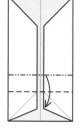

You could stop now as this is a wine glass. However, if you would like a shorter wine glass with a stand, then make a pleat, first making the valley fold and then the mountain so that it touches the base of the wine glass.

7

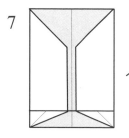

Turn over.

8

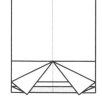

Valley-fold down the two corners to make a stand. Valley-fold the bottom edge upward to shrink the wine glass base to taste.

9

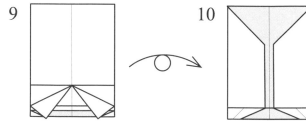

Turn over.

10

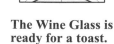

The Wine Glass is ready for a toast.

Peace Sign

Here's how to turn a piece of paper into the **peace** of paper. The model is closely related to the beginning steps of Mr. Smiley on page 65. In addition to being a peace sign, this model can also be used as a change purse, a medallion or a frisbee.

Thoughts Behind the Folds

Growing up in Berkeley, California, a home of the Peace and Love movement, it's not surprising that I would think to design a peace sign. In high school, I went through a symbolic phase (literally folding symbols). I discovered the border technique in the process of designing this model. **Challenge:** What other models can you come up with using the border technique? **Ideas:** Dancing skeleton, clock striking midnight, bristlecone pine tree, hot cross bun, Grand Prix race track, Mississippi River, NO scissors sign, NO boomerangs sign.

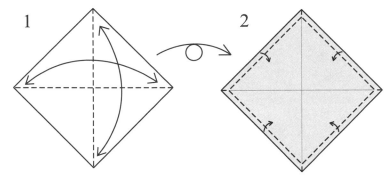

1

Begin with white side up. Valley-fold and unfold both diagonals. **Turn over.**

2

Create an equal border all around by valley-folding the sides in and pinching the corners so that they stick up. The final thickness of the lines of the Peace Sign will be double that of the border.

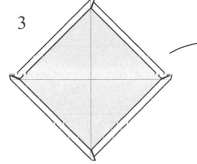

3

Like this. **Turn over.**

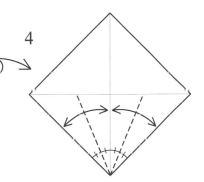

4

Valley-fold and unfold a Kite Base. But don't let the valleys cross the crease.

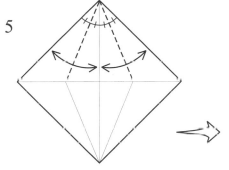

5

Valley-fold and unfold a Kite Base the other way.

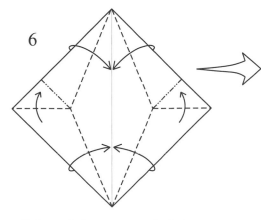

6

Using existing creases, pinch the side corners so that they stick up.

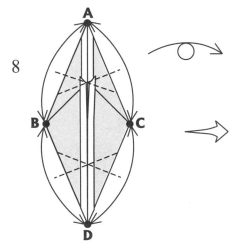

7

Flatten the model, forming a Fish Base.

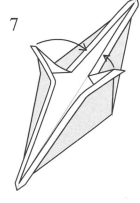

8

Valley-fold and unfold **A** to **B**, **A** to **C**, **D** to **B** and **D** to **C**. **Turn over.**

9

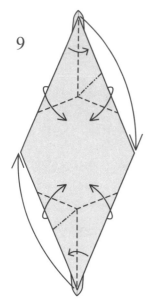

Rabbit-ear both ends along existing creases, first making the valley creases. The mountain creases form themselves naturally when you collapse the rabbit ears to one side.

10

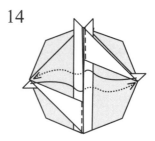

The two flaps on this side are extra. You can make them into two hugging snakes, two kissing swans, or two dancing lightning bolts, but the best thing to do is to tuck them inside the model by following the next four steps. If you find these four steps too difficult you can skip them and go to step 15. You will still make a peace sign, but it will have two extra flaps on the back. To tuck the flaps inside the model, first unfold the rabbit ears made in step 9.

11

Here is a three-dimensional alternative to steps 5 through 9 of Mr. Smiley (page 65). Spread open the bottom of the model from behind; it won't lie flat. The next view is in perspective looking at the spread-open end (the other end appears in the distance).

12

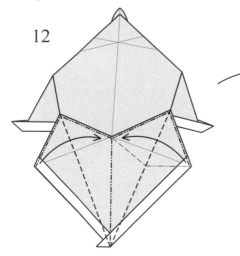

Locate the heart shape (**shaded dark**) and pinch mountain folds along the top of the heart. Valley-fold the sides of the heart into the center and collapse the flap to one side or the other. **Turn over.**

13

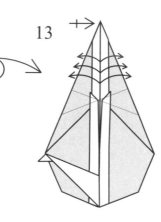

Find peace from within. Then repeat steps 11–12 on the top.

14

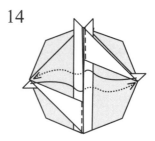

Once again you can turn the extra points into two kissing crane heads, but it's better to tuck them inside the change purse. That's right; this model is also a change purse!

15

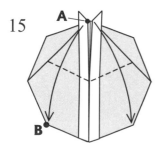

Valley-fold the left flap down bringing point **A** to point **B**. Do the same with the right flap.

16

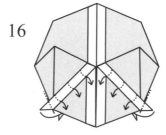

Widen the two limbs of the peace sign by bringing out paper from behind. When this is accomplished the ends of the limbs should wrap very nicely around the corners of the octagon.

17

The peace of paper has been attained. Display it as a reminder of our search for peace within us and around us.

Multiple Rippling Deltoid Design

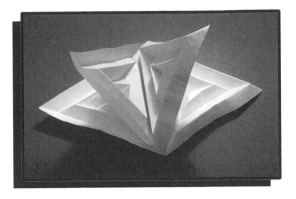

If one Rippling Deltoid is neato, then what is multiplying it fourfold? Neato-neato-neato-neato! For best effect, use paper the same color on both sides. However, for best understanding of the diagrams use two-color paper.

1

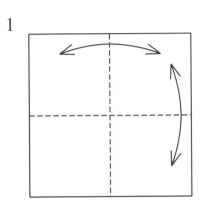

White side up, valley-fold and unfold both ways in half.

2

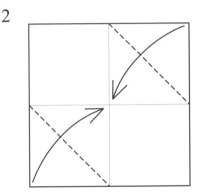

Valley-fold opposite corners to the center.

3

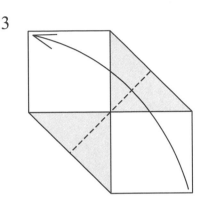

Valley-fold in half.

4

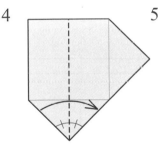

Valley-fold vertically on the near layer.

5

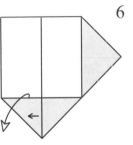

Pull out the paper.

6

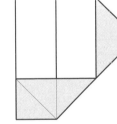

Turn over.

7

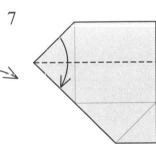

Valley-fold horizontally on the near layer.

8

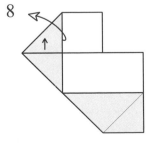

Pull out the paper.

9

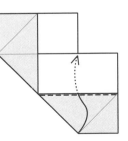

Valley-fold the bottom edge upward, slipping it underneath the near layer.

10

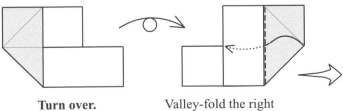

Turn over.

11

Valley-fold the right edge, slipping it underneath the near layer.

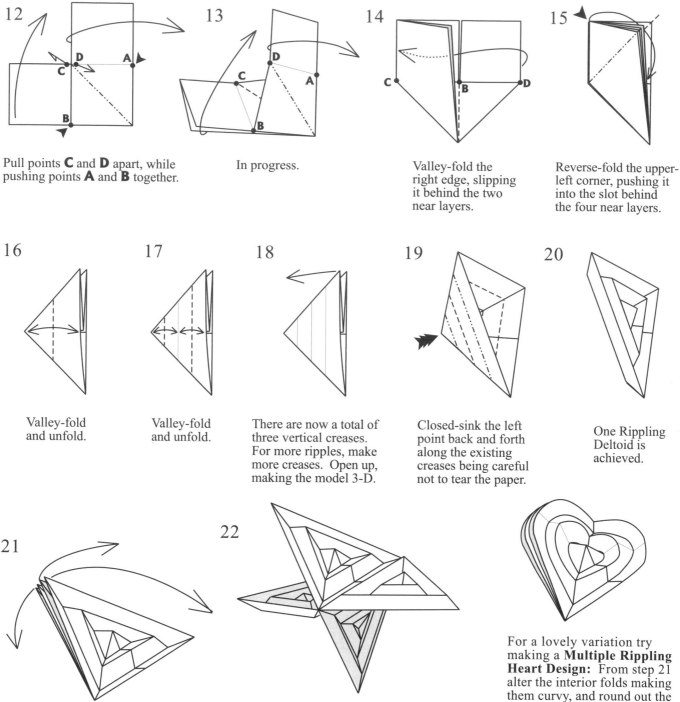

12 Pull points **C** and **D** apart, while pushing points **A** and **B** together.

13 In progress.

14 Valley-fold the right edge, slipping it behind the two near layers.

15 Reverse-fold the upper-left corner, pushing it into the slot behind the four near layers.

16 Valley-fold and unfold.

17 Valley-fold and unfold.

18 There are now a total of three vertical creases. For more ripples, make more creases. Open up, making the model 3-D.

19 Closed-sink the left point back and forth along the existing creases being careful not to tear the paper.

20 One Rippling Deltoid is achieved.

21 Say the magic words, and multiply the model by separating the layers.

22 The Multiple Rippling Deltoid Design has been suddenly synthesized.

For a lovely variation try making a **Multiple Rippling Heart Design:** From step 21 alter the interior folds making them curvy, and round out the sides with mountain folds and reverse folds. This variation looks much better with paper colored red on both sides.

Thoughts Behind the Folds

While experimenting with the Pinwheel Base, I came across four pyramids inlaid in each other. From there I saw a window of possibilities which included the Multiple Rippling Deltoid Design (the name came later). Then, with much exploration, I found a simple folding method devoid of pinwheels. **Challenge:** Make the rippling triangles spiral instead of concentric. Also, what other multiple models can you come up with? **Ideas:** Three-pointed star, Star Trek emblem, dormant volcano, dented contact lens, headless crane doing a somersault in a strobe light.

Musical Notes

Fa-Do-Sol-Mi

The final tune depends on the key signature, the clef, and whether or not you're standing on your head.

1

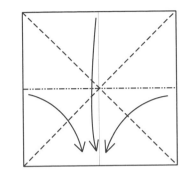

This model works best in foil. Begin by folding a Waterbomb Base.

2

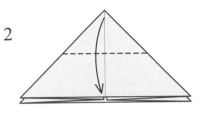

Valley-fold the top corner down to the bottom.

3

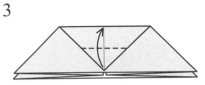

Valley-fold same corner up to the top.

4

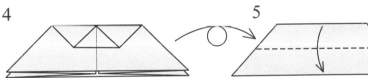

Like this. **Turn the model over.**

5

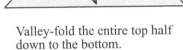

Valley-fold the entire top half down to the bottom.

6

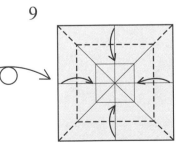

Cover your eyes, hold your nose, plug your ears, and, with your remaining hands... **completely unfold the model!**

7

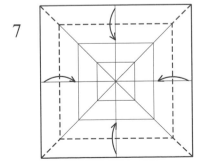

Valley-fold the four sides in along existing creases while pinching at the corners so that they stick up. The model will look like an upside-down table with very short legs.

8

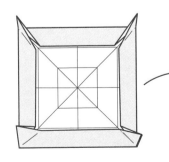

Like this.
Turn the table over.

9

Valley-fold the four sides in along existing creases while pinching at the corners, as was done in step 7.

10

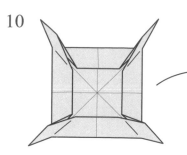

We now have a smaller upside-down table with longer legs.
Turn the table over.

11

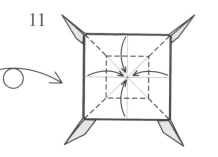

Valley-fold the four sides in along existing creases while pinching at the corners, as was done in step 7.

12

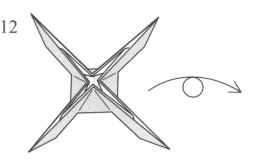

We now have a very small table with extremely long legs.
Turn the table over.

13

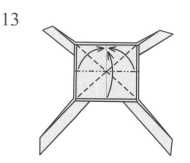

Fold the central square into a Waterbomb Base.

14

Valley-fold and unfold the tip of the near right flap to the center.

15

Swing one flap to the left.

16

Valley-fold and unfold point-to-point. **Careful:** the reference points are not the same as in step 14.

17

Valley-fold to the crease line.

18

Valley-fold the near flap to the right, crease-to-edge.

19

Swing one flap to the right, like turning a page of a book.

20

Valley-fold both flaps as one point-to-point.

21

Unfold both flaps as one.

Thoughts Behind the Folds

The first time I ever designed musical notes was on a school bus with Berkeley High Concert Chorale on our way to compete at the 1991 Reno Jazz Festival. During the eight-hour voyage I offered to teach origami to some fellow classmates and asked them what they would like to learn. My good friend Eveline Séquin requested musical notes, which I had never tried to fold but agreed to try to teach anyway. So I taught and designed it at the same time and it actually turned out quite nice. That's called designing under pressure! Since then the number of notes has doubled and the design approach has evolved greatly, which goes to show that a good idea can be fruitful and multiply.
Challenge: Try to design other musical symbols. Also, what else could this model become? **Ideas:** Golf clubs, chimes, stalagmites, a family of four serpentine swamp creatures sticking their heads out of the water.

22

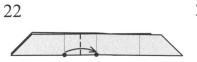

Valley-fold the front left flap over to the right, placing crease on crease.

23

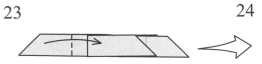

Valley-fold on the existing crease.

24

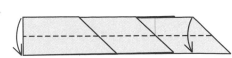
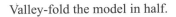

Valley-fold the model in half.

25

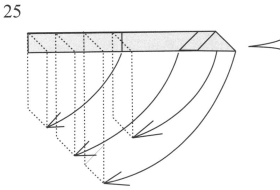

Reverse-fold the four stems down as far as each will go.

26

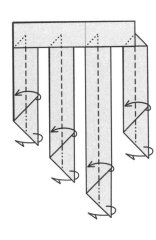

Reverse-fold on the front and the back, narrowing the stems.

27

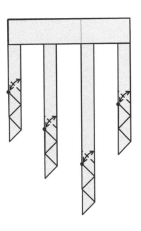

Valley-fold and unfold point-to-edge.

28

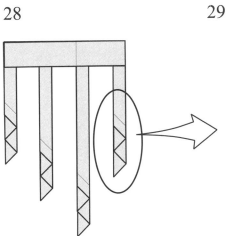

Look closely at one stem.

29

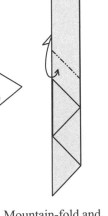

Mountain-fold and unfold, inverting the valley fold made in step 27.

30

Inside-reverse-fold.

31

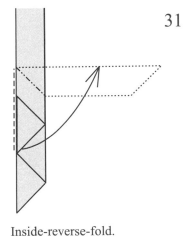

Swing the near flap upward. Sing your favorite song.

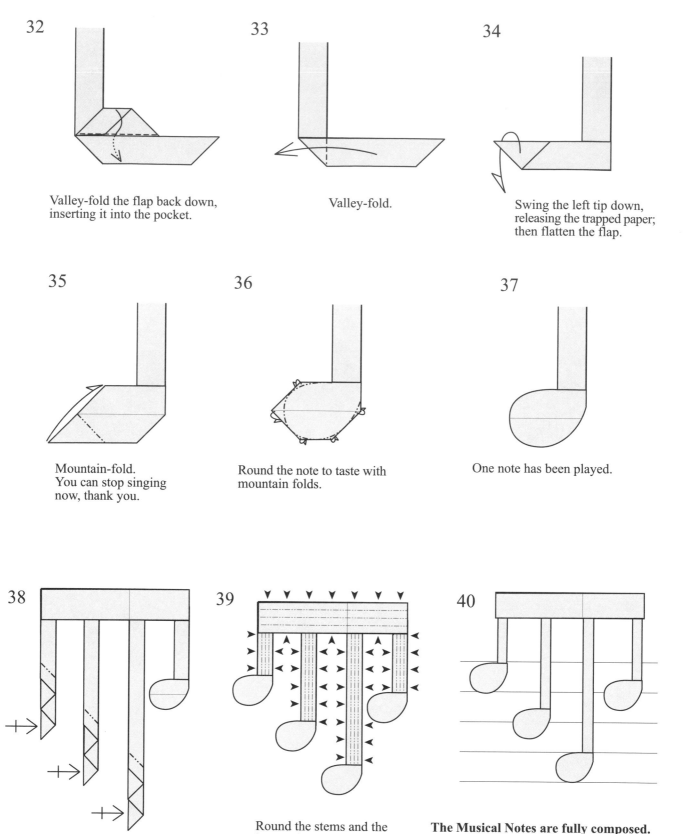

32

Valley-fold the flap back down, inserting it into the pocket.

33

Valley-fold.

34

Swing the left tip down, releasing the trapped paper; then flatten the flap.

35

Mountain-fold. You can stop singing now, thank you.

36

Round the note to taste with mountain folds.

37

One note has been played.

38

Play the other three notes by repeating steps 29–36.

39

Round the stems and the bar to give the model a three-dimensional look.

40

The Musical Notes are fully composed. Now fold a hundred and put them onto staff paper—it's the "Broken Record Lullaby," guaranteed to put you to sleep or drive you crazy if you try to play it!

Dancers

This is a perfect model to fold in the limo on the way to the prom, assuming your date doesn't mind.

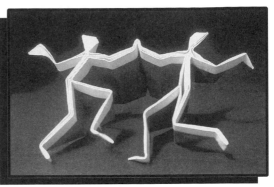

1

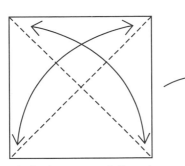

Six-inch paper or foil works fine for this model. Begin white side up. Valley-fold and unfold both diagonals. **Turn over.**

2

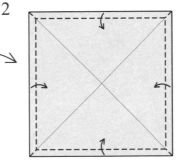

Create an equal border all around by valley-folding the sides in and pinching the corners so that they stick up. The thickness of the border will become the limb thickness of the dancers. An ideal thickness is 1/32 of the side of the square.

3

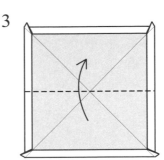

Valley-fold in half.

4

Valley-fold the front down.

5

Reverse-fold along existing creases.

6

Shake, rattle, and roll, and **turn over.**

7

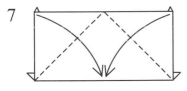

Valley-fold the corners down. The tiny protruding corners should overlap.

8

Make the indicated valley creases, dividing the height into four equal parts. Pleat-sink, first unfolding to step 7.

9

Pleat-sinking in progress. Make the indicated creases and collapse. Not you— the PAPER!

Pleat-sinking in progress.

10

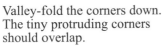

Pleat-sinking is com**pleat**. Swing the nearest right central white corner to the right and flatten. Watch the black dot. **Then repeat on the left.**

In progress.

11

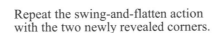

Repeat the swing-and-flatten action with the two newly revealed corners.

12

The next view is from the bottom looking up.

13

From now on, the diagrams will be in stick-figure form, with all the paper hidden behind the lines. Swing the appendages into humanoid form: four bend downward, two bend upward and two remain pointing to the sides.

14

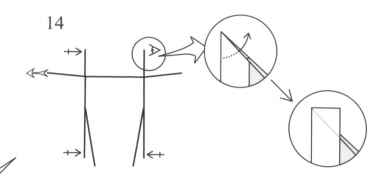

Close-up of the right head from the side view. Pull out border paper from inside. Repeat as indicated. Pull the left person's arms apart causing the body to spread open.

15

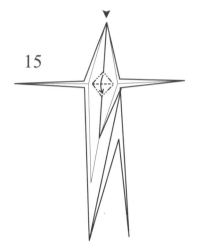

Close-up front view of the left person. The purpose of this fold is to lengthen the arms while shortening the head and body. To do this, pinch the indicated creases. Then pull the arms out as you squeeze the body back together. The amount of paper you squeeze out of the head and body to donate to the arms is up to you. Repeat this process on the right person.

16

View from the side.

Valley-fold the heads, rotating them as shown so that they seem to face each other.

17

Form the joints as you see fit. The black dots are suggestions for where to put the joints.

Thoughts Behind the Folds

For the discovery of the Dancers I give full credit to Becky Brockman, my college sweetheart. The model I had designed and given to her was two people holding hands. Moments later she gave me back the model, with all the joints folded, and exclaimed, "Dancers!" **Challenge:** What other activities can you make the couple play? **Ideas:** Sunbathing, mime in the mirror, sumo wrestling, Twister, double roadkill, two-person mosh pit, E.T. phone home, head standing.

18

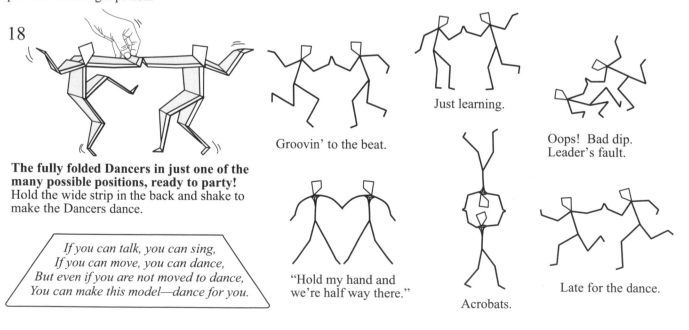

The fully folded Dancers in just one of the many possible positions, ready to party! Hold the wide strip in the back and shake to make the Dancers dance.

If you can talk, you can sing,
If you can move, you can dance,
But even if you are not moved to dance,
You can make this model—dance for you.

Groovin' to the beat.

Just learning.

Oops! Bad dip. Leader's fault.

"Hold my hand and we're half way there."

Acrobats.

Late for the dance.

Dragon

Based on Robert Neale's Dragon, this Dragon has the added features that it stands on its hind legs, has an arrowhead tail and is pleated all over.

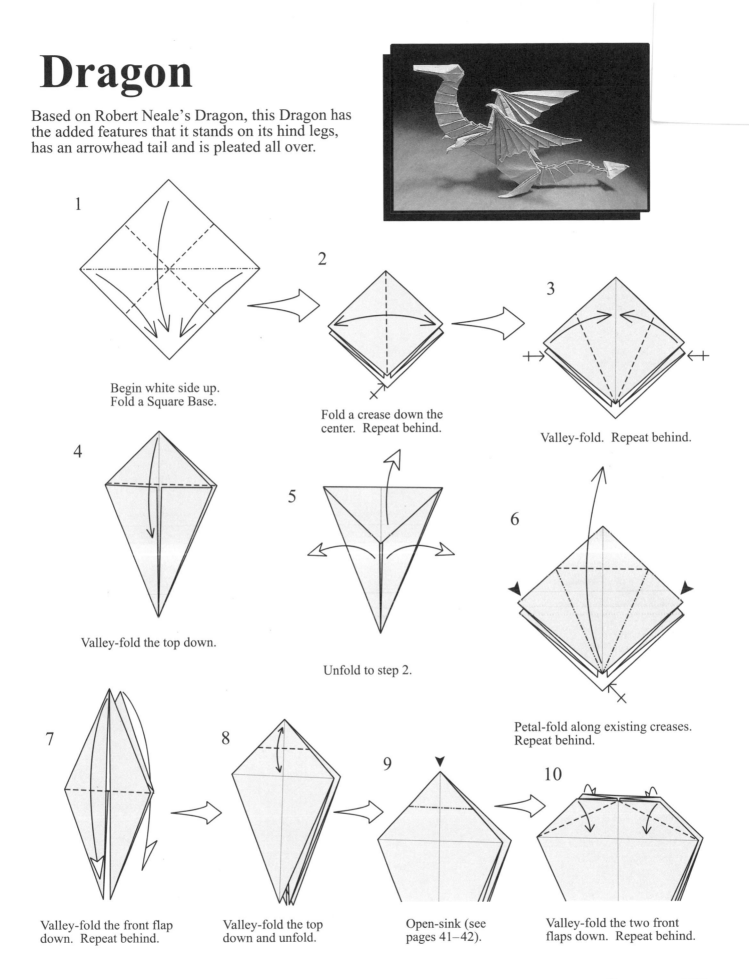

1

Begin white side up. Fold a Square Base.

2

Fold a crease down the center. Repeat behind.

3

Valley-fold. Repeat behind.

4

Valley-fold the top down.

5

Unfold to step 2.

6

Petal-fold along existing creases. Repeat behind.

7

Valley-fold the front flap down. Repeat behind.

8

Valley-fold the top down and unfold.

9

Open-sink (see pages 41–42).

10

Valley-fold the two front flaps down. Repeat behind.

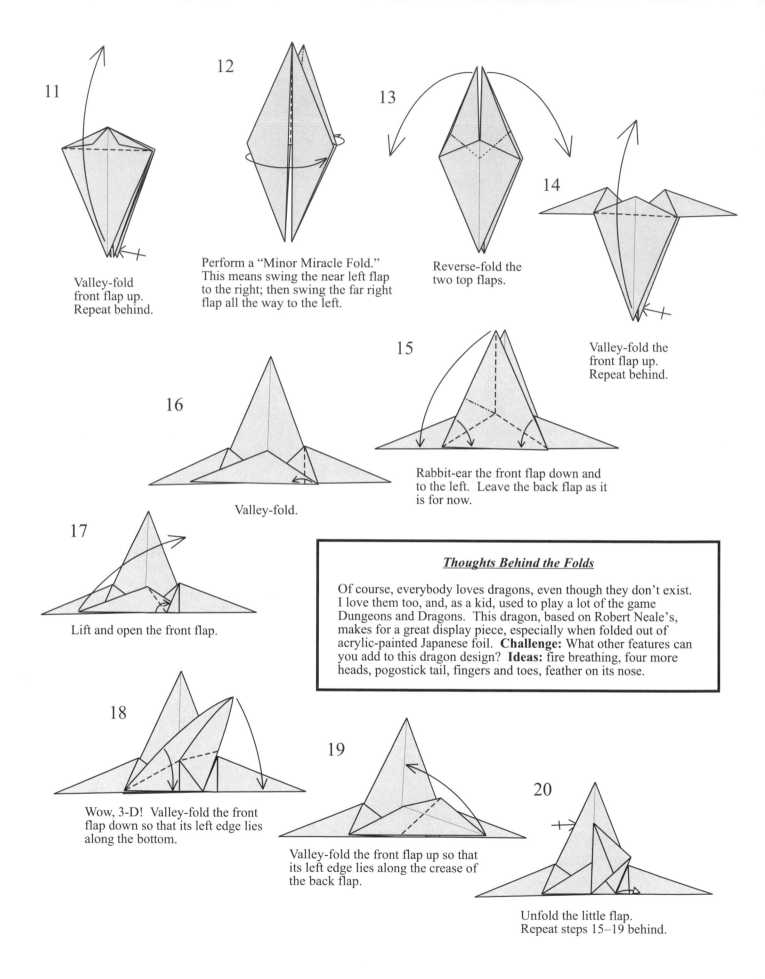

11 Valley-fold front flap up. Repeat behind.

12 Perform a "Minor Miracle Fold." This means swing the near left flap to the right; then swing the far right flap all the way to the left.

13 Reverse-fold the two top flaps.

14 Valley-fold the front flap up. Repeat behind.

15 Rabbit-ear the front flap down and to the left. Leave the back flap as it is for now.

16 Valley-fold.

17 Lift and open the front flap.

Thoughts Behind the Folds

Of course, everybody loves dragons, even though they don't exist. I love them too, and, as a kid, used to play a lot of the game Dungeons and Dragons. This dragon, based on Robert Neale's, makes for a great display piece, especially when folded out of acrylic-painted Japanese foil. **Challenge:** What other features can you add to this dragon design? **Ideas:** fire breathing, four more heads, pogostick tail, fingers and toes, feather on its nose.

18 Wow, 3-D! Valley-fold the front flap down so that its left edge lies along the bottom.

19 Valley-fold the front flap up so that its left edge lies along the crease of the back flap.

20 Unfold the little flap. Repeat steps 15–19 behind.

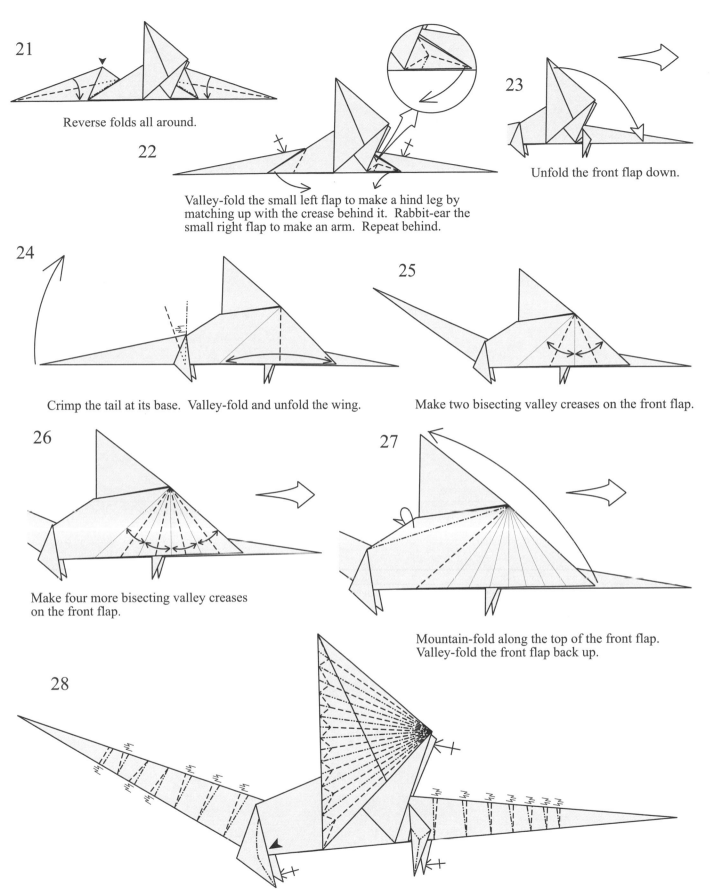

21

Reverse folds all around.

22

Valley-fold the small left flap to make a hind leg by matching up with the crease behind it. Rabbit-ear the small right flap to make an arm. Repeat behind.

23

Unfold the front flap down.

24

Crimp the tail at its base. Valley-fold and unfold the wing.

25

Make two bisecting valley creases on the front flap.

26

Make four more bisecting valley creases on the front flap.

27

Mountain-fold along the top of the front flap. Valley-fold the front flap back up.

28

Using existing creases and adding eight more, pleat the front flap, and for extra thrills, make eight tiny reverse folds, at which point we can now safely call it a wing. Make a wing out of the back flap (repeat steps 23–28). Shape the arms and legs and crimp the heck out of the neck and tail, so that everything looks exactly like the next diagram.

Dragon **139**

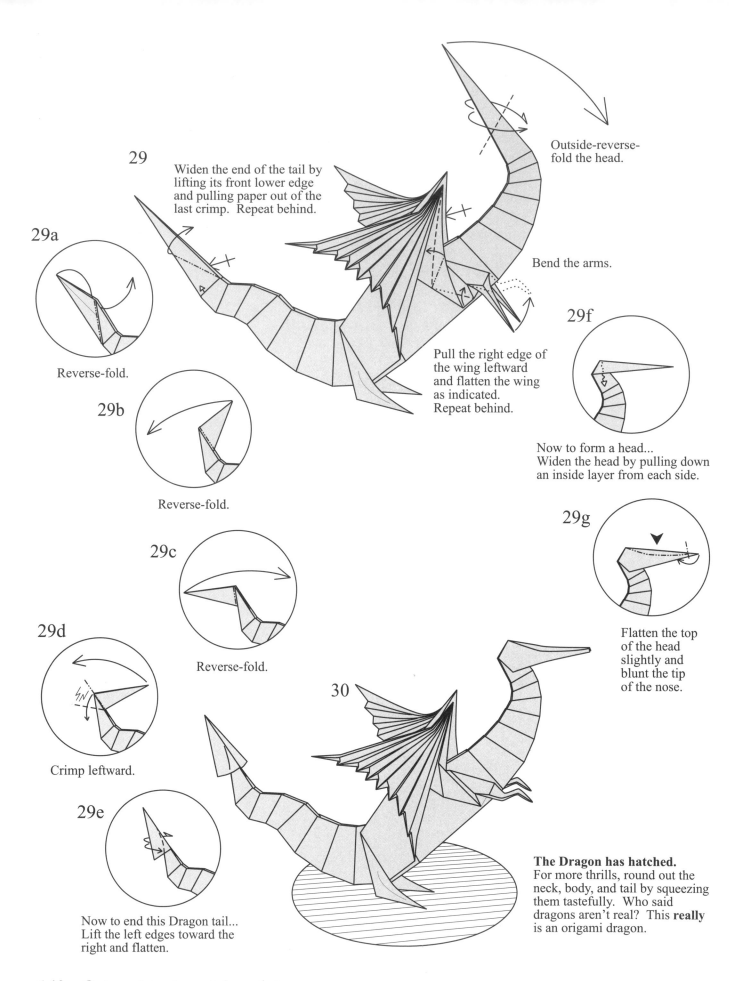

29

Widen the end of the tail by lifting its front lower edge and pulling paper out of the last crimp. Repeat behind.

Outside-reverse-fold the head.

Bend the arms.

29a

Reverse-fold.

29b

Reverse-fold.

29c

Reverse-fold.

29d

Crimp leftward.

29e

Now to end this Dragon tail... Lift the left edges toward the right and flatten.

Pull the right edge of the wing leftward and flatten the wing as indicated. Repeat behind.

29f

Now to form a head... Widen the head by pulling down an inside layer from each side.

29g

Flatten the top of the head slightly and blunt the tip of the nose.

30

The Dragon has hatched.
For more thrills, round out the neck, body, and tail by squeezing them tastefully. Who said dragons aren't real? This **really** is an origami dragon.

Rocking Horse

This model is based on Paul Jackson's Barking Dog, but it doesn't bark and looks and acts nothing like a dog. Doggone it, it's a rocking horse!... hence the title.

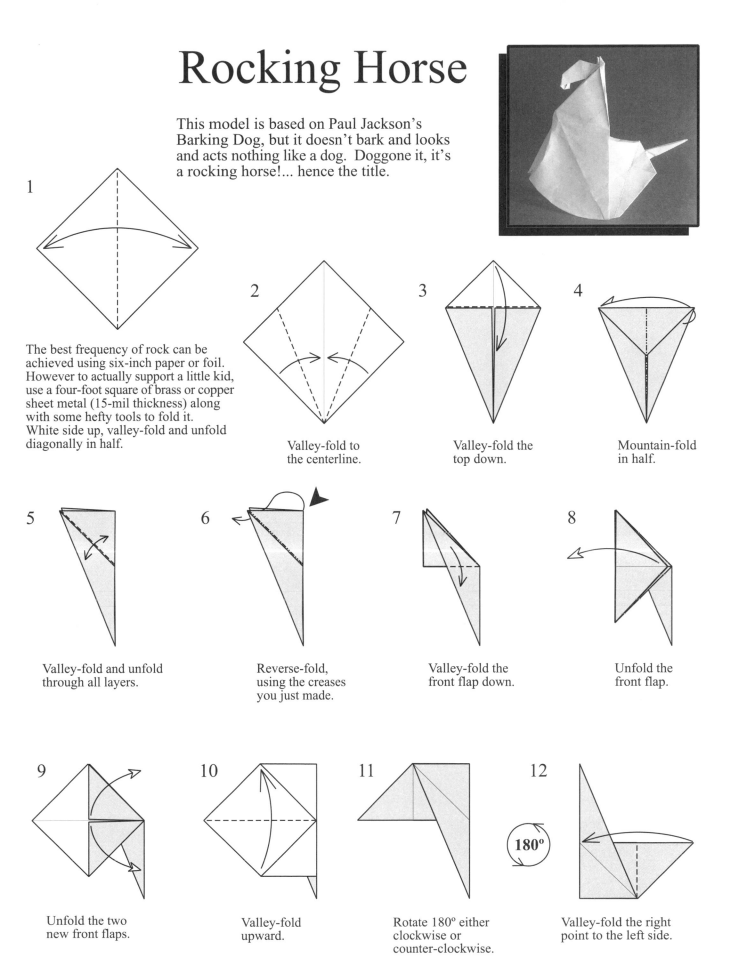

1

The best frequency of rock can be achieved using six-inch paper or foil. However to actually support a little kid, use a four-foot square of brass or copper sheet metal (15-mil thickness) along with some hefty tools to fold it. White side up, valley-fold and unfold diagonally in half.

2
Valley-fold to the centerline.

3
Valley-fold the top down.

4
Mountain-fold in half.

5
Valley-fold and unfold through all layers.

6
Reverse-fold, using the creases you just made.

7
Valley-fold the front flap down.

8
Unfold the front flap.

9
Unfold the two new front flaps.

10
Valley-fold upward.

11
Rotate 180° either clockwise or counter-clockwise.

12
180°
Valley-fold the right point to the left side.

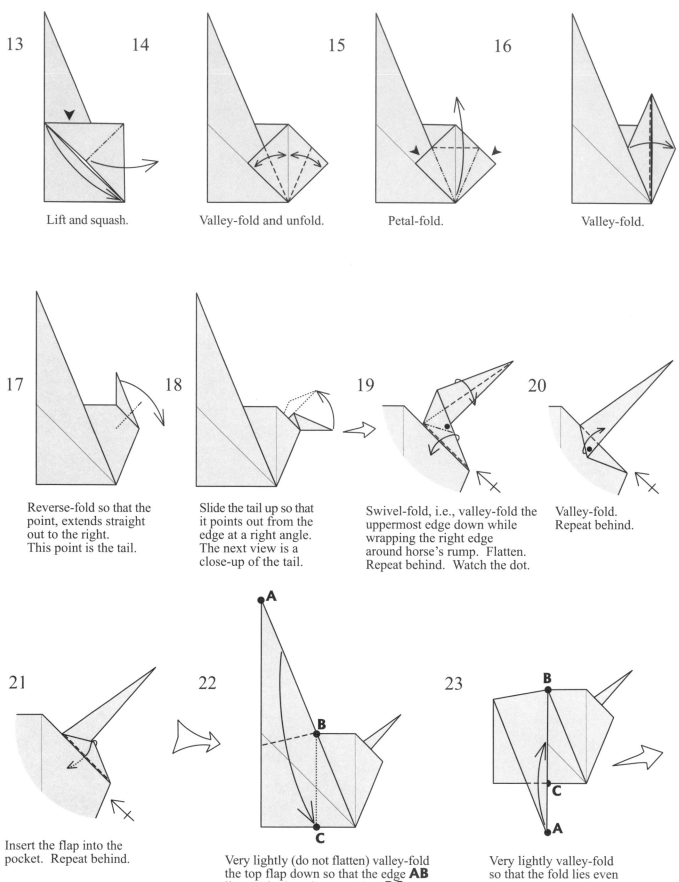

13

14 Lift and squash.

15 Valley-fold and unfold.

16 Petal-fold.

Valley-fold.

17 Reverse-fold so that the point, extends straight out to the right. This point is the tail.

18 Slide the tail up so that it points out from the edge at a right angle. The next view is a close-up of the tail.

19 Swivel-fold, i.e., valley-fold the uppermost edge down while wrapping the right edge around horse's rump. Flatten. Repeat behind. Watch the dot.

20 Valley-fold. Repeat behind.

21 Insert the flap into the pocket. Repeat behind.

22 Very lightly (do not flatten) valley-fold the top flap down so that the edge **AB** lies on the imaginary vertical **BC**.

23 Very lightly valley-fold so that the fold lies even with the bottom edge.

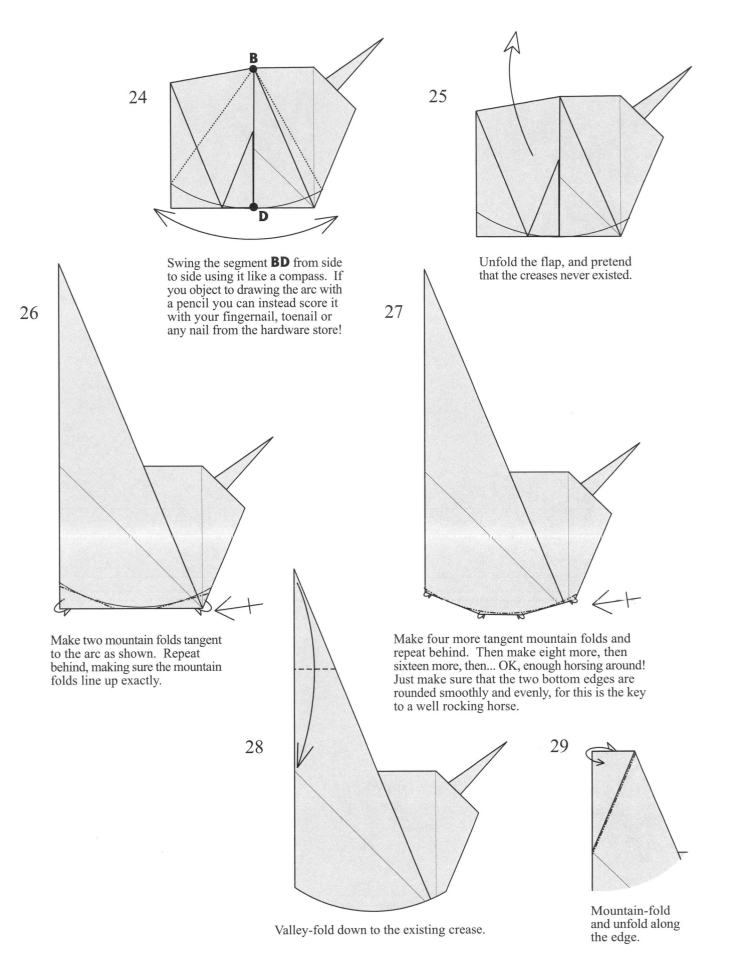

24 Swing the segment **BD** from side to side using it like a compass. If you object to drawing the arc with a pencil you can instead score it with your fingernail, toenail or any nail from the hardware store!

25 Unfold the flap, and pretend that the creases never existed.

26 Make two mountain folds tangent to the arc as shown. Repeat behind, making sure the mountain folds line up exactly.

27 Make four more tangent mountain folds and repeat behind. Then make eight more, then sixteen more, then... OK, enough horsing around! Just make sure that the two bottom edges are rounded smoothly and evenly, for this is the key to a well rocking horse.

28 Valley-fold down to the existing crease.

29 Mountain-fold and unfold along the edge.

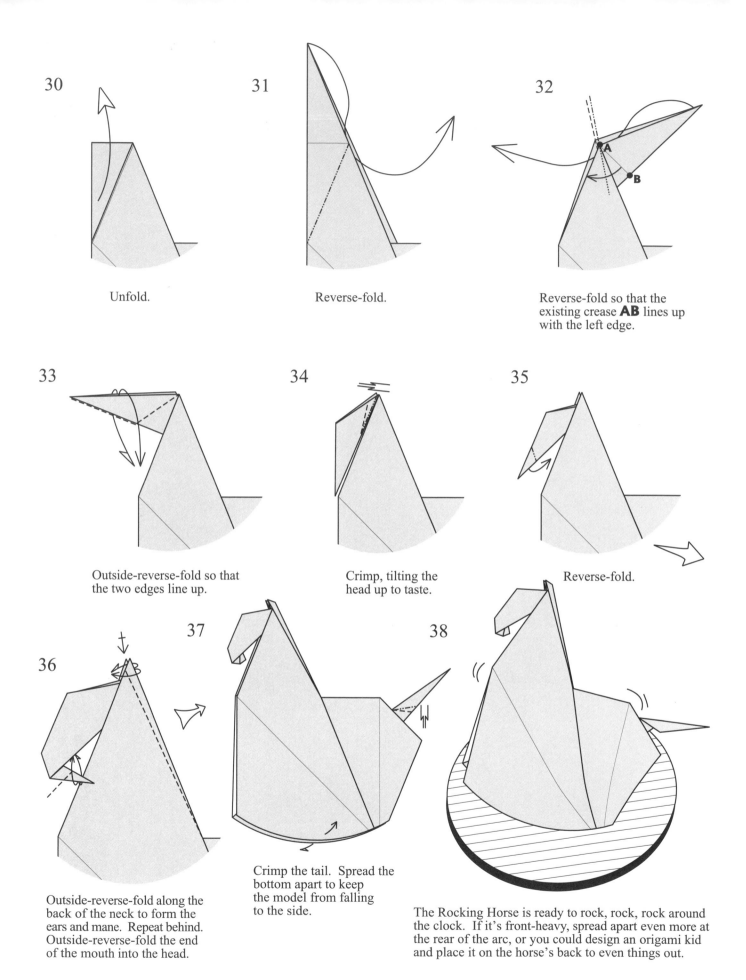

30

Unfold.

31

Reverse-fold.

32

Reverse-fold so that the existing crease **AB** lines up with the left edge.

33

Outside-reverse-fold so that the two edges line up.

34

Crimp, tilting the head up to taste.

35

Reverse-fold.

36

37

Outside-reverse-fold along the back of the neck to form the ears and mane. Repeat behind. Outside-reverse-fold the end of the mouth into the head.

Crimp the tail. Spread the bottom apart to keep the model from falling to the side.

38

The Rocking Horse is ready to rock, rock, rock around the clock. If it's front-heavy, spread apart even more at the rear of the arc, or you could design an origami kid and place it on the horse's back to even things out.

Menorah

Fold this model out of a sheet of brass and it can actually hold burning candles. Even a Menorah folded from paper can hold burning candles, but be aware that when the candles burn down, the model will likely burn up!

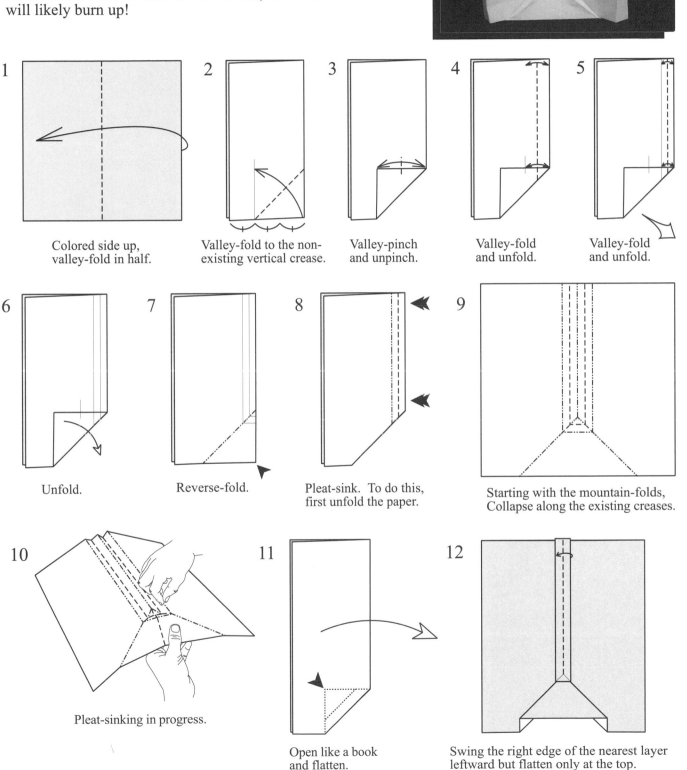

1 Colored side up, valley-fold in half.

2 Valley-fold to the non-existing vertical crease.

3 Valley-pinch and unpinch.

4 Valley-fold and unfold.

5 Valley-fold and unfold.

6 Unfold.

7 Reverse-fold.

8 Pleat-sink. To do this, first unfold the paper.

9 Starting with the mountain-folds, Collapse along the existing creases.

10 Pleat-sinking in progress.

11 Open like a book and flatten.

12 Swing the right edge of the nearest layer leftward but flatten only at the top.

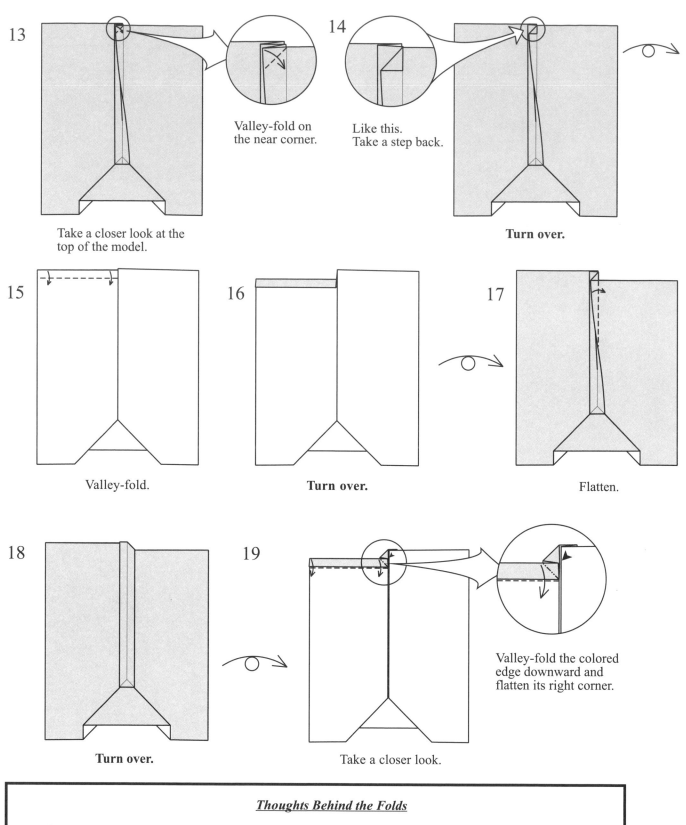

13 Take a closer look at the top of the model.

Valley-fold on the near corner.

14 Like this. Take a step back.

Turn over.

15 Valley-fold.

16 **Turn over.**

17 Flatten.

18 **Turn over.**

19 Take a closer look.

Valley-fold the colored edge downward and flatten its right corner.

Thoughts Behind the Folds

I enjoy very much celebrating Chanukah, which is why I've made many attempts at folding a menorah. In designing this menorah, my goal was simplicity. Although it's certainly not a simple model, it's much less complex than my previous attempts which were based on obtaining ten long narrow appendages (nine candleholders and a stem). **Challenge:** What other models can you simplify by utilizing the interior of the square? **Ideas:** Tree, leaf, fence, ladder, train tracks, bicycle wheel, rainbow, rolling hills, Niagara Falls.

20

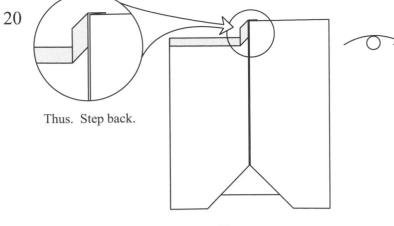

Thus. Step back.

Turn over.

21

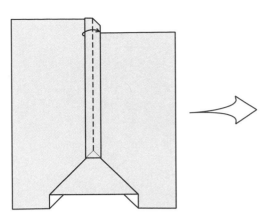

Repeat steps 12–20 on the left side.
For the next 10 steps ignore the
lower part of the model.

22

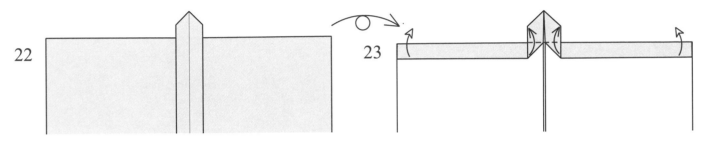

Turn over.

23

Swing the colored flaps upward.

24

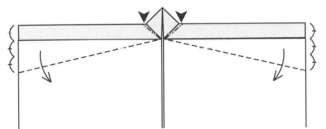

Valley-fold on the left and the right. Squash at
the center to make the folds lie flat.

25

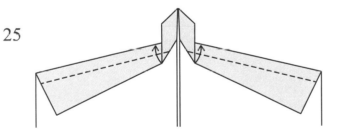

Valley-fold. These folds are parallel
to the upper edge.

26

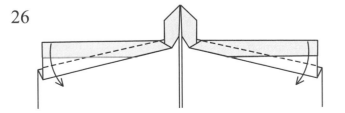

Valley-fold, lining up with the edge in back.

27

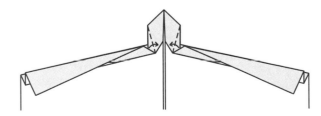

Valley-fold, pulling out the trapped paper.

Menorah **147**

28

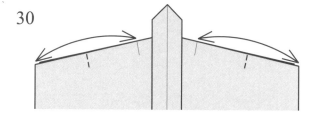

Turn over.

29

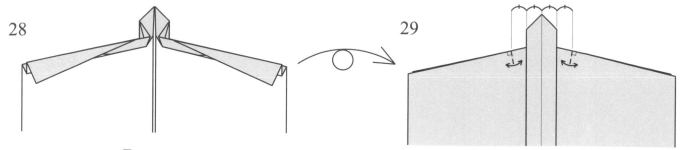

Valley-pinch and unpinch.

30

Valley-pinch and unpinch.

31

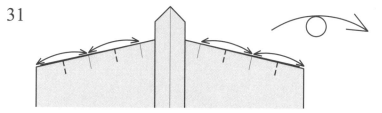

Valley-pinch and unpinch.
Turn over.

32

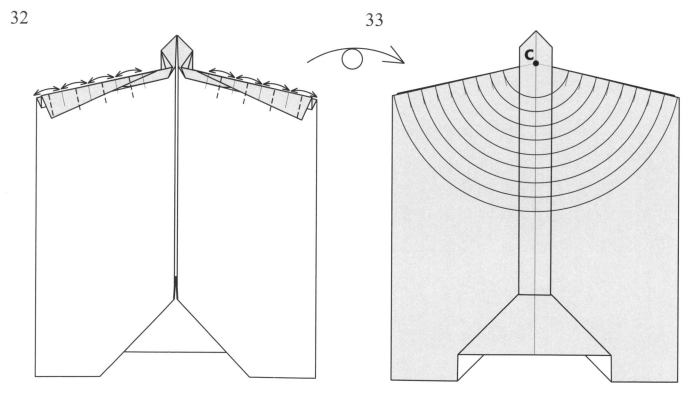

Valley-pinch and unpinch.
Turn over.

33

C.

Here's where using a compass is a really good idea. Fixing the compass to point **C**, draw (or score) the indicated arcs. Then skip to step 37. For a compass-free method of generating the arcs follow steps 34–36.
Compass Tip: If you paper-clip a piece of cardboard onto point **C**, you can avoid puncturing the paper.

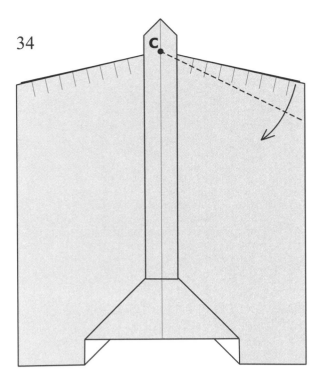

Pretend to make a valley fold through point **C**, BUT DON'T ACTUALLY FLATTEN IT.

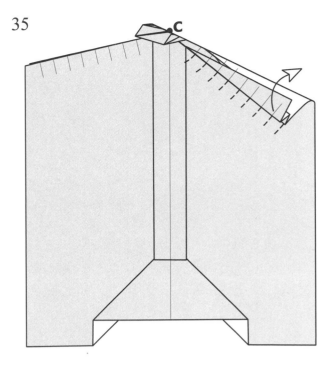

Using your fingernail (or other scoring device), copy the existing pinch marks onto the bottom layer. Then undo the pretend valley fold.

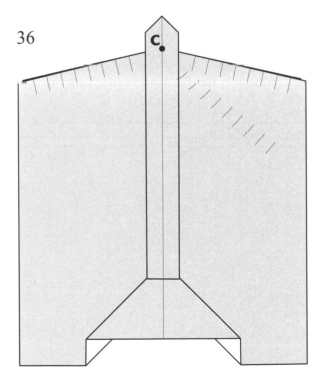

Repeat steps 34–35 over and over making the pretend valley fold go through point **C** at many different angles until all of the arcs are fully scored.

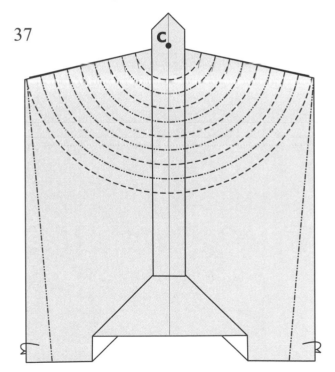

Make the indicated mountains and valleys along the existing scored arcs. How much do they get folded? Stop when the top edge of the menorah is roughly horizontal. Then, mountain-fold the left and right edges but do not flatten them. They should point straight back so that the menorah can stand.

38
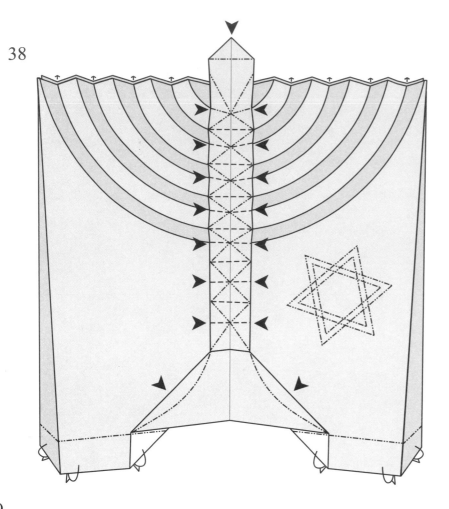

a. Sink the middle to form a holder for the shammes (the middle candle). Create pockets for the other candles by making eight reverse folds along the back layer of the top edge. Make these reverse folds as you see fit: bigger pockets hold bigger candles.

b. OPTIONAL: By pushing in at the sides, turn the central pillar into a stack of semi-open Waterbomb Bases. To do this most cleanly, completely unfold the model and make the mountains and valleys indicated in step 39. Then, refold the model incorporating the new folds.

c. OPTIONAL: For extra decoration, how about creasing a Star of David? You may either eyeball the creases, or, for utmost precision, construct them using a compass and straight edge. Regardless, make the creases as sharp as possible, so that they can be seen.

d. Shape the base to taste. Mountain-fold the bottom edges behind even with the bottom of the base.

39

Step 38**b** in progress. The clean method of making the central pillar.

40
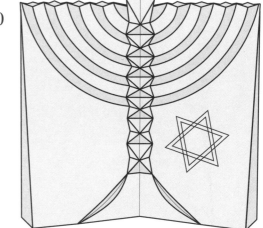

The Menorah is fully fashioned and ready for seasons of joy and thanksgiving.

Crab

What's this? An ordinary animal model by Jeremy Shafer?! How astonishing! How amusing! This Crab, a remnant from my animal-folding past, is included in this book because it's fun to fold and easier than most other crabs (at least for me!).

1

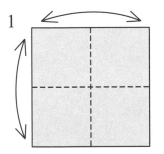

For best results, use foil at least twelve inches square. Begin with the colored side up. Valley-fold in half and unfold both ways.

2

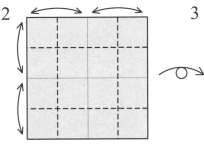

Valley-fold and unfold to make fourths. **Turn over.**

3

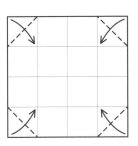

Valley-fold the corners.

4

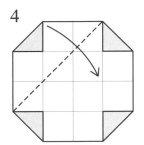

Valley-fold.

5

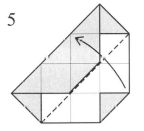

Valley-fold.

6

Valley-fold.

7

Unfold to step 4.

8

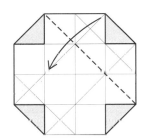

Repeat steps 4–7 on the other side.

9

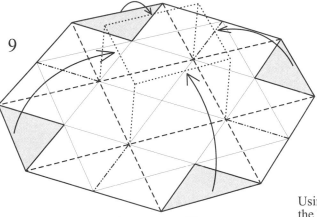

Using existing creases, lift up the corners to form a box.

10

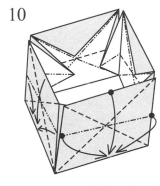

Using existing creases, fold each side of the box into a Waterbomb Base: i.e., push the center of each square side of the box toward the base of the box while pulling the black dots down as shown.

11

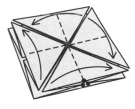

Valley-fold four flaps.

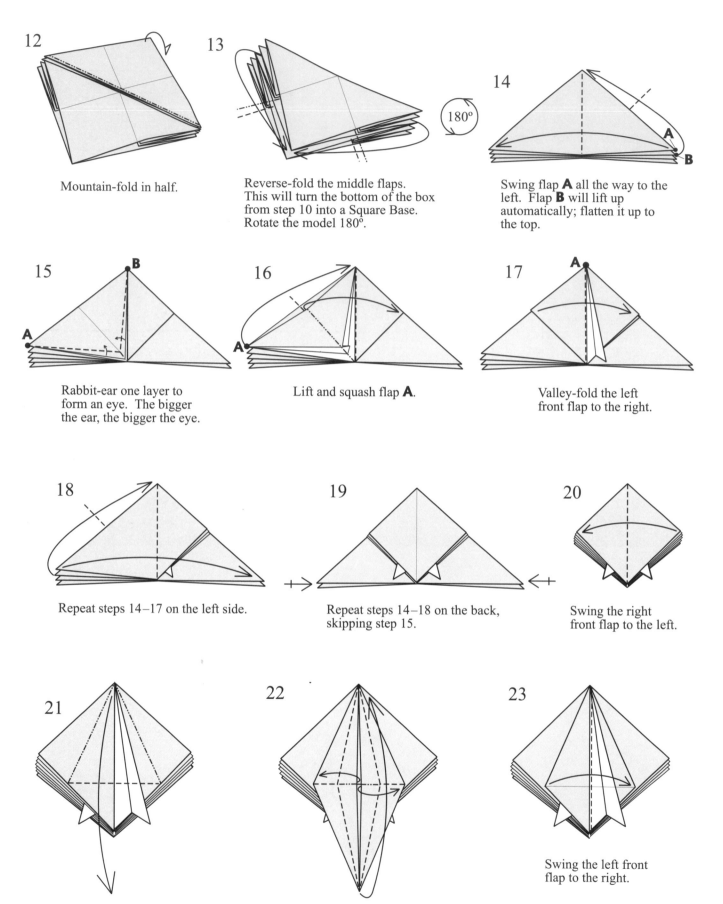

12

Mountain-fold in half.

13

Reverse-fold the middle flaps.
This will turn the bottom of the box
from step 10 into a Square Base.
Rotate the model 180°.

14

Swing flap **A** all the way to the
left. Flap **B** will lift up
automatically; flatten it up to
the top.

15

Rabbit-ear one layer to
form an eye. The bigger
the ear, the bigger the eye.

16

Lift and squash flap **A**.

17

Valley-fold the left
front flap to the right.

18

Repeat steps 14–17 on the left side.

19

Repeat steps 14–18 on the back,
skipping step 15.

20

Swing the right
front flap to the left.

21

Petal-fold downward.

22

Pull the central edges to the
outer edges of the petal while
closing the petal upward.

23

Swing the left front
flap to the right.

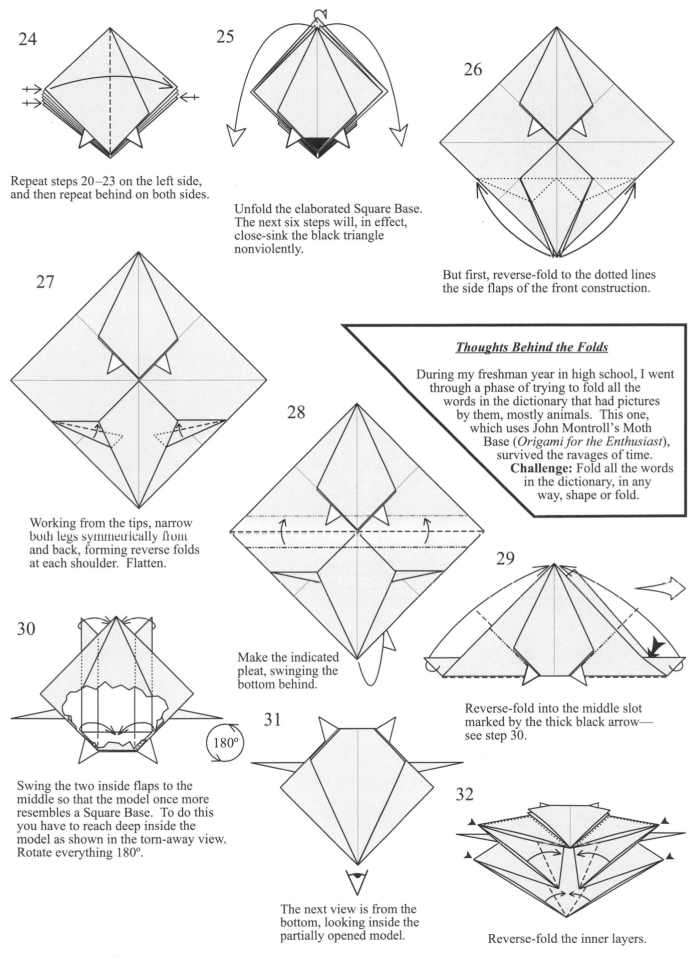

24

Repeat steps 20–23 on the left side, and then repeat behind on both sides.

25

Unfold the elaborated Square Base. The next six steps will, in effect, close-sink the black triangle nonviolently.

26

But first, reverse-fold to the dotted lines the side flaps of the front construction.

27

Working from the tips, narrow both legs symmetrically front and back, forming reverse folds at each shoulder. Flatten.

__Thoughts Behind the Folds__

During my freshman year in high school, I went through a phase of trying to fold all the words in the dictionary that had pictures by them, mostly animals. This one, which uses John Montroll's Moth Base (*Origami for the Enthusiast*), survived the ravages of time. **Challenge:** Fold all the words in the dictionary, in any way, shape or fold.

28

Make the indicated pleat, swinging the bottom behind.

29

Reverse-fold into the middle slot marked by the thick black arrow— see step 30.

30

Swing the two inside flaps to the middle so that the model once more resembles a Square Base. To do this you have to reach deep inside the model as shown in the torn-away view. Rotate everything 180°.

31

The next view is from the bottom, looking inside the partially opened model.

32

Reverse-fold the inner layers.

Crab **153**

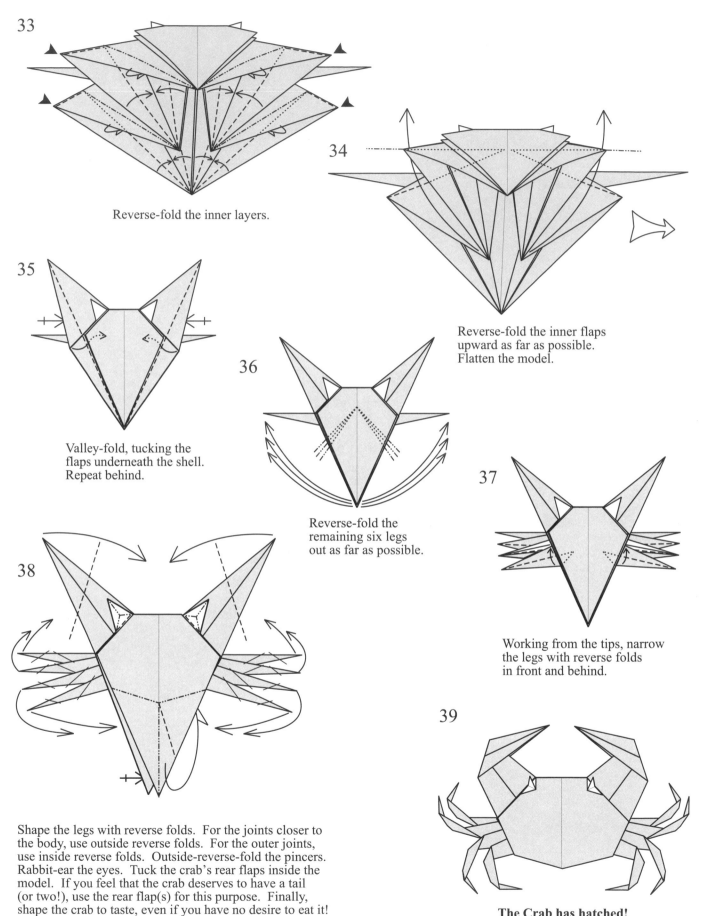

33

Reverse-fold the inner layers.

34

Reverse-fold the inner flaps
upward as far as possible.
Flatten the model.

35

Valley-fold, tucking the
flaps underneath the shell.
Repeat behind.

36

Reverse-fold the
remaining six legs
out as far as possible.

37

Working from the tips, narrow
the legs with reverse folds
in front and behind.

38

Shape the legs with reverse folds. For the joints closer to
the body, use outside reverse folds. For the outer joints,
use inside reverse folds. Outside-reverse-fold the pincers.
Rabbit-ear the eyes. Tuck the crab's rear flaps inside the
model. If you feel that the crab deserves to have a tail
(or two!), use the rear flap(s) for this purpose. Finally,
shape the crab to taste, even if you have no desire to eat it!

39

The Crab has hatched!

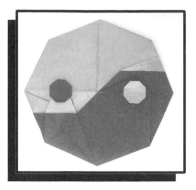

Double Yin Yang

Come gather around, 'tis time to learn
Something much more than a fish or ring—
Come fold ye this symbol of ancient times:
The Double Yin Yang of Tao Te Ching.

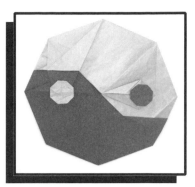

1

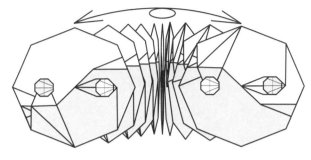

Corner to corner, crease to crease,
Let the whole journey thus commence;
We'll trek us across the endless folds
And hope that these diagrams make some sense.

7

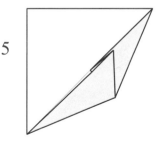

Is a falling tree silent
    if no one's around?
Is a diagram absent
    when there's no fold?
No! No! In absence
    is presence profound
like **flipping aback**
    to the side of old.

2

6

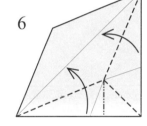

Valley-the-fold
    and undo the fold;
The Taoist Te Ching
    has much to tell.

Life is much like
    origami designed
Diagrammed, folded
    and played with by ear:
By nature we're all
    life designers in kind
Creative **rabbit-ear**ing
    radiant cheer.

3

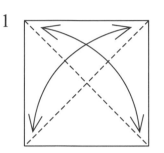

Of patterns relived,
    of tales retold
By sight by touch
    by taste or smell.

4

Rabbit-the-ear... Take time to listen
To nothing but silence, so we can hear
Our breath, our heart and our intuition,
To find our right path and leap without fear.

5

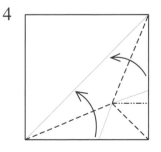

To walk on water, to swim in earth,
To carve the metal, to forge the wood,
To juggle the fire in merry mirth
We dig up and **over turn** sorrow for good.

8

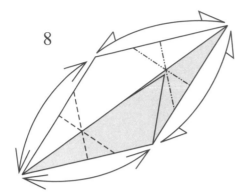

On one end we valley it point-to-point;
The other requires a mountainous hike.
This model like paper has two sides conjoined
That though contrast in color in look look alike.

9

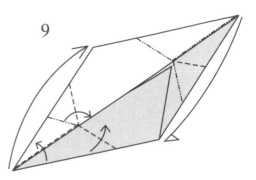

Rabbit-the-ear, both corners fly:
One goes in front, the other behind.
The Yin is the earth, the Yang, the sky;
The Yin is our body, the Yang, our mind.

10

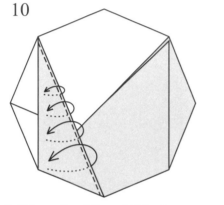

Pull 'em all out those hidden layers,
Swing 'em around and lay 'em in front;
We take a small moment to say our prayers
for soon we'll attempt a challenging stunt.

11

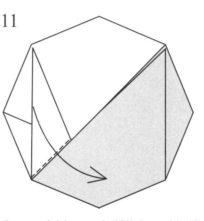

Our model is now half light and half dark,
But still all its features are left untold;
On trickier folds we must embark,
But first, make a trivial valley fold.

12

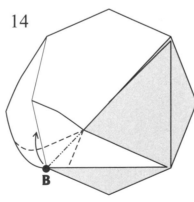

Now crease both those perpy pendiculars—
Look to point **A** to guide the way;
Make both these creases shine like stars
And make sure they both run into point **A**.

13

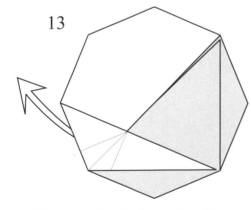

Get ready-set-go for that radical ride
By pulling the back layer out from behind;
Make this back paper peep out the side.
The next drawing shown is the 3-D kind.

14

Reverse-fold point **B**, a radical pleat—
The crease marks existing show where at;

15

Now we're in process (still in 3-D)
Of collapsing the flaps so all lies flat.

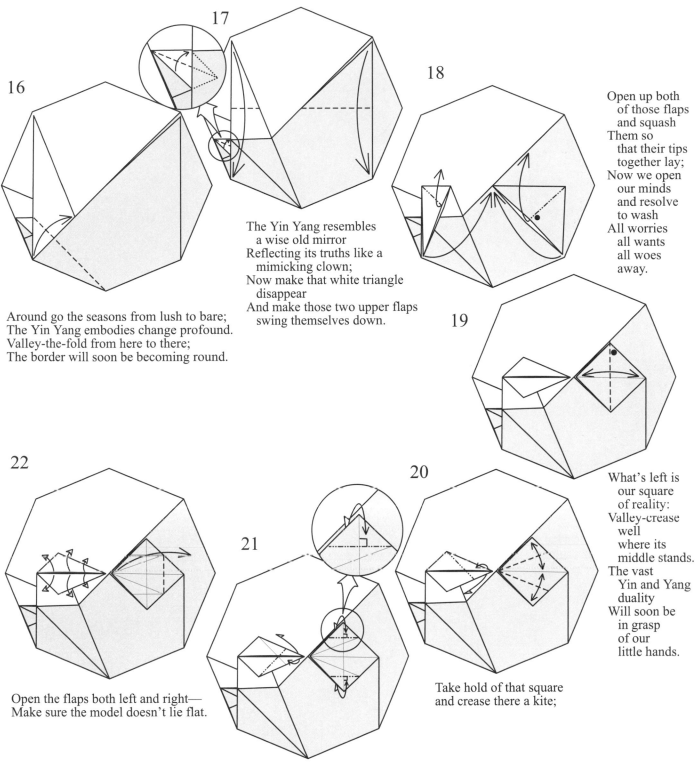

16

Around go the seasons from lush to bare;
The Yin Yang embodies change profound.
Valley-the-fold from here to there;
The border will soon be becoming round.

17

The Yin Yang resembles
a wise old mirror
Reflecting its truths like a
mimicking clown;
Now make that white triangle
disappear
And make those two upper flaps
swing themselves down.

18

Open up both
of those flaps
and squash
Them so
that their tips
together lay;
Now we open
our minds
and resolve
to wash
All worries
all wants
all woes
away.

19

What's left is
our square
of reality:
Valley-crease
well
where its
middle stands.
The vast
Yin and Yang
duality
Will soon be
in grasp
of our
little hands.

20

Take hold of that square
and crease there a kite;

21

The ends of the creases put mountains at;

22

Open the flaps both left and right—
Make sure the model doesn't lie flat.

Thoughts Behind the Folds

The idea to fold a yin yang came from looking through the dictionary for pictures to fold. At first I was just trying to make it one-sided, but my design ended up with two extra flaps on the back, which gave me the idea of making it two-sided and iso-area. The idea of writing all the directions in poetry was simply a naive, immense undertaking that took forever and will never be repeated. **Challenge:** Rewrite this entire book in poetry... and then get a life!

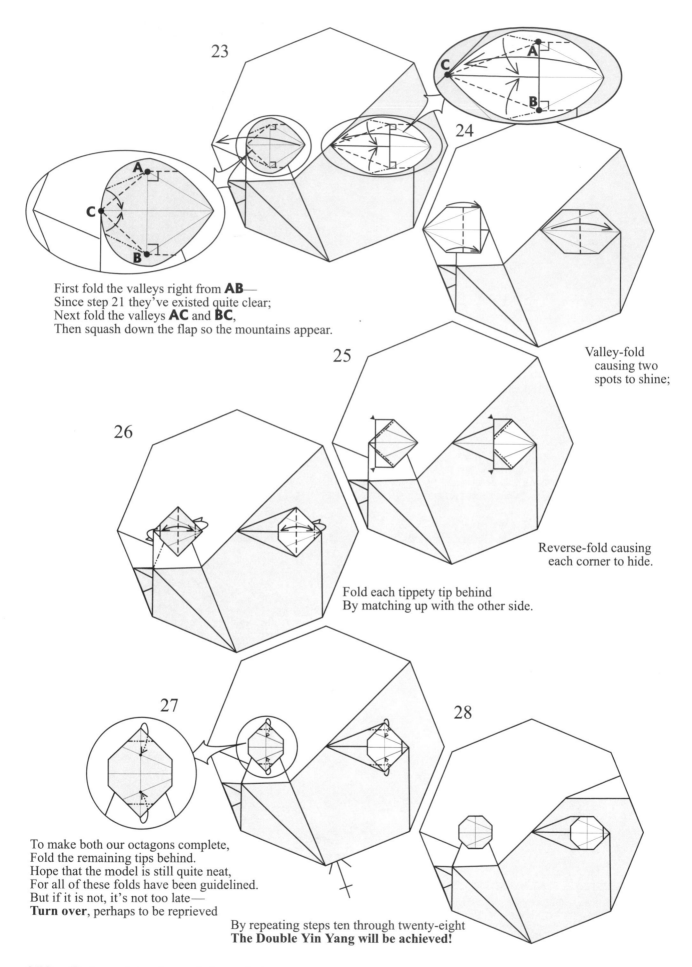

23

24

First fold the valleys right from **AB**—
Since step 21 they've existed quite clear;
Next fold the valleys **AC** and **BC**,
Then squash down the flap so the mountains appear.

Valley-fold
causing two
spots to shine;

25

26

Reverse-fold causing
each corner to hide.

Fold each tippety tip behind
By matching up with the other side.

27

28

To make both our octagons complete,
Fold the remaining tips behind.
Hope that the model is still quite neat,
For all of these folds have been guidelined.
But if it is not, it's not too late—
Turn over, perhaps to be reprieved

By repeating steps ten through twenty-eight
The Double Yin Yang will be achieved!

Star of David

Be amused as your audience of stargazers is astonished that this woven Star of David is from one square, no cuts!

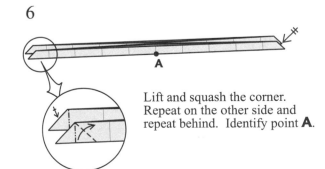

1

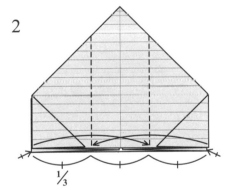

For best results, use Japanese foil ten inches square or larger. Make sure that you have folded Two Permanently Interlocking Rings (page 48). Begin by folding a Waterbomb Base, colored side out. Divide its height into 16ths. It doesn't matter whether you use mountains or valleys. Valley-fold and unfold the **Top** to the first 16th thereby making a 1/32 crease. Valley-fold and unfold the front **Side Tips** at the 1/16 mark and then valley-fold (and **don't** unfold) them at the 6/16 mark. Repeat behind on the back **Side Tips**.

2

Valley-fold the front in thirds. Repeat behind.

3

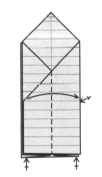

Valley-fold. Repeat on the flap underneath, and then repeat everything behind.

4

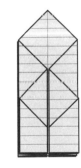

Unfold to the Waterbomb Base.

5

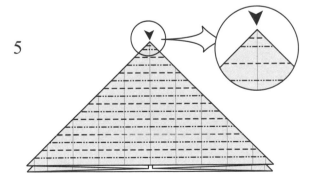

Pleat-sink completely including the top 1/32nd. If you are unfamiliar with pleat-sinking, first fold Two Interlocking Rings (page 46), and then Musical Notes (page 131).

6

Lift and squash the corner. Repeat on the other side and repeat behind. Identify point **A**.

Star of David **159**

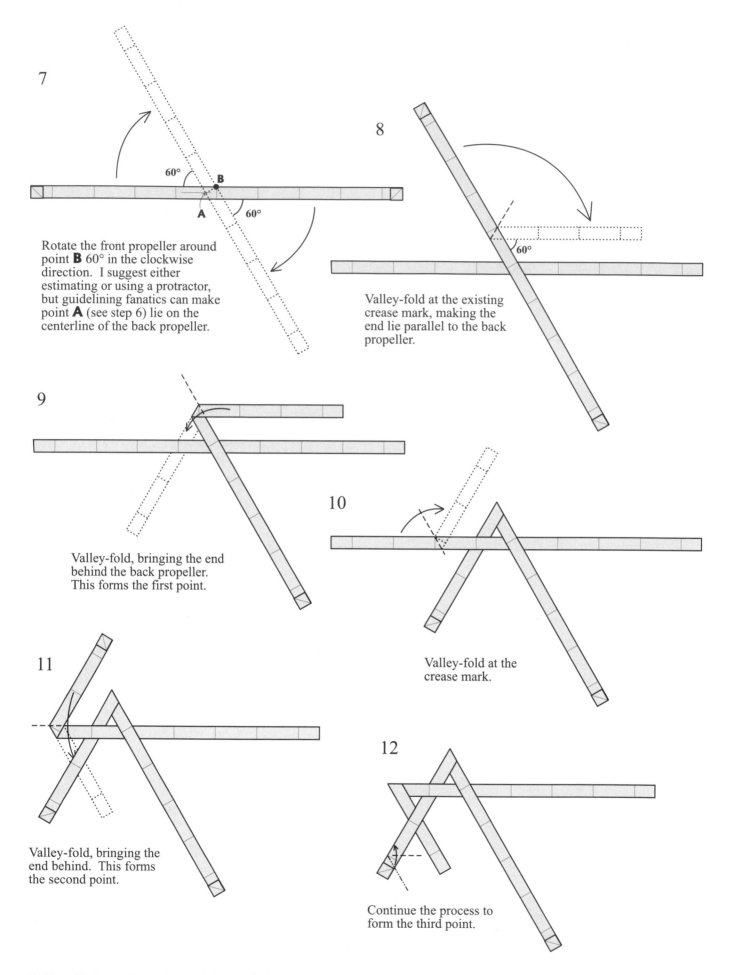

7

60°   **B**

60°

A

Rotate the front propeller around point **B** 60° in the clockwise direction. I suggest either estimating or using a protractor, but guidelining fanatics can make point **A** (see step 6) lie on the centerline of the back propeller.

8

60°

Valley-fold at the existing crease mark, making the end lie parallel to the back propeller.

9

Valley-fold, bringing the end behind the back propeller. This forms the first point.

10

Valley-fold at the crease mark.

11

Valley-fold, bringing the end behind. This forms the second point.

12

Continue the process to form the third point.

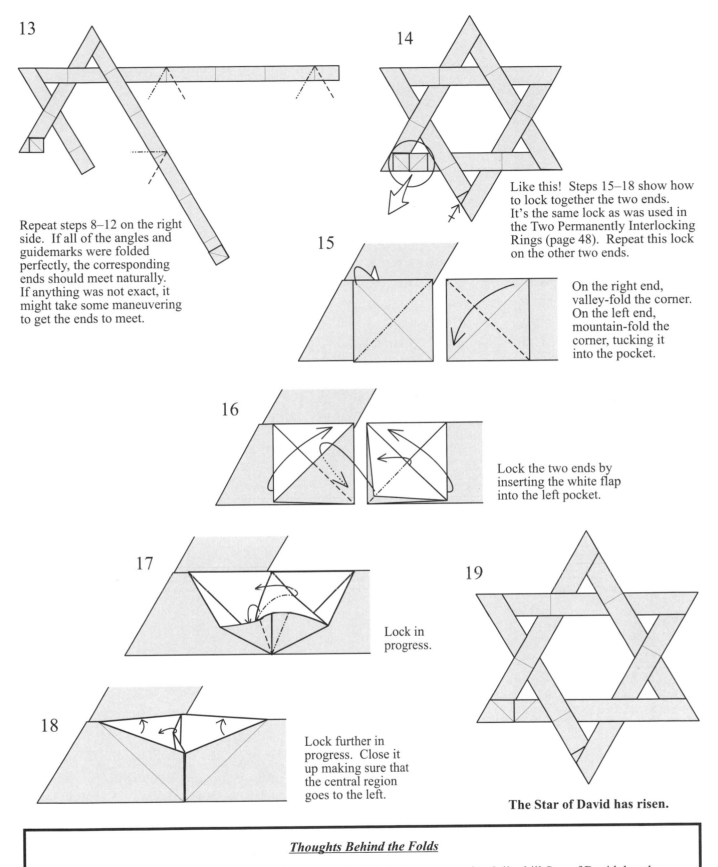

13

Repeat steps 8–12 on the right side. If all of the angles and guidemarks were folded perfectly, the corresponding ends should meet naturally. If anything was not exact, it might take some maneuvering to get the ends to meet.

14

Like this! Steps 15–18 show how to lock together the two ends. It's the same lock as was used in the Two Permanently Interlocking Rings (page 48). Repeat this lock on the other two ends.

15

On the right end, valley-fold the corner. On the left end, mountain-fold the corner, tucking it into the pocket.

16

Lock the two ends by inserting the white flap into the left pocket.

17

Lock in progress.

18

Lock further in progress. Close it up making sure that the central region goes to the left.

19

The Star of David has risen.

Thoughts Behind the Folds

My inspiration to fold a Star of David came from seeing Fred Rohm's very popular dollar bill Star of David, but the design came directly from the Two Interlocking Rings. Finding the exact guidelines was the trickiest part of the design process. There are endless other potential models hidden in the sunken Waterbomb Base. **Challenge:** Design something from the sunken Waterbomb Base. **Ideas:** Dancing snakes, working scissors, cutoff braid, Saturn, eight-pointed star.

Spider Web

Editor's disclaimer: No spiders were evicted in the designing, folding, or diagramming of this model.

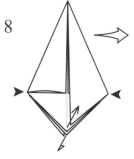

1
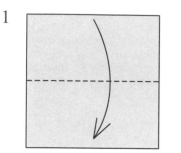

Use fly paper for best results! Colored side up. Valley-fold the top down to the bottom.

2

Valley-fold on the left. Mountain-fold on the right.

3

Open the middle pocket while pushing in at the sides.

4
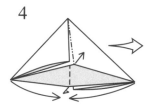

In progress.

5

The Square Base is complete. Valley-fold to the centerline on both sides.

6
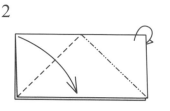

Pull out the two inner flaps.

7

Mountain-fold on the left. Valley-fold on the right.

8

Open the middle pocket while pushing in at the sides.

9
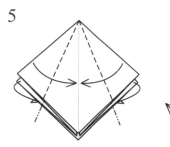

In progress.

10

Pleat-sink tastefully. To do this, first make mountains and valleys through all layers as shown— the more pleats, the more strands of web. When all the pleats are in place, unfold the model completely.

11
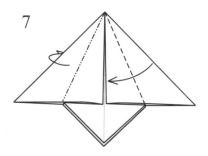

Pleat-sinking in progress. Starting with the concentric octagons, rearrange the existing creases as indicated. It's easiest to move outside in. Then fold it back up. If you get **stuck**, call it a completed model... "Sticky Web of Creases."

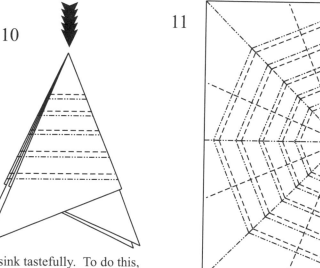

162 *Origami to Astonish and Amuse*

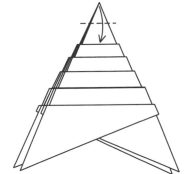

12

The model has been pleat-sunk.
Valley-fold the top down.

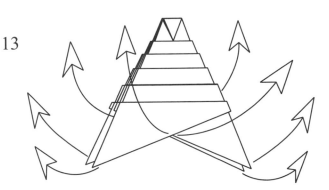

13

Open up the model from underneath. Don't let any of the horizontal
folds unfold. With the colored side up, squash the model flat any
which way. Randomness is good. Make sure the back flaps are
all flattened to the same direction (clockwise or counterclockwise).
Don't let the top unfold.

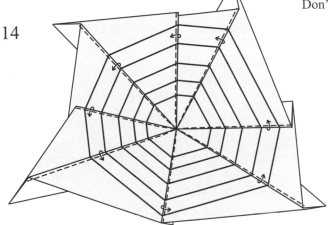

14

Form valley folds near each radial edge,
making the edges into thin spokes that stick up.

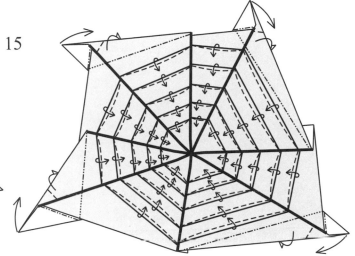

15

Valley-fold near the concentric folds so that the
edges stick up. These new folds should be curved.
Mountain-fold the outside edges behind, flattening
the white tips as indicated.

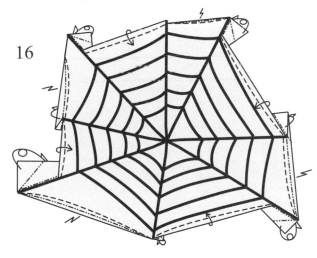

16

Pleat along the outside edges to form the outermost
strands of web. Mountain-fold each colored corner twice.

17

The Spider Web has been woven.
Throw some stinky glue on it and it
might even catch you some bugs.
Fold it out of a dollar bill and it might
even catch some capitalists!

Thoughts Behind the Folds

The idea of folding a spider web came from walking around my back
yard looking for subjects to fold. I came upon a nice little spider named
Charlotte who had spun a very pretty web, which I decided to try to
design in paper. **Challenge:** Try making Charlotte positioned in the
center of the web. Next, try writing words in the web.

$ Pyramid

Turn your dollars into something
worth something. House your savings
in dollar pyramids. But remember,
do not sell this pyramid for less than a dollar!

1

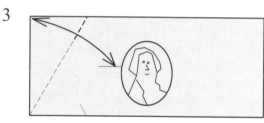

Begin with a crisp dollar bill face up.
Valley-pinch in half just to the left
of the oval.

2

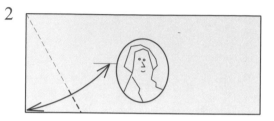

Anchoring the crease at the upper left corner,
bring the lower left corner to the existing pinch
mark, and put a pinch mark at the bottom edge.

3

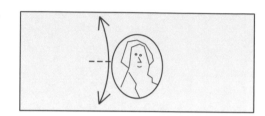

Bring the upper left corner to the existing
pinch mark, and put a pinch mark at the top edge.
Turn over.

4

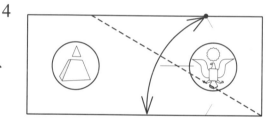

Bring the bottom edge to the upper pinch
mark and crease sharply.

5

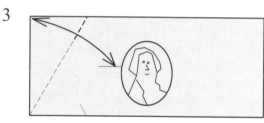

Bring the top edge to the lower pinch mark
and crease sharply.

6

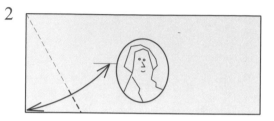

Valley-fold the lower right corner
to point **A** and unfold. Valley-fold the
upper right corner to point **B** and unfold.
Turn over.

7

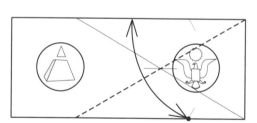

Valley-fold bisections and unfold.

8

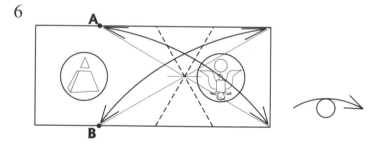

Mountain-fold and unfold. **Turn over.**

9

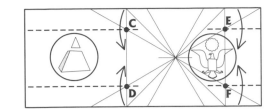
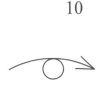

Valley-fold to the left of points **C** and **D** and to the right of points **E** and **F**. **Turn over.**

10

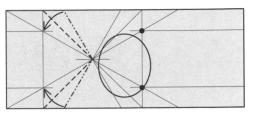

Pleat along existing creases. The model will not lie flat.

11

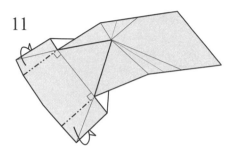

Mountain-fold.

12

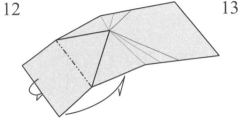

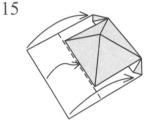

Mountain-fold.

13

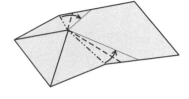

Pleat along existing creases. The model still will not lie flat, darn it!

14

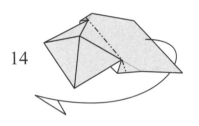

Mountain-fold.

15

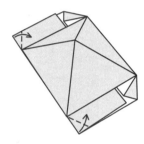

Valley-fold the protruding edge underneath the pyramid.

16

Valley-fold.

17

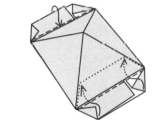

Insert the remaining tabs into the pyramid so that they touch the inside surfaces of the walls.

18

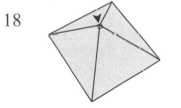

If you plan to balance an Eagle on the Pyramid, then make a tiny closed sink at the top. If you want to be precise about it you have to unfold the model completely and make the mountain folds individually. If you would rather fake it, simply poke the top in with a pointed tool.

19

The Pyramid has been built. And it didn't even take thousands of slaves hundreds of years.

Thoughts Behind the Folds

The idea of designing the Pyramid came out of a search for a stand for the Balancing Eagle. Looking at the back of a dollar bill, I saw the eagle and pyramid and knew right away that the pyramid would make the perfect stand. I've long enjoyed folding geometrical models and find it to be good mind exercise (which is partly why I majored in math in college). Compared to many of my other models, the Pyramid was rather straightforward to design, since it has such a clear form. The challenge was to find a design with a good lock that wasted as little paper as possible and then find a clean diagrammable folding method free of visible extra creases. **Challenge:** What other geometrical solids can you design? As an extra challenge, see if you can use any extra flaps to make something zany. **Ideas:** Flying walking tetrahedron, duck on a magic cube, slug-infested octahedron, stellated icosahedron (more zany than it sounds... I almost went crazy once trying to fold it!).

Balancing $ Eagle

Tired of trying to balance your checkbook? Try this model instead. It's much easier to balance and more fun too!

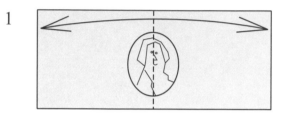

1 Begin face up. Valley-fold and unfold in half.

2 Make valley pinches at the sides.

3 Make two more valley pinches at the sides.

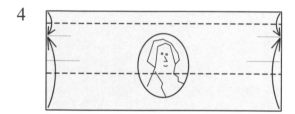

4 Valley-fold the top and bottom edges to the crease marks you just made.

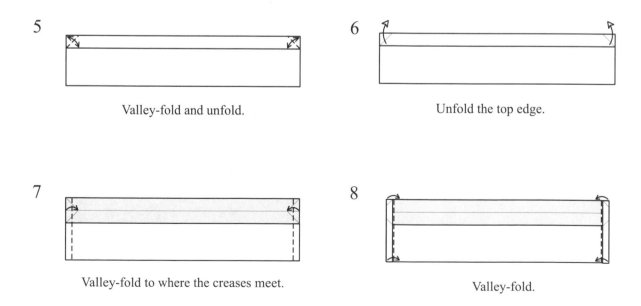

5 Valley-fold and unfold.

6 Unfold the top edge.

7 Valley-fold to where the creases meet.

8 Valley-fold.

9

Valley-fold.

10

Valley-fold.

11

Valley-fold.

12

Outside-reverse-fold.

13

Outside-reverse-fold.

14

Valley-fold the near flap down.

15

Valley-fold the wings together, while making a Fish Base out of the body.

16

Valley-fold and unfold. Think thirds!

17

Sink.

Thoughts Behind the Folds

The idea of folding the Balancing Eagle came from seeing the plastic version in a toy store. Since the wing span was so much greater than the distance between the head and tail, I resorted to starting from a rectangle. Whenever I drift away from the purity of the square, I like to first try taking refuge in the security of the dollar bill, which I know will at least appeal to a large number of American folders. Once I had succeeded in designing the dollar bill Balancing Eagle, my next task was to design a stand for it, which I thought should also be from a dollar, but what to make? Staring at the dollar, the pyramid on the back side jumped out at me and the rest was history. My final challenge was to readjust the eagle design to make the eagle and pyramid on the dollar come out on the wing tops of the eagle. **Exercise:** Visit a toy store and search for subjects to fold.

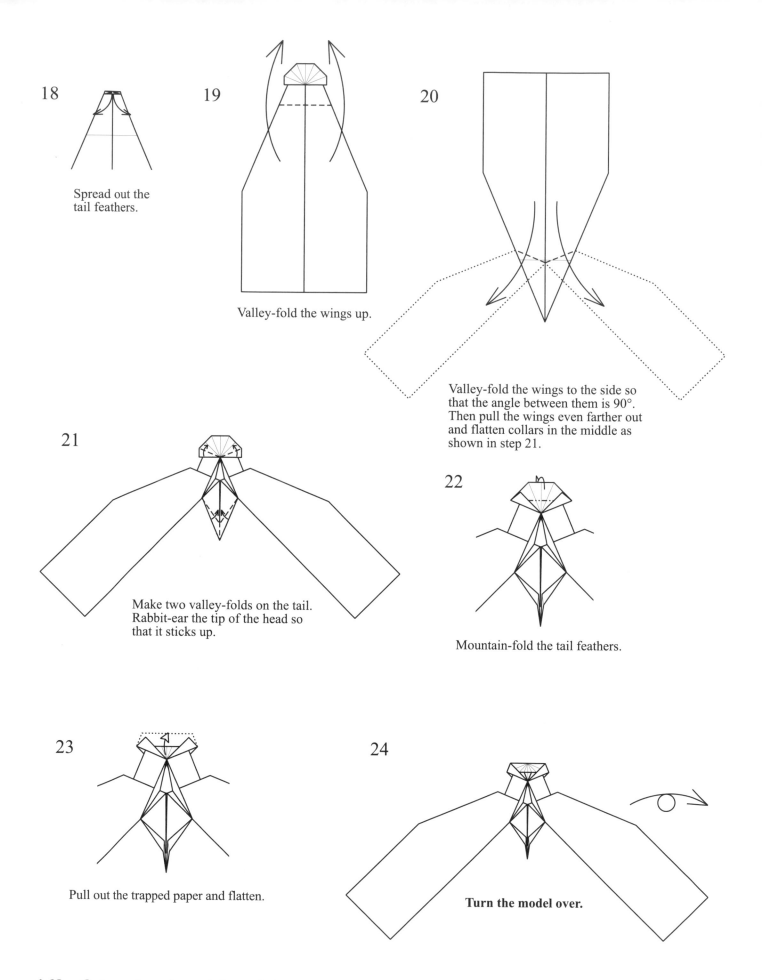

18

Spread out the
tail feathers.

19

Valley-fold the wings up.

20

Valley-fold the wings to the side so
that the angle between them is 90°.
Then pull the wings even farther out
and flatten collars in the middle as
shown in step 21.

21

Make two valley-folds on the tail.
Rabbit-ear the tip of the head so
that it sticks up.

22

Mountain-fold the tail feathers.

23

Pull out the trapped paper and flatten.

24

Turn the model over.

25

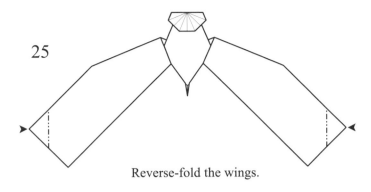

Reverse-fold the wings.

26

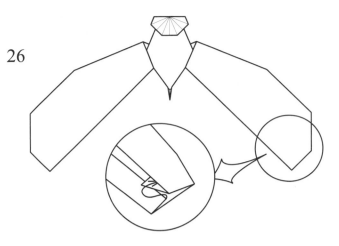

Make the end of the wing lock nicely by inserting the lower layer into the upper layer.

27

Valley-fold and unfold.

28

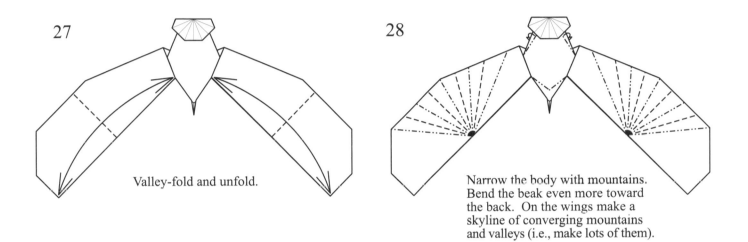

Narrow the body with mountains. Bend the beak even more toward the back. On the wings make a skyline of converging mountains and valleys (i.e., make lots of them).

29

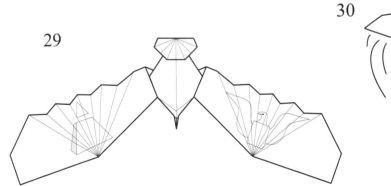

The Eagle has soared into existence.
If done correctly, the pyramid on the dollar bill should end up on the right wing and the eagle should end up on the left wing. (From the Eagle's perspective.)

30

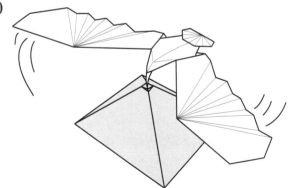

Now try to balance the Eagle on the Pyramid (or your finger). Reposition the beak until you find the center of balance. Then, take him for a spin!

Dollar Bill Cuboid

If you like cubist art, then this model is for you!
Six cubes from just one dollar! Just goes to
show, a dollar can still go a long way.

Warning: Although the Dollar Bill Cuboid can be folded out of a crisp dollar bill (hence
its name!), it is advisable at least for your first try to use a larger rectangle. The dimensions
need not be exact, just around 3 by 7, but the paper must be an exact rectangle, and all
creases must be made razor sharp!

1

Begin colored side up, or if you are using a dollar
bill, begin face up. Valley-fold in half and unfold.

2

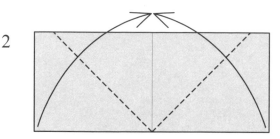

Paper-airplane-fold up.

3

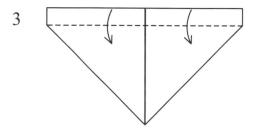

Valley-fold both edges down so that the
resulting creases lie on the hidden back edge.

4

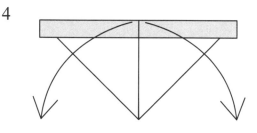

Open out to form a 1 by 2 rectangle.

5

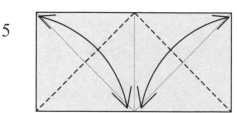

Valley-fold and unfold.

6

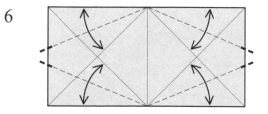

Valley-fold and unfold the edges to the
diagonals, but actually crease only at the left
and right edges (where boldly diagrammed).

7

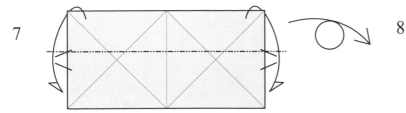

Mountain-fold the top edge behind so that the fold touches the left and right edges exactly at the crease marks made in step 6. This fold must be so exact that even an electron microscope should not be able to detect any error! **Next, turn the bill over.**

8

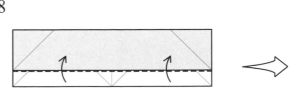

Valley-fold the bottom edge upward.

9

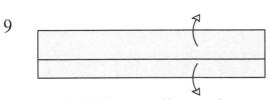

Unfold the top and bottom edges.

10

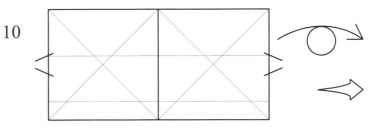

Turn over.

11

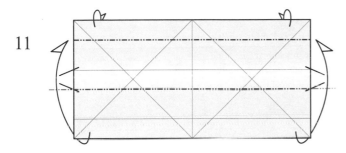

Repeat steps 7–10, beginning by folding the bottom edge behind with the same molecular accuracy as in step 7.

12

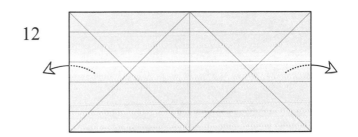

Unfold the bill completely.

13

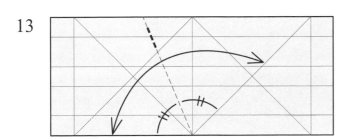

Bisect the indicated angle, but actually crease only where boldly diagrammed: **- - - -** .

14

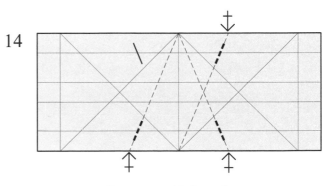

Repeat step 13 three times.

15

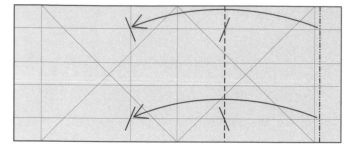

First, make the valley fold so that it goes through the two internal crease markers on the right (made in step 14). Then make the mountain fold so that it lies on the two left crease markers. Note that this mountain fold is different from the nearby existing crease.

16

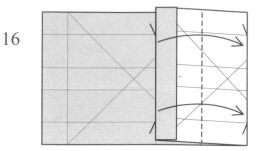

Valley-fold so that edge meets edge.

17

Unfold completely.

18

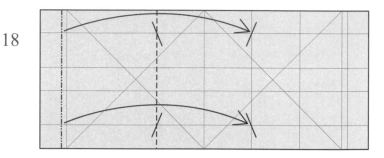

Once again, make the valley fold so that it goes through the two internal crease markers on the left (made in steps 13–14). Then make the mountain fold so that it lies on the two right crease markers.

19

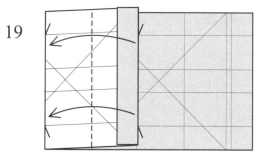

Valley-fold so that edge meets edge.

20

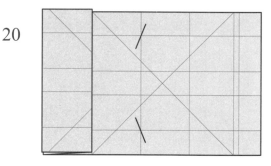

Unfold completely.

21

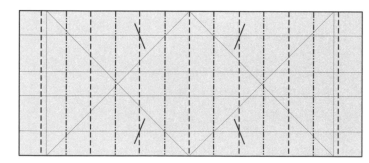

Using the existing creases as the valley folds, make a paper fan.

22

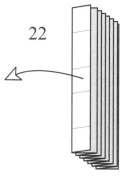

Play with the fan. Cool off. Then unfold it and go on to the next step.

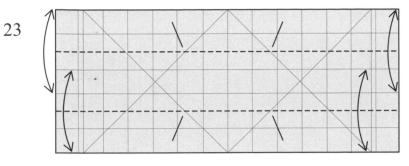

23

Valley-fold top and bottom edges to the indicated horizontal creases and unfold.
These creases are really unnecessary, and create extra creases on the final
model, but you may find them useful for steps 25–28.

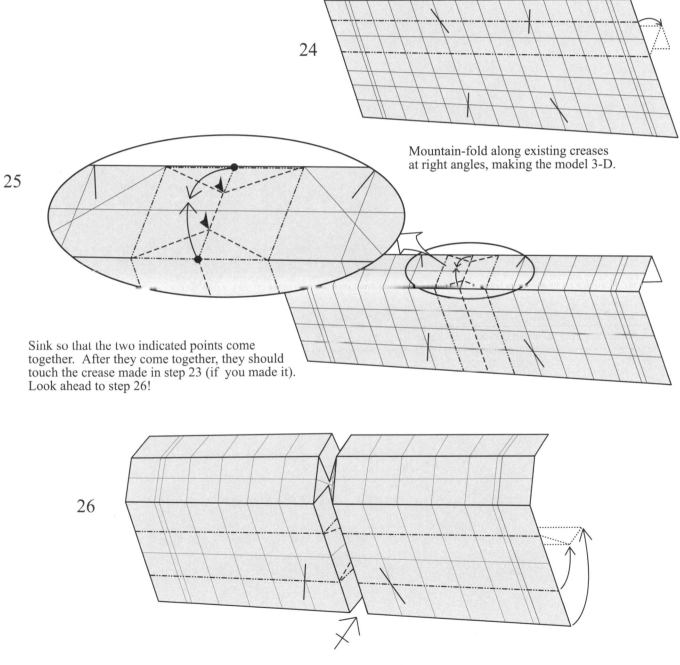

24

Mountain-fold along existing creases
at right angles, making the model 3-D.

25

Sink so that the two indicated points come
together. After they come together, they should
touch the crease made in step 23 (if you made it).
Look ahead to step 26!

26

Repeat steps 24–25 on the lower

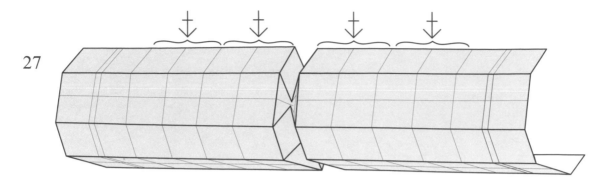

27

Repeat steps 25–26 on the four indicated segments.

28

Make four rabbit-ear-like folds, resulting in the collapse of both ends.

29

Play the accordion. Leave it in its outstretched position and go on to the next step.

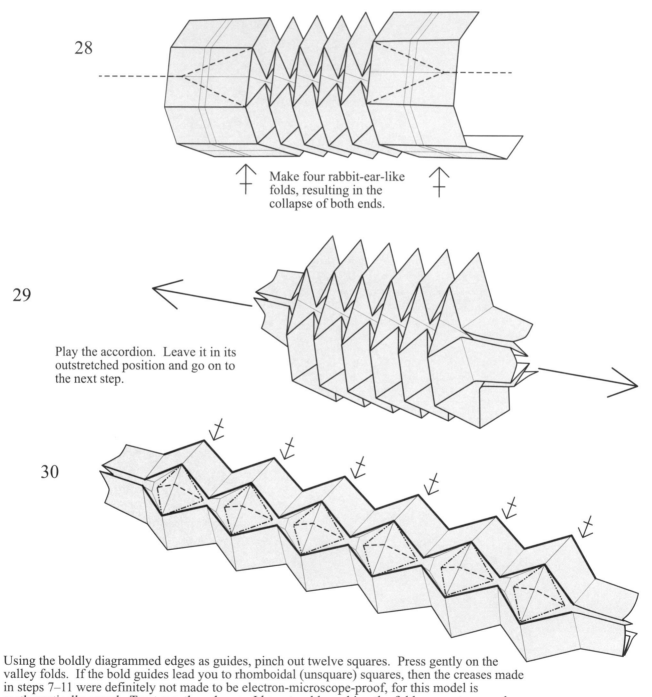

30

Using the boldly diagrammed edges as guides, pinch out twelve squares. Press gently on the valley folds. If the bold guides lead you to rhomboidal (unsquare) squares, then the creases made in steps 7–11 were definitely not made to be electron-microscope-proof, for this model is mathematically sound. Trust me, though even I have trouble making the folds accurate enough.

31

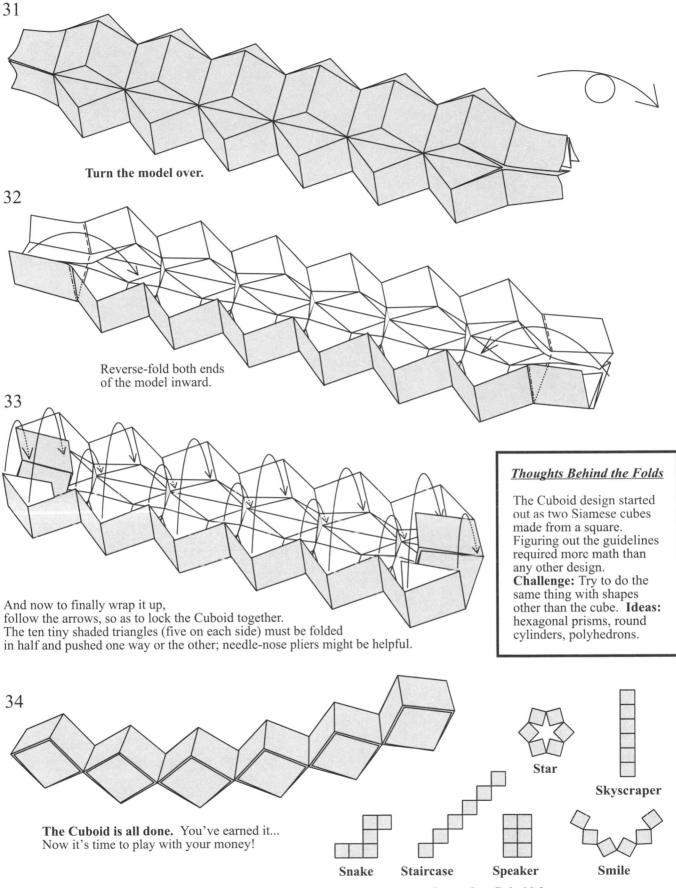

Turn the model over.

32

Reverse-fold both ends
of the model inward.

33

And now to finally wrap it up,
follow the arrows, so as to lock the Cuboid together.
The ten tiny shaded triangles (five on each side) must be folded
in half and pushed one way or the other; needle-nose pliers might be helpful.

Thoughts Behind the Folds

The Cuboid design started
out as two Siamese cubes
made from a square.
Figuring out the guidelines
required more math than
any other design.
Challenge: Try to do the
same thing with shapes
other than the cube. **Ideas:**
hexagonal prisms, round
cylinders, polyhedrons.

34

The Cuboid is all done. You've earned it...
Now it's time to play with your money!

Snake   **Staircase**   **Speaker**   **Smile**

Star

Skyscraper

Just a few Cuboid forms.

Eight (or 2n) Interlocking Rings

This impossible-looking model is from one square, no cuts!
Theoretically there is no limit to the number of rings
that can be folded using this method. However it's no
piece of cake. The prerequisite for this model is the ability
to fold Two Permanently Interlocking Rings (page 48).

1

Begin with a three-inch square sheet of
paper. Just kidding! Japanese foil thirty
inches square or larger is recommended.
Colored side up, valley-fold and unfold
both diagonals.

2

Valley-fold and unfold
two opposite corners to
the center.

3

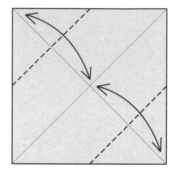

Make four new valley-creases,
thereby dividing the line **AB** into
eight equal sections. **Turn over.**

4

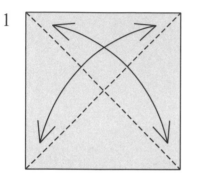

Make the two indicated pleats. The best
way to do this is to pinch up the two
existing mountain creases that are next to
the diagonal, **C-D**, and lay them both onto
C-D, thereby making two new valley folds.

5

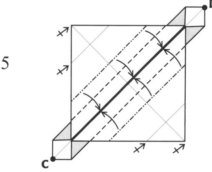

Repeat step 4 on each of the
other four parallel creases, and
fold the two corners in as well.

6

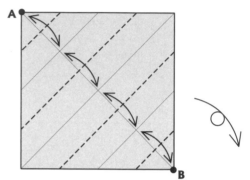

Notice there are eight white
diamonds. To fold twelve rings,
we would need twelve white
diamonds. Unfold the two
rearmost folds.

7

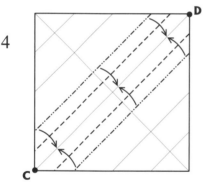

(22.5°)

Valley-fold and unfold
edge-to-edge, bisecting
the indicated angles.
Rotate the model 22.5°
counterclockwise.

8

(22.5°)

Valley-fold and
unfold on the front
layer only. Rotate
the model 22.5°
counterclockwise.

9

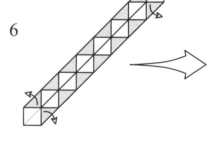

Valley-fold and
unfold on the
front layer only.

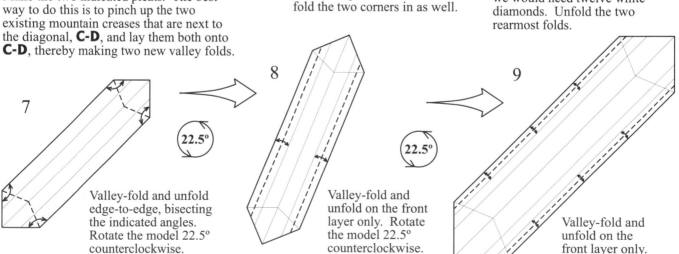

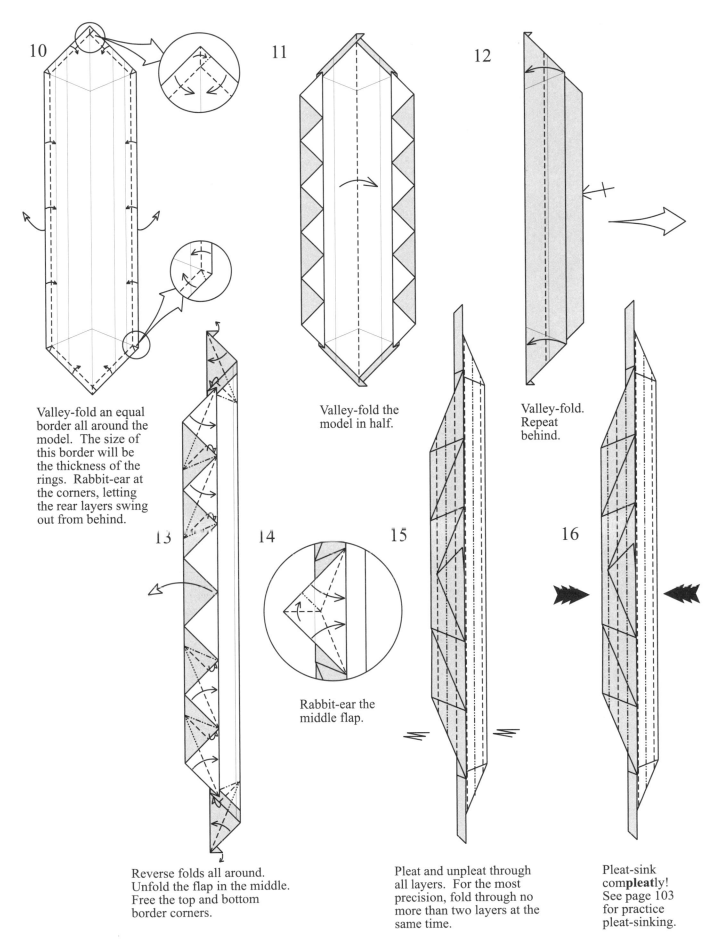

10

Valley-fold an equal
border all around the
model. The size of
this border will be
the thickness of the
rings. Rabbit-ear at
the corners, letting
the rear layers swing
out from behind.

11

Valley-fold the
model in half.

12

Valley-fold.
Repeat
behind.

13

Reverse folds all around.
Unfold the flap in the middle.
Free the top and bottom
border corners.

14

Rabbit-ear the
middle flap.

15

Pleat and unpleat through
all layers. For the most
precision, fold through no
more than two layers at the
same time.

16

Pleat-sink
com**pleat**ly!
See page 103
for practice
pleat-sinking.

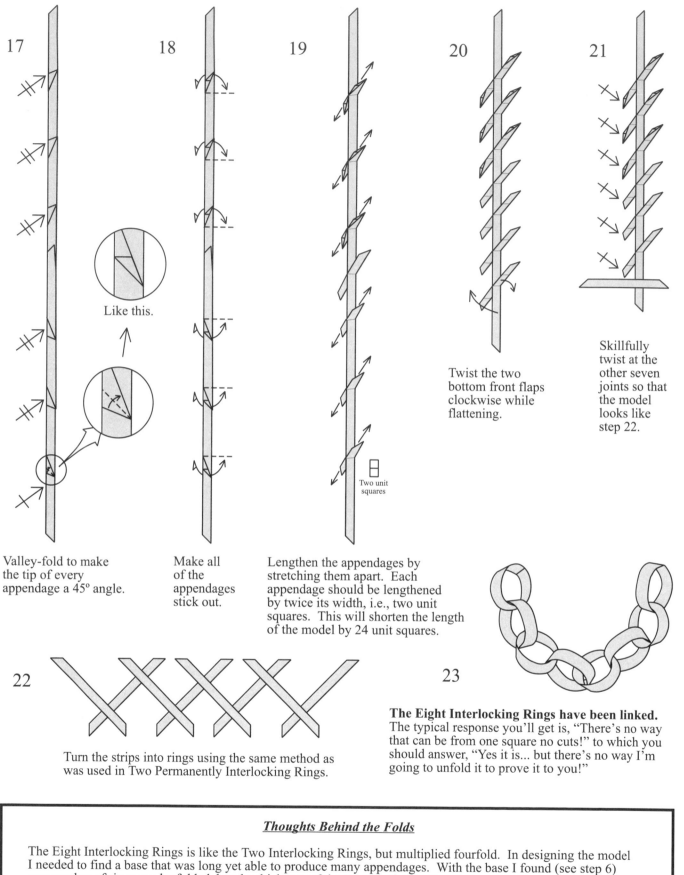

17

18

Like this.

19

20

21

22

23

Valley-fold to make the tip of every appendage a 45° angle.

Make all of the appendages stick out.

Lengthen the appendages by stretching them apart. Each appendage should be lengthened by twice its width, i.e., two unit squares. This will shorten the length of the model by 24 unit squares.

Two unit squares

Twist the two bottom front flaps clockwise while flattening.

Skillfully twist at the other seven joints so that the model looks like step 22.

Turn the strips into rings using the same method as was used in Two Permanently Interlocking Rings.

The Eight Interlocking Rings have been linked. The typical response you'll get is, "There's no way that can be from one square no cuts!" to which you should answer, "Yes it is... but there's no way I'm going to unfold it to prove it to you!"

Thoughts Behind the Folds

The Eight Interlocking Rings is like the Two Interlocking Rings, but multiplied fourfold. In designing the model I needed to find a base that was long yet able to produce many appendages. With the base I found (see step 6) any number of rings can be folded, but the thickness of the paper is the limiting factor. **Challenge:** How many interlocking rings can you make? Also, what else can this model be? **Ideas:** Centipede (step 20), millipede, fence (step 22), very crooked railroad tracks (step 22), tire tread marks (step 22), Christmas tree paper chain (step 23).

Models from the Heart

No need for money
Gifts of love are worth much more
Equal rich and poor

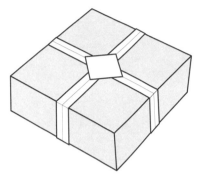

Origami

In Creasing Peace Fully All Ways.

**Thanks to the story of Sadako and the 1000 Cranes,
the traditional crane has become a symbol of world peace.
Folders hope that in the 21st century origami will be increasingly used
to help bring peace and compassion to Earth and all its inhabitants.
This section is devoted to models that express love and friendship—
models we can send to our loved ones and
use to help generate new loved ones.**

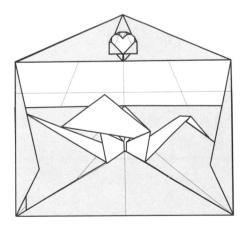

Butterfly Heart Card

This makes a great first model to teach to a large class because it's easy and exercises the imagination. When teaching it, I ask the students at each step what they think the model looks like.

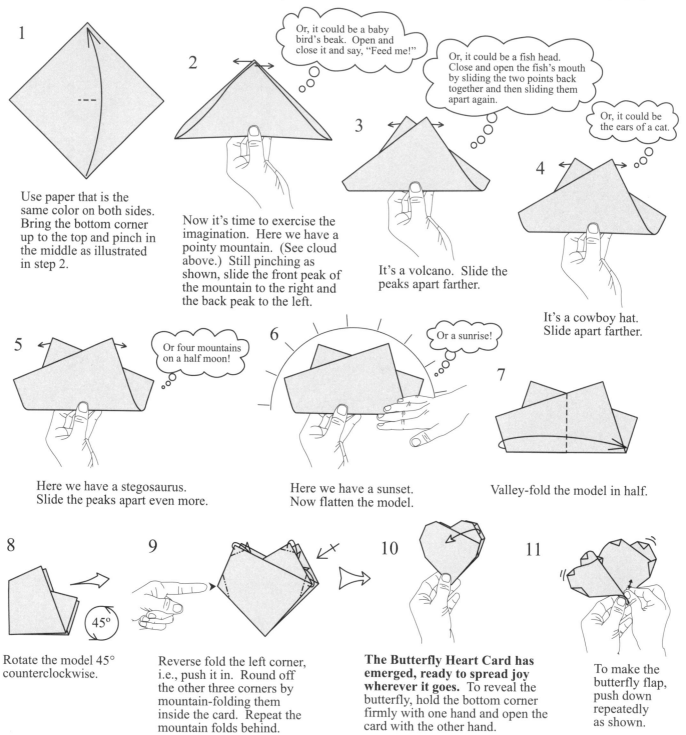

1

Use paper that is the same color on both sides. Bring the bottom corner up to the top and pinch in the middle as illustrated in step 2.

2

Or, it could be a baby bird's beak. Open and close it and say, "Feed me!"

Now it's time to exercise the imagination. Here we have a pointy mountain. (See cloud above.) Still pinching as shown, slide the front peak of the mountain to the right and the back peak to the left.

3

Or, it could be a fish head. Close and open the fish's mouth by sliding the two points back together and then sliding them apart again.

It's a volcano. Slide the peaks apart farther.

4

Or, it could be the ears of a cat.

It's a cowboy hat. Slide apart farther.

5

Or four mountains on a half moon!

Here we have a stegosaurus. Slide the peaks apart even more.

6

Or a sunrise!

Here we have a sunset. Now flatten the model.

7

Valley-fold the model in half.

8

Rotate the model 45° counterclockwise.

9

Reverse fold the left corner, i.e., push it in. Round off the other three corners by mountain-folding them inside the card. Repeat the mountain folds behind.

10

The Butterfly Heart Card has emerged, ready to spread joy wherever it goes. To reveal the butterfly, hold the bottom corner firmly with one hand and open the card with the other hand.

11

To make the butterfly flap, push down repeatedly as shown.

Cubist
Heart Card

Take heart! Here's a heart card that's so simple to fold that even the world's most celebrated novices will be able to tackle it with ease.

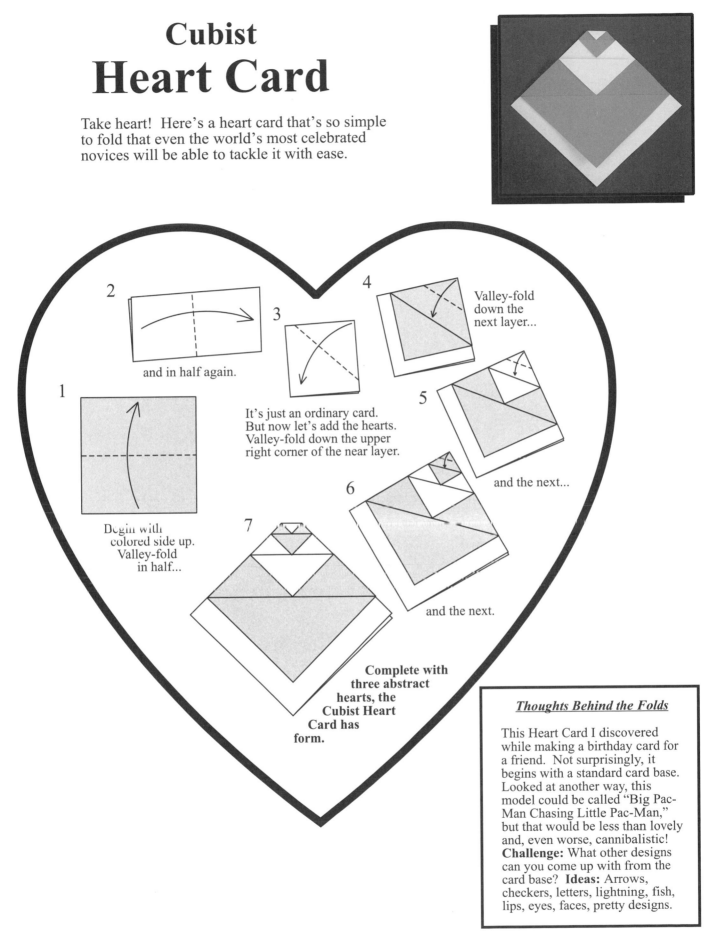

2

and in half again.

3

It's just an ordinary card. But now let's add the hearts. Valley-fold down the upper right corner of the near layer.

1

Begin with colored side up. Valley-fold in half...

4

Valley-fold down the next layer...

5

and the next...

6

and the next.

7

Complete with three abstract hearts, the Cubist Heart Card has form.

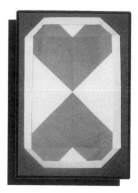

Window
Heart Card

This model demonstrates that folding that which isn't a heart can outline and reveal that which is.

1

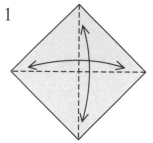

Colored side up. Valley-fold and unfold diagonally in half both ways.

2

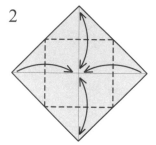

Valley-fold the four corners to the center. Unfold the top and bottom corners.

3

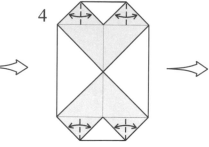

Valley-fold. Jump for joy!

4

If you're in a hurry, **skip to step 7** and estimate the valley folds. But, to capture the octagonal beauty of the model, valley-fold and unfold as shown above.

5

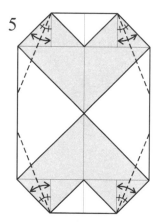

Valley-fold and unfold to the existing vertical crease.

6

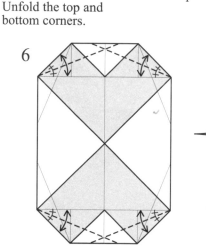

Valley-fold and unfold to the existing horizontal crease.

7

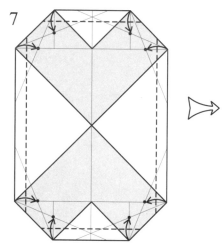

Valley-fold to the intersections of the existing creases (i.e., to the black dots).

8

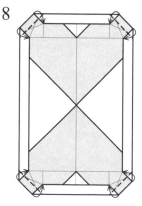

Valley-fold to complete the octagonal rounding of the hearts. You may stop jumping now.

9

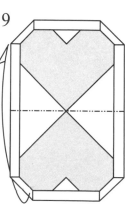

Mountain-fold in half, making a card with a heart on each side.

10

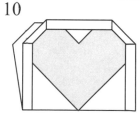

The Window Heart Card has come into view. Now, open the card, hold it up to a light and see how the light shines through. For the ultimate stained glass effect, fold the model out of translucent paper.

Thoughts Behind the Folds

This model came about from playing with Glassine, a colorful, translucent paper. Notice that the tops of the hearts are halves of regular octagons. **Challenge:** What other designs can you come up with using this technique of folding the outline of the subject? **Ideas:** Hourglass (make from step 9), moon and stars, shooting star, black cat, witch on a broomstick.

Blintz Envelope

It would take a pretty nosy mail carrier to break into this envelope. This model also makes a great spinner. Simply open out the pockets and blow on it at the proper angle.

1

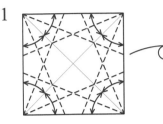

White side up. First, crease both diagonals. Then valley-fold and unfold kites in all directions. **Turn over.**

2

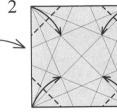

Valley-fold the corners to the intersections of the existing creases.

3

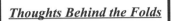

Mountain-fold on the existing crease. **Turn over.**

Thoughts Behind the Folds

The goal of this model was to make an aesthetic, efficient, durable, easy-to-fold, sensible, sendable envelope. I started with a traditional tato design (steps 1–7 skipping step 3) and tried to make it more secure, resulting in this model. **Challenge:** Experiment with step 7. See what designs you can make on the front of the envelope by folding the flaps symmetrically.

4

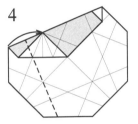

Valley-fold on the existing crease.

5

Do it again.

6

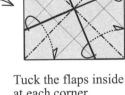

And again, but this time tuck the flap inside at the top. Oh, but first, it's time to fill the envelope with goodies.

7

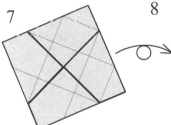

Turn over.

8

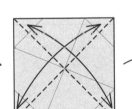

Valley-fold and unfold through all layers. **Turn over.**

9

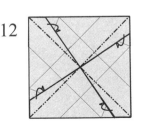

Tuck the flaps inside at each corner.

10

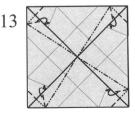

The well-sealed Blintz Envelope is ready to address, stamp and send. Uh oh, did you forget to fill it with goodies? If so, unfold to step 6 and do so.

11

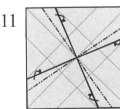

For an extra strong lock, begin at step 9. Mountain-fold the flaps to the diagonals.

12

Tuck the flaps inside.

13

The fully folded Extra Strong Blintz Envelope. For an even stronger lock, tuck the flaps inside again, pulling each corner toward the middle.

14

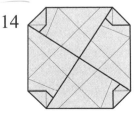

The fully folded Ultra Strong Blintz Envelope. If you're tired of folding, blow the model up like a balloon and you'll have yourself a fine pillow.

Envelope

For all you practical folders, here is a clean, sturdy envelope that won't even get mangled by the mail carriers! What's more, if you don't mind your envelope being unfolded by its recipient, you can write a letter on the white side, and your letter can then be folded into its own envelope, as follows.

1

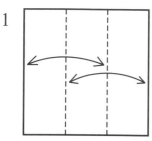

For a mailable Envelope, use paper no smaller than ten inches square. White side up, valley-fold and unfold in thirds.

2

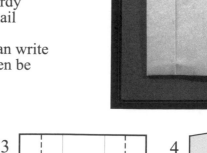

Here's one way to fold thirds. Holding as shown, fiddle with the folds until they line up.

3

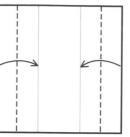

Valley-fold the sides inward to meet the existing creases.

4

Like this. **Turn the model over.**

5

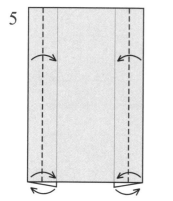

Valley-fold the sides inward to meet the existing creases, letting the two rear flaps swing to the outside.

6

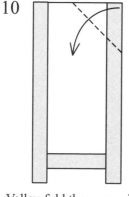

Like this. **Turn the model over.**

7

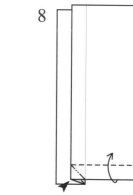

Valley-fold and unfold at a 45° angle.

8

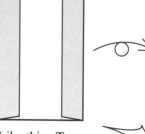

Valley-fold the bottom edge upward and flatten the lower corners.

9

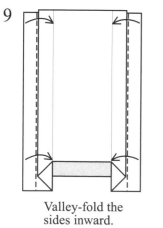

Valley-fold the sides inward.

10

Valley-fold the upper right corner to just past the middle of the model.

11

Valley-fold the upper left corner, making it even with the right flap.

12

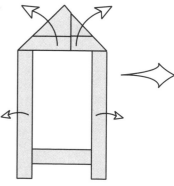

Like this. Unfold the model to step 9.

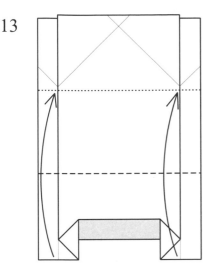

13

Valley-fold the bottom up to
just below the existing creases.

14

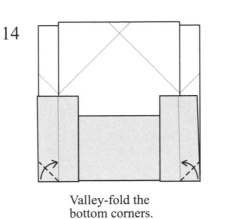

Valley-fold the
bottom corners.

15

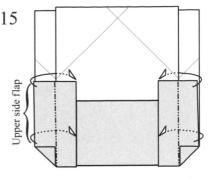

Upper side flap

Mountain-fold the upper side
flaps, tucking them into the
rearmost pockets.

Thoughts Behind the Folds

I used to require myself to design a new envelope every time I wrote a letter
to a friend. That's why I was often such an untimely pen pal. The goal of
this design was to make an envelope that looked and acted like a standard
envelope and could be sent safely through the mail without tape.
Challenge: Design an envelope filled with something punny like a letter
from the alphabet, a note from the C-major scale, or a bill from a duck.

16

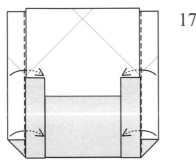

Valley-fold the side
flaps, tucking them
into the side pockets.

17

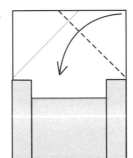

Valley-fold the
upper right
corner along the
existing crease.

18

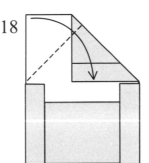

Valley-fold the
upper left
corner along the
existing crease.

19

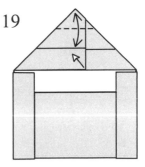

Valley-fold and unfold
the top. Lift and open
the upper left flap,
thereby exposing the
different layers.

20

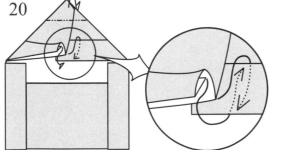

Lock the left and right flaps together by
wrapping the lower part of the left flap
around the lower part of the right flap, as
indicated by the arrows. Mountain-fold the
top behind, along the existing crease.

21

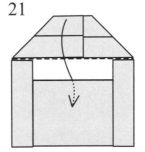

**The Envelope is crafted, ready
to seal.** To do this tapelessly,
first valley-fold the top down,
tucking it inside the envelope.

22

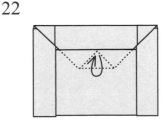

Then, reach inside the envelope
and wrap the tip of the
envelope flap around the layer
in front of it. Finally, violate
the doctrines of pure origami by
addressing, stamping and
sending the envelope... but
don't you dare use tape!

Envelope **185**

Off the Wallet

This extremely versatile cardholder is filled with pockets galore in which you can store everything from your fake ID cards to your confetti collection. This model will appeal to your origami sensibilities and make you want to send **off the wallet** of old to the dump.

1

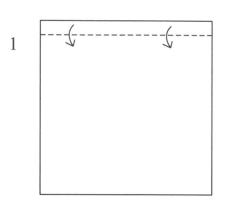

This model works best from a twelve-inch square of paper. Pages cut from a calendar work especially well. White side up, valley-fold the top edge arbitrarily down.

2

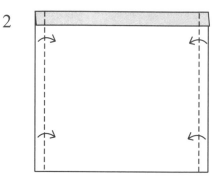

Valley-fold the side edges in, to taste.

3

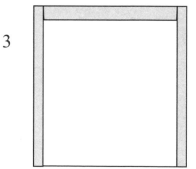

About like this. **Turn over.**

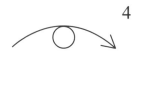

4

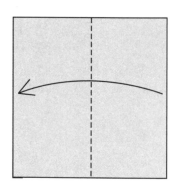

Valley-fold in half.

5

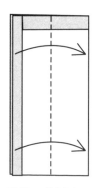

Valley-fold the near flap in half.

6

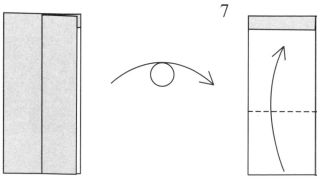

Turn over.

7

Valley-fold up yonder.

8

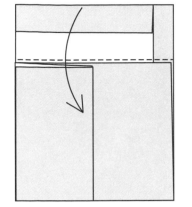

Valley-fold down yonder.

9

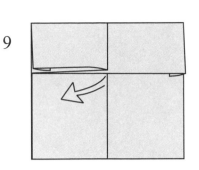

Pull out the hidden flap to somewhere where you can see it.

10

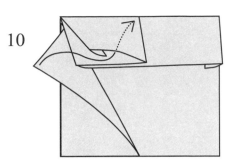

Stick it in that pocket, somewhere where you can't see it.

11

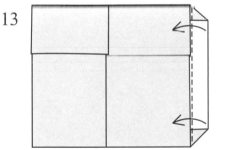

On both sides, wrap the flaps around the layer behind.

12

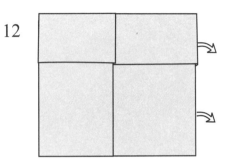

The wallet has about nine pockets. If you want one of them to be a change purse, pull out a flap.

13

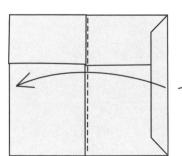

Close the purse pocket.

14

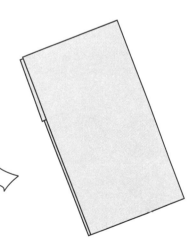

Off the Wallet is officially finished. Close it up.

15

This paper fun is as good as done; so call it a wallet and "son of a gun"— you've just won one! Two three plus four pockets for cards and money to store.

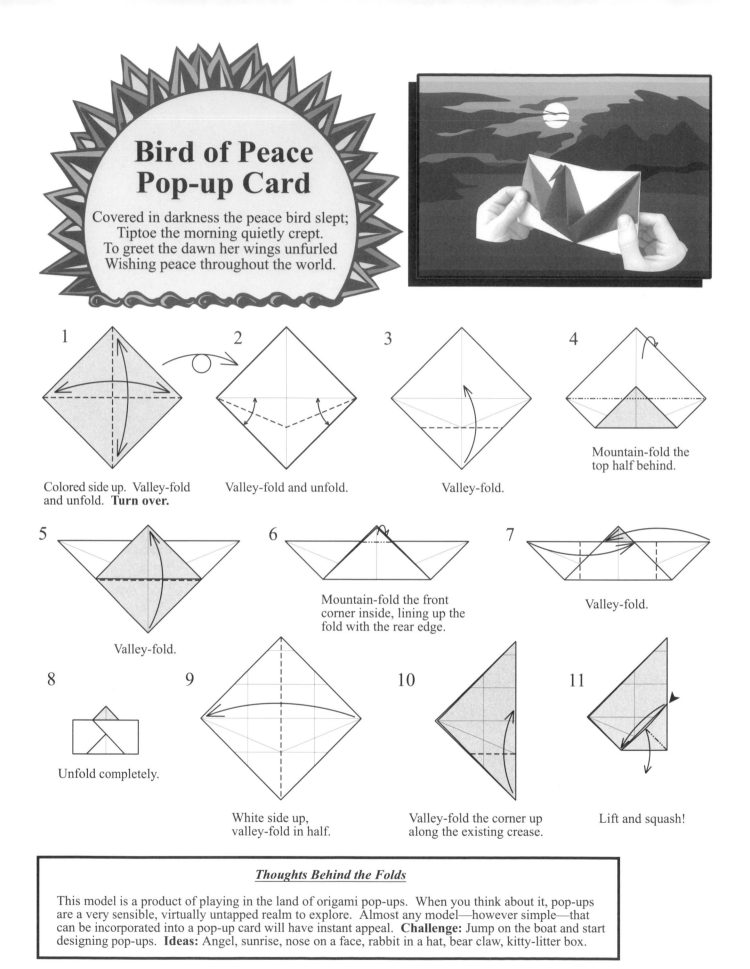

Bird of Peace Pop-up Card

Covered in darkness the peace bird slept;
Tiptoe the morning quietly crept.
To greet the dawn her wings unfurled
Wishing peace throughout the world.

1

Colored side up. Valley-fold and unfold. **Turn over.**

2

Valley-fold and unfold.

3

Valley-fold.

4

Mountain-fold the top half behind.

5

Valley-fold.

6

Mountain-fold the front corner inside, lining up the fold with the rear edge.

7

Valley-fold.

8

Unfold completely.

9

White side up, valley-fold in half.

10

Valley-fold the corner up along the existing crease.

11

Lift and squash!

Thoughts Behind the Folds

This model is a product of playing in the land of origami pop-ups. When you think about it, pop-ups are a very sensible, virtually untapped realm to explore. Almost any model—however simple—that can be incorporated into a pop-up card will have instant appeal. **Challenge:** Jump on the boat and start designing pop-ups. **Ideas:** Angel, sunrise, nose on a face, rabbit in a hat, bear claw, kitty-litter box.

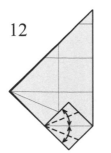

12

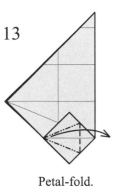

13

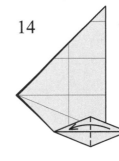

14

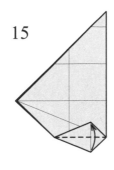

15

Valley-fold and unfold.

Petal-fold.

Valley-fold.

Valley-fold.

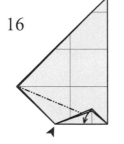

16

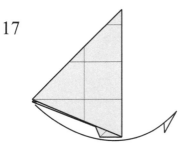

17

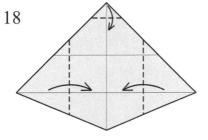

18

Reverse-fold (i.e., push the point in) along existing creases.

Swing the back flap out from behind. The back of the model won't lie flat.

Make valley folds along existing creases.

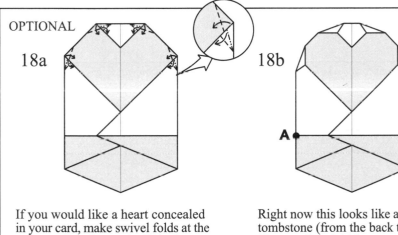

OPTIONAL

18a

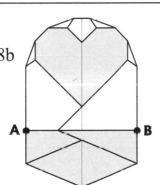

18b

If you would like a heart concealed in your card, make swivel folds at the corners. But the card will look slightly nicer if you skip this option.

Right now this looks like a lovely tombstone (from the back too), or if you valley-fold between **A** and **B**, it's a love seat.

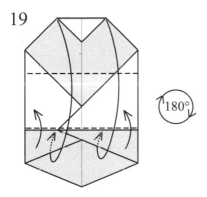

19

Valley-fold the top down and the bottom up on the existing creases. As you do this, slip the top edge into the pocket. Rotate the model 180°.

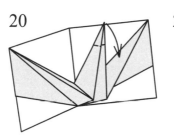

20

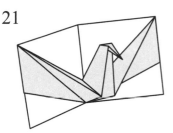

21

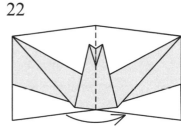

22

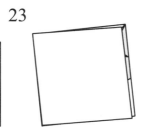

23

Reverse-fold the head. **It's a Bird! It's a Plane! It's...**

...just a bird. **Indeed, the Bird of Peace has been spotted...**

...and is now looking straight at you. Close the card.

The Bird of Peace is enclosed for safe keeping. This model can also be used as a wallet.

Bird of Peace Pop-up Card **189**

Diamond Heart Ring

This is a perfect model to teach on a first date... assuming you find your date romantically interesting.

1

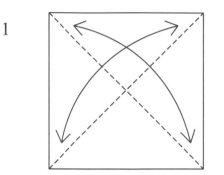

Begin with a three-inch square of foil, white side up. (For cats use a six-inch square—see photo.) Valley-fold and unfold diagonally in half both ways.

2

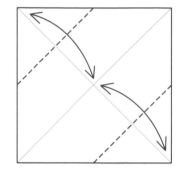

Valley-fold and unfold opposite corners to the center.

3

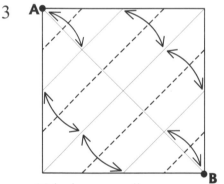

Make four new valley creases, thereby dividing the line **AB** into eight equal sections.

4

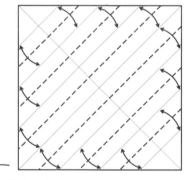

Make six new valley creases in between existing creases. Do not add creases to the corner triangles. **Turn the model over.**

5

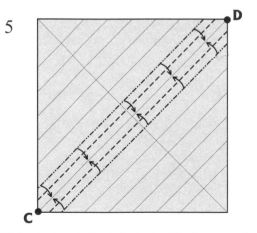

Make the two indicated pleats. The best way to do this is to pinch up the two existing mountain creases that are next to the diagonal, **C-D**, and lay them both onto **C-D**, thereby making two new valley folds.

6

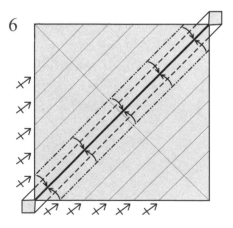

Repeat step 5 on each of the other ten parallel creases.

7

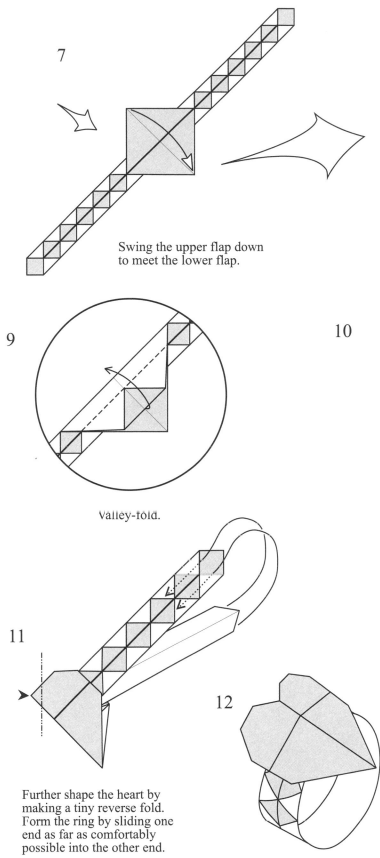

Swing the upper flap down to meet the lower flap.

8

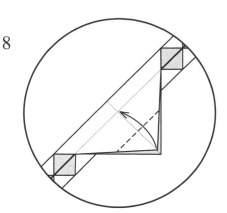

Valley-fold this same flap back up to meet the centerline.

9

Valley-fold.

10

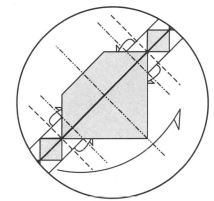

Shape the heart by pleating the sides. Mountain-fold the heart in half.

11

Further shape the heart by making a tiny reverse fold. Form the ring by sliding one end as far as comfortably possible into the other end.

12

The Heart Ring has been crafted. Now fold it out of a sheet of 24K gold and you'll have a wedding ring.

Thoughts Behind the Folds

I came up with the Diamond Heart Ring in my high school chemistry class while inconspicuously experimenting with pleats in the back row. First I discovered the diamond strip, then the ring, and finally folded a heart from the square on top. I tested out the model by giving it to the girl in the second row, on whom I had a crush. I was turned down (presumably for being too forward), but this model would play a major role in all my future romance!

Challenge: What else can you fold out of the square on top?

Ideas: Peace sign, star, rose, blinking eyes, mask, picture frame, pearl in a clam, waffle, dental finger cup.

Peace Ring

No more turbulent relationships!
Put this ring on your partner's finger
and enjoy living in peace forevermore!

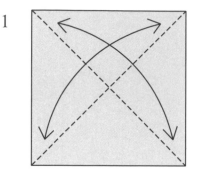

1

Foil is recommended. A three-inch square
sheet will make a ring that fits nicely on an
adult finger. However, for the first time
you might want to start with a larger sheet.
Colored side up, valley-fold and unfold
diagonally in half in both directions.

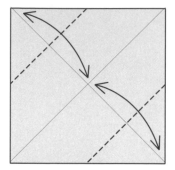

2

Valley-fold and unfold opposite
corners to the center.

3

Valley-fold and unfold,
lining up crease to crease.

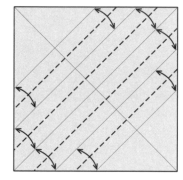

4

Valley-fold and unfold again, this
time making four new creases.
Turn the model over.

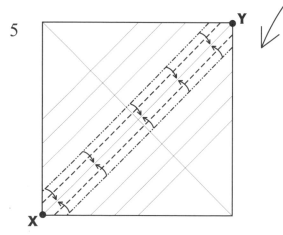

5

Make the two indicated pleats. The best way to do
this is to pinch up the two existing creases that are
next to the diagonal, **X-Y**, and lay them both onto
X-Y, thereby making two new valley folds.

6

Repeat step 5 on each of the
other six parallel creases.

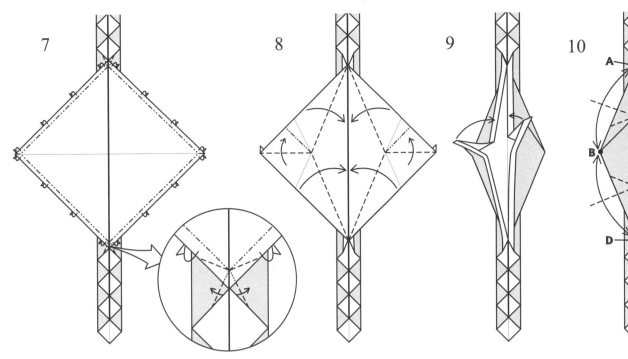

7

Create an equal border around the square by mountain-folding along the edges. The line thickness of the peace sign will be double the chosen thickness of this border. What happens at the corners? Rabbit-ear at the left and right and reverse-fold at the top and bottom.

8

Fold a Fish Base.

9

Fish Base in progress.

10

Through all layers, valley-fold and unfold **A** to **B**, **A** to **C**, **D** to **B**, and **D** to **C**.

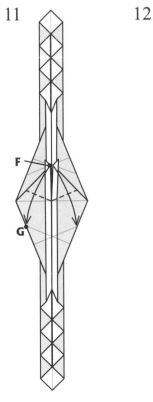

11

Valley-fold the left flap down bringing point **F** to point **G**. Do the same with the right flap.

12

Mountain-fold the lower portion of the model behind, folding through points **R** and **S**.

13

Valley-fold the front end to the right.

14

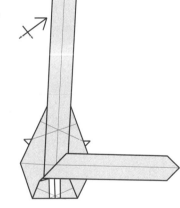

Repeat steps 12 and 13 on the top.

15

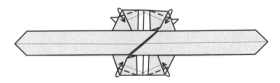

Valley-fold along the creases existing on the rear layer (front side of the peace sign).

16

Turn over.

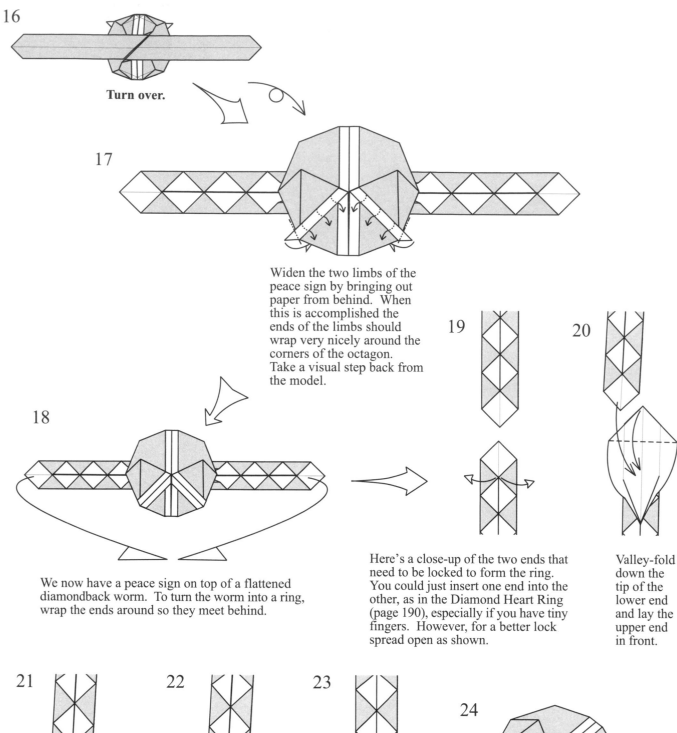

17

Widen the two limbs of the
peace sign by bringing out
paper from behind. When
this is accomplished the
ends of the limbs should
wrap very nicely around the
corners of the octagon.
Take a visual step back from
the model.

18

We now have a peace sign on top of a flattened
diamondback worm. To turn the worm into a ring,
wrap the ends around so they meet behind.

19

20

Here's a close-up of the two ends that
need to be locked to form the ring.
You could just insert one end into the
other, as in the Diamond Heart Ring
(page 190), especially if you have tiny
fingers. However, for a better lock
spread open as shown.

Valley-fold
down the
tip of the
lower end
and lay the
upper end
in front.

21

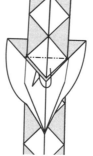

Mountain-fold
the corners of
both ends.

22

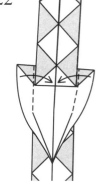

Close the sides
of the newly
joined ends.

23

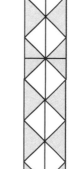

The ends are now
locked. Round the ring
and peace sign to taste.

24

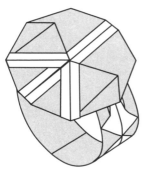

The Peace Ring is declared.
A significant treasure for a
significant other!

Crane Envelope

The crane, signifying peace, coupled with the envelope, signifying "Yes, I got mail!" is sure to bring tidings of comfort and joy far and wide.

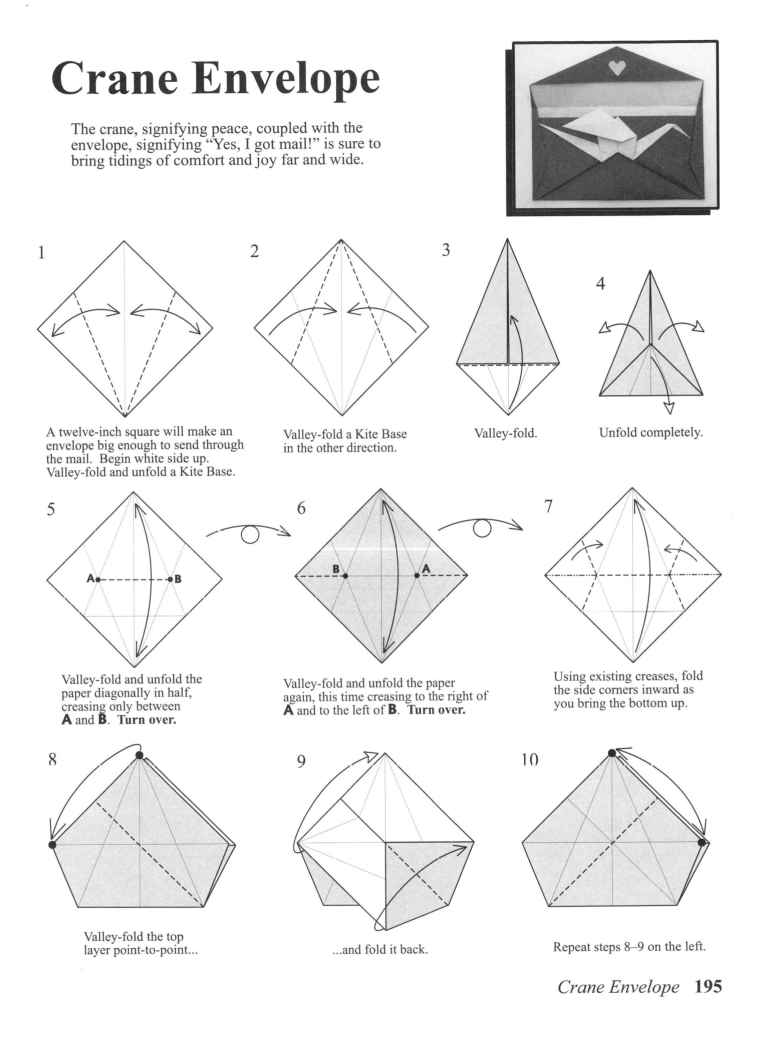

1

A twelve-inch square will make an envelope big enough to send through the mail. Begin white side up. Valley-fold and unfold a Kite Base.

2

Valley-fold a Kite Base in the other direction.

3

Valley-fold.

4

Unfold completely.

5

Valley-fold and unfold the paper diagonally in half, creasing only between **A** and **B**. **Turn over.**

6

Valley-fold and unfold the paper again, this time creasing to the right of **A** and to the left of **B**. **Turn over.**

7

Using existing creases, fold the side corners inward as you bring the bottom up.

8

Valley-fold the top layer point-to-point...

9

...and fold it back.

10

Repeat steps 8–9 on the left.

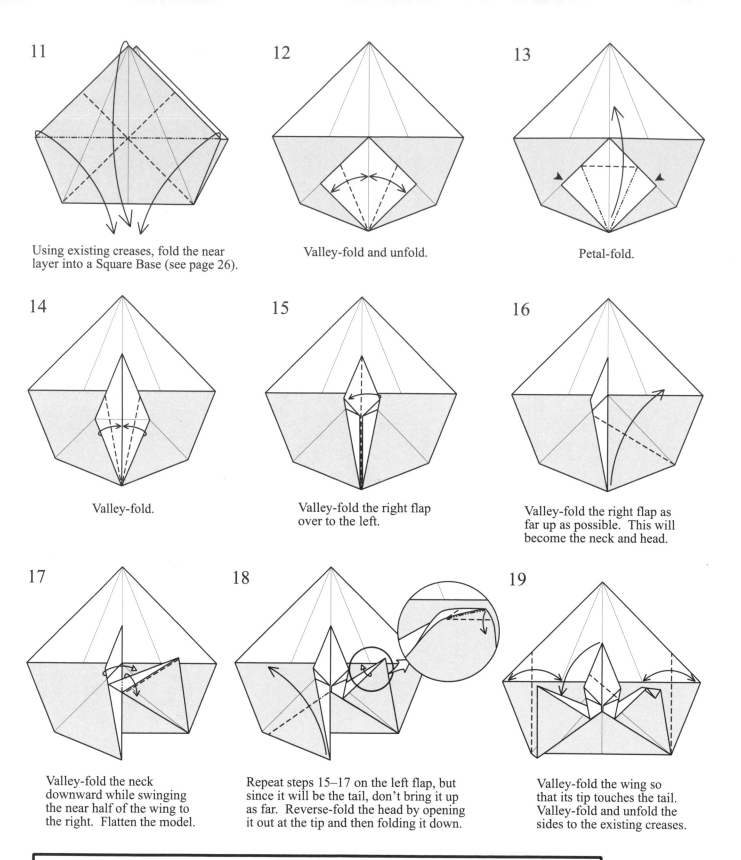

11

Using existing creases, fold the near layer into a Square Base (see page 26).

12

Valley-fold and unfold.

13

Petal-fold.

14

Valley-fold.

15

Valley-fold the right flap over to the left.

16

Valley-fold the right flap as far up as possible. This will become the neck and head.

17

Valley-fold the neck downward while swinging the near half of the wing to the right. Flatten the model.

18

Repeat steps 15–17 on the left flap, but since it will be the tail, don't bring it up as far. Reverse-fold the head by opening it out at the tip and then folding it down.

19

Valley-fold the wing so that its tip touches the tail. Valley-fold and unfold the sides to the existing creases.

Thoughts Behind the Folds

The Crane Envelope is an example of my isolation technique. The idea is to try to use only part of the paper to fold a given model and then use the rest to make something else. **Challenge:** What else can you put on this envelope? **Ideas:** Peace sign, heart, butterfly, dragon in front of volcano, white rainbow, lightning bolt, scary mask, frog catching fly, fish chasing bait, nosy mail carrier.

20

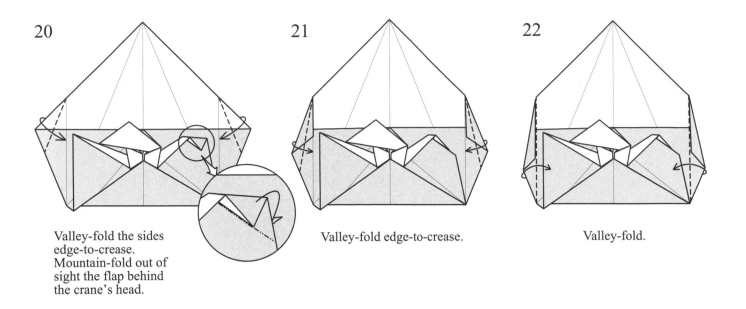

Valley-fold the sides edge-to-crease. Mountain-fold out of sight the flap behind the crane's head.

21

Valley-fold edge-to-crease.

22

Valley-fold.

23

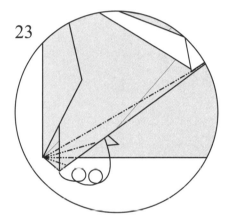

With mountain folds, tuck in the left flap, making the model look more symmetrical.

24

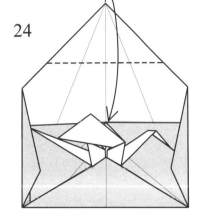

Valley-fold the top down.

25

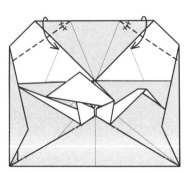

Valley-fold, aligning the top edge with the existing crease.

26

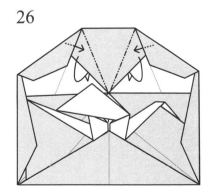

Pull out paper from within the folds made in step 25 in order to make the indicated mountain folds.

27

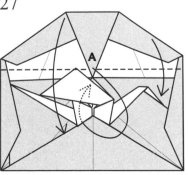

Valley-fold the envelope flap down and seal the envelope by tucking point **A** underneath the crane as far up as it will go.

28

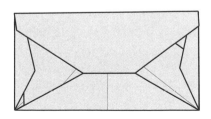

The sealed Crane Envelope is ready to fly. Plain on the outside, but *Crane* on the inside.

Crane Envelope **197**

Crane in Love Envelope...

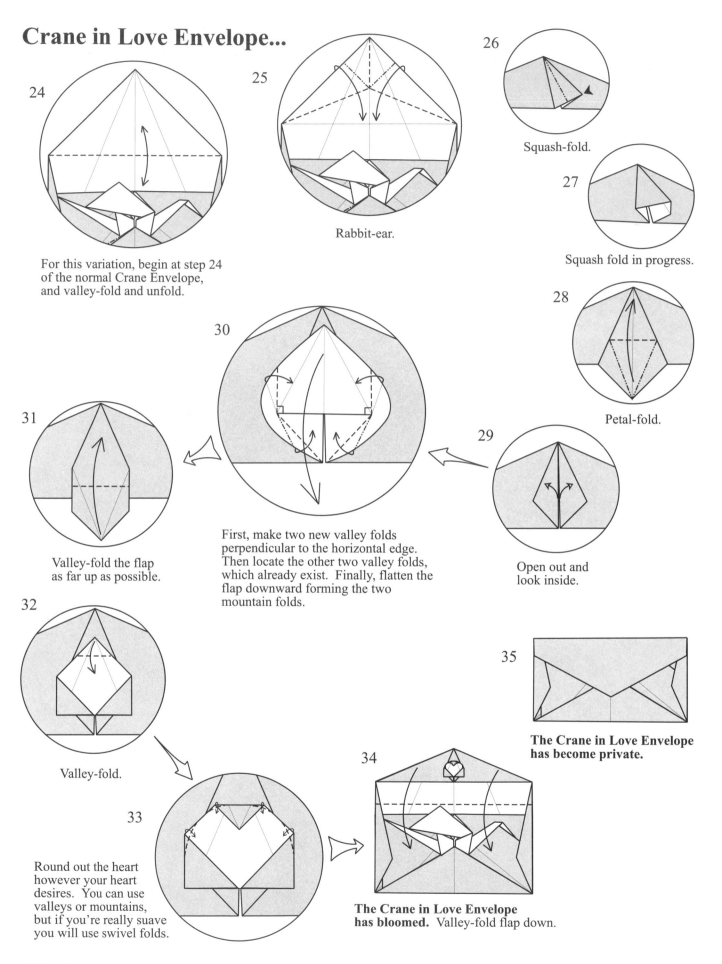

24

For this variation, begin at step 24 of the normal Crane Envelope, and valley-fold and unfold.

25

Rabbit-ear.

26

Squash-fold.

27

Squash fold in progress.

28

Petal-fold.

29

Open out and look inside.

30

First, make two new valley folds perpendicular to the horizontal edge. Then locate the other two valley folds, which already exist. Finally, flatten the flap downward forming the two mountain folds.

31

Valley-fold the flap as far up as possible.

32

Valley-fold.

33

Round out the heart however your heart desires. You can use valleys or mountains, but if you're really suave you will use swivel folds.

34

The Crane in Love Envelope has bloomed. Valley-fold flap down.

35

The Crane in Love Envelope has become private.

Beating Heart Card

Is your heart tired of beating? Then just relax, and let this card do all the beating for you.

1

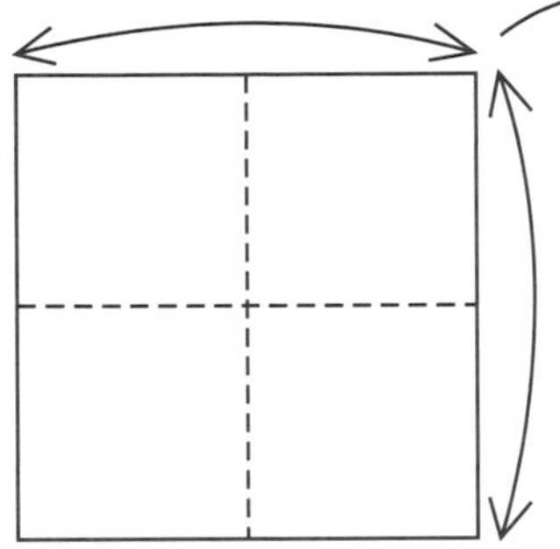

This model works best in six-inch paper or foil. Begin white side up. Valley-fold in half and unfold both ways. **Turn over.**

2

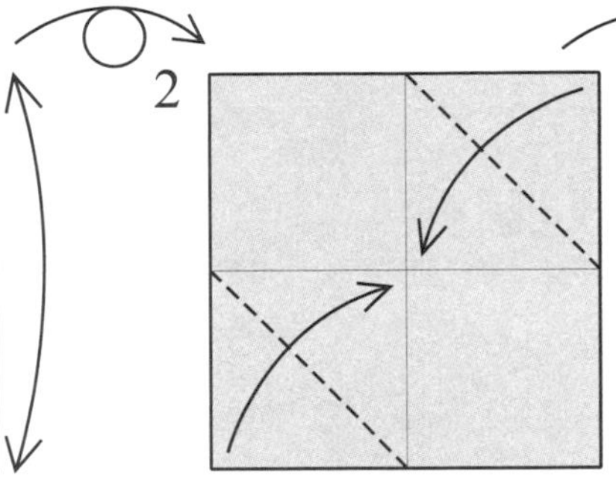

Valley-fold.
Turn over.

3

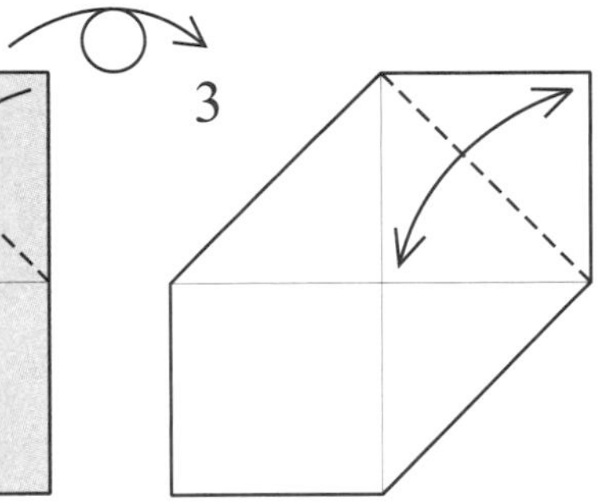

Valley-fold and unfold.

4

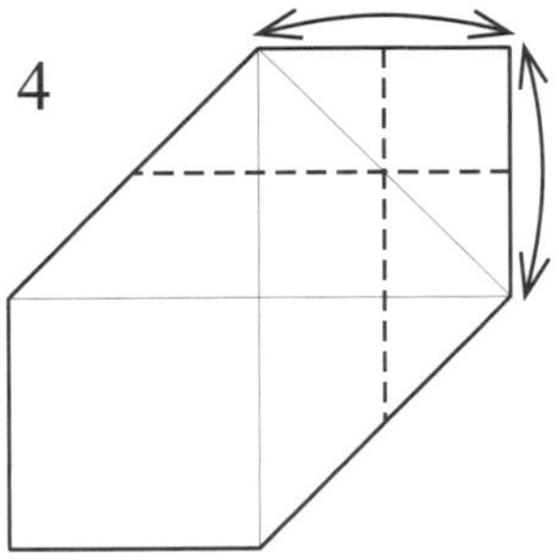

Valley-fold and unfold.

5

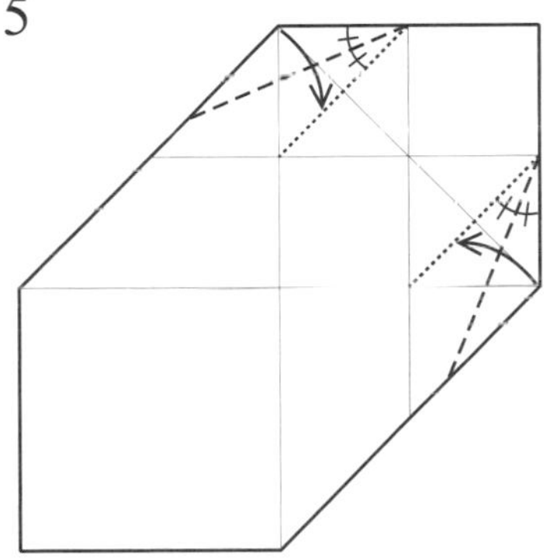

Valley-fold to the imaginary dotted line.

6

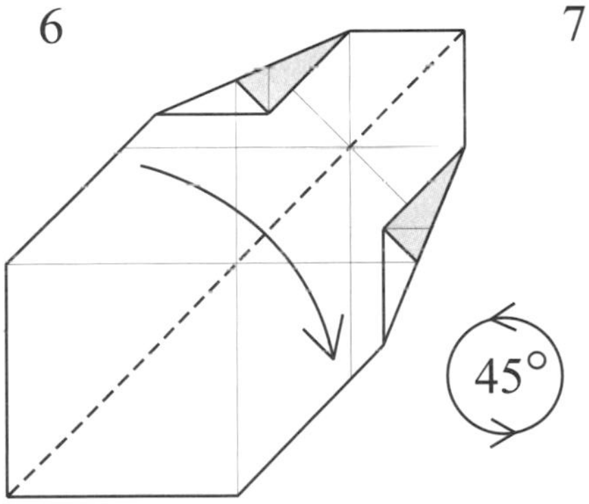

Valley-fold in half.
Rotate 45° counterclockwise.

7

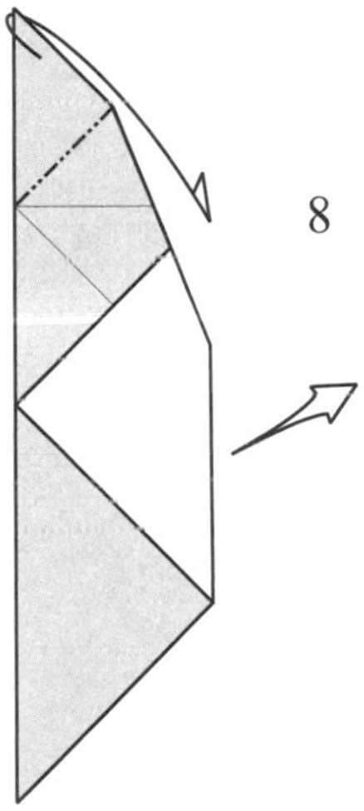

Mountain-fold, bringing the top corner to the back.

8

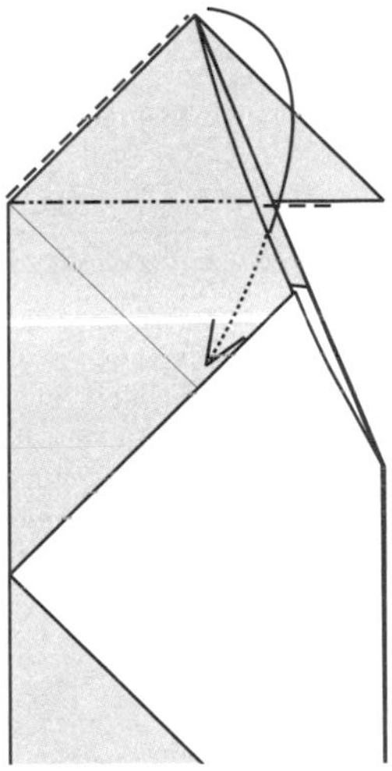

Reverse-fold into the indicated slot.

9

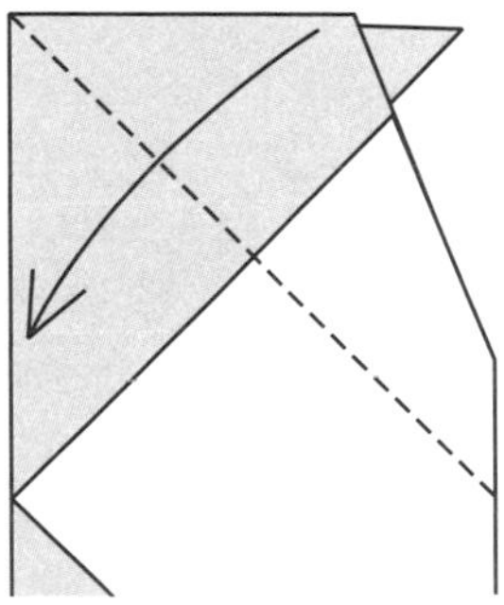

Valley-fold downward the front flap only.

10

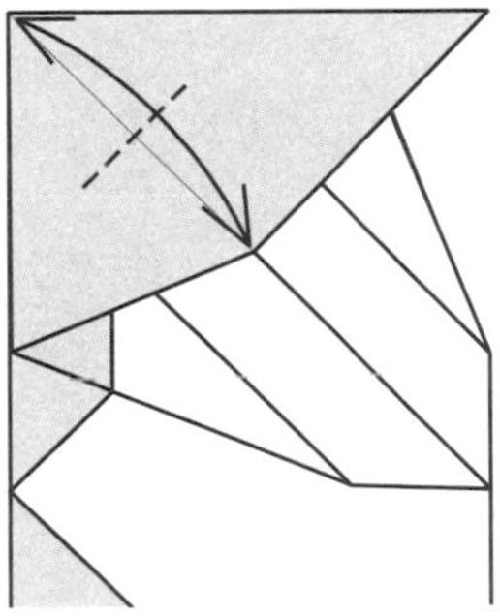

Make a faint crease mark.

11

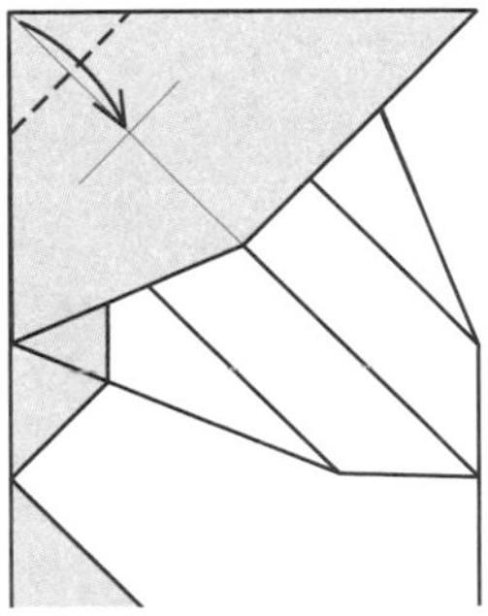

Valley-fold.

12

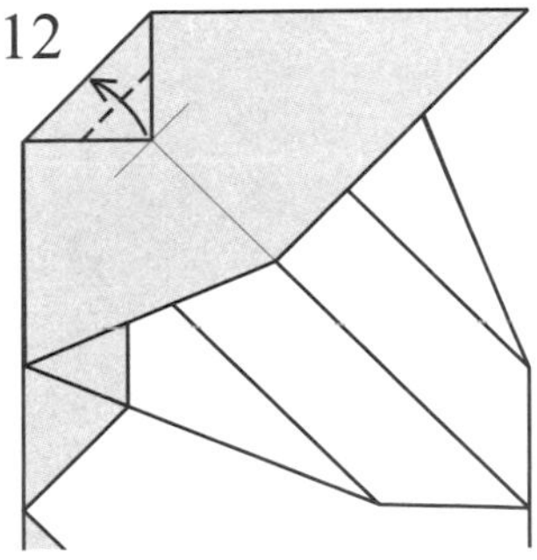

Valley-fold.

13

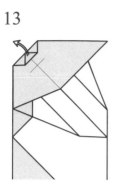

Unfold to step 10.

14

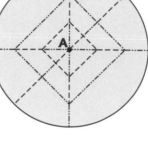

Pleat-sink the top left corner. To do this, first unfold corner **A**. The following enlarged diagram shows **A** after it has been unfolded.

15

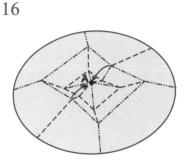

Pleat-sinking in progress. Along the existing creases, make the indicated folds, starting by pinching the outside square of mountains and then pinching the inside square of valleys.

16

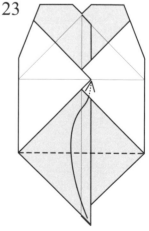

Pleat-sinking further in progress. Return the model to the configuration shown in step 13, incorporating the new folds.

17

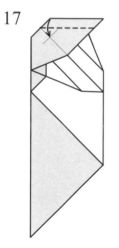

Make a horizontal valley fold on the top front flap.

18

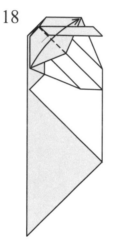

Valley-fold, swinging the left front flap up.

19

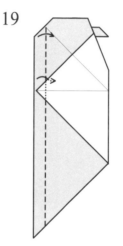

Make a vertical valley fold along the left edge. Place the left edge underneath the white corner.

20

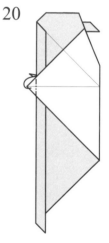

Mountain-fold the front white corner behind the left edge; don't fold the matching back corner.

21

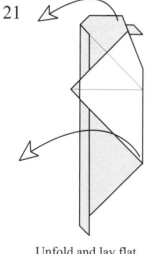

Unfold and lay flat like opening a book.

22

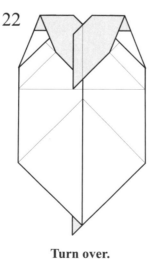

Turn over.

23

Valley-fold, tucking the tip underneath the white flap.

24

Valley-fold in half.

25

Turn over.

26

Closed-sink the flap into
the center of the heart
(i.e., push it in being careful
not to tear the paper).

27

Valley-fold the tiny
white triangle in half.

28

Valley-fold the even
tinier flap, tucking
it behind the bottom
tip of the heart.

29

Mountain-fold the sides of the
heart behind, making sure that
the folds go through point **A**
on each side.

30

"Wrinkle-fold" the sides of the heart
back into view. In other words, roll
the indicated edges outward, pulling
paper out from behind the heart.

31

Round out the heart to taste with
a series of mountain folds, or
you can wait till the end to do
the rounding.

32

Valley-fold the Heart Card in half.

33

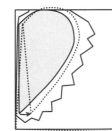

Torn-away view of the heart enclosed in the card.
Reach inside the card and slide the bottom corner of
the heart out slightly. The folds on the top of the heart
will also need to be slightly adjusted in order to make
the closed card lie flat again. This small alteration
makes the heart beat outward rather than downward.

34

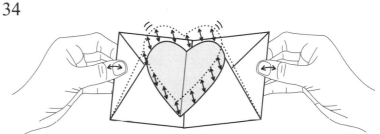

The Beating Heart Card is alive and well.
Pull out on the sides of the card, and the heart
will beat.

Star of Peace

No need to cut paper to produce multiple cranes. There's enough paper in this one square model to make cranes go around and around the world in peace to share.

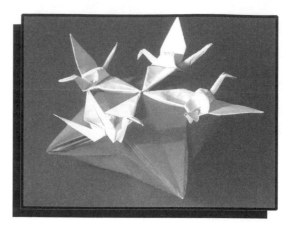

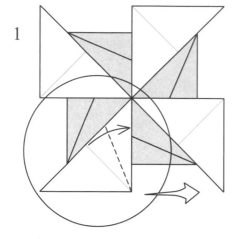

1

Use foil no smaller than ten inches square or paper no smaller than fifteen inches. Begin by folding steps 1–29 of the Folding the Blintz Base (page 228). Valley-fold one of the triangles.

2

Close-up view of one triangle. Valley-fold.

3

Valley-fold.

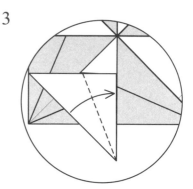

4

Valley-fold and unfold on all white layers.

5

Half-a-petal-fold on the front layer.

6

Half-a-petal-fold again.

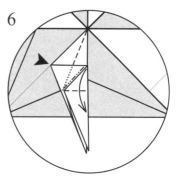

7

Unfold to step 1.

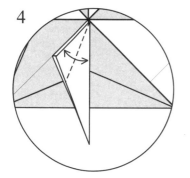

8

Collapse along the existing creases.

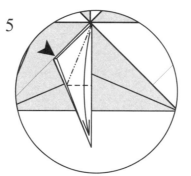

9

Lift and squash.

10

Petal-fold to form a Bird Base.

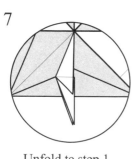

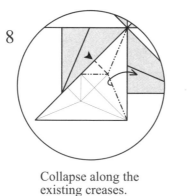

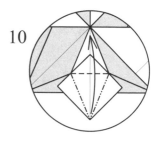

11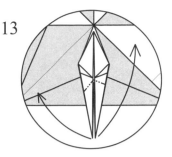

Valley-fold on
the front layer.

12

Mountain-fold.

13

Reverse-fold to form the
head and tail.

14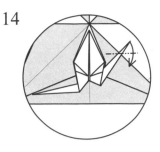

Reverse-fold the head.

15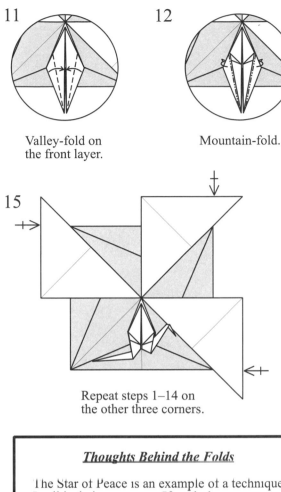

Repeat steps 1–14 on
the other three corners.

16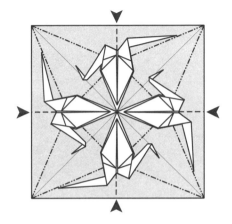

At this point you should have four cranes on a square. The possibilities for folding this square are endless. One good idea is to try folding it into yet another crane, so the model could be called, "Getting a Ride on Mama's Back." You could also fold a birdbath or a bird's nest. A really tasteless idea is to fold the square into a Monolithic Rubblestone Boulder (page 245). It could be called, "Four Birds with One Stone." The best idea is to follow the above diagram; push in at the sides. To do this, it helps to continually inflate the model through the hole in the center.

Thoughts Behind the Folds

The Star of Peace is an example of a technique I call isolating squares. If a whole square can be made out of just one corner, then at least four models can be made from one square.
Challenge: What else can you make from an isolated square other than a crane?
Ideas: Hand, foot, heart, diamond, spade, club, four-pointed star, mermaid, peace sign.

17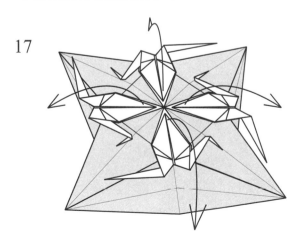

Fold out the wings and puff out the backs of the cranes.

18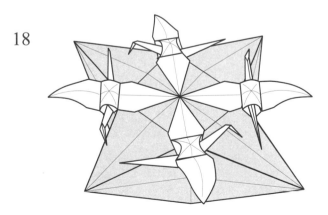

The Star of Peace has risen. This model also makes a fine vase for a flower. If folded from foil with the foil side inside, you can even fill it with water... but that wouldn't be pure... unless perhaps if you use purified water.

Interlocking Diamond
Heart Rings

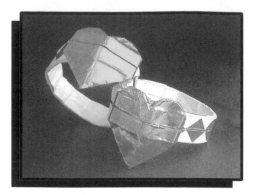

Giving this model to your soul mate will demonstrate that you are very dedicated... at least to the art of origami! This model is a toughy—no piece of wedding cake!

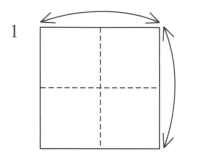

1

Use Japanese foil at least ten inches square. Begin white side up. Valley-fold and unfold in half both ways.

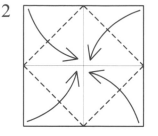

2

Valley-fold all four corners to the center.

3

Turn over.

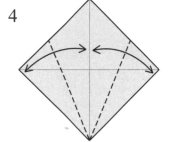

4

Valley-fold and unfold.

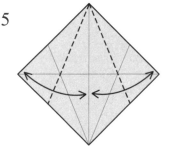

5

Valley-fold and unfold.

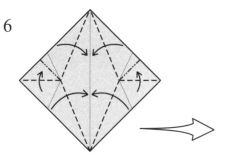

6

Fold a Fish Base.

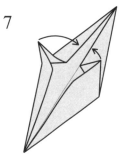

7

Fish Base in progress.

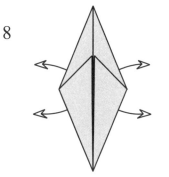

8

Bring out the back flaps.

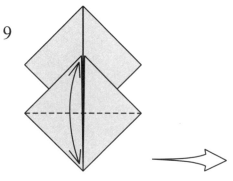

9

Valley-fold and unfold.

10

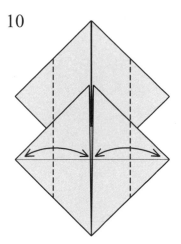

Valley-fold and unfold the side corners to the center, creasing through all layers.

11

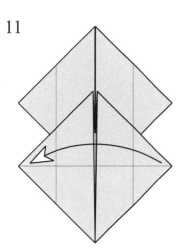

Swing the near right flap over to the left.

12

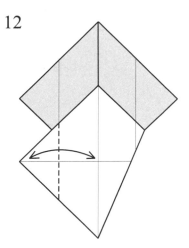

Valley-fold and unfold the swung-over white flap only.

13

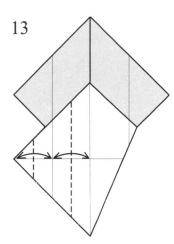

Valley-fold and unfold crease-to-crease, for a total of two new creases.

14

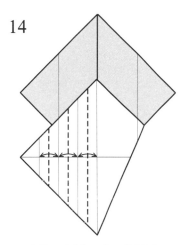

Valley-fold and unfold, for a total of three new creases.

15

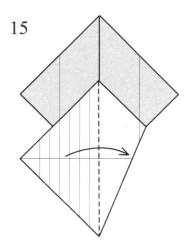

Swing the white flap back over to the right.

16

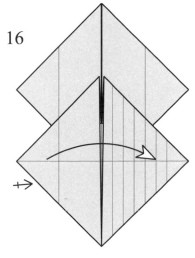

Repeat steps 11–15 on the left side.

17

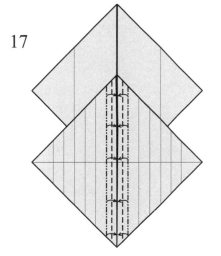

Pinch along the two innermost existing mountain creases and lay them on the center, forming a pleat on each side. The valley folds are new.

18

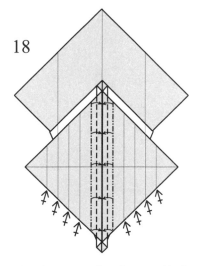

Continue to make pleats until all of the existing creases have been carried to the center.

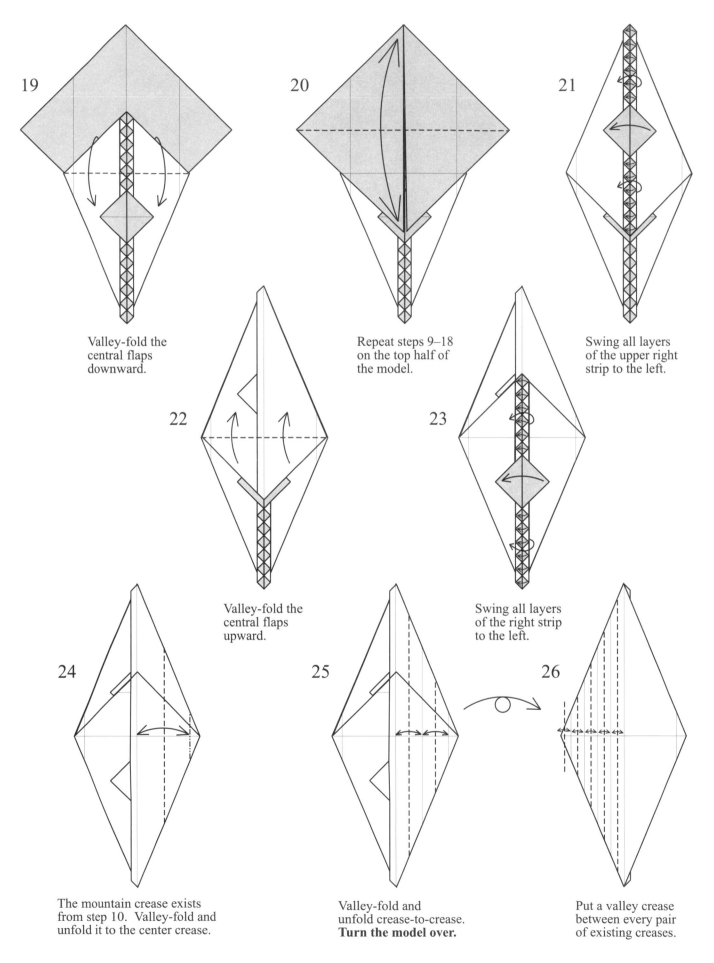

19

Valley-fold the
central flaps
downward.

20

Repeat steps 9–18
on the top half of
the model.

21

Swing all layers
of the upper right
strip to the left.

22

Valley-fold the
central flaps
upward.

23

Swing all layers
of the right strip
to the left.

24

The mountain crease exists
from step 10. Valley-fold and
unfold it to the center crease.

25

Valley-fold and
unfold crease-to-crease.
Turn the model over.

26

Put a valley crease
between every pair
of existing creases.

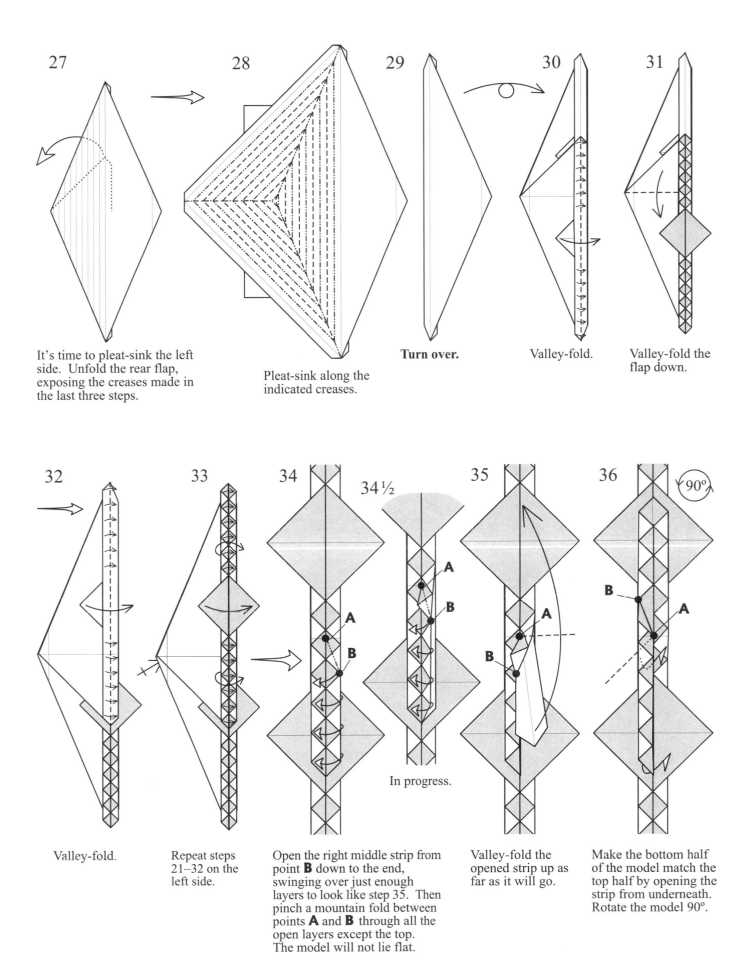

27

It's time to pleat-sink the left side. Unfold the rear flap, exposing the creases made in the last three steps.

28

Pleat-sink along the indicated creases.

29

Turn over.

30

Valley-fold.

31

Valley-fold the flap down.

32

Valley-fold.

33

Repeat steps 21–32 on the left side.

34

Open the right middle strip from point **B** down to the end, swinging over just enough layers to look like step 35. Then pinch a mountain fold between points **A** and **B** through all the open layers except the top. The model will not lie flat.

34½

In progress.

35

Valley-fold the opened strip up as far as it will go.

36

Make the bottom half of the model match the top half by opening the strip from underneath. Rotate the model 90°.

90°

37

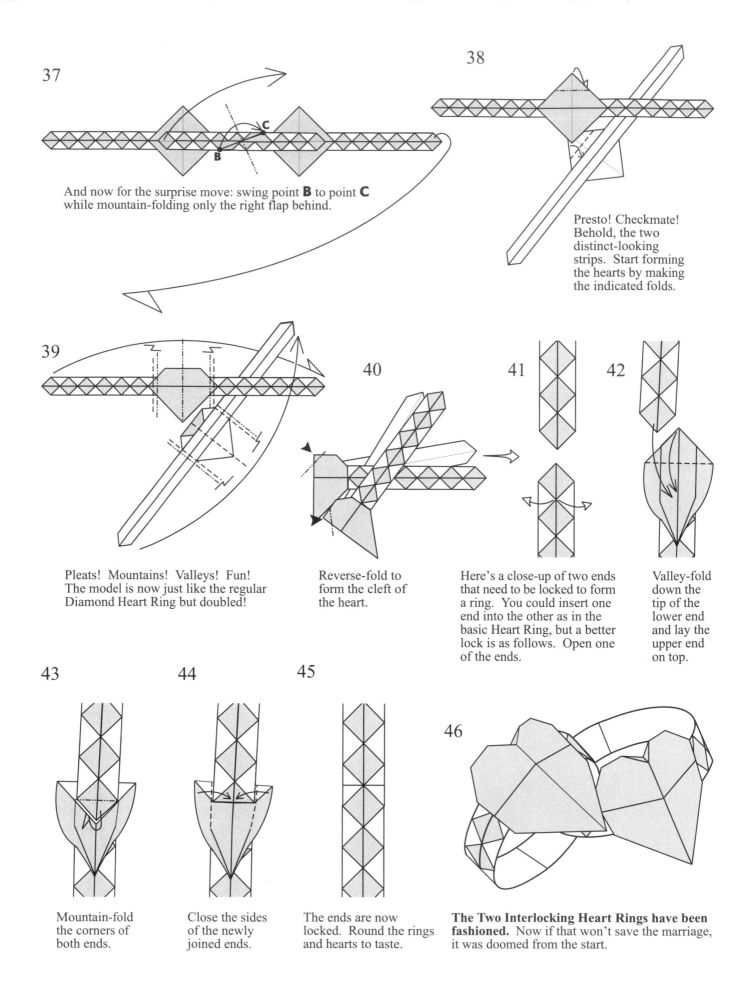

And now for the surprise move: swing point **B** to point **C** while mountain-folding only the right flap behind.

38

Presto! Checkmate! Behold, the two distinct-looking strips. Start forming the hearts by making the indicated folds.

39

Pleats! Mountains! Valleys! Fun! The model is now just like the regular Diamond Heart Ring but doubled!

40

Reverse-fold to form the cleft of the heart.

41

42

Here's a close-up of two ends that need to be locked to form a ring. You could insert one end into the other as in the basic Heart Ring, but a better lock is as follows. Open one of the ends.

Valley-fold down the tip of the lower end and lay the upper end on top.

43

Mountain-fold the corners of both ends.

44

Close the sides of the newly joined ends.

45

The ends are now locked. Round the rings and hearts to taste.

46

The Two Interlocking Heart Rings have been fashioned. Now if that won't save the marriage, it was doomed from the start.

Present Box

Although this model isn't nearly as impossible to fold as it looks, it is a complex model. If simplicity were the goal, why not instead use a cardboard box, some wrapping paper, and some ribbon? But, since we're origami purists, we must do things the hard way.

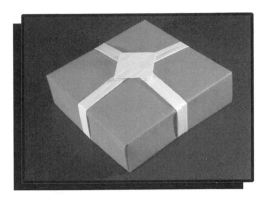

1

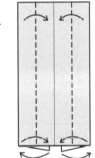

A ten-inch square will make a 3 by 3 by 1 box. Use paper or foil. Begin with white side up. Valley-fold in half and unfold.

2

Valley-fold the sides to the center.

3

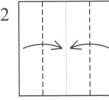

Turn over.

Thoughts Behind the Folds

This model came from the back row of my high school economics class. My friend Nathan Parker, who saw me folding, passed me a note challenging me to fold an "**X**" (as pictured below) I quickly folded a sloppy Blintz Base and passed it to him. He sent me back a note saying, "But can you make the "**X**" on top?" My solution to that was to add pleats to the "**X**" to raise it. That night I played with this model and managed to develop it into a present box. Nathan's birthday party was a few weeks later, and you can guess how I wrapped my present to him. **Challenge:** What else can Nathan's Challenge evolve into? **Ideas:** Quadrate cross, vehicle intersection, Excalibur, knight's shield, four-spoked wheel, bow tie on a cigarette.

Nathan's Challenge

4

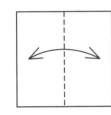

Valley-fold the sides to the center, letting the two back flaps swing to the outside. Ideally, make these folds by reaching underneath so as not to make extra dents in the paper.

5

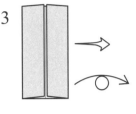

Turn over.

6

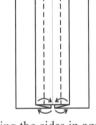

Swing the sides in again as in step 4, letting the two back flaps swing outward.

7

Turn over.

8

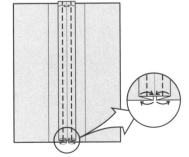

Swing again as in step 4.

9

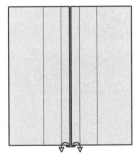

Completely unfold the model and **turn over.**

10

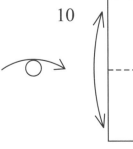

Repeat steps 1–9, making the creases horizontal instead of vertical.

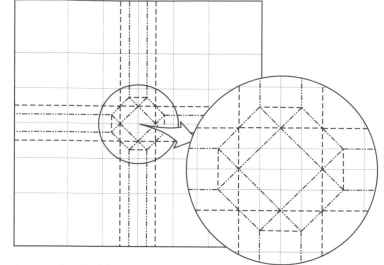

11

12

Start out by pinching the mountains so that
they protrude. Then make the indicated folds.

Step 11 in progress.
Be assertive with the paper—
it might need some coaxing.

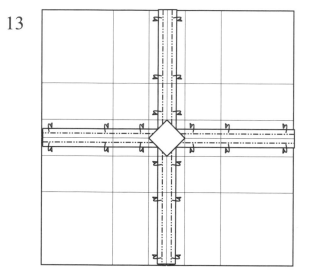

13

Narrow the ribbon-to-be by mountain-folding its
sides to the far side of the ribbon. Note that these
mountain folds extend beneath the center square.

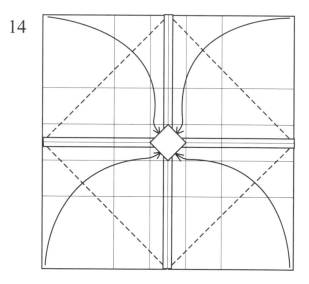

14

Valley-fold the four corners to the
center, tucking them behind the ribbon.

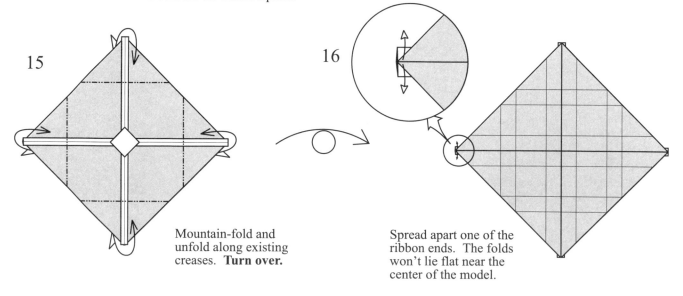

15

Mountain-fold and
unfold along existing
creases. **Turn over.**

16

Spread apart one of the
ribbon ends. The folds
won't lie flat near the
center of the model.

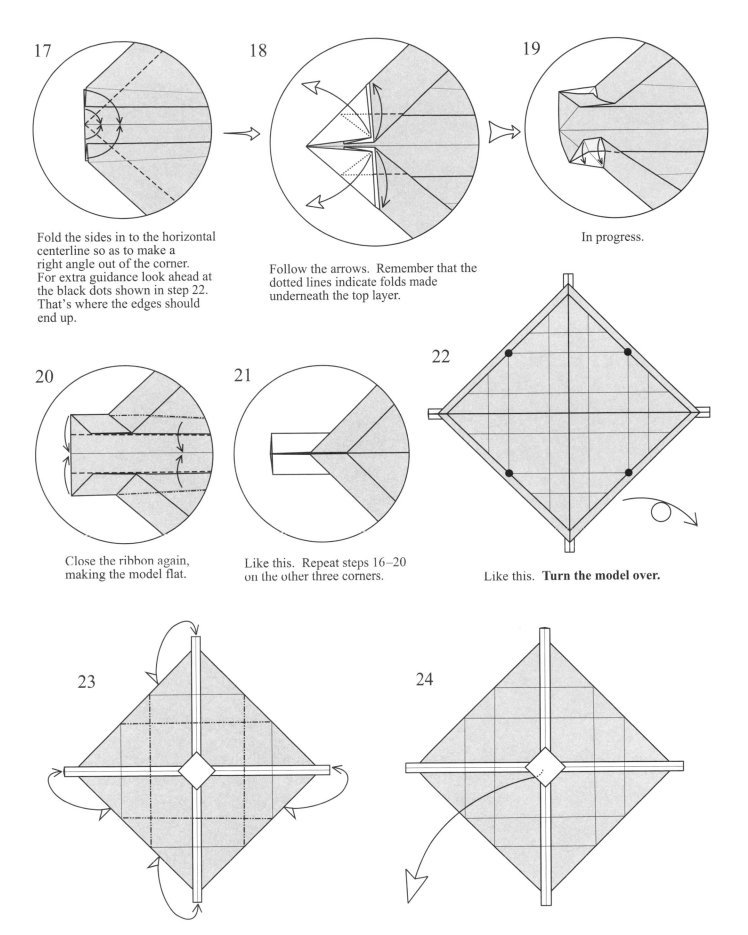

17

Fold the sides in to the horizontal centerline so as to make a right angle out of the corner. For extra guidance look ahead at the black dots shown in step 22. That's where the edges should end up.

18

Follow the arrows. Remember that the dotted lines indicate folds made underneath the top layer.

19

In progress.

20

Close the ribbon again, making the model flat.

21

Like this. Repeat steps 16–20 on the other three corners.

22

Like this. **Turn the model over.**

23

Mountain-fold and unfold.

24

Pull one corner out from behind the ribbon.

25

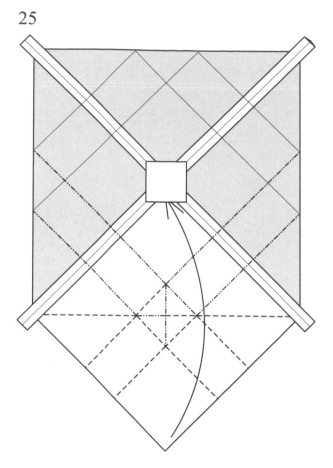

This next tricky move will lock the corner of the box. Make the indicated folds while bringing the edges back behind the ribbon. The center mountain segment is the only new crease; the rest are preexisting.

26

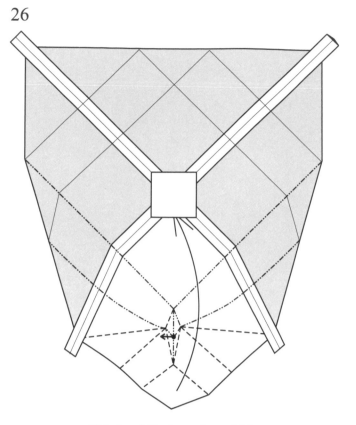

This is a 3-D view of step 25 in progress. Collapse the center mountain segment to the left.

27

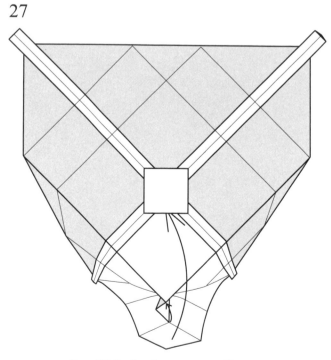

Step 25 further in progress. Close the newly locked corner of the box.

28

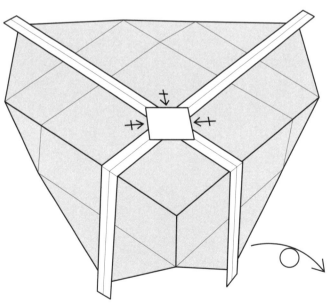

Fold complete. Now do steps 24–27 on the other three corners of the box. **Turn the box over.**

29

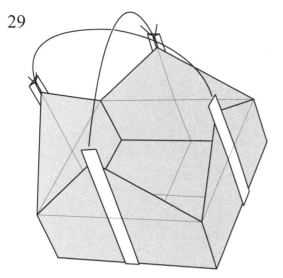

Now for the conceptually easy, but technically very difficult, final closure of the box. **The concept:** Slide one ribbon end into the ribbon end across from it. Do the same with the other two ends. **The technique:** Keep at least two fingers inside the box to use as support. You will find that this is quite difficult to do when trying to secure the final lock, for how can you keep two fingers inside a box that is already closed? Well, where there is a will, there is a way, but if you don't object to the use of tools, this would be an ideal time to use them. A butter knife is perfect, for it can slip inside the cracks to give you the support that you need.

30

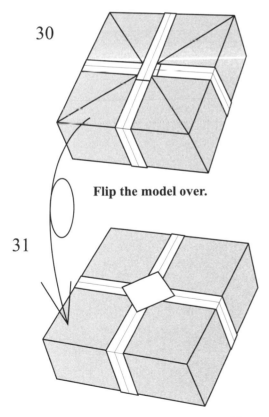

Flip the model over.

31

The Present Box is all wrapped up. It's complete even with nothing in it—a gift worth leaving empty, or filling with another very special gift.

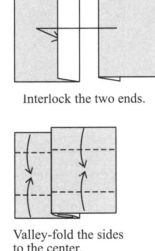

Origami for the Almost Deranged

Even for optimists, there are times
when it seems that the world has finally gone insane.
During these trying times, keeping a sense of humor,
however dark and cynical that humor may be,
is crucial to not losing one's mind.

Hence this final section is devoted
to helping those on the edge
to avoid falling into full derangement.

But even if you aren't on the verge of losing your mind,
I hope you'll find this section at least worth a few good laughs!

Origami Square

This model is from one square piece of paper,
no cutting, gluing, drawing on, or folding!

Author's note: A six-inch square creates
a six-inch by six-inch model.

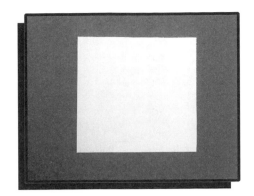

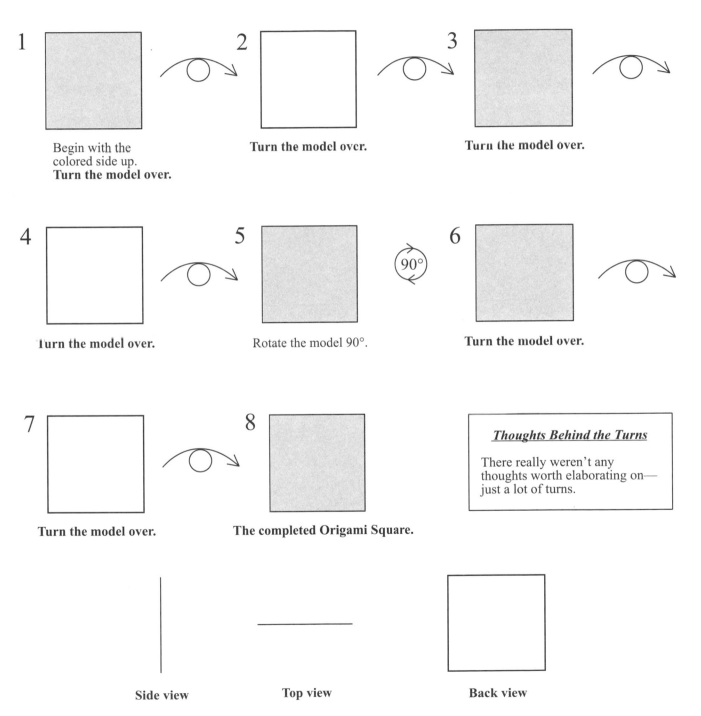

1 Begin with the
colored side up.
Turn the model over.

2 **Turn the model over.**

3 **Turn the model over.**

4 **Turn the model over.**

5 Rotate the model 90°.

90°

6 **Turn the model over.**

7 **Turn the model over.**

8 **The completed Origami Square.**

Thoughts Behind the Turns

There really weren't any
thoughts worth elaborating on—
just a lot of turns.

Side view

Top view

Back view

Transvestite Puppet

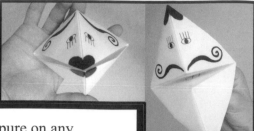

OK... so this is not pure origami. In fact, it's not very pure on any account, but, surely, purely almost deranged. I hope that you enjoy showing this puppet to your friends, and that they stay your friends.

1
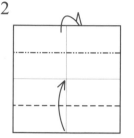

Begin white side up. Valley-fold and unfold both ways.

2
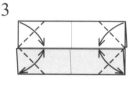

Valley-fold the bottom edge to the center crease. Mountain-fold the top edge to the center crease.

3
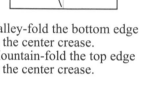

Valley-fold and unfold the bottom corners. Valley-fold and **don't** unfold the top corners.

4
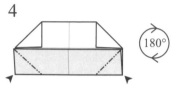

180°

Reverse-fold the bottom corners. Rotate the model 180°.

5
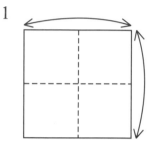

Insert the bottom half of the model into the frontmost pocket of the top half. In the end, this bottom half will independently take on the form of the puppet, and can be pulled back out to reveal... the Ghost of the Transvestite Puppet. Oooooooooooh!

6
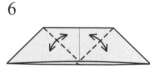

Valley-fold and unfold.

7
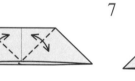

Open out the bottom, and press down on the top. The model will not lie flat.

8
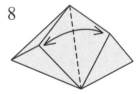

Valley-fold and unfold repeatedly; you are closing and opening the mouth of the Monsieur.

9
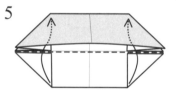

Transvestite Puppet is finished.
If you do not mind breaking the puritan rules of origami in the name of being almost deranged, draw the above face on the model (otherwise, enjoy a blank puppet). Swing together the Monsieur's goatee and toupee (from behind), and voilà, the transvesting is complete...

10

...C'est la Madame.
What else can this model be? **Ideas:** Tweezers, clam, gas mask, pig snout, ear plug, goggles, bra.

11
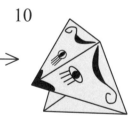

The modular approach: Make two puppets and assemble them into a **Transvestite Cube.**

12
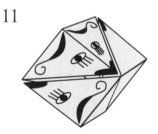

Or assemble them into a **Transvestite Footstool.**

216 *Origami to Astonish and Amuse*

BARF Bag

Make sure to have this dandy state-of-the-art BARF bag on hand at all Bay Area Rapid Folders meetings. It's equipped with an extra wide bottom for superior containment!

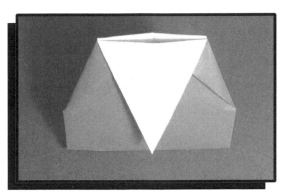

1

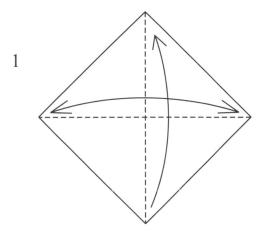

Begin with a very large sheet of waterproof paper, white side up. Valley-fold and unfold the vertical diagonal. Valley-fold the horizontal diagonal.

2

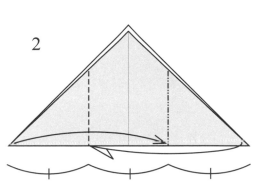

Divide the base of the model into thirds by folding the left side in front and the right side to the back.

3

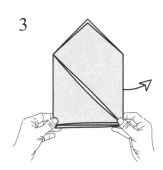

Fiddle with the folds until the thirds are exact. Then unfold the back flap.

4

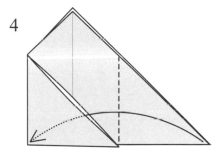

Valley-fold the right flap, inserting it into the pocket of the left flap.

5

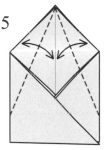

Valley-fold and unfold.

6

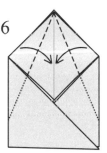

Valley-fold the sides of the inner flap, letting them go underneath the front layer to complete the fold.

7

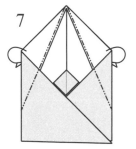

Mountain-fold the side flaps to the back.

8

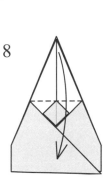

Valley-fold one flap down.

9

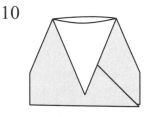

Mountain-fold the other flap behind.

10

The BARF Bag has been provided. It can also be used as a change purse or Halloween candy bag, but not if it has already been used for its primary purpose.

Unfortunate Bungee Jumper

Obviously the cord was either too weak or too long!
What else can this model be called? To be warm
and fuzzy, you can call it a "Hug Me Now Card."
But to stay with the Almost Deranged theme, here are
some good names: "Belly Flop," "Windshield Splat,"
"Stretched to the Limits," "Limb Stretcher," or for you ultra almost deranged folders, roll it up and say,
"Guess what kind of bean burrito this is." Unroll it and exclaim, "A HUMAN being burrito!"

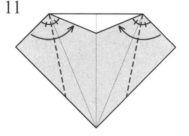

1

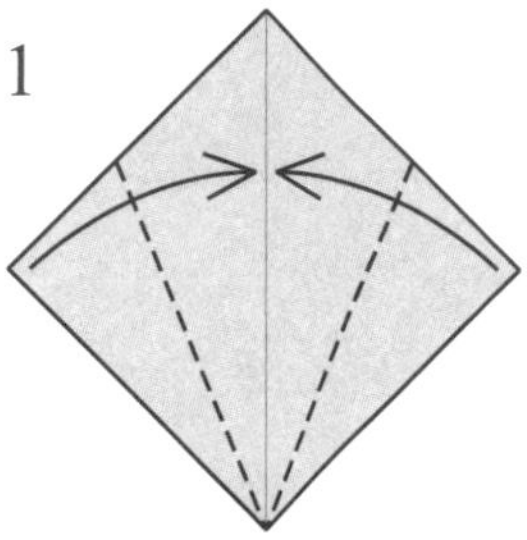

Begin colored side up.
Fold a Kite Base.

2

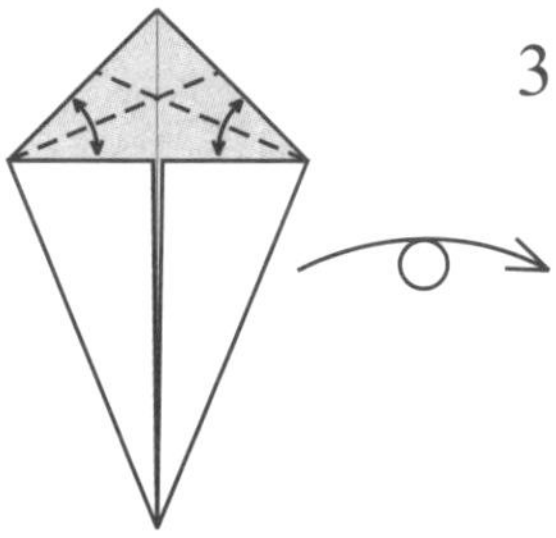

Valley-fold and
unfold. **Turn over.**

3

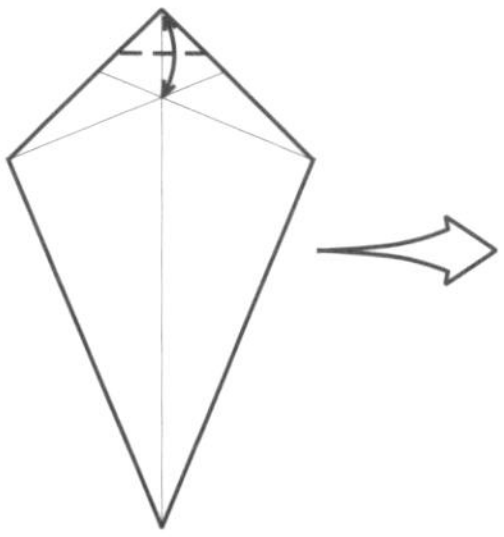

Valley-fold
and unfold.

4

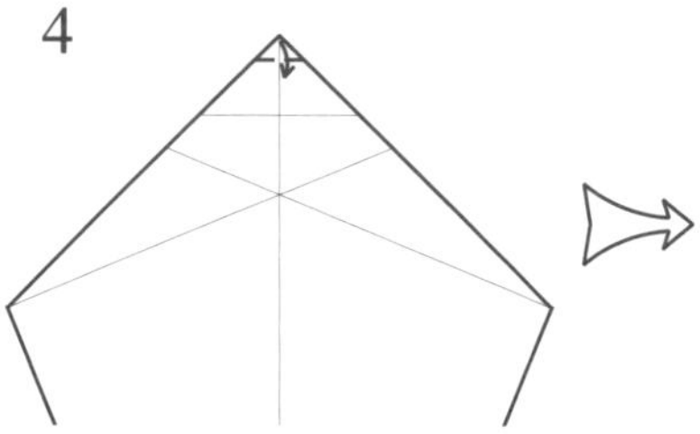

Valley-fold the tip down.

5

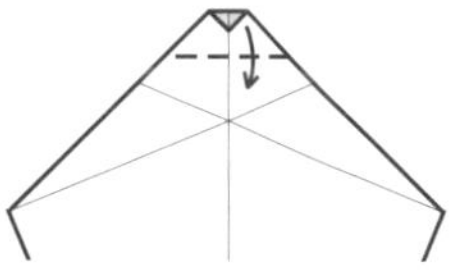

Valley-fold.

6

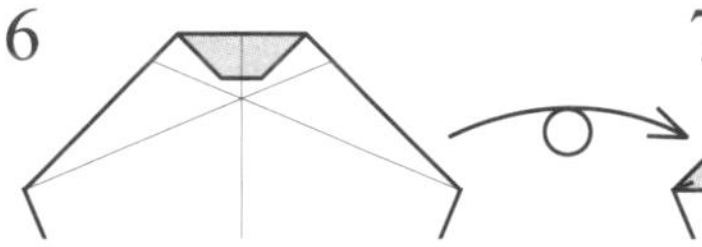

Turn over.

7

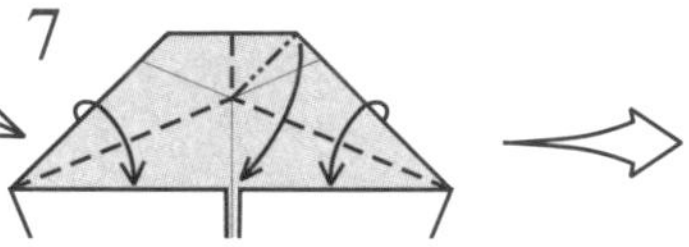

Rabbit-ear using
existing creases.

8

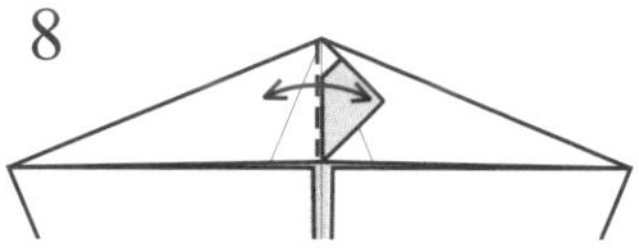

Swing the head to
the left and then
back to the right.

9

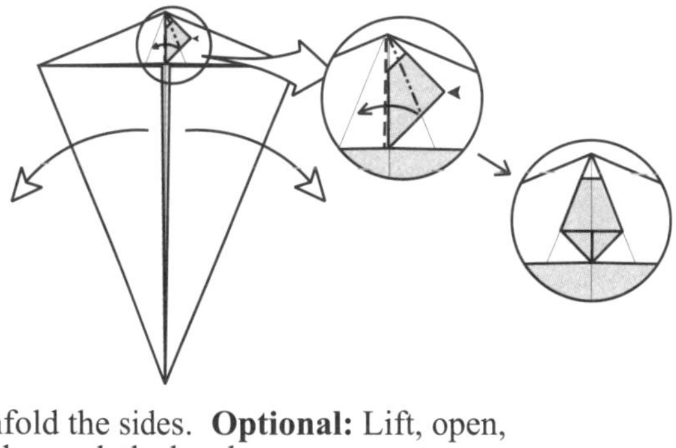

Unfold the sides. **Optional:** Lift, open,
and squash the head.

10

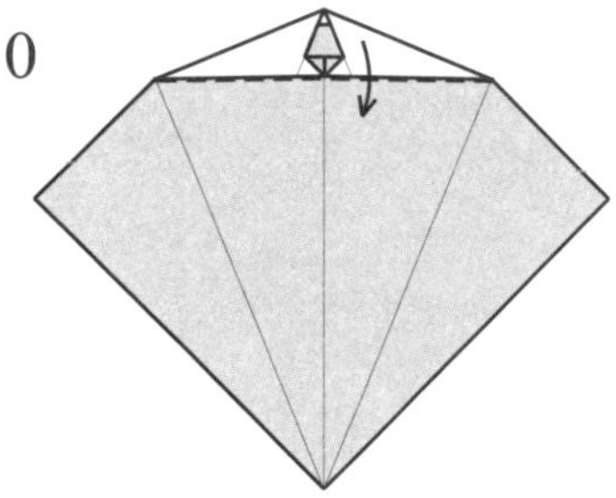

Valley-fold the head down.

11

Valley-fold edge-to-edge.

12

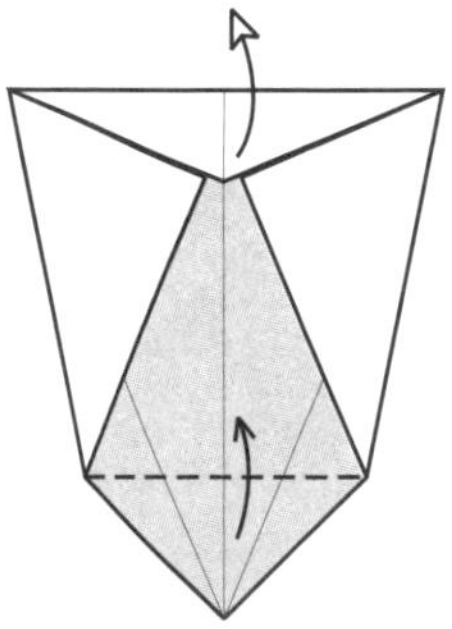

Swing the top flap up.
Valley-fold the bottom flap.

13

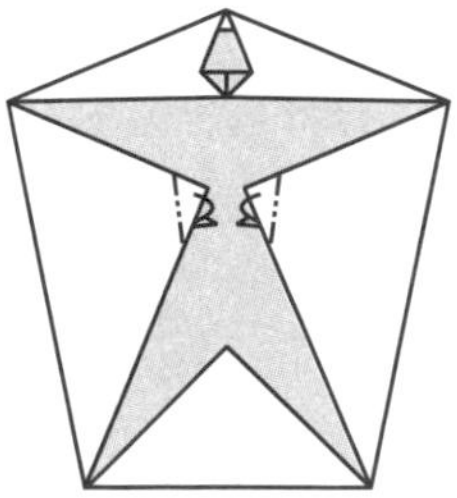

Mountain-fold the
corners behind.

14

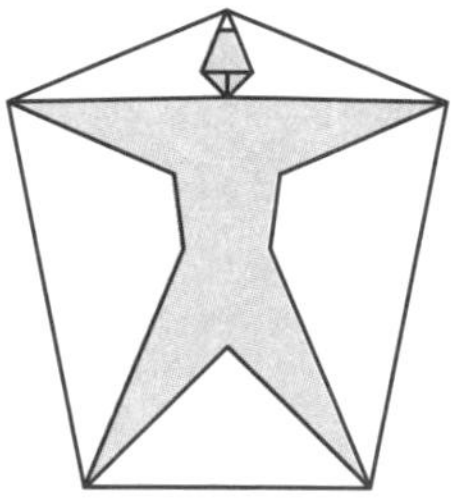

**The Unfortunate Bungee Jumper has landed,
having completed his final jump.**

Folder

Not only is this model simple, but it's useful too. It lets you organize loose papers! Put order back into your life now with this revolutionary new origami model!

1

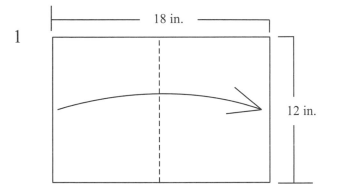

Begin white side up. Valley-fold the paper in half.

2

The Folder has been successfully folded. Repeat step 1 twenty times to obtain twenty folders.

Strobe Light

For the best effect use black paper coated with plutonium on one side.

1

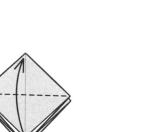

Begin with a Square Base. Valley-fold the front flap up. Repeat behind.

2

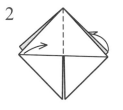

Make one corner stick out forward and another stick out toward the back.

3

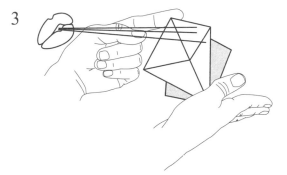

The Strobe Light has been fabricated. Hold the model either between two fingers or between two hands making sure to place the two loose ends together. Blow on the top part and the model will spin, creating a strobe.

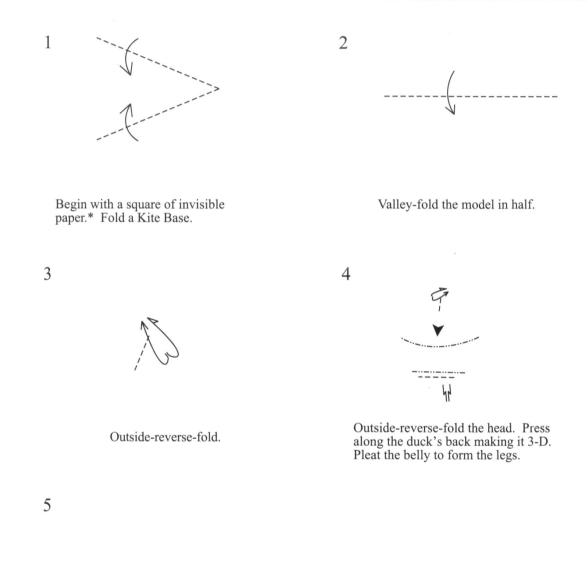

Invisible Duck

Such fine art, you can't even see it!

Here's a model that **ain't no quack!** It looks the same no matter how you fold it or how you hold it!

1

Begin with a square of invisible paper.* Fold a Kite Base.

2

Valley-fold the model in half.

3

Outside-reverse-fold.

4

Outside-reverse-fold the head. Press along the duck's back making it 3-D. Pleat the belly to form the legs.

5

Front view.   **Side view.**   **Back view.**

The Invisible Duck is complete.
Display it proudly for all to view.

*Invisible paper can be purchased from your local con artist or manifested via hallucinogens.

Happy Halloween!
Jack-O'-Lantern

The average American folds thousands of articles of clothing every year, without ever achieving anything recognizable. What a sad waste of folds! Now you can put an end to mindless folding, with this all-new, simple-to-fold T-shirt Jack-O'-Lantern.

Author's disclaimer: No pumpkins were butchered in the designing, folding, or diagramming of this model.

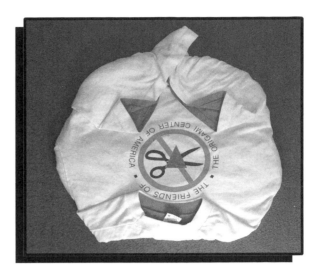

1

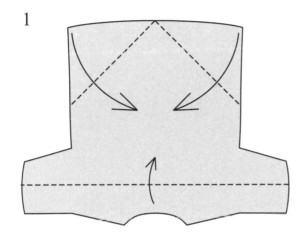

Begin with a T-shirt, back side up, upside down, and colored side out. If you can't find a T-shirt colored only on the outside, consider either using paint or lining the inside with a second T-shirt. Valley-fold as indicated.

2

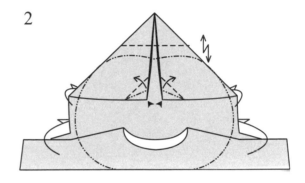

Round out the lower half with mountain folds. Pleat at the top to make a stem. Squash-fold the eyes (or if you prefer, "pumpkin-fold").

3

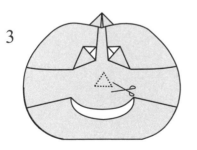

Now for the nose...
Cut along the dotted lines on the front layer only.
Don't hesitate; it's just a shirt.

4

The Jack-O'-Lantern has been carved.
Put a candle inside and it's ready to be displayed on your doorstep.

Upside-Down Heart

Ever had one of those days when the milk of human kindness just won't flow? When you feel your heart has been worn out, misunderstood, and bent out of shape? Well, you're not alone. Take heart, maybe what we need are some different viewpoints like those in this model. **So get the worries off your chests and fold them into shapely Upside-Down Hearts!**

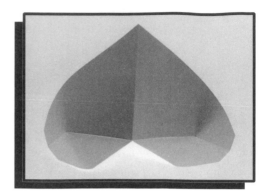

1 Begin white side up. Valley-fold and unfold in half diagonally. Valley-fold diagonally in half in the other direction.

2 Valley-fold and unfold, creasing only at the top.

3 Valley-fold just the front flap to the top edge. The fold line starts at the black dot. The model should refuse to lie flat.

4 Valley-fold and unfold from the black dot to the corner.

5 Unfold to step 3.

6 Repeat steps 3–5 on the right side.

7 Now do just step 3 on both sides at the same time. Flatten the middle flap to the left. This fold is a rabbit ear in disguise.

8 Valley-fold the end of the middle flap down to the center line. The fold line goes through the black dot. Flatten the flap with a squash. A pumpkin also works. Make tiny valley folds on the side corners.

9 Pull the center flap outward to make a nice stand for the Upside-Down Heart. **Turn over.**

10 Valley-fold and unfold to define the left and right ventricles. Shape them to taste. Turn the heart upside down.

11 **The Upside-Down Heart has BUSTED into existence.**

"Who's Staring at my Rump?"

Or alternatively, **Squashed Elephant**

This model is essentially Charles Esseltine's
Millennium Falcon, mistakenly identified by me at a
Bay Area Rapid Folders (BARF) meeting.

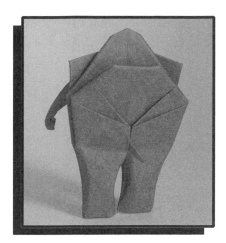

1

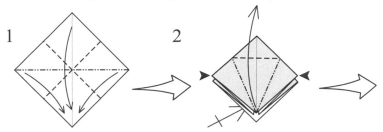

Begin by folding a
Square Base.

2

Petal-fold on both sides,
making a Bird Base.

3

Valley-fold the
front flap down;
the valley fold
touches the top of
the middle layer.
Then fold the
tip upward.

4   **4a**   **4b**

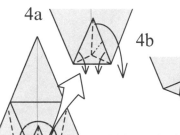

Rabbit-ear the front flap
so that it protrudes
downward (4a and 4b).

Valley-fold the sides
inward to narrow the legs.
Repeat behind.

5

Mountain-fold the two
corners, wrapping them
around just the nearest layer.

6

Make a tiny
mountain fold.
Turn over!

7

Valley-fold at
right angles
and unfold.

8

Rabbit-ear.
Don't think
about pink
elephants.

9

Pleat to form the ears. Shorten
the legs with reverse folds that go
up into the trunk. Perhaps you can
reverse-fold the ends again to form
tusks, but that might upstage the
main attraction—THE RUMP!
Turn over.

10

Shape the legs
and trunk to taste.

11

The Squashed
Elephant is completely
in view—THE END.

Walking Boat

This is my dream boat, for it was designed in a dream. I dreamt that I was folding a piece of paper and it became a walking boat. When I woke up I realized, "Hey, that works!" and I was able to reconstruct the folding method. I wish all dreams were that productive!

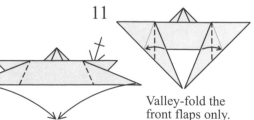

1

White side up. Valley-fold in half both ways.

2

Valley-fold.

3

Lift and squash.

4

Valley-fold the front layers upward.

5

Turn over.

6

Valley-fold; this will cause the bottom to swing upward. The model won't lie flat.

7

Form the horizontal valley fold so that it is even with the edge in back; swing the bottom up to the top, collapsing along existing creases.

8

Valley-fold so that the halves of the near top edge lie along the vertical centerline; roll the adjacent raw inner edges outward to the outer folded edges and flatten. Watch the black dot. This process is shown in progress at the right. Repeat behind.

8a

In progress.

8b

Right front complete. Repeat behind and on the left.

9

Pinch the indicated mountain folds. Swing the flaps to the outside (the valley fold is on an existing crease) and pull the top down, making the model lie flat. Repeat behind.

10

Valley-fold the front flaps back down again. Repeat behind.

11

Valley-fold the front flaps only.

12

Pinch mountain folds down the centers of the near legs, and bend the tips rightward to form feet. Repeat behind.

12.5

The Walking Boat is all ready... to take a walk!

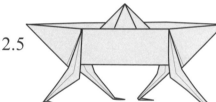

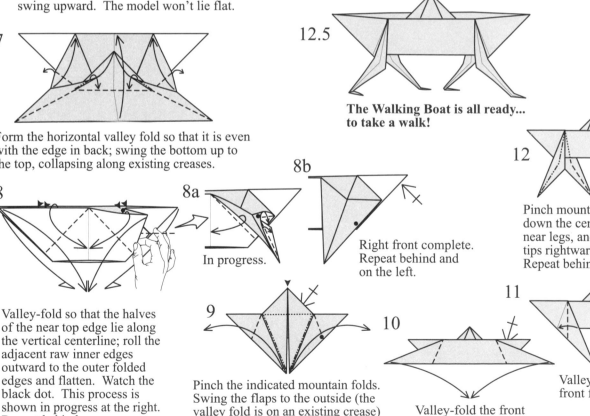

Clogged Artery

This model is not nearly as almost deranged as the real life tragedy it depicts. Heart attacks and strokes happen when arteries get clogged with fatty deposits. The main culprit in this is overconsumption of saturated fats and cholesterol, i.e., animal products. Alas, this unhealthy diet is as widespread in our society as the fast-food chains that promote it. Now, simply by folding this origami model, you too can experience what a clogged artery is like without having to eat all that animal fat, and without dying from it!

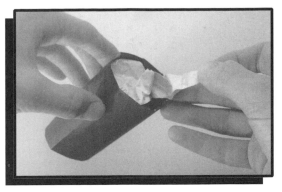

1

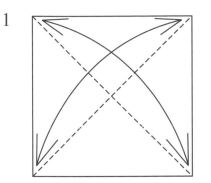

Begin white side up.
Valley-fold and unfold in
half diagonally both ways.

2

Valley-fold and unfold a kite.

3

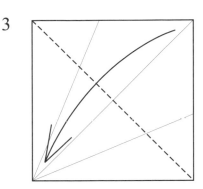

Valley-fold.

4

Valley-fold.
Learn CPR.

5

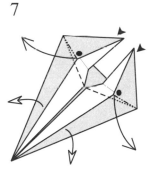

Mountain-fold
and unfold.

6

Lift and squash-fold
outward. No new creases
need be made.

7

In progress.

8

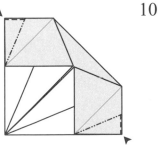

Valley-fold and unfold.

9

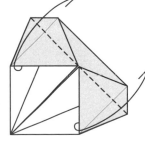

Reverse-fold.

10

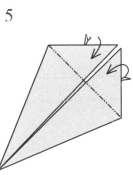

Valley-fold.

11

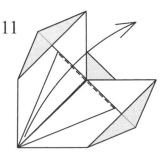

Valley-fold.

12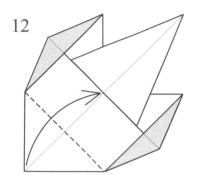

Valley-fold.

13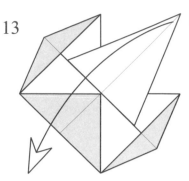

Swing down the flap.

14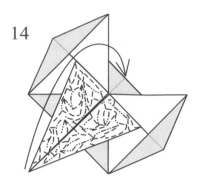

Crumple the flap making it look as gross as possible. Dipping the flap in lard gives it a nice touch. The pointy end of the yucky flap should come to the center of the folded edge. For more folding tips, see Monolithic Rubblestone Boulder (page 245).

15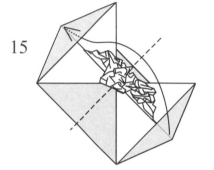

Valley-fold the model in half, slipping one side into the pocket of the other side. You needn't flatten the model.

16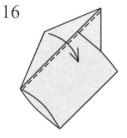

Valley-fold the pocket and its contents downward in order to hold the artery together.

17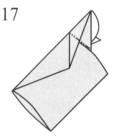

Reverse-fold, tucking the flap inside the tube.

18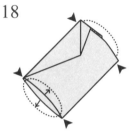

Round out the arterial segment.

19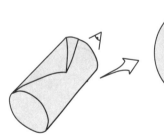

The artery has been formed. The next view is looking into the back side of the segment.

20

As we can see, the artery is completely clogged (make it so if it's not already). So we must perform open-heart surgery to extract the atherosclerotic deposit. To do this, grasp the end of the yucky flap of fat, and slowly slide it out from the artery. While performing this operation, be sure to give your audience a melodramatic look of disgust.

21

The offending matter has been removed, and so blood can once again pass through freely, at least until the next clogging occurs.

Unopenable Envelope

Befuddle your friends with this insidious model. How can it be unfoldable?
Because what you can push you can't always pull, as we'll soon see.

1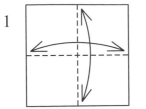

Start with ten-inch
paper, white side up.
Valley-fold and unfold.

2

Valley-fold. Due to the creep factor
you might want to make all folds
fall just short of their guidemarks.

3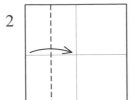

Valley-fold.

4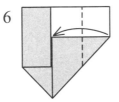

Valley-fold.

5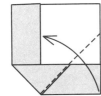

Valley-fold.

6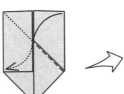

And yet another valley fold.
If you want to put something
inside, now is the time.

7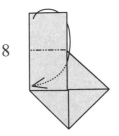

Valley-fold, slipping the
corner underneath the
surface of the left side.

8

Reverse-fold the top
so that it too goes
underneath the
surface of the left side.

9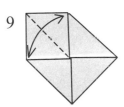

Valley-fold and
unfold on the
near layer only.

10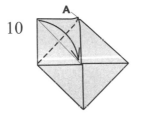

Valley-fold. Note where flap **A**
is. The next two steps are tricky.
If you can't tackle them, it's OK;
skip to the Consolation Version.

11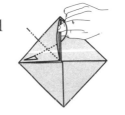

Mountain-fold the inside flap (flap **A**)
deep into the model. You may have
to push and shove a little or use tools
(a key is very fitting for the task).

12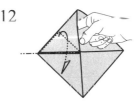

Reaching in with your
finger, mountain-fold the
inside flap even deeper
into the model.

13

The fully locked
Unopenable Envelope.
Now see if you can unfold it
without tearing it? Not even
I can. Once you feel
confident, bet your worst
friend $5 s/he can't unfold it
without tearing it.

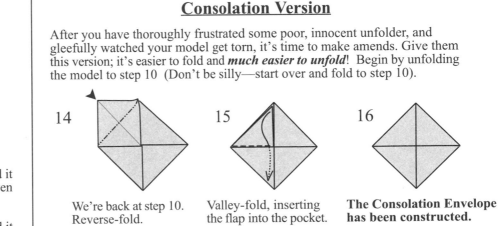

Consolation Version

After you have thoroughly frustrated some poor, innocent unfolder, and
gleefully watched your model get torn, it's time to make amends. Give them
this version; it's easier to fold and *much easier to unfold*! Begin by unfolding
the model to step 10 (Don't be silly—start over and fold to step 10).

14

We're back at step 10.
Reverse-fold.

15

Valley-fold, inserting
the flap into the pocket.

16

**The Consolation Envelope
has been constructed.**

Folding the Blintz Base

This model, inspired by the cover of *Folding the Universe*, by Peter Engel, is a tribute to the famous M.C. Escher drawing. But instead of two hands drawing themselves, here are four hands **folding** themselves. Wouldn't it be nice if paper were to behave that way in real life?

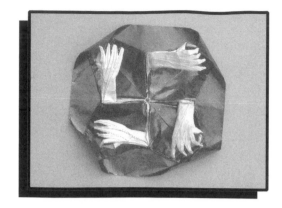

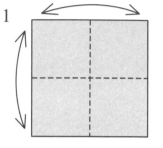

1

Foil at least ten inches square is recommended. Begin with the colored side up. Valley-fold in half and unfold both ways.

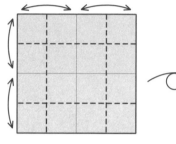

2

Valley-fold and unfold to make fourths. **Turn over.**

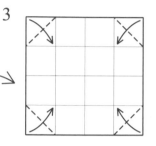

3

Valley-fold the corners.

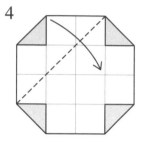

4

Valley-fold.

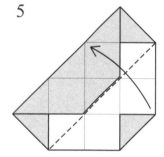

5

Valley-fold.

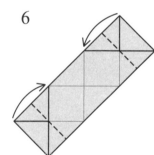

6

Valley-fold.

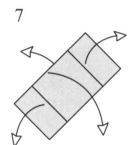

7

Unfold to step 4.

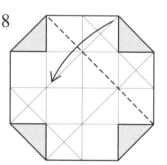

8

Repeat steps 4–7 on the other side.

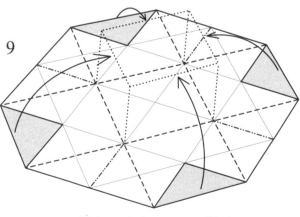

9

Using existing creases, lift the corners to form a box.

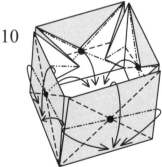

10

Using existing creases, fold each side of the box into a Waterbomb Base: i.e., push the centers of the sides (see black dots) toward the empty space of the box.

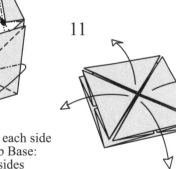

11

Unfold the four corners.

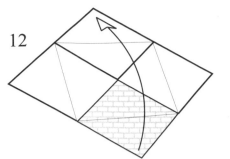

12

Open out and swing the brick-shaded square up to the top.

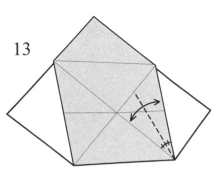

13

Valley-fold and unfold, bisecting the indicated angle.

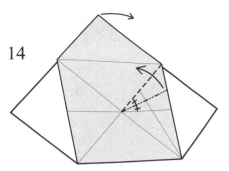

14

Pleat. The mountain fold, which is new, bisects the two existing creases. The model will not lie flat.

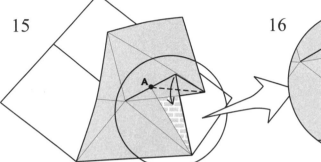

15

Valley-fold the flap down so that the fold line touches point **A**. The purpose of the next twelve steps is to eliminate the brick-shaded triangle through a series of swivel folds. Don't even think about using scissors instead.

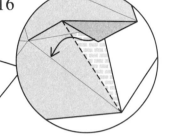

16

Valley-fold along the existing crease, pulling paper out from behind the dark-shaded triangle and flattening it.

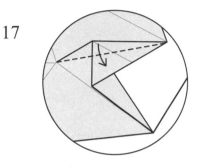

17

The first swivel fold is complete. Valley-fold the flap down...

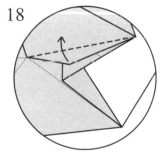

18

...and bring it back up.

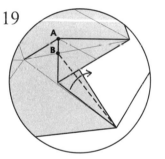

19

Valley-fold at point **B**.

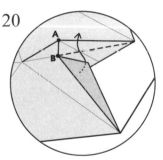

20

Valley-fold along the existing crease, pulling out paper from behind the dark-shaded triangle and flattening it.

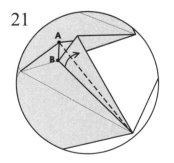

21

The second swivel fold is complete. Valley-fold the flap...

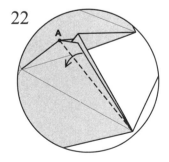

22

...and bring it back.

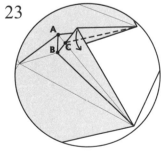

23

Valley-fold at point **C**.

Folding the Blintz Base **229**

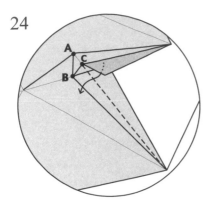

24

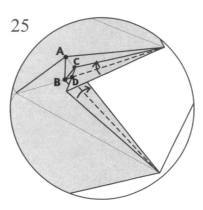

25

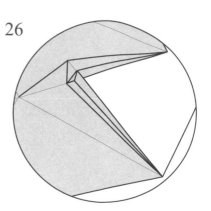

26

Valley-fold along the existing
crease, pulling paper out from
behind the dark-shaded triangle
and flattening it.

The third swivel fold is complete.
Continue swivel-folding until
nothing sticks out beyond the
underneath edges. Once you get
the hang of it, it's much faster to
do the swivel folds in one step as
illustrated above.

Like this.

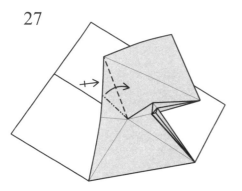

27

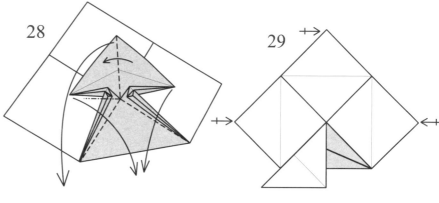

28

29

Repeat steps 13–26 on the other side.

Rabbit-ear, collapsing to the left.

Bye-bye 3-D.
Repeat steps 12–28 on
the other three corners.

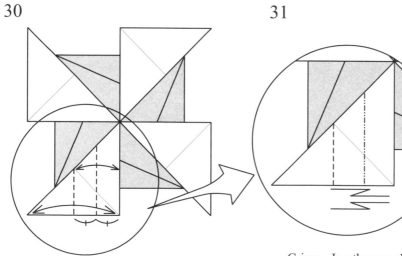

30

31

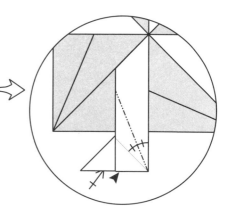

32

We will now fold the circled white triangle
into a hand. Make the indicated valley creases.

Crimp. In other words,
make two reverse folds.

Reverse-fold the indicated corner,
bisecting the indicated angle. Repeat
this on the other side of the hand.

33

Valley-fold and unfold on the left side. Reverse-fold the two shaded right flaps.

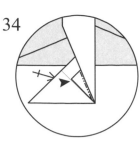

34

Reverse-fold. Repeat behind.

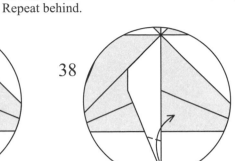

35

Crimp.

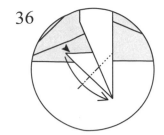

36

Reverse-fold.

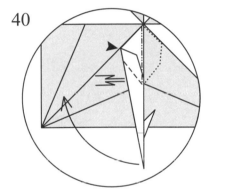

37

Reverse-fold. Repeat behind.

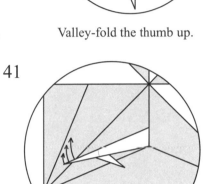

38

Valley-fold the thumb up.

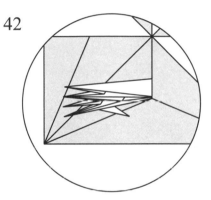

39

Valley-fold the wrist in half.

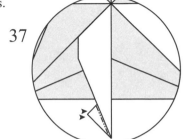

40

Crimp the wrist, swinging the hand to the left. To do this, you must close-sink the base of the wrist; its final position is indicated by the dotted line.

41

Spread open the fingers.

42

Sculpt the hand tastefully and let it grab the nearest corner.

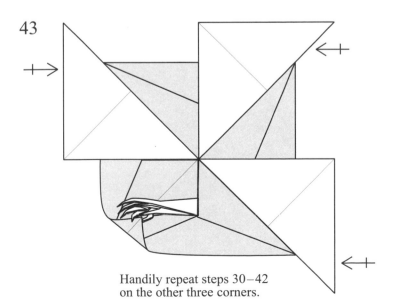

43

Handily repeat steps 30–42 on the other three corners.

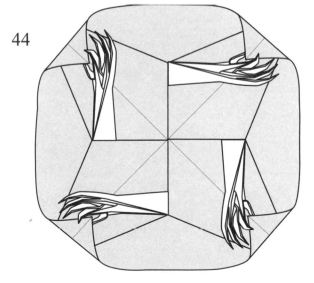

44

Folding the Blintz Base is complete... or at least forever in process!

Folding the Square Base

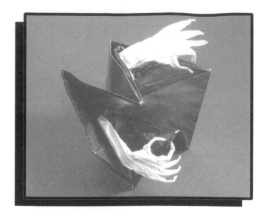

If you prefer Square Bases to blintzes, try this variation. Since four hands trying to fold one piece of paper might get a little too handy, this version has just two hands, a right and a left.

1
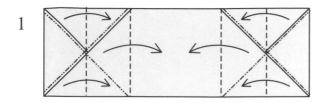

Begin with step 6 of Folding the Blintz Base. Fold both ends into Waterbomb Bases, and fold them to the center.

2
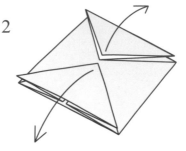

Unfold the corners (top layer only).

3
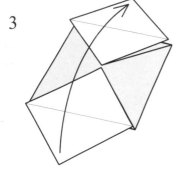

Swing the front corner across to the back corner, unfolding one of the Waterbomb Bases made in step 1.

4
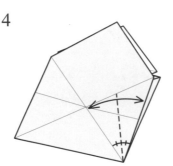

Follow steps 13–40 of Folding the Blintz Base on both hands, but change the orientation of one of the hands at step 28 to make it a left hand.

5
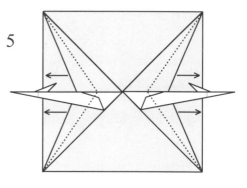

Slide the hands outward so that the colored edges meet the sides of the square and then flatten.

6
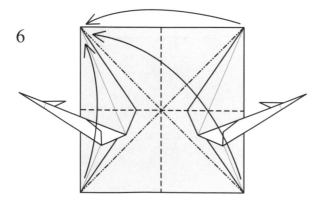

Fold a Square Base and sculpt the hands to taste as shown in steps 41–43 of Folding the Blintz Base.

7

Folding the Square Base has been handmade. Is it not handsome?!

Folding the Flapping Bird

With four hands coming out of a square sheet of paper, it's easy to see that the possibilities are endless (e.g., try "Folding the Nail Clippers"), but for now let's stick to simple traditional origami and fold a dear little Flapping Bird, or less affectionately, A Flapping Bird from Hell!

1

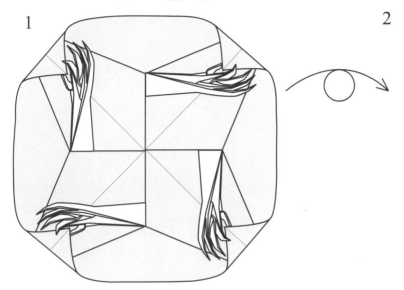

Begin with the completed Folding the Blintz Base. Uncurl the corners and **turn the model over.**

2

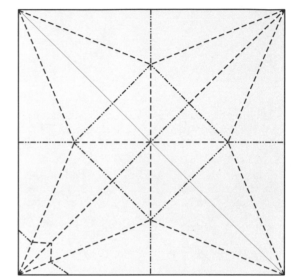

Fold the Flapping Bird and shape the hands to taste. See page 27 of the Basics section for directions if you don't know how to fold the bird.

3

Thoughts Behind the Folds

Once I discovered how to make a hand from the corner, I started inserting hands in all sorts of origami models. **Challenge:** What other models would benefit from having hands reach out of them? **Ideas:** Pit of despair, walking table, walking boat, hand plant, cemetery, handbag, handkerchief, handgun, handbook, handyman, handsaw, handstand.

Folding the Flapping Bird has been reached.

Man Swatter

Creator's disclaimer: The title, "Man Swatter," was chosen because it rhymes with *manslaughter*. Any feminist overtones to the title are purely accidental and do not reflect the creator's wish for mankind.

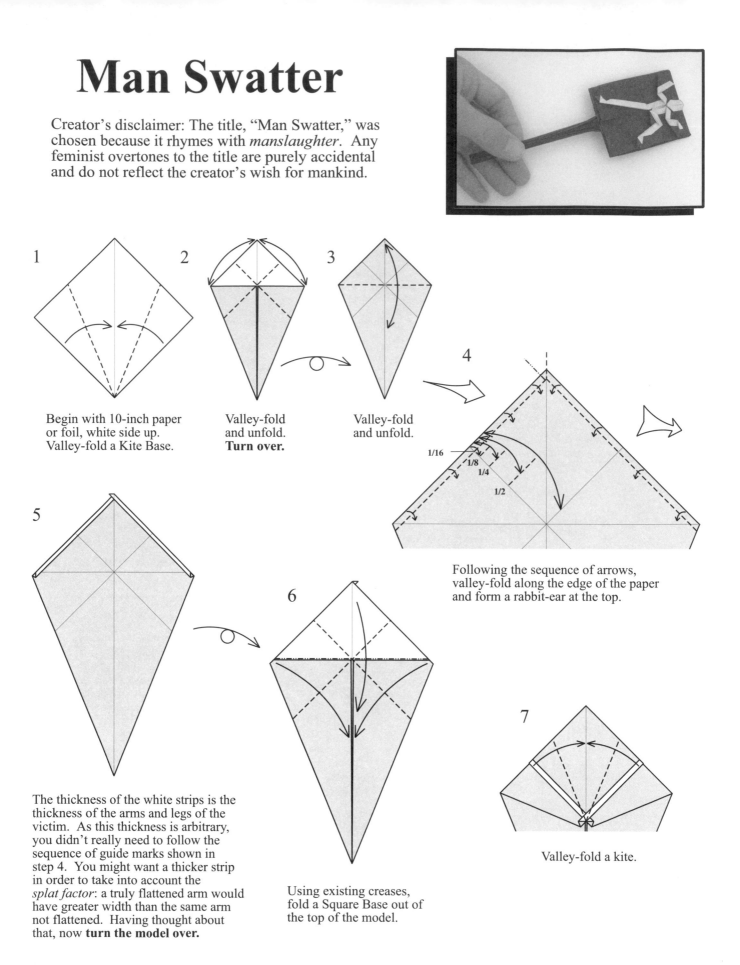

1 Begin with 10-inch paper or foil, white side up. Valley-fold a Kite Base.

2 Valley-fold and unfold. **Turn over.**

3 Valley-fold and unfold.

4
1/16
1/8
1/4
1/2

Following the sequence of arrows, valley-fold along the edge of the paper and form a rabbit-ear at the top.

5 The thickness of the white strips is the thickness of the arms and legs of the victim. As this thickness is arbitrary, you didn't really need to follow the sequence of guide marks shown in step 4. You might want a thicker strip in order to take into account the *splat factor*: a truly flattened arm would have greater width than the same arm not flattened. Having thought about that, now **turn the model over.**

6 Using existing creases, fold a Square Base out of the top of the model.

7 Valley-fold a kite.

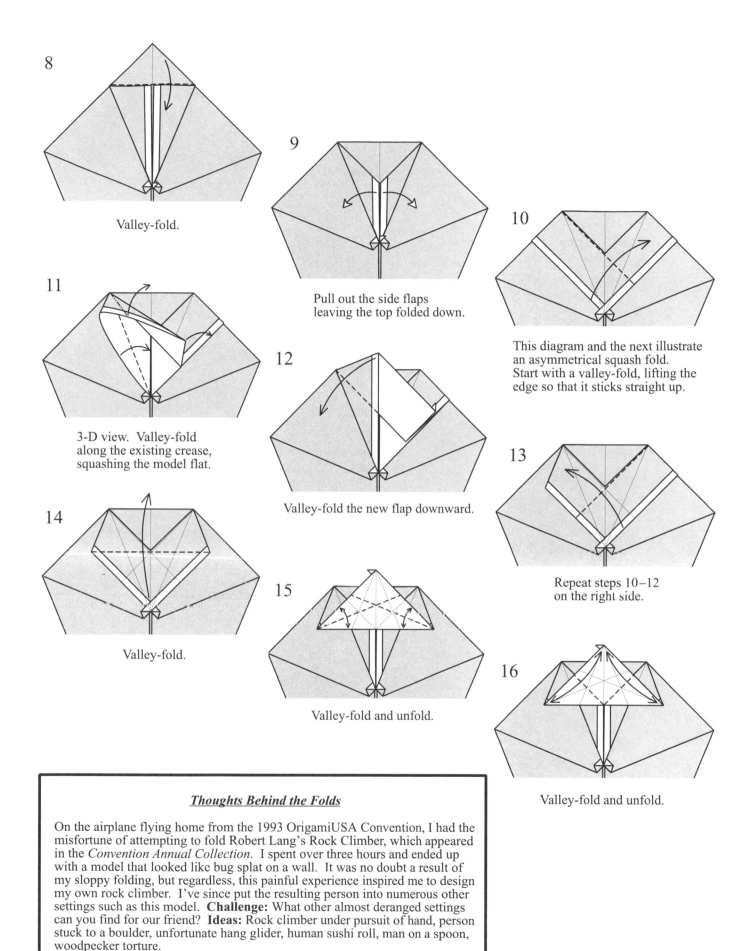

8

Valley-fold.

9

Pull out the side flaps
leaving the top folded down.

10

This diagram and the next illustrate
an asymmetrical squash fold.
Start with a valley-fold, lifting the
edge so that it sticks straight up.

11

3-D view. Valley-fold
along the existing crease,
squashing the model flat.

12

Valley-fold the new flap downward.

13

Repeat steps 10–12
on the right side.

14

Valley-fold.

15

Valley-fold and unfold.

16

Valley-fold and unfold.

Thoughts Behind the Folds

On the airplane flying home from the 1993 OrigamiUSA Convention, I had the
misfortune of attempting to fold Robert Lang's Rock Climber, which appeared
in the *Convention Annual Collection*. I spent over three hours and ended up
with a model that looked like bug splat on a wall. It was no doubt a result of
my sloppy folding, but regardless, this painful experience inspired me to design
my own rock climber. I've since put the resulting person into numerous other
settings such as this model. **Challenge:** What other almost deranged settings
can you find for our friend? **Ideas:** Rock climber under pursuit of hand, person
stuck to a boulder, unfortunate hang glider, human sushi roll, man on a spoon,
woodpecker torture.

17

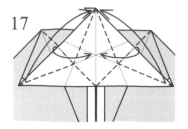

Follow the indicated mountains and valleys, to form, in effect, two rabbit ears.

18

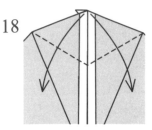

Valley-fold to expose the victim's head for the first time.

19

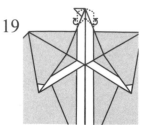

Open and flatten the tip, making it rounder as the top of a head ought to be.

20

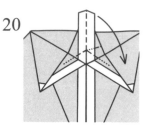

Rabbit-ear.

21

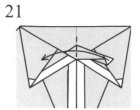

Swing the head over to the left.

22

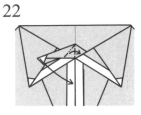

Squash the head tenderly.

23

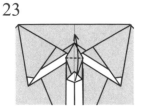

Bring the head up.

24

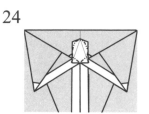

Round the head with mountain folds.

25

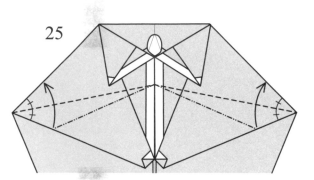

Pleat to cause the legs to spread apart. Make the valleys first, then the mountains, which end up horizontal.

26

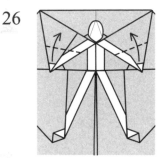

Valley-fold the arms.

27

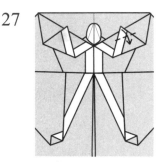

Valley-fold down at least one hand. Note that placement of the limbs is open to interpretation.

28

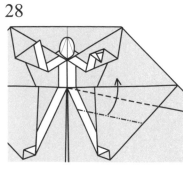

Pleat the leg.

29

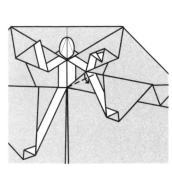

Valley-fold.

30

Pull trapped paper out from behind the leg to restore the leg's width.

31

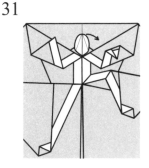

Tilt the head and make any other adjustments you consider fit for a swatted man.

236 *Origami to Astonish and Amuse*

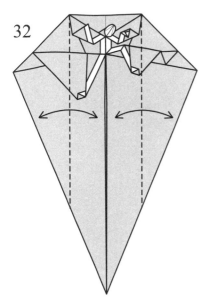

32

The man is complete. Now for the swatter. Valley-fold and unfold, making vertical creases.

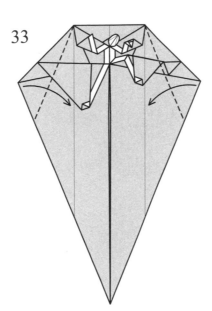

33

Valley-fold.

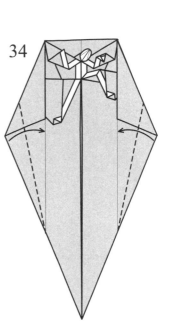

34

Valley-fold. Scratch that itch on your leg.

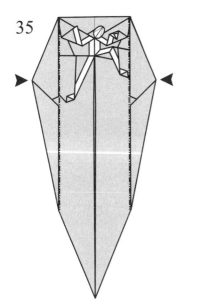

35

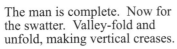

Closed-sink. In other words, shove in the sides so that they disappear.

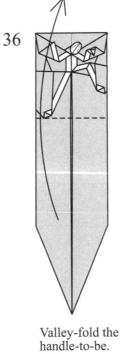

36

Valley-fold the handle-to-be.

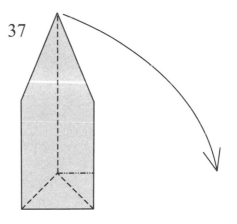

37

Rabbit-ear.

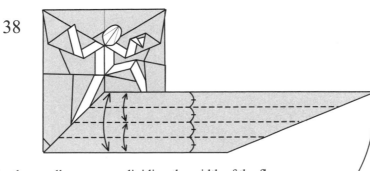

38

Make three valley creases, dividing the width of the flap into four equal partitions. Then unfold to step 36.

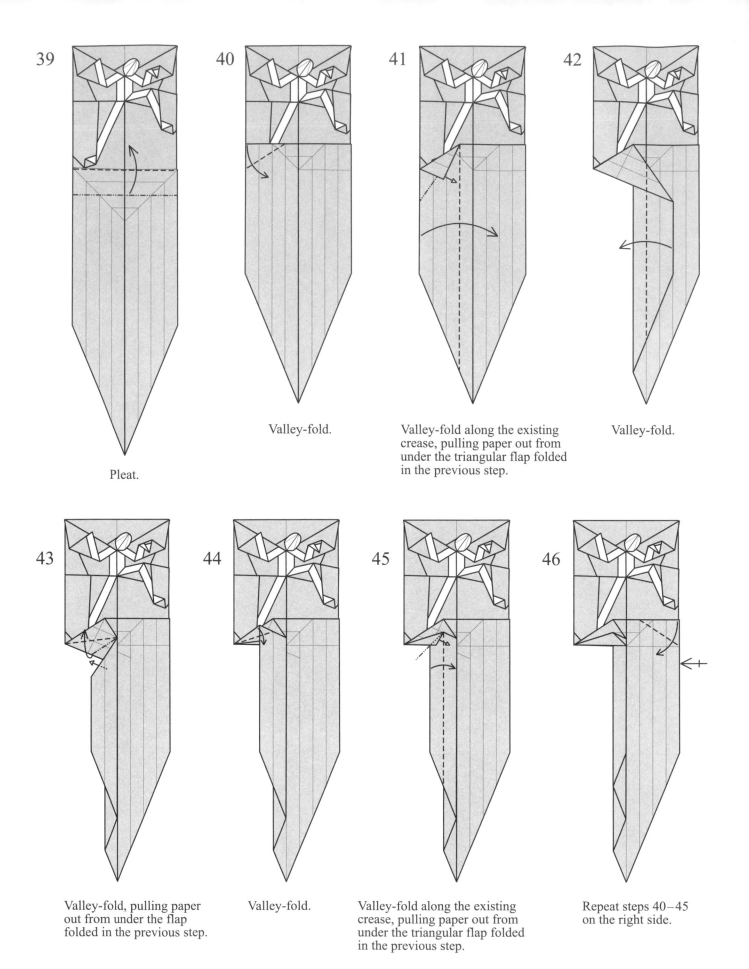

39 Pleat.

40 Valley-fold.

41 Valley-fold along the existing crease, pulling paper out from under the triangular flap folded in the previous step.

42 Valley-fold.

43 Valley-fold, pulling paper out from under the flap folded in the previous step.

44 Valley-fold.

45 Valley-fold along the existing crease, pulling paper out from under the triangular flap folded in the previous step.

46 Repeat steps 40–45 on the right side.

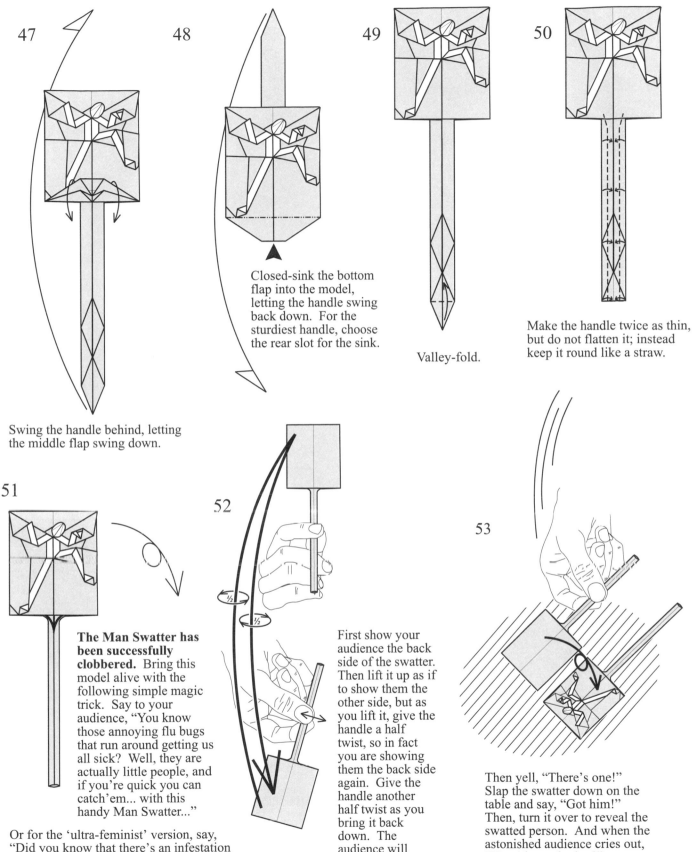

47

Swing the handle behind, letting the middle flap swing down.

48

Closed-sink the bottom flap into the model, letting the handle swing back down. For the sturdiest handle, choose the rear slot for the sink.

49

Valley-fold.

50

Make the handle twice as thin, but do not flatten it; instead keep it round like a straw.

51

The Man Swatter has been successfully clobbered. Bring this model alive with the following simple magic trick. Say to your audience, "You know those annoying flu bugs that run around getting us all sick? Well, they are actually little people, and if you're quick you can catch'em... with this handy Man Swatter..."

Or for the 'ultra-feminist' version, say, "Did you know that there's an infestation of sleazy [or pesky] men running around these days? That's why I always carry around this handy Man Swatter, so that whenever I see one..."

52

First show your audience the back side of the swatter. Then lift it up as if to show them the other side, but as you lift it, give the handle a half twist, so in fact you are showing them the back side again. Give the handle another half twist as you bring it back down. The audience will quickly conclude that the swatter is blank on both sides.

53

Then yell, "There's one!" Slap the swatter down on the table and say, "Got him!" Then, turn it over to reveal the swatted person. And when the astonished audience cries out, "How'd you do that?" you say, "It's all in the folds—you have to fold the model to understand how it works."

Unfortunate Suitor

Message to the Unfortunate Suitor:

True, everybody plays the fool sometimes,
but if you can't laugh a little, it's no longer play.
So, cheer up! There will be many more high-heel
shoes in the future to be squashed by, and
who knows, you might even find one that fits.

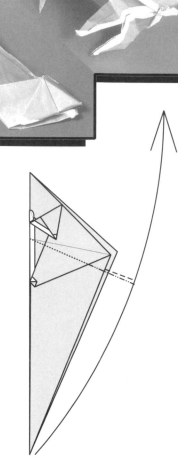

26

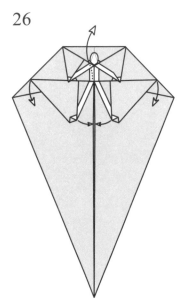

Begin with step 26 of the Man Swatter.
Undo the pleats made in step 25.
Pull the flap out from behind
the suitor's head.

27

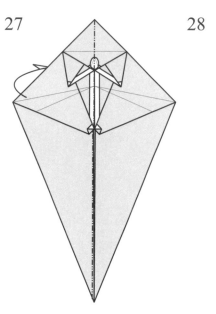

Mountain-fold the entire
model in half.

28

Reverse-fold the bottom, lining up
the fold with the existing creases
made in step 25.

29

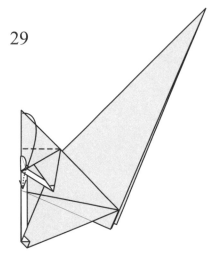

Valley-fold the flap,
tucking it inside the pocket.

30

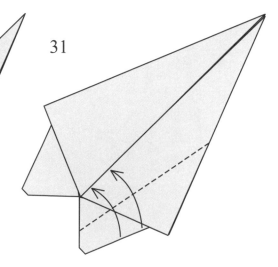

Open the reverse-folded flap.
Include the arm in the opening
action.

31

Valley-fold edge-to-edge.

32

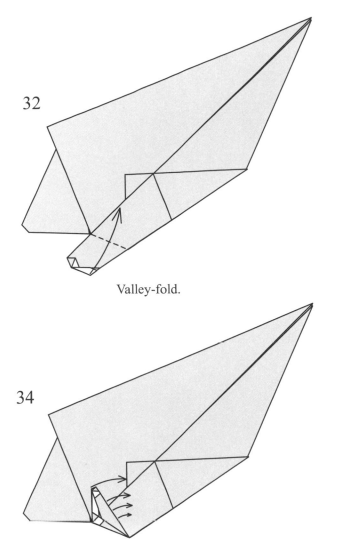

Valley-fold.

33

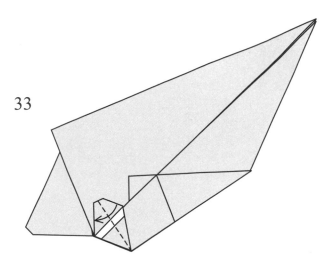

Valley-fold edge-to-edge.

34

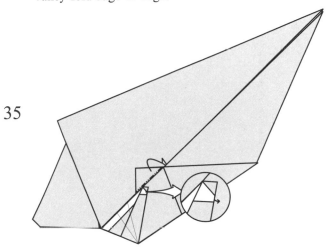

Pivot the flap to the right,
releasing trapped layers.

35

Mountain-fold the small flap, tucking it inside
the model. With a tiny rightward pull you can
restore the tip of the suitor's toe, which was cut
off in step 34. But this is optional, as a cut-off
toe here or there might actually enhance the
model's appearance.

36

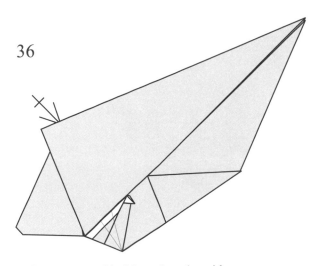

Repeat steps 31–35 on the other side.

37

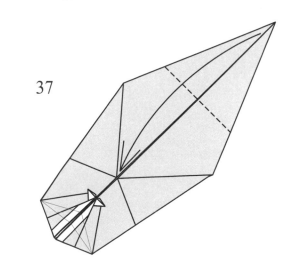

Valley-fold. This flap will soon
become the high heel.

38

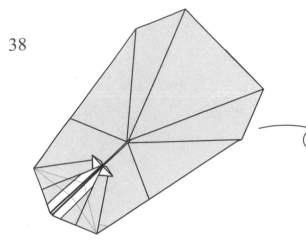

Turn the model over.

39

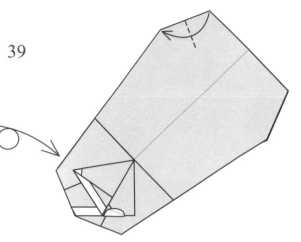

Valley-fold point-to-point,
but flatten only a short segment.
Let the rear flap swing out.

40

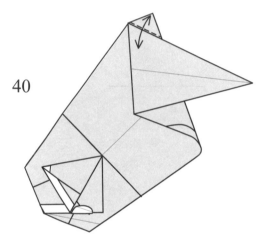

Valley-fold and unfold.

41

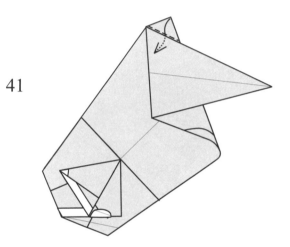

Valley-fold, tucking the little flap
behind the big flap.

42

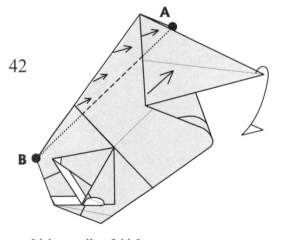

Make a valley fold from
A to **B**, on the far layers only.
Swing the right flap to the rear.
Nothing should lie flat.

43

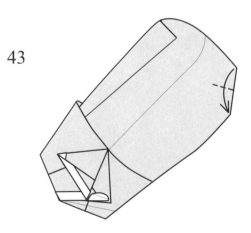

Repeat steps 39–42 on the right.

44

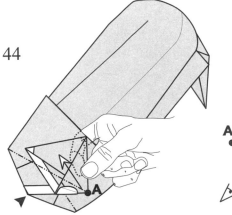

Reach in with your index finger, and puff out point **A**, forming a pyramid-like thing that protrudes.

45

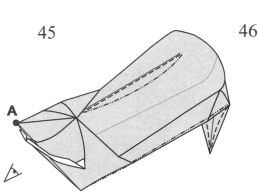

Shape the arch of the shoe with a curved pleat. Shape the high heel with curved valley folds. The next view is of the unfortunate suitor, tragically squashed by this elegant shoe. Surely it must have been an accident! He was simply in the wrong place at the wrong time. **Turn over** to see what we've done...

46

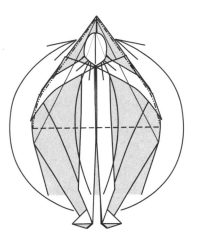

Oh, my! What a shame! Poor fellow! We had better cover up the evidence. To do this, swing up the legs and forcibly drag them all the way up so that the bottoms of the feet lie underneath the top of the head. To achieve this it is necessary to redefine the sides of the toe with mountain folds, which will also serve to shape the shoe.

47

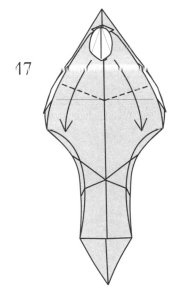

The evidence has been successfully covered up. All that remains is a round dot, and if questioned, we can just call that a tack stuck in the shoe. But, for you almost deranged folders who aren't afraid to show the truth, valley-fold the legs back down to reveal to the police that what was thought to be "a tack in the shoe" is in fact...

48

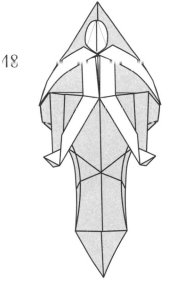

"Attack of the Shoe!"
The Unfortunate Suitor
has been safely executed.

49

And here we have our lovely high-heel shoe, which should be shaped to taste even though this is a tasteless model.

Carbon Atom

Even though this is a pureland model (all valley folds), it's so difficult that even particle scientists can't seem to get past step 10. But perhaps they're just not using thin enough paper.

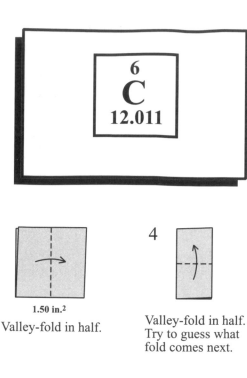

1

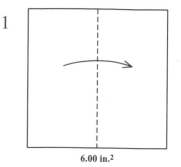

6.00 in.²

For best results use an extremely thin six-inch square of paper, preferably no more than 10^{-13} microns thick. Begin with white side up. Valley-fold in half. Make sharp creases.

2

Valley-fold in half.

3

Valley-fold in half.

1.50 in.²

4

Valley-fold in half. Try to guess what fold comes next.

5

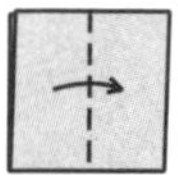

3.75 X 10⁻¹ in.²

Valley-fold in half. Remember: only wimps use tweezers.

6

Valley-fold in half.

7

9.38 X 10⁻² in.²

Valley-fold in half. Hope you don't find this model too repetitive; we've only just begun.

8

Valley-fold in half.

9

2.34 X 10⁻² in.²

Valley-fold in half. Remember to make sharp creases.

10

Valley-fold in half.

11

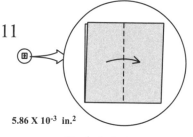

5.86 X 10⁻³ in.²

Exploded view. Valley-fold in half.

12

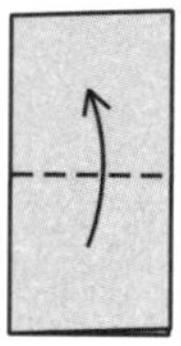

Valley-fold in half.

13

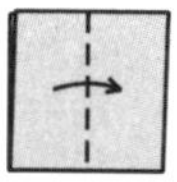

Valley-fold in half.

14

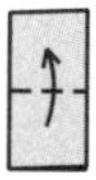

Valley-fold in half.

15 ... Continue valley-folding in half.

1.46 X 10⁻³ in.²

3.66 X 10⁻⁴ in.²

Valley-fold in half. No microscopes please.

...23

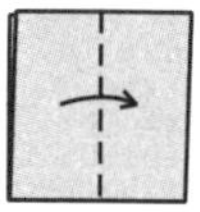

1.43 X 10⁻⁶ in.²

Valley fold in half. Electron microscopes are not allowed.

...31

5.59 X 10⁻⁹ in.²

Valley-fold in half. Warning: Fusion reaction may occur resulting in extremely large release of energy. Wear safety glasses. Fold at your own risk.

32

2.79 X 10⁻⁹ in.²

Valley-fold in half.

33

1.40 X 10⁻⁹ in.²

The completed Atom.

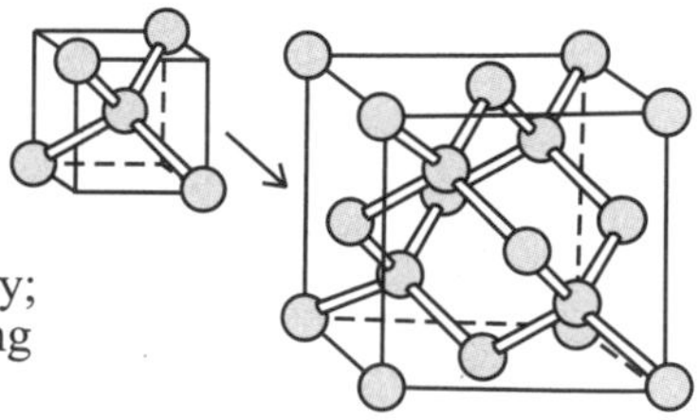

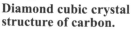

Diamond cubic crystal structure of carbon.

The modular approach: Fold at least 1,000,000 units. For charcoal, assemble randomly; no need for locks; the units will stick together on their own. For a challenge try arranging them in hexagon sheets to form graphite. When you've mastered that try folding your graphite sheets into fullerene molecules, better known as Bucky Balls. For a money-making venture, try assembling the carbon atoms into diamond, as pictured to the right.

Monolithic Rubblestone Boulder

Here is an elegant model of such stunning intricacy that even the Robert Langs of paperfolding might find it to be over their heads. I have managed to fold it only once. But don't give up yet, because the model's sensational final result more than makes up for its difficulty. **BEWARE:** The guidelines are subtle, but do exist and can readily be found in the realm of chaos theory.

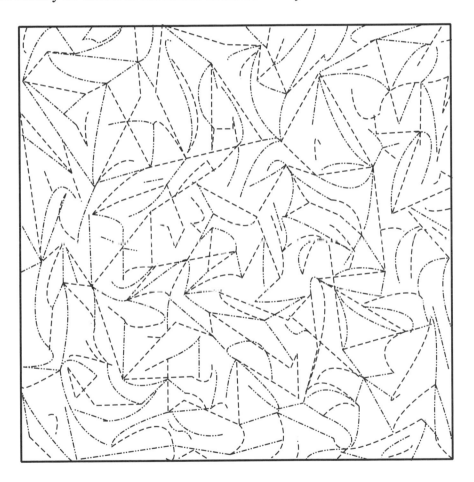

In order to begin to fathom the incredible aesthetic genius infused into this masterpiece, it is imperative that the crease pattern be followed exactly. To do this, first pinch all of the indicated mountains and valleys. Then, starting at the sides and moving inward, carefully collapse each fold, thus achieving the **Monolithic Rubblestone Boulder**.
In addition to its striking appearance, the Monolithic Rubblestone Boulder is a fantastic action model. The action is most stunning when the model is folded in great quantity—folding a thousand is ideal and good luck too! For the dramatic action, place the boulders at the top of a steep hill and then roll them down. An origami avalanche!

Running Car

Warning: This model is not really intended to be folded while driving on the road. Friends don't let friends drive while folding.

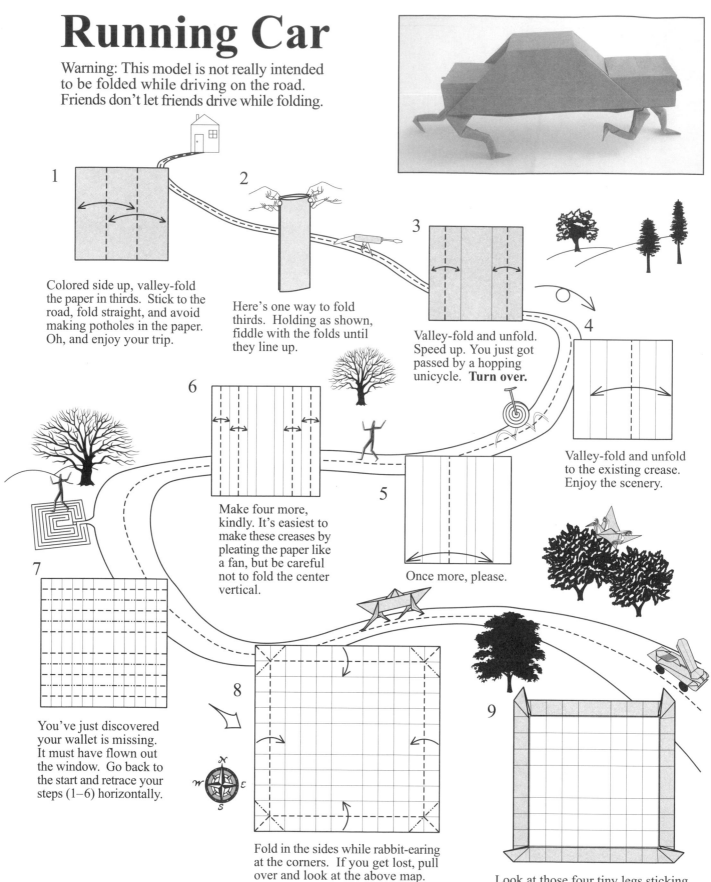

1 Colored side up, valley-fold the paper in thirds. Stick to the road, fold straight, and avoid making potholes in the paper. Oh, and enjoy your trip.

2 Here's one way to fold thirds. Holding as shown, fiddle with the folds until they line up.

3 Valley-fold and unfold. Speed up. You just got passed by a hopping unicycle. **Turn over.**

4 Valley-fold and unfold to the existing crease. Enjoy the scenery.

5 Once more, please.

6 Make four more, kindly. It's easiest to make these creases by pleating the paper like a fan, but be careful not to fold the center vertical.

7 You've just discovered your wallet is missing. It must have flown out the window. Go back to the start and retrace your steps (1–6) horizontally.

8 Fold in the sides while rabbit-earing at the corners. If you get lost, pull over and look at the above map.

9 Look at those four tiny legs sticking out. These legs will grow fourfold, by the end of this trip. **Turn over.**

10

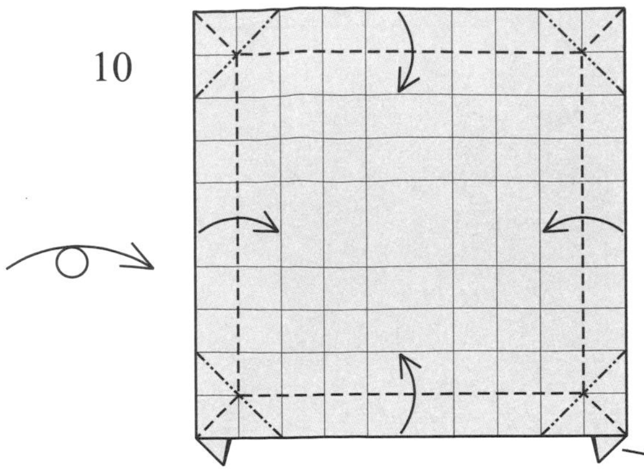

Once again, valley-fold the sides in while rabbit-earing the corners. Now you're rolling, I mean running... Look out! You just ran over that hopping unicycle.

11

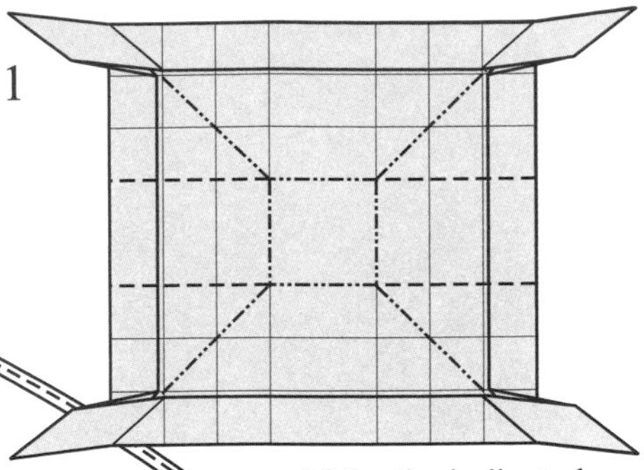

Make the indicated mountains and valleys. The terrain is no longer flat.

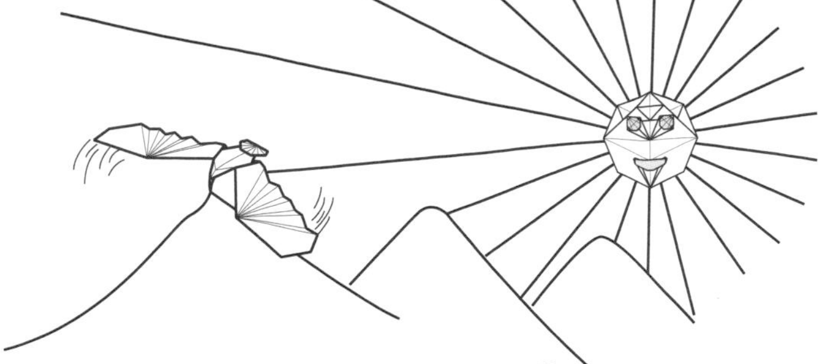

12

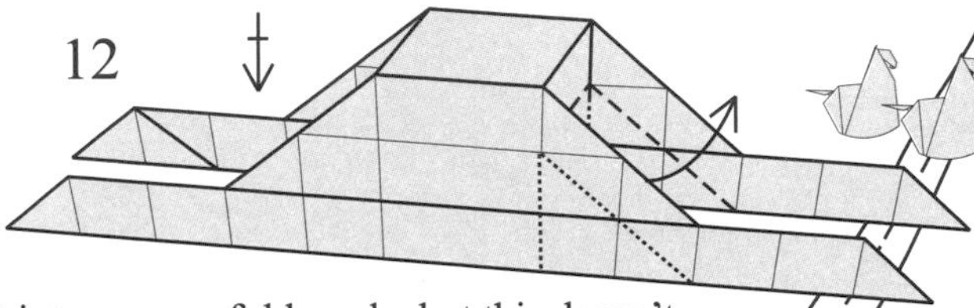

Time to shift into reverse fold mode, but this doesn't mean unfold the model. Reverse-fold to form the trunk of the car. Repeat on the other side to form the hood.

13

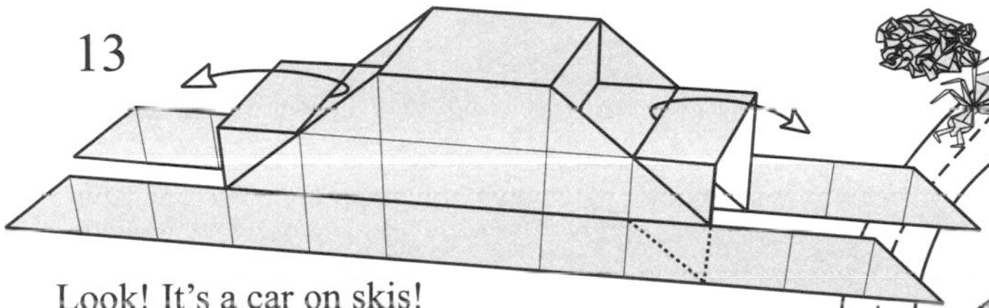

Look! It's a car on skis! Elongate the car by pulling the top layers outward. Partially unfolding will make this easier.

14

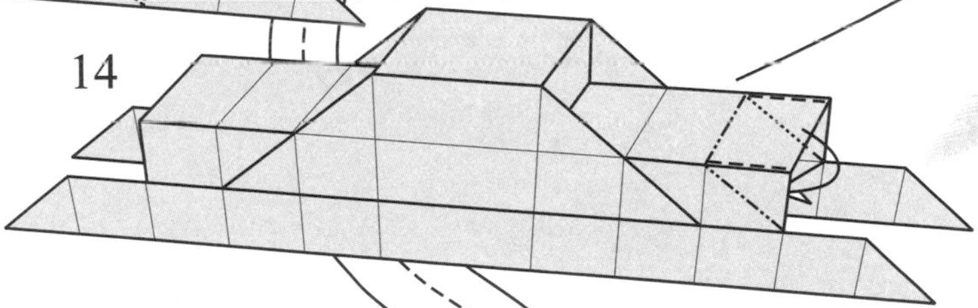

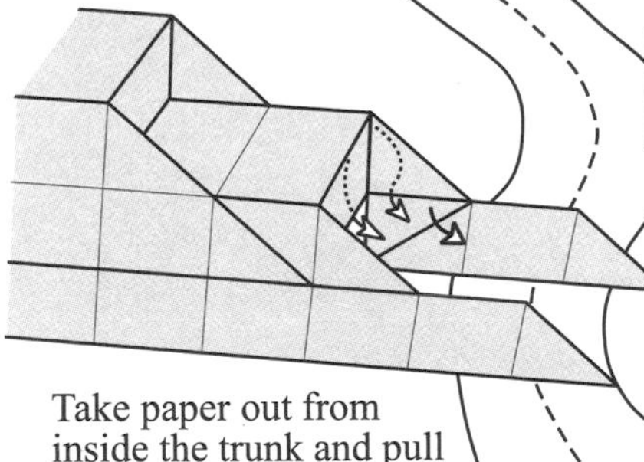

Reverse-fold the trunk to make it look less like the hood.

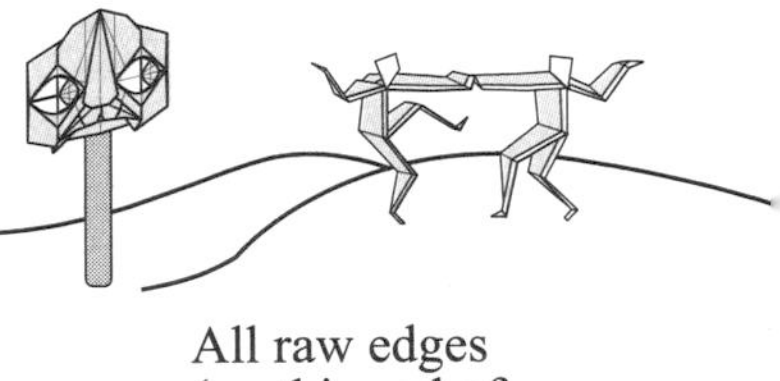

15

Take paper out from inside the trunk and pull it down to the ground.

16

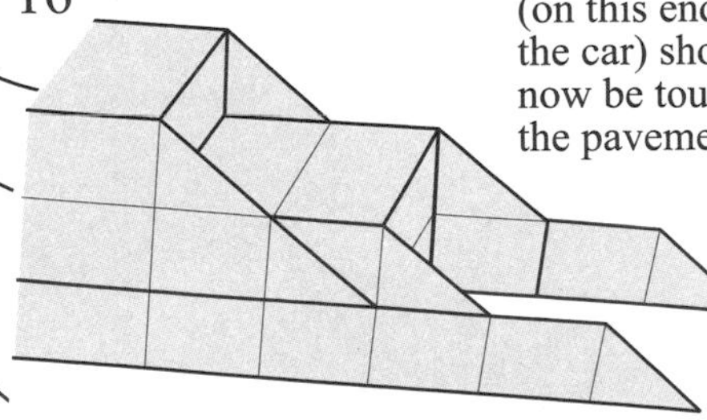

All raw edges (on this end of the car) should now be touching the pavement.

Rocking Horse X-ing

CAUTION
LOOSE GRAVEL
WATCH YOUR STEP

SPEED LIMIT 55

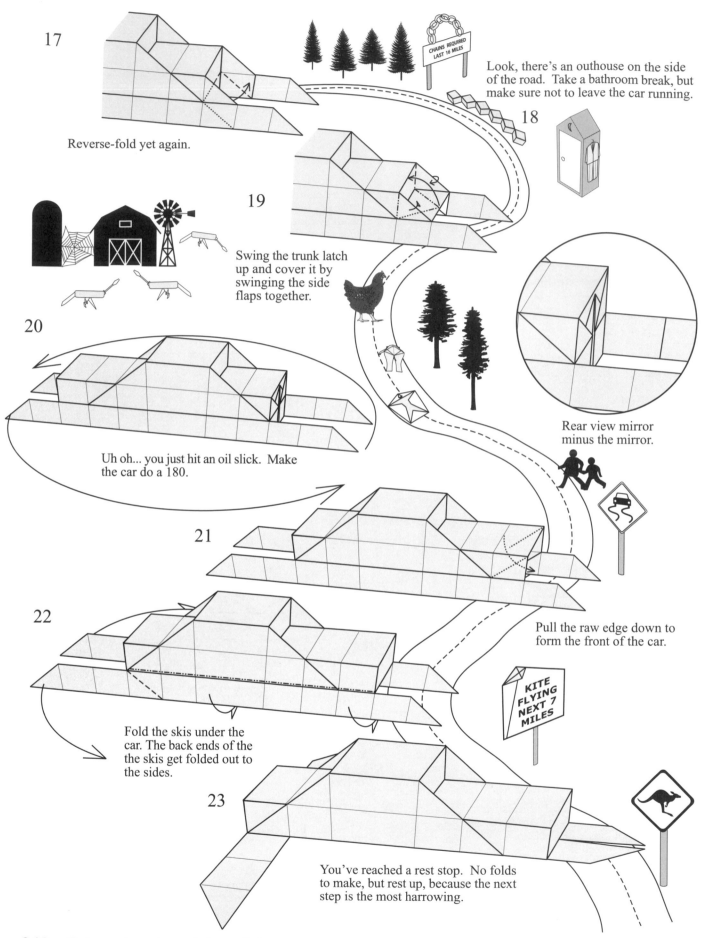

17

Reverse-fold yet again.

Look, there's an outhouse on the side of the road. Take a bathroom break, but make sure not to leave the car running.

18

19

Swing the trunk latch up and cover it by swinging the side flaps together.

20

Uh oh... you just hit an oil slick. Make the car do a 180.

Rear view mirror minus the mirror.

21

Pull the raw edge down to form the front of the car.

22

Fold the skis under the car. The back ends of the the skis get folded out to the sides.

23

You've reached a rest stop. No folds to make, but rest up, because the next step is the most harrowing.

CHAINS REQUIRED
LAST 16 MILES

KITE FLYING NEXT 7 MILES

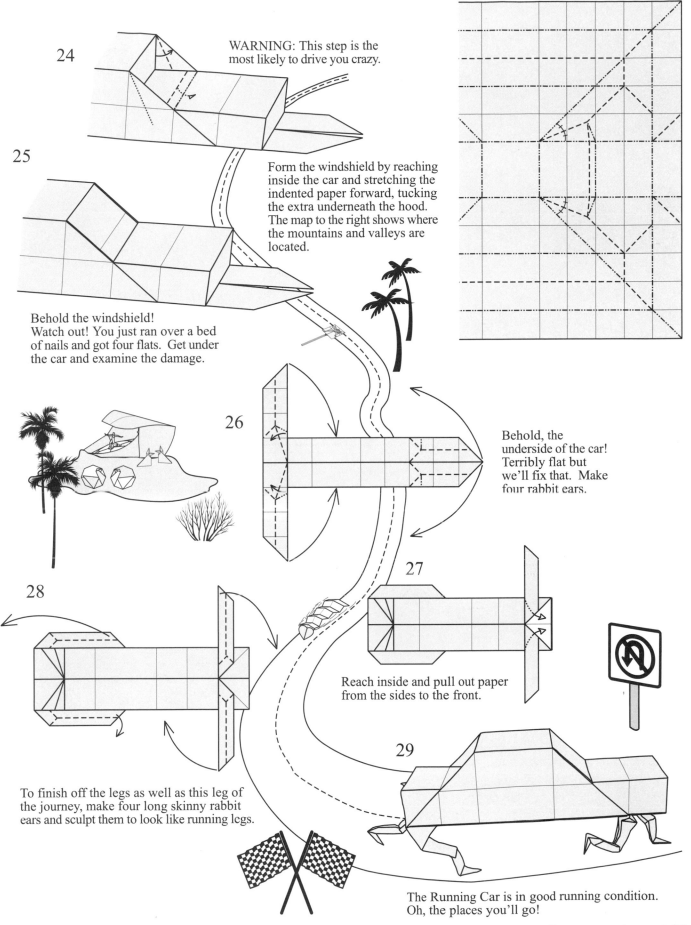

24 WARNING: This step is the most likely to drive you crazy.

25

Form the windshield by reaching inside the car and stretching the indented paper forward, tucking the extra underneath the hood. The map to the right shows where the mountains and valleys are located.

Behold the windshield! Watch out! You just ran over a bed of nails and got four flats. Get under the car and examine the damage.

26

Behold, the underside of the car! Terribly flat but we'll fix that. Make four rabbit ears.

27

Reach inside and pull out paper from the sides to the front.

28

To finish off the legs as well as this leg of the journey, make four long skinny rabbit ears and sculpt them to look like running legs.

29

The Running Car is in good running condition. Oh, the places you'll go!

About the Author

Jeremy Shafer has been designing origami models since the age of ten, and has traveled around the world teaching and exhibiting his work. He lives in Berkeley, California, and is editor of the newsletter for the Bay Area Rapid Folders (BARF).

He is a professional entertainer whose act includes juggling torches and fireballs, riding a flaming unicycle, and folding a Flapping Bird out of burning paper. His other passions include salsa dancing, handwhistling, and mastering nine-ball juggling. He spends his summers teaching kids how to juggle and unicycle at Camp Winnarainbow, a circus-arts camp in northern California.

Resources

OrigamiUSA
15 West 77th Street
New York, NY 10024-5192
U.S.A.
(212) 769-5635
www.origami-usa.org

Bay Area Rapid Folders (BARF)
www.barf.cc

Joseph Wu's Origami Page
www.origami.vancouver.bc.ca
   (This is the most comprehensive online
   source for origami information with
   hundreds of links to other origami sites.)